bo

18.

Cathal Gannon
The Life and Times of a Dublin Craftsman 1910–1999

Cathal Gannon

The Life and Times
of a Dublin Craftsman
1910–1999

CHARLES GANNON

THE LILLIPUT PRESS
DUBLIN

First published 2006 by
The Lilliput Press
62–63 Sitric Road, Arbour Hill
Dublin 7, Ireland
www.lilliputpress.ie

ISBN 10-DIGIT   1 84351 086 3
ISBN 13-DIGIT   978 1 84351 086 4

10 9 8 7 6 5 4 3 2 1

Set in 12 pt on 14 pt Perpetua
Printed in England by MPG Books, Bodmin, Cornwall

In memory of my father

Contents

Quonam consilio, quaeso, fanum pulcherrimum et ad Euterpen rite colendam idoneum parabis nisi architectum qui columnas excudit in honore habeas? Vos ergo, Academici, qui Musarum cultores exsistitis, hunc virum, organorum musicorum fabricatorem callidum et spectatum, acclamatione celeberrima cumulare debetis.

How, I ask, can one expect to have a handsome temple well fitted for celebrating the rites of Music unless one holds in honour the mastercraftsman who shapes the columns? All in this company who cultivates the Muses should bestow the accolade of their applause on this very skilled and highly regarded maker of musical instruments.

(From the oration given at the conferring of Cathal's honorary MA degree at Trinity College, Dublin on 6 July 1978.)

Foreword

When, many years ago, I had the pleasure of meeting Cathal Gannon at the Old Dublin Society gatherings in what is now the Civic Museum in South William Street, I was immediately struck by the store of knowledge that he carried around in his head. Another member of the ODS at that time, Professor Kevin B. Nowlan, remarked that Cathal was always full of out-of-the-way information. It seemed that Cathal, who shared my passion for Georgian architecture, was interested in many different things: music, musical instruments, history, art, literature, horology and antiques – he could talk about any of these subjects with ease and a great deal of authority. Added to this was his infectious sense of humour, which endeared him to everyone he met. I introduced him to my father, Bryan Guinness (Lord Moyne), who was fascinated to hear of his talents, especially his ability to make harpsichords, for which he really became famous. Ultimately Bryan invited him, his wife and son to live at Knockmaroon, beside the Phoenix Park, where there was a flat in the stable courtyard.

Mariga and I encouraged Cathal and his wife Margaret to join the Irish Georgian Society, which we formed in 1958, and they attended many of the meetings and outings that were organized over the following years. One of the expeditions was to Glin Castle in County Limerick.

Cathal and his brother Jack helped in the restoration of Leixlip Castle when I purchased it and was frequently a guest of ours at home. He stayed over a period of eight weekends when Mariga and I were away, in order to restore a Broadwood grand piano of mine. The Gannons were frequently invited to the birthday parties that we gave for our children, Patrick and Marina, who were about the same age as their son Charles. When I bought

Castletown to save the house and make it the headquarters of the Irish Georgian Society, Cathal's ingenuity with the locks and skill at mending the main staircase banister was invaluable.

Cathal was a wonderful individual: full of life, good spirits, humour and fascinating stories. Anyone who is interested in delving into the life of a man who, despite such humble beginnings, achieved so much and enriched the lives of so many will, I am sure, enjoy reading this book.

Desmond Guinness, December 2003

Acknowledgments

*T*he publication of this book was made possible by the generous financial support of RTÉ and Diageo Ireland; my thanks to Cathal Goan, Director General of RTÉ and Pat Barry, former Director of Corporate Affairs, Diageo Ireland.

It would have been almost impossible to write this biography without the co-operation and help of my late father, Cathal Gannon, who was so patient and generous with his time, allowing me to question him repeatedly and tape his interesting conversations and huge collection of anecdotes over the years.

Other people who must be thanked include Antony Farrell and Nicola Sherwell of The Lilliput Press, with whom it was so pleasant to work, and Professor Kevin B. Nowlan, who very kindly allowed me to interview him at his home and who subsequently read the entire typescript and wrote the Postscript. Thanks to the Hon. Desmond Guinness, who kindly furnished me with a Foreword, Malcolm Proud, who wrote the Afterword, George and William Magan (who supplied me with a copy of his book, *The Story of Ireland*) and John Boles, who read and checked the section on Dolphin's Barn. Desmond McInerney also read the entire typescript, offered opinions and gave me much-needed encouragement, and Joe O'Donnell read my first efforts and offered valuable advice.

Eibhlin Roche and Clare Hackett of the Archives Department, Diageo Ireland deserve special mention as they granted me access to files and photographs that had been carefully preserved over the years. Both were extremely helpful, efficient and supportive. Permission to reproduce Diageo photographs and an article from the Guinness *Harp* magazine was kindly granted by Chad Dowle, Trade Mark Manager, Diageo.

Patrick Horsley, who completed Cathal's four last harpsichords in England, kindly posted me photocopies of all the letters and cards that Cathal had written to him over the years and allowed me to quote extracts from them. This correspondence was of enormous interest to me as it helped in putting together the large jigsaw that was my father's busy life and allowed me to see things from my father's point of view.

Many others supplied help and gave me valuable information: my father's (and now my) good friend Anthony Harrison; June Stuart (widow of my father's best friend, William) who allowed me to rummage through her collection of Dublin Directories; John Beckett, who also agreed to be interviewed and taped by me; William Mullen, who himself videotaped my father and interviewed him; Aengus Devine, who interviewed Cathal on tape for a project; the late Kieran Hickey of B.A.C. Films Ltd, who also interviewed Cathal; the late Barbara Durack of the Television Archives Department of RTÉ, who unearthed information and videotapes for me; members of the staff in the Radio Archives Department of RTÉ; Amy Kerr and Emma Keogh of the RTÉ Stills Library (who permitted me to reproduce some of their photographs); staff of BBC Northern Ireland, who managed to find original film footage of my father in his workshop; Dr Stan Corran (now deceased) who wrote to me concerning my father; Paul Doyle of the National Museum of Ireland; Eoin McVey of *The Irish Times* (who gave me permission to quote from the newspaper and to reproduce a photograph); Gerard O'Regan, Editor of the *Irish Independent*. I also wish to thank Emer Buckley, Patricia Agnew, Joan Doyle, Arthur Agnew, Werner Schürmann (who wrote to me from Germany), Kieran Egar, Marie O'Neill, Carol Acton, Andrew Robinson, Dr Anna Lee, David Boles, Veronica Smith Murphy, Al Byrne, Rhoda Draper and, last but not least, Gillian Smith, who has been a great champion of my father over the years and was instrumental in setting up the Cathal Gannon Early Music Room in the Royal Irish Academy of Music.

Preface

On a long, summer's afternoon, an elderly lady from the village of Crumlin,
then rather isolated, was driving her grandchildren in a trap with a gentle-
man ass between the shafts. When passing near the brickworks, the animal
spied a female of his own species in a field. Nature asserted herself and the
gentleman ass dragged the trap, old lady and children over a ditch and
through a hedge. They finished up their afternoon in the Meath Hospital. As
Thomas à Kempis says: 'a joyful setting out is often a sorrowful coming home'.

It was explained to us children that these asses for years past had been at
'daggers drawn' and disliked each other. With childish innocence we accepted
this explanation.

I believe I was about seven or eight years of age when this happened; it
was one of my early memories of the Crumlin Road.

*T*his was the somewhat promising start of my father's autobiography, but
sadly it progressed little further than this. No amount of encouragement would persuade him to write another word; Cathal Gannon was a
talker, not a writer. It is a pity that he did not persist, for he would probably
have employed this Dickensian style of writing (Dickens being his favourite
novelist) to great comic effect. From this small fragment, one can instantly
get the measure of Cathal's impish sense of humour.

My father was blessed with a remarkable memory. Always reluctant to
talk about himself, he could recount many entertaining stories about the various people that he had encountered throughout his long and busy life. He
seemed to know everybody and everyone seemed to know him. He was
known to most people as 'the man who made the harpsichords'; many did
not know that this was only one of the many crafts that he had mastered.

His story is not one of rags to riches – he was never rich in the monetary sense – but rather one of obscurity to recognition. Despite a poor start
in life and little chance of success, he conquered his timidity and the sense

of hopelessness that haunted him, taught himself everything he needed to know, and in time became a person respected by many for his skills. He was ultimately awarded with not just one but two honorary MA degrees for his contribution to music-making in Ireland.

As he steadfastly refused to put pen to paper, I realized that the only way to write the story of this remarkable man was to switch on a tape recorder, question him and record what he had to say. Fortunately he fell in with this plan and agreed to be interviewed. The recording sessions, conducted over a period of years, yielded many hours of valuable material, which later I transcribed and finally formed into this account.

Because of Cathal's modesty and reluctance to reveal much about his inner self, it has been difficult for me to write about his personality, especially in the first part of this book, which deals with his life up to the time when I was born; essentially I am writing about a man whom I never knew. As the second part of the book is a more personal and subjective account of my father, I have more to say about the man himself and his character. The bulk of the text, however, is packed with the amount of detail and digressions that Cathal, I feel, would have approved of, for the simple reason that he loved to enliven his own conversation in this way.

Upon checking these snippets of information during the course of writing this book, I discovered that my father's memory was not as faultless as I had imagined it to be. Indeed, I noticed that over the years he had begun to 'embroider' his stories, as most people do when repeating anecdotes. Many of them, therefore, may bear little resemblance to the truth and consequently my rendition of them may be regarded more as fiction than fact. As many unfortunate colleagues of Cathal's in Guinness's Brewery were lampooned and teased by him and others, I have taken the precaution of slightly altering their names in order to protect their identity.

As my father's life was so packed with incident and as his circle of acquaintances was so wide, not all of the original material could be incorporated into this book, due to space constraints. For those interested in reading the full, unabridged text, a copy can be found in the National Library of Ireland, Kildare Street, Dublin 2.

Cathal Gannon
The Life and Times of a Dublin Craftsman 1910–1999

PART ONE

Cathal Gannon 1910–55

One

*C*harles William Gannon (later renamed Cathal by an aunt in order to distinguish him from his father who bore the same name) was born on 1 August 1910 in the Rotunda Hospital, Dublin. Before the birth, his mother was unable to rest, due to some medical students who were having a party upstairs and singing a popular song of the time, 'Yip I Addy I Ay'. Cathal, therefore, was able to claim that he was born to the sound of music. He continued with it for the rest of his life, though, as he commented, on a somewhat higher plane.

Apparently his was a difficult birth. The first thing his mother heard when she came out of the anaesthetic was the astounding news that Dr Hawley Harvey Crippen, who had murdered his wife by poisoning, had been arrested with his mistress whilst fleeing from England, via Belgium, on a ship bound for Canada.

Cathal was also born in the year of Halley's Comet. He dreaded that he might 'go out with it', but fortunately he lived for many more years after its return.

The first of August was a Monday and his father claimed that Cathal's birth had spoiled his bank holiday. Mr Gannon worked as a carpenter in McLaughlin and Harvey's, a reputable Dublin firm of building contractors in Dartmouth Road, Ranelagh (a suburb in the south of the city), and at that stage earned the princely sum of 35s. per week. During Christmas week of 1910 he was sacked. A note received some days afterwards informed him that back money was due to him. He went to the office and received an envelope containing 2s. 6d. Cathal's first Christmas was a lean one; his parents were glad to have their dinner in Cathal's grandmother's house.

During the following January, Mr Gannon started work in the Guinness Brewery (or Guinness's Brewery as Cathal and his colleagues always called it) and remained there until he retired in 1948 at the age of sixty-five.

Charles Gannon senior was born in 22 Upper Clanbrassil Street, Dublin, near the Grand Canal, in 1883. He was one of seven children; he had two brothers and four sisters. When he was about eight or nine years of age he served as an altar boy in the nearby church attached to the Passionist monastery at Mount Argus, Harold's Cross. He distinctly remembered the renowned Blessed Charles of Saint Andrew – the humble Dutch priest who had been sent to Ireland to encourage the developing Passionist community and who had devoted his life to frugality, prayer, and, despite ill health, endless blessings and healings of the sick. Mr Gannon recollected how, on locking up the church one evening, it was discovered that Father Charles was missing. The door of the church was opened and he was found at the altar, praying. Mr Gannon spoke of how he had been forcibly removed and how he had been told that he would catch cold whilst kneeling in the freezing church. This indeed would have been typical of the man who, towards the end of his life, immersed himself in prayer to the exclusion of everything else.

As a boy, Mr Gannon was often sent on the unpleasant errand of bringing his father home from the pub for his dinner. It is possible that his father's drinking habits had caused a rift in the family, as money that he should have inherited was given instead to his sister. Consequently, Mr Gannon abhorred alcohol for the rest of his life and discouraged drinking at home. Cathal benefited from his father's strict rule and drank only a little when socializing.

Mr Gannon attended the Christian Brothers' school in Synge Street and hated it. Cathal was told that his father took out his revenge on one of the teachers, who was beating him, by 'splitting' him with a slate. Despite this, Mr Gannon would send all his sons to the same school in later years; either his dictum was 'if it was good enough for me, it will be good enough for you', or the modest school fees were the deciding factor, money being scarce at the time.

On one particular evening, when Mr Gannon was aged thirteen, he completed the most difficult homework that he had ever been given, and was told by his father, 'You may put away your school books now – you're starting work tomorrow.' He began his working life as an apprentice carpenter in McLaughlin and Harvey's at six o'clock the following morning. As Cathal laconically remarked, 'That was the way they did things then.'

The working day was long and hard: six o'clock in the morning until six in the evening and until two on Saturdays. Having served his apprenticeship, Mr Gannon became a carpenter. It is not known whether he actually liked working for the company or not; he simply regarded himself as being lucky to have constant employment. His supervisor was rather put out when he became friendly with Sir Henry McLaughlin, and this ultimately led to his dismissal during the week before Christmas, 1910.

Before he was married, he was sent to do interior woodwork for a big mansion in Killarney and then some panelling for Clonsilla Lodge, County Dublin, then owned by the St George family. The house was burned at a later stage and the land now belongs to St Joseph's Hospital.

Whilst working in Clonsilla, Mr Gannon stayed in a railway engine shed that had been converted into four little cottages and which was located some distance from the bridge over the Royal Canal. However, he was soon driven out of it by fleas. He therefore opted to travel all the way from his home in Clanbrassil Street to Clonsilla by bicycle, often accompanied for part of the journey by his fiancée, Susan Mary Kelly, who then proceeded to her place of work.

Susan was born in 1882. Like the Gannons, she came from a family that had its roots in Francis Street, at the heart of Dublin's Liberties. Despite such humble beginnings, the Kellys were well read and would have an important influence on young Cathal's development. Susan was sent to school in Warrenmount Convent, Blackpitts, a short walk from her home. Later, it appears, she was sent to an orphanage after her father suddenly left home. She never spoke about this. It seems that she remained there until she was old enough to work.

In the early 1900s she went to work for the Ravensdale Mill Stores and continued there until she was married. She started working at the head-quarters on Wellington Quay, selling seeds, flour and meal, and later moved to other branches, including one in Clanbrassil Street, where she met Mr Gannon. He was a very handsome man with a swarthy complexion and Susan mistook him for a Jew. This was not too surprising, as many Jewish families lived in the vicinity of the South Circular Road at that time.

Another one of the five branches of the Ravensdale Mill Stores was in Baggot Street, where Susan finally became manageress, earning 30s. a week. Here she met quite a number of interesting people – the wives of all the important senior council, judges and the like – who came to buy pet food. A frequent visitor to the shop was the cabinetmaker James Hicks, who worked nearby in Pembroke Street. Thanks to him, she became knowledge-able about old furniture. Later, Cathal would note her good taste as regards furnishings at home. She also knew the Honourable Thomas Lopdell O'Shaughnessy KC, who was the County Court Judge and Recorder of Dublin and who was a great collector of snuff boxes and silver. Count and Countess Plunkett, the parents of Joseph Mary Plunkett, frequented the shop. Another customer was Lady Lumsden, wife of Sir John Lumsden, who was head of the medical department in Guinness's Brewery. When customers such as these invited Susan to afternoon tea, Mr Drake, her employer, always allowed her to go.

One morning, around 1905, when she was walking to work, a tall Panhard car drew up beside her and either a doctor's or barrister's chauffeur invited her to take a lift. She sat beside him and was driven to the shop in Baggot Street. As motor cars were something of a novelty at that time, she was aware of everybody looking at her. This was the first time she had travelled by car and she was justifiably pleased with herself.

When she journeyed in to work one morning on April Fool's Day, she counted nineteen coal carts parked outside the headmaster's house of the High School in Harcourt Street. Each of the two-wheeled carts would have carried a ton of coal. Obviously some pupils had organized this prank, copying the more famous incident that had taken place in London years previously. The coalmen were standing around the hall door of the house talking to one another and somebody could be seen on the steps.

One of Susan's friends was a lady by the name of Miss Gordon, proprietor of the Irish Lace Shop in Mary Street. This, in fact, was just half a shop; the premises had been divided in two. Displayed in the window were samples of Carrickmacross, Limerick and French lace pinned to pieces of white or brown paper. This shop always fascinated Cathal and he often stopped to look in the window when on his way to technical school in the 1920s.

Miss Gordon's opinion on lace was often sought when private houses were to be auctioned and she frequently invited Susan to join her when visiting these residences. Susan accompanied her one day in 1905 or 1906 to 77 St Stephen's Green, now Loreto Hall, which had been lived in by the eccentric Miss Augusta Elizabeth Magan. Miss Magan was descended from one of the oldest royal houses, the O'Conors of Connaught. The house, bought in 1820, had been lived in by the family until Miss Magan's death in 1905.

According to Cathal's mother, by the time 77 St Stephen's Green was to be auctioned it had been neglected for some thirty or forty years and the curtains were falling off the windows. The kitchen was in its 1820 condition and had not been modernized. As it happened, the lace that was to be examined had become discoloured and moth-eaten: it was worthless. Whilst there, Susan found an antique oval mahogany table and a square piano by the English maker Tomkison. Her friend Mr Hicks attended the auction and secured the table for 9s. and the piano for 8s. The table is still in use and the piano probably still exists somewhere in Dublin.

In 1909, Susan Kelly married Mr Gannon and the couple spent a short honeymoon in Avoca, County Wicklow. Mr Gannon was then earning 36s. – just 6s. more than his wife. They had saved the grand total of £36 for setting up house and the two articles of furniture with which they started married life were the aforementioned table and piano. They lived at first in a rented flat in a large Georgian house near Mount Pleasant Square, Ranelagh, beside the railway bridge. In 1910, the elderly lady who owned the house decided to sell her property and offered it to Mr Gannon for £200, which he could not afford.

The family was now obliged to move to a small artisan's dwelling: 31 Darley Street in Harold's Cross, close to the Grand Canal and South Circular Road. This, then, is the house where Cathal's parents lived when he was born. Darley Street is one of several narrow side streets off the main road and it is lined on each side by terraced houses. Cathal could remember a large room downstairs with a staircase leading from it. There was a little scullery at the back and an outdoor toilet. Upstairs there were two bedrooms.

As a baby, Cathal was put into a playpen that his father had made from an old tea chest. Mr Gannon had placed a smooth hand rail around the top, fitted castors to the bottom and lined the inside with a rug. This contraption was pushed under the table when not in use, then pulled out after mealtimes for Cathal's amusement.

Sometime in 1911 a baby competition was run by a magazine called *Lady of the House*, in which a photograph of Cathal appeared. The original print, now sepia in colour, shows a chubby though unremarkable boy some ten or eleven months old with long, fair hair and the distinctive heavy eyelids of the Gannon family; the face and expression is instantly recognizable. It came as no surprise to Cathal that he did not win the competition. Cathal always spoke critically of his own looks and behaviour, describing his face as 'twisted like the handle of a jug'.

He very clearly remembered the Tomkison square piano that his mother had bought in Miss Magan's house. A 'square' piano was the type of piano owned by the average person during the late-eighteenth and mid-nineteenth centuries. The instrument was actually rectangular in shape, was a little higher than a table and stood on either four or six legs. In about 1820, a grand piano would have cost a hundred guineas, whereas a square piano would have only cost twenty-five to thirty.

The little piano in the front room in Darley Street was a handsome instrument. On one occasion, when Cathal was playing under it, one of the legs somehow became detached and rolled across the floor after him. This frightened him and caused nightmares for a few days afterwards. It was a good enough reason to remember the piano clearly.

Cathal was certainly in contact with early keyboard instruments from his childhood, for he recollected seeing another square piano soon afterwards. The occasion was his removal from Darley Street to the home of his maternal grandmother, Susan Mary Kelly, and his spinster aunts, Cissie and Peggy Kelly: 289 South Circular Road, then called Priestfield House, near Dolphin's Barn. This occurred in 1912 when his brother Jack was due to be born. His mother brought him to a little shop by the Grand Canal, near Harold's Cross Bridge, to speak to the owner, who had undertaken to move Cathal's cot and belongings to his aunts' house by horse and cart (or 'horse and car' as Cathal always said). Cathal distinctly remembered standing in the front of the shop, holding his mother's hand and looking into the little parlour at the back through an open door. In the room was a square piano. Amazingly, at just a year and ten months old, Cathal knew exactly what it was.

Two

*B*efore we proceed any further with Cathal's story, let us pause at this point to outline a brief history of his parents' families.

The name Gannon comes from County Mayo. It is derived from the Irish patronymic *Mag Fhionnán*, meaning 'son of Fionnán', which means white or fair. At one time very few Gannons were listed in the telephone directory for the Dublin area.

The first Gannon known in Cathal's family is listed in the 1794 edition of Wilson's Dublin Directory, a section of the grandly titled *Treble Almanack for the year MDCCXCIV. Containing I. Watson's Irish Almanack, II. Exshaw's English Court Registry, III. Wilson's Dublin Directory*. In it, Cornelius Gannon is listed as a tobacconist working at 130 Francis Street. His name appears in the directories each year until 1814; he appears to have died in 1816. Cornelius would have been Cathal's great-great-great-grandfather. Whilst it is impossible to determine Cornelius's status, it would seem that he lived comfortably enough in rented accommodation, first at 130 Francis Street and then at number 135. It was not unusual for people of his class to move from one address to another. During his lifetime, Francis Street would have been a respectable enough address, although there undoubtedly were tenement houses then; the decline took place during the mid-nineteenth century and later.

It appears that one of Cornelius's daughters married into a family by the name of Cunningham, who were clay pipe makers and who lived a few doors away. Cathal's grandfather told him that he spent some years of his childhood in this house.

Cathal's grandfather also told him that Cornelius was a very clever man. As he was good at mathematics, the tinsmiths who lived around Francis

Street and nearby Engine Alley used to consult him if they wanted the capacity of a utensil to be calculated. Making such a calculation would be child's play nowadays, but at that time it was regarded as being difficult.

Cathal was also told by his grandfather that Cornelius was a brother of the Gannons who lived in the house at Cornmarket where Lord Edward Fitzgerald was given shelter for a few days in 1798 before his arrest in Thomas Street.

Unfortunately, we know nothing about the next generation; interestingly, the name Gannon seems to disappear from the records of the Church of St Nicholas of Myra, Francis Street. This may well coincide with the exodus of upper-class people from the district to better and more fashionable areas in the suburbs.

Cathal's great-grandfather, William Gannon, was born sometime around 1816 and died in 1900. He lived in 135 Francis Street and his profession was described as a 'house carpenter'. This effectively meant that he was a carpenter who was available for hire. He also worked, possibly in a temporary capacity, in Guinness's Brewery some time before 1858. Apparently he knew Sir Benjamin Lee Guinness, who died in 1868. He appears to have had a row with Sir Benjamin, the result of which was his dismissal or perhaps his own decision to leave the company.

William and his family then journeyed to Naul in north County Dublin, where he supervised the building of a large mansion, though it is not known for whom. William's son, Charles William, was aged eight at this time and was there when his little sister slipped backwards and fell off the kitchen table, hit her head against the ground and died. She was buried in the little graveyard in Naul.

In 1882, William Gannon and his family, having lived at various addresses around the city, followed the general trend and settled down in Mountpleasant Avenue in the suburb of Rathmines, not far from where other members of the extended family lived. The Gannons had risen a notch on the social ladder and become a little more respectable.

William's son Charles William was born in 1850. Just to confuse matters, this combination of names would be used for the next three generations. As noted earlier, Charles lived for a while with Mrs Cunningham in Francis Street. However, he too moved towards the suburbs and lived for most of his life in 22 Upper Clanbrassil Street, a house near Clanbrassil Bridge on the Grand Canal. The house has long since been demolished.

This house had a basement and two storeys above. Cathal remembered the long back garden, which extended from the house to the back of Wellington Barracks (now Griffith College) and contained apple trees. At one period, before Cathal's time, horse-trams used to run along the road by the house, having been helped over the steep bridge by extra horses that were stationed near the Gannons' house.

Charles William, who was a rather religious man and who belonged to the Franciscan Third Order, worked in his younger days at Martin's, the woodworkers, with the famous Matt Talbot – a reformed chronic alcoholic who, inspired by a priest, followed a strict regime of total abstinence, prayer, fasting and generosity. During Charles William's last days in the Hospice for the Dying, Cathal presented him with a book that had been written about Matt Talbot. He read it and returned it to Cathal, saying, 'I enjoyed reading that but I don't believe a word of it. I knew Matty Talbot better than I know you, and he was a very dependable man, but he was a terrible man for drink.' Charles William agreed that Matt had attended Mass regularly and that he had given up drinking, but said, 'I don't believe all this about wearing chains around his waist.'

Charles William was then employed as a carpenter in Guinness's Brewery. He started work at six o'clock every morning. His job was to look after the directors' office furniture, make any little alterations that were needed and have his work done before these exalted members of the staff arrived at nine or ten o'clock.

The men's wages were paid in sovereigns or half sovereigns, along with shillings and other coins. In the basement of his house, Charles William had a huge kitchen table with three-inch square legs. Cathal often watched as his grandparents turned the table upside down, extracted a cork from one of the legs and spilled out the money that was kept inside it.

Charles William married Catherine Beggs in 1876; she was born in Dorset Street in 1851. Apparently she had a lovely singing voice. According to Cathal, she was a very competent woman and made money go to its full extent.

She had magnificent white hair, which she brushed and did up before retiring to bed every night. Cathal never saw her wash her hair, which led him to believe that maybe there was something wrong with it. Recently I unearthed the only photograph of her that exists. It shows an elderly woman with strong features, a wrinkled face and silvery hair.

An old lady once said to Cathal, 'You know, the Gannons were very respectable – they always had their own house.' At the time Cathal did not know what she meant but later realized that most carpenters in that period could only afford to live in tenement houses. The fact that the Gannons always had a house of their own was quite an achievement. According to the Dublin Directories, Charles William is listed as the tenant of 22 Clanbrassil Street from 1892 until 1927, when he died. Cathal's grandmother finally gave up the house in about 1930 when she went into St Monica's, the old ladies' home at Belvidere Place, near Mountjoy Square.

Cathal generally spoke about his father's family out of a sense of duty, but always spoke with more enthusiasm about his mother's.

His mother's lineage begins with a small drop of ancient Irish aristocracy. Cathal was told that his mother's grandmother, Margaret McDermott of Elphin, County Roscommon, was related to the great MacDermot family and thus descended from the Princes of Coolavin, rulers of Connaught. I have been unable to find any definite proof of this connection, but in all probability Margaret was related – albeit distantly – to the family, if one is to believe the anecdotal evidence. MacDermot is the spelling used by the illustrious family, yet Margaret appears to have spelt her name McDermott – the version recorded twice in the baptismal records of the Church of St Nicholas of Myra, Francis Street.

Margaret was a Protestant and had to be received into the Catholic Church in 1837 in order to marry Michael Byrne, who was a humble apothecary and who worked in 102 and then 111 Francis Street. As we have noted, the Gannons resided at number 135 during the 1860s. One may guess that Margaret's deep love for Michael caused her to renounce her faith and marry below her station; in doing so she incurred the wrath of her family and was disowned by them.

One of Margaret's daughters was Susan Mary Byrne. She was born in 1844 at Newmarket, near the Coombe. She was sent to the nearby Warrenmount Convent, at that time run by Carmelite nuns, who were later transferred to Harold's Cross. At the age of five she was put standing on a chair by the nuns, who undid the stitches and let down the hem of her skirt, which they considered to be too short. Her parents then took her away from the school as a protest.

When Susan was twelve, her mother died and she took on the role of rearing the family of eight and looking after her father. She subsequently never went to work. By and large, her life was hard and uneventful, but she had the pleasure, in her young days, of hearing Charles Dickens reading publicly in Dublin on two occasions when he came to Ireland. Her father brought her to hear him in the Rotunda, and she remembered an old deaf lady interrupting Mr Dickens by banging her stick on the floor and demanding that he speak louder.

In about 1870, Susan married Philip Kelly and for some years they lived in a fine, elegant house in Gloucester Street. Philip lived fairly well and at one time was an importer of Russian furs. He was also lessee of the Queen's Theatre for a few years. He and Susan then moved to a small house in Lombard Street, off the South Circular Road; Cathal thought that business might have gone bad and a more modest lifestyle was necessary.

It appears that although Philip was a well-liked man, he was a street angel and house devil. On the other hand, Susan was rather pious. One day a row took place in the house and Philip stormed out, never to return. Nobody knew what happened to him. As a young man he had been to sea and it is thought that perhaps he became a sailor again.

Naturally, when he left, the breadwinner went and it was up to Susan to run the house on slender means. She took in needlework for Pim's in George's Street and her daughters helped her with the work. However, Cathal's mother was too young at the time and was packed off to an orphanage, as we have seen in the first chapter. Cathal never knew any of this until one of his aunts told him the story before she died.

Cathal remembered Susan singing beautifully, accompanied on the piano by one of her daughters, on Sunday evenings. When older, she became rather fussy. It was a common occurrence for her to work herself up into a tizzy on Saturday evenings in her preparations for Sunday, which was an important day for her. She used to say to her daughters, 'Have you got your *articles* ready for tomorrow morning?' Despite this, as Cathal remarked, she was a 'grand old character'.

Cissie, whose correct name was Esther Kelly, was one of Susan's daughters and one of Cathal's two aunts who lived in Priestfield House on the South Circular Road when Cathal was a child. She was a teacher by profession; she started as a monitoress or assistant teacher in Francis Street National School and finished up as headmistress. Cathal did not seem to know what subjects she taught; no doubt teachers at that time and in that particular type of school were expected to teach all subjects. She was highly proficient in Irish; she began to study the language after the change of government in 1922.

Filthy, decayed tenement houses, crowded with people, abounded in the Francis Street area at that time. Despite the grinding poverty – many survived on little more than bread and tea – the people in these close-knit communities were extraordinarily cheerful and good-humoured. Cissie Kelly was in constant contact with these 'rough diamonds' and loved them; she regarded them – especially the women – as being decent, hard-working people. Although the overworked wives were frequently abused and beaten by lazy, drunken husbands who squandered what little money they had on alcohol, there was very little crime amongst the community and doors were always left open. Cissie often heard talk of people who lived in a tenement house with 'a shut hall door and water on the landing': that was judged to be the epitome of luxury.

Although Cissie was very precise about grammar – Cathal never heard any bad grammar in Priestfield House – she had a great sense of humour. When she came home from school in the afternoon she always had some funny incident to talk about, such as a row or a mother complaining about a child being beaten, repeating what had been said and how it had been said.

Cissie was pious and fond of going to the church at Mount Argus near Harold's Cross, home of Father Charles. She attended all the various ceremonies there, and often brought young Cathal to them. Excursions were organized regularly by the church and Cissie often joined them. She was one of what the other priests referred to as 'Father Gerald's girls'. Father Gerald, from Northern Ireland, officiated at Mount Argus for many years and founded a women's sodality.

For some inexplicable reason, she nicknamed Cathal 'bop man'. He enjoyed her company immensely.

Cissie's sister, Cathal's other aunt, was Margaret Kelly, better known as Peggy. Born in 1874, she was the eldest of the family. Her first job was in White's china shop in Marlborough Street, Dublin, beside the old Abbey Theatre. It appears that she earned a half-crown (2s. 6d.) per week. Mr White was a very old man then; he was in his late eighties or early nineties. Peggy spoke of seeing packing cases in the shop that had lain unopened since the 1820s; they contained Wedgwood china designed by John Flaxman (1755–1826). She remembered one of the big cases being opened and an employee taking out the china, which she then had the pleasure of handling. This encouraged her to take an interest in china and porcelain.

Peggy worked in White's for a number of years; after this she opened a little sweetshop in Marlborough Street and worked in that for a while.

Peggy seems to have been an unsettled person. She decided that she wanted to be a nurse and subsequently went to England, where she studied in Crumpshill, Manchester. She became a nurse, returned home and was attached for a while to Portobello Home on the banks of the Grand Canal at Rathmines Bridge. She was working there on 25 April 1916 and from the window saw Francis Sheehy Skeffington, the socialist, pacifist and feminist, being arrested and brought to Portobello (Cathal Brugha) Barracks.

At some stage in the early 1900s, Peggy nursed an old lady in Cork whom Edith Somerville had used as a prototype for Flurry Knox's grandmother in *Some Experiences of an Irish R.M.* Peggy described her as being a very old lady in her nineties with hands 'like the talons of a bird of prey', but with magnificent diamond rings on her fingers. Peggy subsequently introduced young Cathal to the book, from which he often quoted in later life.

Peggy then became a lady's companion. She lived with various families, including Sir John and Lady Lumsden, the Westbys of Roebuck Castle and the Turbetts of Owenstown House, Dundrum. She also nursed big families in the country. As she was well read and interesting, she was obviously considered to be good company by these exalted people. Consequently her manner became rather grand and, according to Cathal, she spoke beautifully. It was no wonder then that Cathal developed an English accent at a young age. That soon changed when he went to school, where he was ridiculed for speaking in such a manner.

Despite Peggy's polished manners, she was erratic and unpredictable. She was also possessed of a very fiery temper.

She took Cathal under her wing and brought him to such places as the National Museum and National Gallery in Dublin. She also took him to auctions and drew his attention to different types of porcelain; and she brought him around the many second-hand shops in Dublin, including the Iveagh Market in Francis Street. She was full of knowledge and had a great influence on the young boy. Thanks to Peggy, Cathal saw many things that he took notice of and never forgot; she was a landmark in his life.

Cathal's uncle John also lived in Priestfield House with his mother and sisters. Uncle John spent much of his time 'out with the boys'; he was a friendly character and 'a great one for playing billiards and slugging beer'.

Being the eldest of his family, Cathal was sent regularly to the house when his mother was giving birth to his brothers and sisters (Jack, Willie, Maureen and Ethna). He spent many happy days there. They expected him to stay every weekend, but often he overstayed his welcome and his father used to say, 'I think it's time you came home and got to know your brothers and sisters a little bit better.'

Three

The Gannon family moved from Darley Street to Longford Terrace on the Crumlin Road in 1913, the year of the notorious Dublin baton charge when the police prevented the labour leader Jim Larkin from addressing the crowds during the famous lock-out. On 31 August Cathal's father was cycling through Sackville Street (now O'Connell Street). He saw Larkin, disguised as an elderly clergyman, being helped out of a cab and into the hallway of the Imperial hotel. A couple of minutes afterwards he appeared on a balcony, without the disguise, and addressed the crowd below. He was immediately arrested by members of the Dublin Metropolitan Police who were nearby. A very cruel baton charge then ensued. Mr Gannon jumped on his bicycle and cycled as quickly as he could out of Sackville Street, along Westmoreland Street and into George's Street. He went into a shop to buy a newspaper and while he was describing the scene to the girl behind the counter he saw men trudging up the street with blood streaming from their heads.

Cathal distinctly remembered his father coming home and telling his mother that he had seen the baton charge. Mr Gannon showed Cathal how he had twisted his bicycle around and cycled away. Cathal remembered every detail of the conversation.

At some stage during the year the family moved to a terraced house on the Crumlin Road, not far from the Grand Canal and Harold's Cross. Mr Gannon had always wanted a nicer house, in more rural surroundings. The house, now 82 Crumlin Road, was at that time 20 Longford Terrace. It was opposite Carnaclough House, now Loreto College. The Gannons' house was the fourth last on the Crumlin Road, and after that there was open country.

For Cathal it was an idyllic place to live because of its tranquillity and rural atmosphere. Cathal, and later his brothers, slept in the back bedroom and during summer nights it was difficult to sleep due to the unceasing calls of the corncrakes in the fields. It was so quiet that they were able to hear an occasional motor car horn hooting some two miles away in Crumlin village. Even then some of the cars had electric lights. The lights would flicker on the bedroom wall; the car would come nearer and nearer, then pass the house and all would be quiet once again.

Opposite the house was a tennis club, where young ladies and gentlemen dressed in white could be seen playing lawn tennis. From here to the back of Mount Argus Church – one could see the steeple and bell turret from the house – were fields. There was an uninterrupted view of the Dublin Mountains; a view that Cathal, aged eighteen, sketched in pencil at the back of his Palgrave's *Golden Treasury*.

On summer evenings it was customary for the family to push up one of the sash windows at the front of the house and sit in chairs, looking at the tennis matches and the scenery beyond. Occasionally they saw a fire in the mountains; either it was the work of picnickers or farmers who might have set a whole bank of brushwood on fire. Cathal fondly remembered the pleasure afforded to him by this restful scene. He would often use a telescope to watch motor cars going slowly up the mountains.

Sometimes they sat at the back of the house, facing the old St James's Gate football club, owned by Guinness's Brewery, where men played football or ran around exercising. Sometimes Brewery pensioners engaged in walking races and competed against each other.

The playing fields were bordered by large trees along the nearby Herberton Lane, now Herberton Road. A tall wall ran along by the road and on top of it was a corrugated iron fence, which increased the height of the wall to ten or fifteen feet. The trees grew inside the wall; one particular tree leaned well into the field and a huge branch projected from it. On it a pulley had been mounted and from it a very heavy weight was suspended. One or two individual members of a tug-of-war team used to pull this weight up and it could be heard thumping back to the ground when they let it go.

The back of the house also looked towards the Grand Canal, Herberton Bridge and to the area later to be called Rialto. One could also see what was then known as the Old Soldiers' Home, now the Royal Hospital, Kilmainham. Cathal's eyes were keen when he was young and he could see the time on the elegant clock tower. He often peered at it in the morning when he got up.

Cathal could distinctly remember the interior of the family house. It was one of twenty-four houses built around 1912 and the Gannons were the first residents to live in it. Cathal lived there until he was married in 1942.

The house had three bedrooms upstairs, two rooms downstairs – a front sitting room and a kitchen-cum-living room with a range in it – and a projecting scullery, containing a stove, at the back. A gas cooker was added later. Over the scullery was a bathroom containing a toilet. By the standards of the time, it was quite a good house; it was certainly an improvement on Darley Street. Cathal believed that the rent was 16s. a week, which would have been nearly half his father's weekly wages.

The back bedroom was let for a few years, until Mr Gannon 'got on his feet', to two sisters, the Victorys; Cathal described them as being very nice and kind to the children. They disappeared every morning and came back late in the evening, so they were rarely seen.

There were small gardens at the back and front, and in the back garden Mr Gannon kept poultry, so the family always had eggs. During the years of World War I, Mr Gannon sold all his eggs to a grocer in nearby Dolphin's Barn. For years he kept a careful record of his transactions and accounted for every penny that he spent. He used to have about sixty hens and he reckoned that he made £1 a year out of each one. When a hen had stopped laying, he would sell it or else kill it for his own use, and so there was always chicken for the family's meals. Thanks to Mr Gannon's industry and economy, the family was able to live in reasonable comfort. They lived frugally but were happy.

At the other side of the hen run in the back garden was Mr Gannon's little workshop, in which he made furniture for the house during his spare time. Lying against the wall of the house was a stack of timber, with which Cathal spent many happy hours playing. Mr Gannon used to acquire second-hand timber in Guinness's Brewery. The children used it to make imaginary aeroplanes and afterwards, when they had finished, they put it back the way they had found it.

Mr Gannon was a very methodical man. He cut the boys' hair – they never went to the barber's – and repaired their shoes. He was also a great jam maker. Vegetables came from the plots of land that he owned. He was fond of eating rabbits, especially young ones. Cathal hated the sight of them and never liked the taste.

Distance often lends enchantment and an elderly person is inclined to glorify the past, but perhaps Cathal should have been believed when he said that the taste of meat was wonderful then, especially pork. No doubt this was due to the healthy upbringing of the animals and the lack of chemical additives. It was difficult not to yield to the temptation of nibbling offcuts whilst carving.

Cathal's mother was a great maker of yeast bread. She also baked wonderful cakes and never, as far as Cathal knew, used a weighing scales. Instead, she measured her ingredients in an old cup without a handle. The only scales they had in the house was an old spring balance, which was very inaccurate.

Apart from some good paintings that were in the family home, two were remembered vividly by Cathal for different reasons. One, on a mahogany panel, of no great merit, depicted Crom Castle in Northern Ireland. Mr Gannon saw great possibilities in the wood and used it to make a table. Consequently, in order to see the picture it was necessary to crawl under the table.

In Cathal's bedroom hung a head-and-shoulders portrait of an old man with a beard. It was very well painted – the picture was oil on canvas and it had a gilt frame – but nobody knew who the man was. Cathal thought that his mother had probably bought it at an auction for a shilling. At a later stage Cathal and his brother Jack found that their trousers could be affixed to the painting and buttoned around it, so that the man appeared to have legs. Jack pinned his stockings to the legs, creating feet. Cathal then conceived the idea of 'finishing it off', and fashioned a penis using a rolled up handkerchief, which he attached to the trousers. His mother came upstairs at this point and caught the boys. He never saw the painting afterwards.

There were a few other pictures in the house that were typical of the period: 'Scotland Forever' and 'The Roll Call' by the Victorian artist Lady Butler and some old black-and-white prints of her paintings. When Cathal was older he began to buy eighteenth-century prints, mezzotints and oil paintings, and frame them. By the time he left the house, there were several good pictures on the walls. He left some behind and gave others away.

The Gannon household was the only one in the terrace with imported Swiss net curtains in the windows, which Mrs Gannon bought from Jackson's house-furnishing shop in Camden Street. Cathal did not know if they met with the neighbours' approval. Most people had lace curtains, which they starched and ironed. Sometimes they pinned them together so that they could not pull apart. This, in Cathal's eyes, 'gave a terrible drab appearance'.

The Gannons' net curtains hung down to the floor; according to Cathal, his parents were years ahead of their time in some respects.

Mr Gannon wallpapered the interior walls of the house himself. The work was accurately done and the wallpaper was butt joined, edge to edge – never overlapped. Mr Gannon favoured a paper with a restrained pattern and an oatmeal background.

Another fashion of the period was to have a chair rail in the hall. The wall under the rail was painted in white enamel and above the rail it was painted red. There was also a brass rail by the hall door, which prevented people rubbing against the wall.

From an early age Cathal was always aware of the bad taste in furniture of the period. He despised the then-fashionable art nouveau decor but had to put up with a certain amount of it at home: 'It was the thing to have it', as he said. The pattern books that his father used were produced during the 1890s and were influenced by the style of that time. According to Cathal, he tried to be modern but just could not be modern enough.

Four

*L*ike all young children, Cathal amused himself by playing. Toys were not abundant in the Gannon household, but what they had were appreciated to the full.

Cathal could remember lorries made of tin and the flat, two-dimensional drivers inside them that dissatisfied him. He also played with German clockwork toys, which if turned upside down revealed that they were made out of salvaged tin boxes with various designs and words printed on them. They only cost a few pence.

On Cathal's fourth birthday he was given a large clockwork saloon car and he played with it for many years. It was kept on a shelf and ceremoniously taken down every so often for his use. He often wondered what it might be worth nowadays.

Favourite chasing games amongst the children were 'tip and tig' and 'relievio'. Cathal used to join skipping games and play with tops. However, he did not participate in as many games as some of the other children did, often not being very interested in them.

He and the children would often play 'shop' and buy things with 'chaney' money: pieces of broken china on which fragments of willow pattern could often be seen. Another favourite recreation was playing with marbles, which the children never seemed to buy – they were usually given to them or else they acquired them in some other manner.

Most children like to indulge in some sort of 'divilment'; Cathal and his companions were no exception. Indeed, Cathal's penchant for playing pranks started at an early age. At night they used to tie a piece of string across the road from one lamp post to another and knock off people's hats.

Another trick was to tie the knockers of adjacent houses together. The children would give the string a tug to knock at one of the doors, then run to a hiding place to watch the results. They also used to tie a button on to a piece of thread, pin the thread to the edge of somebody's window, pull it from the other end and tap on the glass.

During the daytime they would place a fake parcel on the ground and attach a length of thread to it. When somebody bent down to pick it up, they would jerk it away.

Cathal spent much of his childhood playing with the children of the Healy family, who lived on the other side of Crumlin Road in Towerfield House, which was at the end of a long avenue. It was a lovely country house, set in fields.

Cathal was often sent to the farm for buttermilk. The Healys used to ask him to repeat 'a pennyworth of buttermilk' several times because of the English accent that he had acquired from his maternal aunt, Peggy Kelly. Cathal would then have to struggle home with about a gallon of buttermilk in a big tin can – so big that he could hardly carry it. It was a delicious drink with meals and was frequently used for making bread.

The Healys were close friends of the family; the Gannons often visited them for musical evenings. They were well off and owned a good piano. Various people used to sing and one of the daughters would 'scrape' a violin. The Gannons usually went to the Healys' house on Christmas Day.

A great celebration was organized when the Healys' son was ordained a priest. They rigged up a stage in a barn and performed little amateur plays that they wrote themselves. Much later, Cathal remembered his brother Jack playing a part in Lady Gregory's *Spreading the News*.

An old quarry in one of the Healys' fields looked like an amphitheatre. It was here that Cathal witnessed an open-air meeting known as an *aeriocht*. He was told afterwards by someone that he had seen Patrick Pearse addressing the assembled crowd. There was also Irish dancing and traditional music. A photograph of the event in a newspaper many years later helped to jog Cathal's memory. He remembered being brought to the quarry when he was about five years of age by a girl who lived nearby. There were uniforms and flags; people marched up from Dolphin's Barn and went into the field. The children followed afterwards. Although Cathal could rightfully claim that he had seen Patrick Pearse, he really had just a hazy recollection of him.

A pool of water had formed in the bottom of the quarry, which added a certain amount of charm. It was a very peaceful spot; one could sit on the banks and admire the view. People used to walk around the area, exercising their dogs.

Halfway along the Crumlin Road on the opposite side, near Mount Eagle House (the home of the McKeons, who were dairy people), was a spring. Cathal and his young companions often knelt down beside the well and drank the beautifully clear water, which Cathal said was most refreshing.

Heading southwards from the junction between the Crumlin Road and Herberton Lane was the Dark Lane, now Sundrive Road. For some reason, Cathal always referred to this as the Dark Lanes. It was twisty and narrow, about one mile long, and led to the Kimmage Road. It was quite lonely here; there were high hedges on each side and it was dark. Cathal could remember every house along this lane, such as Carnaclough House at the corner and the fine early nineteenth-century Rosebush House on the other side, with its pleasant gardens and brick gazebo. At the junction stood a lovely laburnum tree where Cathal often sheltered from the rain. Along the laneway was a house that was supposed to be haunted – it was said that a hangman had once lived in it – and farther on was a terrace of red-bricked houses where the employees of the one-time nearby brickworks lived. Water had filled the areas that had been dug and consequently there was a series of small lakes amid grassy knolls to the left of the lane.

As an example of how quiet the surroundings could be in this part of Dublin, Cathal liked to recount the following story. Years later, he used to visit a family who were builders and who had a shop on the Kimmage Road, at the end of the Dark Lane. One night in about 1930 he walked home from their house after a party. The lights of the city could be seen to the right and the place was as silent as could be imagined. Cathal had an antique verge watch in his pocket and he could hear it ticking. He passed some people and saluted them. He wondered if they could hear the sound of his watch. Naturally, his hearing was very keen then and he could not sleep in a room in which a clock was ticking, despite his love of clocks. I can remember him placing his wind-up alarm clock under the bed so that it would not disturb him.

The Dark Lane disappeared in the 1930s, when Corporation houses were built along the widened road.

Going in the opposite direction, northwards to the Grand Canal from the Crumlin Road, was Herberton Lane, now Herberton Road. At the junction with the Crumlin Road, where the Garda barracks is now, was Grovefield Villa, a fine Regency house. Next came a couple of small two-storeyed Georgian houses on the left. A little beyond them were Grovefield Cottages: five single-storeyed houses with half doors. The doors were always open and the owners often looked out and greeted the passers-by. On Saturday nights somebody played a melodeon. A few of the people who lived in these cottages were well known for coming home a little drunk. They worked hard, had a few drinks and in the evening they could be heard being brought home. After that, all went quiet.

Farther along Herberton Lane, past the junction with Keeper Road (a mere laneway in Cathal's time) was Springfield House, home of the Richardsons. William and Thomas Richardson were lime burners, coal and cement merchants and general carriers. Guinness's Brewery used their services on a contract basis until 1960. As Springfield House was surrounded by a high wall, it could only be seen when a car went in or came out of the gates. Stables for all the horses were situated behind Grovefield Cottages. The horses and carts left for the city, one after the other, at about seven o'clock every morning. This was the first sign of life to be heard around Longford Terrace when Cathal was young; he and the family knew that it was time to get up.

In summer the drivers drank in Mangan's pub at Dolphin's Barn Bridge nearby and by the time they left it was nearly midnight. As it was hardly worthwhile going home, they slept in Richardsons' field. A bell was rung at about six or seven o'clock in the morning, and they got up and reported for work.

Herberton Bridge crossed the Grand Canal a little farther on; beyond were the Flanagans' market gardens. Women could be seen working there all day long with an overseer watching them. When they had finished at five or six o'clock in the evening, they queued in the stable yard of Flanagans' house, Portmahon Lodge, on the southern side of the canal, and were paid for each day's work. At one time they earned a shilling and a penny per day. Old Alderman Michael Flanagan, father of 'The Bird' and 'The Pope' Flanagan, sat with a cape over his shoulders and paid each woman.

At the junction of Herberton Lane and the South Circular Road was a house named Valencia and nearby were the Rhubarb Fields, also owned by the Flanagans.

A few steps farther northwards brought one to the main line of the Grand Canal that led to the harbour at James's Street – now part of the Luas line to Tallaght. Over this stretched the old Rialto Bridge, high and steep like its namesake in Venice. Its correct name was Harcourt Bridge, after the first Earl of Harcourt. Because of its shape, cars frequently became stuck on the top. The bridge was reconstructed and the approaching roads made higher in 1939. Near the bridge were small cottages with poultry running around outdoors.

The popular name of the bridge, Rialto, was applied to the nearby Rialto Lodge and Cottage; later it referred to the whole area.

The South Circular Road lead eastwards from Herberton Lane to nearby Dolphin's Barn. In the Hollow of the Barn were several eighteenth and nineteenth-century houses, which in Cathal's youth were tenements. These were once fine residences, built to complement the new canal. They were demolished in the 1940s.

There were three public houses in Dolphin's Barn: Mangan's at the bridge, one in Dolphin's Barn itself, and another at the corner of Rehoboth nearby. On Saturday afternoons, people from the village of Crumlin walked to Dolphin's Barn to do their shopping. Others went into town on the tram from Dolphin's Barn, which at that time was the terminus.

In the evening, everyone adjourned to the three pubs, where there were regular rows. They emerged at about ten o'clock, 'well oiled', and made their way along the Crumlin Road, bawling at the top of their voices. An occasional argument would erupt and there would be a dust-up. Because of this, the children in the Gannon household were kept indoors; Mr Gannon forbade them to go near Dolphin's Barn on a Saturday evening.

Cathal could remember walking on cold winter mornings to the freezing church at Dolphin's Barn for eight o'clock Mass. Nobody ever thought of complaining. It was customary to go to early Mass after having fasted for twelve hours in order to receive Holy Communion and then return home for breakfast. One frequently saw people feeling weak in the church because of the cold and not having eaten. The family generally received Holy Communion once a month. Cathal's mother was pious, but could take and make a joke. His father was moderately religious.

In those days, what amounted to an 'admission fee' was charged into the church: one penny for a back seat and threepence for a front seat. The Gannons always sat at the front. Children and people with no money took the one-penny seats in the main body of the church. Some hard-up people chanced their arms by quickly depositing a penny in the three-penny plate when there was a crowd and the collector might not notice; one would be turned back if the incorrect sum were discovered.

A short distance from the church along the South Circular Road was Priestfield House, the home of Cathal's grandmother and aunts. Beside it was the White Heather Laundry, where the Gannons and Kellys had their sheets and some of their clothes laundered. The laundry, which had a contract with the Viceregal Lodge in the Phoenix Park, employed a large number of girls.

Priestfield House still stands out on its own, being built at an earlier period than the surrounding houses, though it has been spoiled somewhat by the addition of modern PVC windows. Apparently it was a relatively unremarkable house inside; it was comfortable and had a front parlour where the piano was kept. This was the instrument that was used to accompany Cathal's grandmother when she sang. Cathal, when older, practised on it before his mother bought him a piano.

Cathal's grandmother, Susan Mary Kelly, who had heard Charles Dickens reading in Dublin, owned a complete set of his works – her father had bought them for her. The house was full of books. Susan and her two daughters were great lovers of Thackeray and could discuss the works of Anthony Trollope at length. At quite a tender age, Cathal delighted in lying on his tummy, in front of the fire, leafing through a collection of journals in bound volumes. They featured pictures of famous places in the world, such as Venice and the pyramids of Egypt, and had captions printed underneath the illustrations. He vividly remembered every illustration in certain books by Dickens, such as *Martin Chuzzlewit*, *David Copperfield* and *Sketches by Boz*. He was particularly fascinated by the intricate frontispiece in *Martin Chuzzlewit*.

An engraving of St Peter's in the Vatican by Piranesi, which hung in the hall of Priestfield House, captured Cathal's imagination and he formed the idea that he would like to climb to the top of the cupola.

An unusual biscuit tin in the scullery, used to store twine, fascinated him. It bore the name of Huntley and Palmer and resembled a marble base on which a statue could be displayed. Cathal reckoned that it must have been made in about 1907.

As at Longford Terrace, Cathal remembered the silence at Priestfield House, especially after the workers had left the White Heather Laundry next door. At around this time a tram could be heard approaching; it would stop and his aunt Cissie would alight. After it had left, silence would descend until around seven o'clock, when the locals would venture out for their evening entertainment. Sundays were particularly quiet; the pace of life was slow and relaxed. On winter mornings, from seven o'clock onwards, the rattling of trams woke Cathal from his slumbers. When frost covered the overhead cables, sparks flew and illuminated the bedroom.

There were few motor cars on the road and they were less noisy. However, their distinctive klaxons could be heard and also the 'pip-pip-pip' as they turned a corner; this sound came from a whistle fitted to the exhaust. Cathal could clearly remember sitting by the fire in Priestfield House on a Sunday afternoon, listening to the occasional noises from outside.

Cathal always had happy memories of his stays with his aunts; he loved going there and felt that it was a house where he had unlimited freedom to do as he pleased. He learned more from his aunts than from anyone else, for they instilled in him an interest in, and an appreciation of, the arts.

During World War I, Cathal's father rented a plot of land halfway up Rutland Avenue, by the Ramparts. The Ramparts was the name given to a long mound between Rutland Avenue and the old City Water Course. A large field had been divided into plots, one of which was Mr Gannon's. Cathal and his brothers used to help him dig his vegetables. A short cut to the field was through Healys' farm. Mr Gannon rented another plot of land in Chapelizod; it was situated near the Catholic church and ran down to the Liffey. He made a handcart, fitted it with old pram wheels and nicely shaped shafts, which were comfortable to hold, and on a Saturday afternoon he loaded this with his forks, shovels and sacks and set off with the children. Exhausted after the work, they wended their way home at six o'clock, the handcart full of potatoes, onions, cabbages or turnips.

On summer evenings, men could be seen working in the plots in their shirtsleeves. Cathal remembered them scraping the mud off their shovels with a piece of slate or a sharp stone. They would pause to talk to one another and then return to their work.

A short distance from Mr Gannon's plot of land off Rutland Avenue, which was near the Grand Canal, a rope-walk ran along the south side of the canal about halfway between Parnell Bridge (popularly known as Sally's Bridge) and Harold's Cross Bridge. Here Cathal saw ropes, hundreds of feet in length, being made in long sheds. He could remember the clicking sound of the hand-powered machines. There were other rope-walks in the vicinity, such as the one at Rialto Bridge, along what was known as Watery Lane.

Very little traffic passed up and down the road on the south side of the

Grand Canal. At Herberton Bridge there was a gate – a simple bar – across the road and from here onwards, heading in the direction of Inchicore, it was private. The gate was only opened on certain occasions by people who lived nearby. However, one could walk along a narrow, bumpy footpath by the banks of a stream that ran parallel to the canal at a distance of some twenty feet. The path was barely wide enough to cycle on. On the left were empty fields, fine mature trees, hillocks, houses and farms. It was pleasant to walk from Herberton to Inchicore Bridge and back in the evenings or on a Sunday afternoon.

Suir Road Bridge, at the junction of the main line of the canal and the branch that had been extended to join the Liffey, did not exist then. Near the junction was an archway known locally as the 'hot arch' because of the hot water that flowed from a nearby cement mill. This part of the canal was used as a swimming pool by the young people, who swam there well into the winter months.

As most of the roads were made of clay and stones, dust abounded during the summer, especially when it was dry. Whipped up by a gust of wind, it billowed down the Crumlin Road and found its way into every hole and corner, so much so that teacups and other utensils had to be stored upside down. Because of the neighbouring farms, flies were a constant source of irritation; windows had to be kept shut or else fly papers were hung in the rooms.

In winter months, rain turned the roads into mud. Excess mud was swept into mounds, which were spaced some twenty to thirty feet apart, and left at the side of the road for a considerable time. They were eventually shovelled into special horse-drawn wooden carts that were used for the collection of rubbish. These rather medieval-looking vehicles had a canvas roof and had the appearance of a caravan. Mud or refuse was thrown in from an opening in the side, near the driver, or else from the back. The bottom of the cart was curved and could swivel; the contents were tipped out by rotating it sideways. The carts had no suspension and went out of use in the 1920s.

In Cathal's youth, the simplest way to get from one place to another was to walk and people were accustomed to walking long distances. Consequently, good sturdy footwear was necessary. As well as shoes, leather boots were commonly worn. In wet weather, dubbin was rubbed into them to make them waterproof. Gumboots came later and then wellington boots.

Besides walking, the most popular and, of course, the cheapest mode of transport was the bicycle. When wet, a cape was used to keep the cyclist dry; leather gaiters were strapped around the legs and laced over one's shoes or boots.

Horses were much in evidence, as were horse cabs, the equivalent of today's taxis. A charwoman who worked for the family, Mrs Ryan, often travelled to the Gannon household by horse cab. It was driven by her husband, a cab driver. Having left her in Crumlin Road, Mr Ryan went off to do his work. He often gave young Cathal a lift to Dolphin's Barn. Despite the musty smell inside the cab, which was probably caused by damp hay, Cathal enjoyed the experience of bumping and swaying as the horse slowly made its way along the road.

In later years, Cathal often travelled by horse cab in funeral processions. All the family funerals used cabs right up until the 1950s. When he was young, his parents left by cab for a funeral one day, leaving Cathal and his brother Jack free to go fishing at Sally's Bridge. Unfortunately, Mr and Mrs Gannon returned by this very bridge and found the boys lying on their bellies, leaning over the water. They were ordered home, slapped and scolded.

The few cars that were driven on the roads when Cathal was young were very distinctive and because of that they could easily be recognized from a distance. It was also possible to make out who was driving them. Cathal could remember the Hatch brothers driving down the Crumlin Road from Drimnagh Castle. Lord Cloncurry of Lyons House, County Kildare often passed in his Model T Ford, sometimes accompanied by his sister. At a later period, when Cathal was fourteen or fifteen, the famous tenor John McCormack was often to be seen driving one of his two Rolls Royces up the road.

Cathal had fond memories of these peaceful outlying areas of Dublin city and could remember every little detail with astounding clarity. The eccentric characters who lived in the vicinity also featured prominently in his recollections of his childhood and formative years.

'Jack the Liar' was the locals' nickname for Johnny Murphy, whose stories were deemed to be unbelievable. Cathal, however, discovered them to be true. Johnny told Cathal in the 1930s how he had stopped a fight between the young George Bernard Shaw and a local lad at his father's place. An article in a newspaper, written by one of Johnny's sons, and which Cathal subsequently read, proved that this event had taken place.

Johnny, who was a gardener, lived in Spencer Lodge at Dolphin's Barn Bridge. When Cathal knew him, he was in his eighties. Johnny used to sit outside his house, which faced the canal, watching all the goings-on.

'Snotty Arthur', whose nickname referred to the permanently dirty state of his nose, sold newspapers along the Crumlin Road. He lived in Cork Street and every day collected his consignment of newspapers at the headquarters of the *Evening Mail* in the city centre. He then made his way towards Crumlin village crying 'Highle Mail! Highle Mail!' ('Herald or Mail!') – the best pronunciation he could manage, thanks to an impairment in his speech. He was taunted by the local lads, who shouted 'Snotty Arthur!' at him. He cursed them by muttering words such as 'funna cunnas'. I shall leave the reader to decipher this salacious remark.

Kitt Watts was a simple, harmless fellow who walked up and down the Crumlin Road and slept in the nearby brickworks, where he was able to find some heat near the kilns. One day Cathal's uncle Larry, who emigrated to America, gave Kitt an old suit that was no longer needed. He accepted it, discarded his old 'duds' and changed into it, probably in a ditch, and returned to strut up and down in front of the house in order to show it off.

On one occasion he was seen carrying a seven-foot long iron girder on his shoulder. Nobody knew where he was going with it. He had probably been told that he might get money for it if he brought it to a certain shop.

On another occasion he developed a sore on his leg and some cruel individual advised him to put red lead on it. As can be imagined, this did not improve matters and he had to be taken into the Union (or workhouse) where medical attention was given to him. Fortunately he survived and was able to continue his perambulations.

'Mad Alec' was supposed to be a spoiled priest but he was nothing of the sort; he was an illegitimate lad who had lived in the workhouse. He was clever and read anything that he could get his hands on. He had the ability to memorize all sorts of things; he liked to pose difficult questions and tax people's knowledge, especially children's. When he was taken back into the workhouse towards the end of his life, he accumulated a huge pile of newspapers which, once read, were slept upon.

A boy who was nicknamed 'Parkie' lived in one of three two-storeyed whitewashed houses in Wellington View, near Dolphin's Barn Bridge. Young Parkie, who used to thwart Cathal because of his knowledge, had to be literally dragged to Dolphin's Barn school every day by his mother and older sister. Cathal could remember his mother calling him in a wavering voice.

'Broken Arse' also lived in Wellington View. He had a deformed leg and was notorious for cadging drink out of anybody who might be inclined to give some to him. Cathal was amused to see him trying to dance whilst drunk, his arms flailing all over the place.

'Nutty' Brennan was an almost permanent fixture in Dolphin's Barn; he used to sit on a wall in the Hollow. He suddenly disappeared for some time; he was probably brought to hospital following a fall. When Cathal's mother mentioned that she had not seen him for quite a while, Cathal and a friend convinced her that he was dead and buried. When she met him some time afterwards, she nearly died of fright.

Billy Baker was a man with Down's syndrome who lived with his two aunts in a house opposite Dolphin's Barn Church, at the end of the Hollow. He frequently attended christenings and loved to pat the babies' heads. One of his aunts gave piano lessons on a 'little tinny piano', which was always out of tune.

At that time, Dublin was full of 'characters' of this sort; they provided great entertainment and added colour to a life that was hard and often full of misery. Thanks to better education and a higher standard of life, they have all but disappeared, leaving us with a rather bland form of society hooked on television, computers and mobile phones.

Five

A t the age of five, Cathal was sent to school at Warrenmount Presentation Convent in Blackpitts, between the South Circular Road and St
Patrick's Cathedral. This convent, which took boys up to the age of ten, was
chosen because of the family's connections with the nuns; Cissie Kelly had
taught there for a while, Cathal's mother had attended the school and his
grandmother had attended when it was run by the Carmelites. Consequently Cathal was treated as a special pupil.

Cathal vaguely remembered his first day there. When his mother had left
him and gone home, he felt miserable until she returned to collect him at
around three o'clock. When he arrived home, he repeated a piece of dog-
gerel that he had learned from a classmate:

> There was an old lady, God bless her,
> Who threw her leg over the dresser.
> A thrupenny nail
> Got stuck in her tail;
> The poor old lady, God bless her!

This was the result of his first day of formal education and his reward was 'a
clatter on the ear'.

As the nuns were very good to him he soon settled down to four years
of happy but uneventful schooling. It seems that he was never chastised. He
and his younger brother Jack walked there every day, in all weather. The navy
blue coats that he and Jack wore were not waterproof and Cathal often came
home saturated, the rain running down the back of his neck. They brought
their lunches with them: sandwiches wrapped in a piece of newspaper, and

milk (or sometimes lemonade) in a HP Sauce bottle.

The distance to the school was about one mile, and it took a good half-hour to walk the journey. Leaving Dolphin's Barn, Cathal and Jack walked along by the canal, crossing it at Sally's Bridge and then turning up what is now the beginning of Donore Avenue. This narrow road swung to the right and brought them to Blackpitts. At this time there were no houses; on one side was the site of Donore Castle and a cotton-spinning mill, and on the other the Tenter and Fairbrothers' fields. A little farther was Verschoyle's glue factory and house. Off the road was the present-day Greenville Terrace, at the corner of which old Mr McEnerny had a sweetshop. Here the boys bought sweets and an occasional toy for a penny. There was another tiny sweetshop at the back of an adjacent house, and nearby was a grocer's shop, which was run by an old man who always wore a straw hat. In his spare time the man made paper bags and stacked them one inside the other. The bags were kept at one end of the counter and were used for holding tea and sugar.

Farther along the road were orchards, where fruit was grown and sold. A small river flowed nearby; Cathal could remember a dead baby being taken out of the water on one occasion.

Finally one reached Blackpitts. The Kennys, who lived in Huntstown House in Finglas (more about them anon), had a dairy beside Warrenmount Convent. Their outhouses, horses and cattle could be seen from the school playground. Pigs, kept in another farm nearby, could be heard grunting and squealing. There were also slaughterhouses in the vicinity.

Signs of poverty were to be seen in and around the school, which was situated within the inner city slums, and many children were barefooted. Frequently, on a Monday, the teacher ordered the boys who had not attended Mass on the previous day to stand in line. Those guilty meekly obeyed and invariably their excuse was 'my boots were in pawn' – they had had no boots in which to walk to Mass. At the time, young Cathal thought they were saying 'my boots were in the pond'.

There was a strong smell of urine in the school; this was due, no doubt, to poor sanitation and the children's dirty underwear. As Cathal belonged to 'a better class of family', he stood out from the rest.

Whilst there, Cathal made his First Holy Communion in the Church of St Nicholas of Myra. After the ceremony, his aunt Cissie cooked him breakfast in the girls' school in Francis Street to save him waiting until he arrived home – it would have taken him a long time to walk back to Longford

Terrace. Cathal supposed that he was aged about seven or eight at this time.

During Cathal's time at Warrenmount, he often encountered the Jews who lived along the South Circular Road. They spoke just a little English. Cathal always admired them and found them pleasant people. They often stood at their doorsteps on the afternoon of the Sabbath at dusk in the winter. Using a mixture of sign language and broken English, they would utter 'gas … gas … turn on the gas' and usher Cathal into a house, where he would light their gas lamps, which they were forbidden to do. He was rewarded with something to eat, such as a slice of unleavened bread.

Their religion also forbade them to walk more than a mile on the Sabbath, though they did foot it to the local synagogue, which was also situated on the South Circular Road.

Young Cathal read and did his homework by the light of an oil lamp; gas was not installed at Longford Terrace until after World War I, in the early 1920s. Electricity was not to come until 1932.

While Cathal received the rudiments of formal education at school, he continued to be influenced by the people around him at home. His taste in good furniture was furthered by perusing a 1902 or 1903 edition of Elizabeth Gaskell's *Cranford*, which his mother owned and often re-read. In it were fine pen-and-ink drawings, very well reproduced, which depicted the furniture of the period. Cathal was intrigued by the amount of detail in the illustrations.

A popular book of the time was *Handy Andy – A Tale of Irish Life* by Samuel Lover, which Cathal found extremely amusing; he roared with laughter when he read it. It seems that his sense of humour was not inherited. Of all his relatives, his aunt Cissie had the best sense of humour.

Cathal's lifelong interest in clocks and watches began at this early stage. He was told that when very young, he would only go to sleep when allowed to clutch an alarm clock in bed. Later he loved to make toy clocks out of Player's cigarette boxes. Using the printed circle on the cover as a guide, he cut out a face and wrote the figures on the white card underneath. He then cut out a pair of hands and pinned them to the face.

If ever he had a chance to acquire a broken clock, he happily accepted it. When he was aged four or five, he went to a house off the South Circular Road where he espied a broken clock on a shelf in a kitchen or scullery. He looked at it so longingly that it was finally fetched down and given to him. He was delighted to bring it home and play with it.

When he was nine or ten years of age, Cathal learned to take clock movements apart, fix whatever was broken, clean and oil them, and assemble them again. Neighbours gave him worn-out or unwanted clocks and soon the house was so littered with broken alarm and American shelf clocks that his father forbade him to bring in any more 'rubbish' as he called it. Fortunately 'Nanna' Kelly, Mrs Gannon's mother, allowed him to house the larger items in her place, Priestfield House.

Pranks continued at home, as well as a certain amount of naughtiness. Coming up to Christmas one year, Cathal's mother bought about three pounds of currants, which she washed and dried before the fire on a clean tea towel, as was her custom. She then went upstairs to do some work in the bedrooms. In her absence, Cathal and Jack decided to sample the currants and ate them all. Mrs Gannon wondered why the children were so quiet.

When the two boys repaired to bed that evening, Jack suddenly announced, 'Mammy, I'm going to get sick,' and the currants shot out of his mouth all over the wall. Mr Gannon was obliged to go downstairs and fetch the fireside shovel and brush in order to sweep up the mess. The consequences of this incident are not recorded but can be imagined.

Christmas itself was never a very elaborate occasion. The children were given toys, which frequently broke when played with – a phenomenon familiar to every child and parent. Invariably this would start a row. The family attended Mass at Dolphin's Barn church in the morning and afterwards they walked home for dinner.

On Christmas night they were invited to the Healys' house, where they enjoyed themselves. Drawing-room songs were sung and accompanied on the piano by a friend, Annie Rogers. The occasion was also used to celebrate Stephanie Healy's birthday, as she had been born on St Stephen's (Boxing) Day. Consequently supper was served at midnight and more jollifications followed. It was great fun for the children to stay up so late.

Christmas at Priestfield House was not so exciting. Cathal's uncle John, who lived with his grandmother and two aunts, used to go out drinking with his pals and would not return in time for dinner. By the time he came home it was spoiled and tempers were frayed.

At nine o'clock in the morning on St Stephen's Day, the Wren boys came hammering on the hall door in Crumlin Road. This was an old traditional custom. They bore a large section of a bush festooned with ribbons and topped with either a dead or imitation wren. They sang songs, accompanying themselves on tin whistles, and recited a poem:

The wren, the wren, the king of all birds
On Saint Stephen's Day was caught in the furze ...
Take off the kettle and put on the pan
And give us a penny to bury the wran.

A penny or a slice of Christmas cake was given to them and they continued their round, knocking on neighbouring doors. Cathal's mother often complained, saying, 'a body can't have a rest on St Stephen's morning'.

In 1915, another member of the family was born: William Francis, better known as Willie. Jack, properly named John Frederic, had been born three years previously.

Apart from what we have already touched upon, World War I made little impact on young Cathal. What he did remember clearly were the incidents that occurred in Dublin in 1916.

Count Plunkett owned Larkfield Mill, near the Dark Lane, in which plans for the Easter Rising had been hatched. The Count's son, Joseph Mary Plunkett, often used to cycle along the Dark Lane. Cathal remembered his mother speaking to him; his bicycle seemed to be very big. Afterwards Cathal asked her who she had been talking to and she replied, 'Joseph Mary Plunkett'. Cathal always remembered the name because of the 'Mary' in the middle.

On Easter Saturday evening of that year, Cissie brought Cathal to Mount Argus, as was her wont. The church was packed with men who had come for confession before the Rising. As Cissie disappeared for what seemed to be a long time, Cathal became restless and began to whinge. A lady said to him, 'Don't worry, your aunt is in the confession box with Father Gerald.' She soon appeared and they walked home together.

It was either over this weekend, or on another occasion when Cissie had brought Cathal to Mass on Sunday, that the altar was hidden by curtains. At some point during the Mass, the curtains were drawn back to reveal the altar in all its glory. Cathal thought this so wonderful that he wanted to see it all over again, but when Cissie brought him the following morning the curtains would not move and had to be coaxed by means of long candle snuffers. Cathal could remember his sense of disappointment.

Cathal and Cissie were certainly at Mass in the church at Mount Argus on Easter Monday when the Rising began. As they were passing by Harold's Cross Green, near the Hospice for the Dying, a woman came out of a house and said, 'Don't bring that child near the bridge – the rebels are out and a little boy has been shot dead.'

They crossed the road and went into the house belonging to Fanny Ryan, a teacher colleague of Cissie's. To amuse Cathal, Miss Ryan played the gramophone for him. Cathal could hear the shooting in the distance – the local people were in their back gardens listening to it – but he was more interested in the gramophone than anything else. He remembered looking under the turntable and seeing a screw, located on the shaft of the motor, which kept appearing as the turntable rotated. Anything mechanical fascinated him. However, he was conscious of volleys of shots followed by periods of silence.

When they felt it was safe to do so, they left, taking a circuitous route by Lime Kiln Lane, at the back of the nearby distillery. They reached the Grand Canal and finally Priestfield House, where Cathal could hear more shooting from the back garden. Somebody called to the door and informed them that the rebels had taken control of the General Post Office. The shooting continued during the night and on the following day Cathal's father called and brought him home.

Soon after this, Cathal remembered his father coming home with a sack of white bread, which he had got in Boland's Mill. The bread was stale, but the family was glad to have it; provisions were hard to come by during the days that followed.

Cathal heard shots ringing out from Kilmainham Gaol one morning not long afterwards. His mother came in to his bedroom and said, 'Say a prayer for the leaders, they're being executed – that's the shooting you heard.'

In the meantime, life went on as usual. Sometime in 1916, Cathal was brought by his mother to the Meath Hospital in Dublin to have his tonsils removed. The famous surgeon and writer Oliver St John Gogarty did the operation and gave young Cathal a 'clip on the ear' when he struggled whilst being carried to the operating theatre. He was then given the anaesthetic.

Within a few hours he was out and walking home with his mother, spitting blood. There was no question of him recovering in hospital.

In the summer of the same year, Cathal spent a fortnight's holiday with his aunt Cissie in Delgany, County Wicklow. Lady Butler, the Victorian artist who painted pictures such as 'The Roll Call' and 'Scotland Forever', had used the small house in which they stayed.

In 1918 Miss Turbett of Owenstown House, Dundrum, whom Cathal's aunt Peggy had served as a lady's companion, invited Cathal and his two aunts to spend a summer holiday at Parkview House in Kilmashogue,

County Wicklow. This was a large two-storey late Georgian house. By staying here, they managed to escape the raging influenza epidemic that ravaged Dublin and the rest of the country; between October 1918 and March 1919, 18,376 people died in Ireland. Although people in the Crumlin Road had suffered and died, the Gannons were unaffected.

The scenery around Kilmashogue was pleasant. Cathal had a happy time clambering up and down the mountains and playing with paper boats in a well.

Earlier in the year, in May, Cathal's sister Maureen had been born. When she was about one year old, Cathal was asked to take her out in the pram and bring her up the Crumlin Road. Cathal brought her out as instructed, but suddenly decided that he would like to take a look at an aerodrome that he had heard about in Tallaght. It was located where the Urney chocolate factory would be built later.

He walked all the way to Tallaght, pushing the pram, and spent a considerable time looking at the planes landing, taking off and doing aerobatics. He was fascinated by what he saw.

He then decided that he should return home. Before leaving, he stopped to buy a twopenny packet of biscuits. When he set off, he was recognized by a local woman, Mrs Dempsey (mother of the famous piper Seán Dempsey), who asked him what he was doing and invited him into her home, the gatelodge of Airton House, to have a cup of tea. Cathal made his excuses, told her that he had eaten some biscuits and said that he must go home. Mrs Dempsey told him to hurry home as quickly as possible and not have his mother worrying.

At Greenhills, Cathal discovered he was heading downhill. Taking advantage of this and the fact that a slight wind was blowing, he gave the pram a good push along the road and sat on it as he freewheeled along. The hood, which was up, acted as a type of sail. It was fortunate that there was very little traffic on the road.

He made good speed and finally arrived home to discover that the family and all the neighbours were out looking for him and Maureen. Cathal could not remember whether or not he got a 'hammering' for being so mischievous – no doubt he did.

Six

*T*he darkest period in Cathal's life began in 1919 when his father decided that it was time to send him to the Christian Brothers' school at Synge Street, off the South Circular Road, despite the fact that he himself had hated the place.

There was a time when Cathal refused to speak openly about his schooling in Synge Street, but eventually the story came out. Like his father, he loathed the place and the type of education that he received there. Apart from the grim atmosphere and the attitude of the Brothers, he hated the High Victorian design of the building. He also disliked St Kevin's Church, which is beside the school. For him it was ugly and a stark contrast to the classical Church of St Nicholas of Myra to which his aunt Cissie used to bring him, and which he loved.

Cathal (and later he and Jack) used to walk to Synge Street from Longford Terrace, though in bad weather he was given threepence for the tram journey from Dolphin's Barn to the school and back: the fare was one and a half pence each way. If the rain eased up and it was possible to run all the way to school, the fare could be spent during the lunch break.

As before, he used to bring his lunch with him and eat it in the school yard. There was no tuck shop and no hot meals were provided for the boys. On the days when they had to go to the gymnasium in the nearby CYMS (Catholic Young Men's Society), Harrington Street, to do half an hour of physical exercises on a hard floor and an empty stomach, he was glad to return home and eat something prepared by his mother.

In the evening it was usual to sit down and attempt four or six sets of homework (or 'exercises' as Cathal always called them), most of which he found very difficult. A book called *Aids to Irish Composition* had been published and another book, for teachers, *The Key to the Aids*, was a translation into Irish of set texts in English. Cathal's aunt Cissie had two copies of the latter; she had ordered an extra copy by mistake. Cathal secretly took one of the copies and kept it. He used it only for reference, for he realized that it would be foolish to 'cog' from it.

When Cathal left school, he gave the book to a companion, Michael Wall, who used it every evening when doing his homework. He shared it with five other classmates and they took care to make different mistakes so as to avoid suspicion. The book was returned to Michael in the mornings. Michael was told by one of the teachers that he would do well in the examinations as he was so good at translating, but of course he and his mates failed miserably.

According to Cathal, the school offered little in the way of encouragement. No credit was given for attempting something in the right manner. If a student did something wrong or made a mistake, he was slapped and made suffer. Cathal often remembered hearing the sound of boys being slapped with a leather strap from outside the school when he passed by many years later.

Cathal's aunts Cissie and Peggy were sympathetic to his misery and provided as much help and comfort as they could. As Peggy was a trained nurse, she took Cathal's temperature when he was unwell and kept him at home until he felt better. Cissie would then write, in a beautiful hand, an excuse note that always began, 'Acting on medical advice ...'.

Religious instruction featured largely, and prayers were said every hour. Every classroom had its own 'single-strike' clock, the bell of which rang just once on the hour to indicate that a lesson had finished. The boys were then obliged to stand up and say some prayers, such as a Hail Mary or Our Father, and sometimes they would sing a hymn. When they sang 'Daily, Daily Sing to Mary', eyes surreptitiously turned on the future President of Ireland, Cearbhall Ó Dálaigh (O'Daly in English) and his face would redden. If anyone was caught looking at him, punishment would be meted out in the usual manner.

Despite the harsh regime, Cathal occasionally gave vent to his latent sense of humour. The boys were regularly brought to the church for Benediction, during which the Latin hymn *Tantum Ergo* was sung. Cathal devised his own version, which I imagine he sang defiantly, perhaps with a twinkle in his eye:

> *Tantum Ergo*
> *Makes your hair grow ...*

What Cathal dreaded most about the school were the Brothers, whom he always described as being cruel. He had the misfortune of being taught, for two years running, by the most notorious teacher of them all, whom we shall call Brother B——. Because of the refinement that had been inculcated by his aunts, Cathal was something of a misfit in such a nationalist school: he did not play sport and showed little interest or ability in mastering the Irish language. He was also of a timid disposition. In later life, Cathal often admitted to being a slow learner, though he did not seem to realize this whilst he was at school.

Brother B——, who hailed from Dingle and was very enthusiastic about the Irish language, was well known for slapping and punishing the students; Cathal described him simply as a brute. Because of Cathal's lack of interest in sport and Irish, B—— decided to single him out. Cathal felt terrorized by him, so much so that he began to sleepwalk. He regularly got out of bed in the middle of the night and put on his clothes, as if preparing to go to school. His parents would hear the disturbance in his room and gently steer him back to bed.

The following incidents may give the reader an idea of B——'s cruelty. Probably the worst offence was not to allow Cathal attend the woodworking class. Mrs Gannon pleaded in vain with him to be more lenient towards her son; his reply was that his leniency would depend on Cathal's enthusiasm for learning Irish.

On one occasion, Cathal was sick just before the Easter holidays. When he returned to school he discovered that, for some unknown reason, he had forgotten to bring a written excuse with him. When his classmates heard about this, they warned him by saying, 'Gannon, you're going to get it!'

When B—— discovered that Cathal had no note to explain his absence, he dragged him up to an empty classroom, where he left him on his own and during the day administered twenty-eight slaps to his left hand, the theory being that it was more painful than the right. Cathal could remember the pain and the weals on his arm where the leather strap had not struck its mark accurately.

B—— also taught Latin and on another occasion ordered Cathal to decline the pronoun *hic/haec/hoc* and write it on the blackboard. Every time he made a mistake, B—— slapped him with a leather strap that had come apart at the end. He had placed chalk dust within the frayed area and a great cloud of white dust arose when the leather landed on Cathal's outstretched hand.

The boys roared with laughter at the spectacle – because they were obliged to do so.

Years later, Cathal met two ladies whilst on holiday in Dingle. They asked him what school he had attended and he replied, 'Synge Street.'

'Oh, the Christian Brothers.'

'Yes.'

'And what master had you got?'

Cathal told them that he had had Brother B— and they asked him what he thought of him. Cathal replied that he was very hard. One of them said, 'You don't have to tell us that, because we happen to be his sisters.' Cathal tried to make his apologies, but they said that there was no need to do so because the happiest day in their life was when their brother left home to join the Christian Brothers. Even they could not abide him.

B— inflicted his brutality on other students also. Cathal was told many years later that he had beaten up a boy so badly and damaged his nose that he returned home in a very bad state, with blood all over his shirt. The boy's stepfather went to the school and 'laid his fists' into Brother B—.

Another boy, who was very tall, became so enraged by B—'s behaviour that he attacked him, beat him up and walked out of the school.

B— showed his shallowness by comparing pretentious people to mahogany veneer on an inferior wood, such as deal or pine. As Cathal was fond of pointing out, the finest of furniture is veneered, it being the only way to achieve the best results. B— also liked to belittle the English and tell his students that the eyes of the world were watching Ireland. The boys were always taught to keep their distance from Protestants. Cathal rebelled by befriending many such people and ultimately by marrying an English woman who was a Protestant.

Another pupil in the same class as Cathal was the writer Brian O'Nolan, who later used the pseudonyms Myles na gCopaleen and Flann O'Brien. Cathal did not know him well. At the time he would have been only twelve or thirteen years of age.

The star pupil of Cathal's class was Cearbhall Ó Dálaigh; he was bright and studious. He was regularly seen reading a book when the other boys were larking about. He often walked home with Cathal to his little one-storeyed house by the Grand Canal, opposite Portobello Barracks, and consoled his unhappy schoolmate. 'Don't mind B—,' he used to say to Cathal, 'he's a very difficult man. Next year you'll be in a better class.'

It can be argued that what Cathal experienced at Synge Street was typical of the period, and that many other students emerged relatively unscathed and rose to prominent positions, like Ó Dálaigh. Whilst the Christian Brothers and their methods of schooling have been criticized, it should be said that B— was an exception and that there were others in the school who performed well as teachers. Unfortunately, B— had such an effect on young Cathal that he succeeded in turning him against the Christian Brothers for the rest of his life. At least we can be grateful that Cathal was not in any way sexually abused whilst at school. Nonetheless, it was a very damaging experience for him; Cathal reckoned that if he had been taught by a sensible teacher, 'a lot of good' could have been got out of him.

According to Cathal, the only reasonable teacher in the school was Brother P. A. Mullen, known as Pa Mullen, who taught him during his last year there. Two other Brothers were known respectively as 'The Gilly' and 'The Golly'. The Gilly was yet another brute, but The Golly was a simple, meek Brother whose passion lay in the collection of pennies for the Holy Childhood, a scheme for helping poor children in Africa – hence his nickname. Upon donating a penny every week, the sum of money was marked up on a special card. If a student was late for school, a good excuse was to say that the card had been left at home and it had been necessary to go back to fetch it. Another ruse was to say, 'I went into the church to say a prayer for the black babies and I was delayed.'

'Oh well, that was a mistake,' was Brother Mullen's mild rebuff.

Brother 'Bang' acquired his nickname from a rude noise he made whilst writing on the blackboard. He was old and a little senile; Cathal only had a vague memory of him.

It seemed to Cathal that the Brothers had a negative attitude to most things, especially to music, though two Brothers did show an interest in this direction. 'Daddy' Cullen gave singing lessons and Brother White, known for some obscure reason as 'Toco', did his best to form a choir. Cathal remembered a part-song by Brahms, which interested him but made little impact on the other students. Brother White organized a small orchestra in which Cathal played the piano. Like the choir, this did not last long. Possibly because he got no encouragement, this Brother left the Order and subsequently married. In Synge Street, the accent was on football and hurling.

The Brothers often warned the boys about the dangers of going near St Stephen's Green and fraternizing with the people who frequented the area.

The students were forbidden to mention the name and the Green was dubbed the 'Lousy Acre'. Needless to say, they were not encouraged to admire the Georgian houses nearby; these were, of course, associated with the British.

Cathal's escape from this narrow-minded attitude was to slip out during his lunch breaks and walk to the nearby Municipal Gallery of Modern Art, then in Clonmell House, 17 Harcourt Street. Cathal loved this elegant Georgian house and could recollect the location of every painting in it. At the head of the staircase was a portrait of Hugh Lane, the first director, who had founded the gallery in 1908. Light shone on the picture from a glass roof.

Here, away from the rough horseplay of his classmates in the school yard, Cathal was able to study the works of Sir William Orpen, Walter Osborne (especially his 'Sick Call') and many other painters. Renoir's famous picture 'Les Parapluies' ('The Umbrellas') would have been there then.

Cathal's thirst for literature was partially satisfied by the small library in Synge Street school. The shelves were filled mostly with what Cathal described as 'Victorian moral tales', though there were some good books. An old Brother ran the library and begrudgingly allowed Cathal to borrow the books that he wanted. He seemed puzzled as to why a boy of twelve or thirteen years of age should be interested in literature that was in any way erudite.

Cathal read several of the popular historical romances by the English author William Harrison Ainsworth, such as *The Tower of London, Windsor Castle* and *Old Saint Paul's*. He later read some of Dickens's novels. At home, Cathal read articles on old Dublin in the evening newspapers.

The boys in Synge Street were occasionally treated to magic-lantern shows. These were staged in the evenings and so the boys had to return to the school to see them. They paid a small admission fee of a few pence. Safe and edifying themes such as views of the Holy Land were chosen; a Brother pointed to details of the projected images with a stick and described the churches and buildings upon which they feasted their eyes. When the monotony was broken by the appearance of a slide that had been inserted upside down, the boys cheered.

Cathal remembered a show with a lighter theme, but with a suitably moralistic ending. It began with a view of a pantry in which a young boy could be seen eyeing jars of jam on the shelves. Subsequent slides showed the boy fetching a stool, standing on it, breaking the glass in the door of a cupboard and squeezing his body in. With his legs still outside, he then began to devour the jam, jar by jar. His stomach became so bloated that he could not extricate himself from the cupboard. At this stage he was discovered by his mother, who could be seen spanking the boy by means of a mechanical slide operated by the projectionist. This scene caused great merriment amongst Cathal and his schoolmates.

Apart from these minor diversions, the Christian Brothers organized nothing else that was vaguely cultural: no visits to museums or art galleries.

From an early age, Cathal had shown an interest in music and had been picking out tunes on his grandmother's piano in Priestfield House. He was keen to learn music. He began to receive formal lessons from a Miss Crosby in Reuben Avenue, off the South Circular Road, when he was aged nine or ten – about the time when he started school at Synge Street. A major drawback was that his parents did not possess a piano; he had to practise on his grandmother's. His teacher employed the old-fashioned method of rapping her students on the knuckles with a pencil when they made mistakes and Cathal soon lost interest. Frustrated, he gave up the lessons a couple of years later. However, he did not lose interest in music and continued to play as much as possible. He was reluctant to let his classmates in Synge Street know that he played the piano for fear of being called a sissy.

Another place that Cathal sometimes visited during his school lunch breaks was the house and workshop of Mr Byrne, the chief piano tuner at Pigott's music shop in Dublin. Mr Byrne lived in Lennox Street, just across from Synge Street. Young Cathal saw many a good piano there, including a beautiful Schiedmayer semi-grand costing £100, which his parents could not afford. His mother regularly went to see what was available. It is possible that Cathal learned the rudiments of piano tuning from Mr Byrne, for he mastered this difficult art at a relatively young age. Cathal had a very sharp ear and appeared to have always been able to tune his own instruments.

A great source of entertainment at this time, and later, was the cinema; Cathal became 'a great film goer'. There were plenty of cinemas in the locality. On Saturday afternoons, when school was over, he and his pals used to foot it to the Princess (better known as 'the Prinner') in Rathmines for the children's programme. The admission fee was about 4d. A dodge was to cradle younger members of the family in the arms, like babies, in the hope that they would be admitted free of charge. Frequently the trick did work. Obviously the person in the box office knew well enough what the children were doing, but took no notice.

The programme normally consisted of silent cowboy films and an occasional Charlie Chaplin comedy. A musical accompaniment was played on a piano, though the larger cinemas often had a piano, violin and cello. When captions appeared on the screen, the older people read them aloud and generally not quickly enough.

At other times, the children went to the Stella cinema, also in Rathmines, in which a lighted fountain played before the curtains opened. Another favourite was the De Luxe in Camden Street. There was also a cinema in Dame Street and in James's Street, near Guinness's Brewery, was the Fountain. Here the children would queue at the door and cheer the owner when he arrived by tram. This immediately put him into bad humour. He would then open up and allow the children in; if they did not behave themselves, he would box them on the ears. He then took a long pole and used it to close the curtains over the windows; this was always greeted by another cheer. His response was to wallop the nearest child.

Cathal's aunt Peggy brought Cathal to good films. He remembered one about the life of Beethoven; it featured scenes of high drama, complete with tears.

Another form of entertainment that Cathal relished was the fairground – in particular the swing boats, on which he generally spent most of his money. He used to swing as long as possible in them and try to go as high as he could. He could remember feeling dizzy and nauseous after one such bout of swinging.

Cathal developed his fertile imagination and art of storytelling at a young age. At this stage the three boys, Jack, Willie and Cathal slept in the same bedroom; Cathal had one bed to himself, and Jack and Willie shared the other. When they went to bed at night, their bedroom was lit by an oil lamp, which was blown out for them. Not yet ready for sleep, they talked to each other quietly in the dark. Cathal seized the opportunity to tell them ghost stories of his own invention, which were listened to with great interest. Cathal frequently terrorized his brothers with tales of hauntings, most of which were set in three wooden pavilions in the tennis club across the road. The inspiration for these ghoulish happenings had come from a visit to the Healy family in nearby Towerfield House; on returning home one dark evening, somebody had appeared enveloped in a sheet and had frightened the boys.

Willie, being the youngest, was the most impressionable. When, after one of Cathal's ghost stories, he became apprehensive and was afraid to go to sleep, Cathal felt that this was 'too good a chance to miss'. He unnerved him further by describing ghosts who disturbed houses and moved furniture about. As Cathal said, 'The poor kid – he must have been driven up the wall altogether!'

Before Willie went to bed one evening, Cathal procured a long piece of cord, which he tied to various pieces of furniture in the bedroom, including the metal fender in front of the fireplace. He then passed the cord under the door. When his unsuspecting brother went to bed and began to fall asleep, Cathal tiptoed out, uttered some ghostly moans and began to pull the cord, so that everything in the room began to move. Poor Willie nearly lost his reason.

Mr Gannon heard Willie screaming and the furniture moving. He ran upstairs to see what was happening and in the process tripped over Cathal, who was trying to avoid him by running downstairs. 'I got a terrible hiding for it,' reported Cathal. 'He had no sense of humour!'

Seven

The audience for Cathal's ghost stories was not restricted to his two brothers. Cathal would think about them, 'French-polish' them and retell them to his school companion Michael Wall, who in turn would relate them to his grandfather, a willing listener who was always ready to hear the next instalment. Cathal was unaware of the fact that Michael's grandfather was enjoying his stories until many years later when the man reminded him of them. He was able to remember them long after Cathal had forgotten them.

At one time, a boy named Kevin Cregan was a classmate of Cathal's, though after a while he was moved to a higher grade of the same class. Unlike Cathal, he was good at Irish. He lived in Rehoboth, close to Dolphin's Barn, and both he and Cathal used to walk home together. Kevin continued at school after Cathal left it and then got a job in the post office. He was then transferred to a country town and the two of them lost touch until about 1939, when they met up again and spent a good deal of time together, as we shall see later.

Michael Wall, whom we have already mentioned, was in the same class as Cathal and lived at 3 Eldon Terrace, on the South Circular Road at Leonard's Corner. He and Cathal used to meet up for walks after they left school.

Another lad who Cathal knocked around with at this time was Jim O'Dea, a nephew of the famous comedian Jimmy O'Dea. Cathal knew him from an early age. Jim never went to the same school as Cathal but he was always around Dolphin's Barn, where he lived. His parents were elderly; his mother was ill and apparently his father was very religious.

When Cathal and his brothers came home from school, they often took a different route along Cork Street, where they stopped at a dark and dusty forge. Although there were several forges in the locality, the boys enjoyed visiting this one the best. Here one could get the pungent smell of singed hoof as the blacksmith fitted red hot horseshoes. These were made on the spot and fitted within half an hour.

The blacksmith always welcomed the schoolboys and chatted to them. Fascinated, they watched him fashion a horseshoe on the anvil, hitting it rhythmically with his hammer. He never rested his hand, for even when he did not hit the horseshoe, he gently hit the anvil, so that, to the boys, it sounded like an echo.

Suddenly he would jump up in the middle of his work and, in his shirt-sleeves, run into Nevin's pub next door for a quick pint, leaving the boys to operate the large bellows over the hearth. They blew it by pulling on a chain; a spring forced the bellows open again.

Cathal remembered some of the events in Dublin during the War of Independence or 'Troubles', as the 1919–21 period was euphemistically called. He very clearly remembered the Black and Tans. These were rough-and-ready troops, many of them jailbirds, sent from England to assist the British military in Ireland in combating Sinn Féin. It was rumoured that they were paid a guinea a day. Many of them came to Ireland to earn easy money, but left in 'wooden cronbies' or coffins.

Cathal saw the Black and Tans everywhere, especially on the way to school. He remembered how they shot an innocent man (maybe a republican), who was washing himself under a tap in a yard in Emerald Square, off Dolphin's Barn Street; he heard women crying and saw an ambulance coming to take away the dead man.

The Black and Tans imposed a curfew in Dublin and other cities from eight o'clock onwards, and to enforce the curfew they patrolled the streets in trucks equipped with powerful searchlights. Only a fool ventured out at night. Anybody caught was questioned and often taken to the nearest barracks, where an overnight stay was necessary in order to await identification the following morning.

When Cathal stayed at Priestfield House, he was often woken by the sound of trucks or by the searchlight if it shone through his bedroom window. People avoided walking down the South Circular Road. However, Cathal's uncle John regularly went out boozing and did not return before the curfew. Cathal's grandmother, who always spoke very precisely, would cry, 'Jesus,

Mary and Joseph! Poor John hasn't come in yet! What is keeping him?'

They would then see one of the trucks coming along, the searchlight sweeping the road ahead. A voice would shout 'Halt!' and a person on the road would be stopped. If the person was out on legitimate business or could produce a permit, he or she would be allowed to proceed.

At last, at about half past ten and after a long, anxious wait, men would be heard singing in the distance and John would stumble into the house. He and his friends would have nipped down side streets in order to avoid the trucks and he would often return after a truck had just passed the house.

Cathal was never caught by the troops; by eight o'clock he was at home doing his homework and later he prepared for bed. The Black and Tans never bothered the children, but it was always possible for them to get caught in crossfire. Cathal remembered a skirmish that began one morning whilst setting off along the South Circular Road on his way to school. He had to run into the porch of a house near Dolphin's Barn post office to shelter from the gunfire. He waited there until the shooting stopped. He could see bullets hitting the walls of the houses in a shower of dust and he saw chunks of masonry falling to the ground. It was a frightening experience. Nearby was a building, later a bank, that had been taken over by the British and was barricaded. The attack seemed to be coming from the other end of the South Circular Road, in the direction of the city centre.

Once the shooting had ceased, the traffic began to move again and Cathal was able to walk to Priestfield House, where his aunts and grandmother were in a terrible state worrying about him, for they knew that he would be passing at around that time. It was fortunate that Cathal was neither seen nor shot.

Cathal remembered the tragedy of seeing a girl lying dead outside the White Heather Laundry beside Priestfield House. She had been cycling along the road and had been overtaken by a military lorry. She did not realize that it was towing another lorry, which ran over her and killed her. Another girl, who was caught in crossfire just as Cathal had been, was shot dead opposite Priestfield House. There was a lot of sadness then and it undoubtedly unnerved many children.

Jim Browne, who lived locally and worked in Guinness's Brewery, had the ability to imitate an English accent very accurately. One cold winter's morning, when he was walking through thick fog on his way to work, a woman stuck her head out of a window and, in a very flat Dublin accent, shouted down at him, 'What time is it, mister?'

'Half past seven, mother,' he replied in the clipped English accent of a Black and Tan trooper. A volley of curses followed him as he continued on his way.

The War of Independence finished in July 1921; the controversial treaty was signed, causing a split, and the Irish Free State came legally into existence in December 1922. Cathal remembered seeing the British troops leaving Wellington Barracks.

The Civil War began in June of that year. Cathal could recollect little about this period, though his brother Jack remembered ambushes in the Dolphin's Barn area and along the Dark Lane. Cathal did remember seeing guns being loaded into cars at Wellington Barracks, in preparation for blowing up the Four Courts. Cathal in later years very much regretted this, especially as so many precious records had been destroyed.

In August, Arthur Griffith died suddenly and Michael Collins was killed. Cathal witnessed the funerals passing along the crowded streets of Dublin and saw Michael Collins lying in state at the City Hall, which was packed with people.

Despite the political upheavals, life went on as usual. As Cathal was interested in history from an early age, he started to collect a few old coins, in particular Georgian pennies and halfpennies, which were easily procured then. He then went on to buy a few books.

At about this time, Cathal received a present of books from a Mrs Sidney Ball – a lady who lived next door to the Gannons in Longford Terrace. She came from Oxford, where her husband had been a professor in St John's College. When he died she came to live in Dublin for a few years. When she left to live in eastern Europe, sometime around 1922, she gave Cathal about two hundred books, many of them classics, and some 78 rpm gramophone records. One of these records fascinated Cathal: Beethoven's 'Kreutzer' Sonata for violin and piano. He played the slow movement of this over and over again, until his father threatened to put his hammer through the record if he played it any more. Cathal considered this to be his first introduction to 'good' music.

Mrs Ball used to encourage Cathal to come into her house and practise on her Broadwood miniature or 'singer's' piano. Cathal found her a very interesting person. Her house was full of books and she knew many important people, such as Countess Markievicz, Darrell Figgis and Mrs Despard of

Roebuck House, Clonskeagh; Cathal often saw these people coming and going. At the time, he only had a vague idea of who they were.

At some stage in the 1920s Cathal joined Kevin Street Library, which at that time was a very impersonal place. The numbers, names and authors of the books were displayed behind a glass panel in the vestibule and beside each one was either a red mark, indicating that the book was out on loan, or a black mark, indicating that it was available. One was required to present one's library ticket to an official behind a counter and shout out the number of a book, which was then fetched. Cathal was reluctant to hesitate over a book or hand it back if he did not like it, as the official was rather snappy. Cathal remembered taking out a large, heavy book entitled *Essay on the Round Towers* by George Petrie, which he somehow carried home and tried to read, but he soon gave it up as he found it so dismal.

Sometime during 1922 Cathal's aunt Peggy brought him to see the newly made doll's house, Titania's Palace, which was displayed at Clerys store in O'Connell Street. Sir Neville Wilkinson, who lived in Mount Merrion House, on the south side of Dublin, had made it for his daughter. Sir Neville, who was in the shop, lifted Cathal up in order to show him the details of the scaled-down house. He drew Cathal's attention to the miniature furniture and showed him some of the tiny pictures, which he took down from the walls.

Cathal saw the masterpiece again at Harrods in 1965. His opinion then was that it was frowsy and that the 1920s decor was in bad taste.

In November 1922, there was great excitement when Tutankhamen's tomb was discovered by Sir Howard Carter in Egypt. Cathal's aunts and grandmother in Priestfield House read the latest newspaper reports, which fascinated Cathal. Cathal remembered how he had read the articles aloud to his grandmother, who was seated in the little back garden. As she was in her latter years and her sight was going, Cathal often read for her. When he stumbled over a difficult word, such as 'sarcophagus', she encouraged him by saying 'break it up into syllables'. From this, Cathal's interest in archaeology developed.

At around this time Cathal went to a festival held in St Mary's College, Rathmines. What attracted him was some type of Egyptian exhibition that featured Tutankhamen's tomb, and the promise of a gift. He paid threepence to enter, but was very disappointed in what was on show. Needless to say, there was nothing from the real tomb to be seen and the gift was simply a lucky bag.

Outside the tent, however, a man was busy cranking the handle of a cine camera as he filmed members of the organizing committee. Young Cathal got in on the act: he stood in the shot, smiled and spoke to a lady. Some time afterwards, various people met him and said, 'Hey, I saw you on the flicks!'

Cathal and his brothers probably encountered 'Professor' Little on their weekly excursions to the cinemas in Rathmines. This eccentric man frequented the area and dressed himself in sackcloth and ashes in an effort to do penance for humanity at large. He wore a sack-like apron and a cross around his neck, and was often seen coming from and going into St Mary's College. He hated to see young women in short skirts; he ticked them off and sometimes gave them a crack of his stick.

He sometimes hired a type of open-air horse cab called an outside car in order to visit a friend in Milltown. He hailed the cab at a stand on the Rathmines Road, paid the driver a shilling and then proceeded to walk behind it, by way of penance.

The most practical way of travelling to Rathmines then was by tram. As mentioned earlier, trams travelled from the city centre to Dolphin's Barn. Another terminus was Rialto Bridge. Cathal and his brothers regularly cycled around the stationary trams in the evenings, having finished school. If the curtains were pulled across the downstairs windows, the conductor told them that the driver wanted to 'rest' and chased them away. The boys did not realize at the time that some of the drivers and conductors were doing anything but resting – they were savouring the delights of a 'lady friend'.

Cathal's aunt Peggy brought him regularly to Howth by tram; it was an outing that she obviously enjoyed. On one occasion it was pouring with rain when they arrived and there was no point in getting off. There was nothing to do but return home. Cathal remembered it being a hot, clammy summer's day. Some nuns, who were sitting near them, had smelly feet; Peggy declared afterwards that they had been travelling 'in an odour of sanctity'.

In around 1922 Cathal heard the Italian coloratura soprano Madame Luisa Tetrazzini singing in the Theatre Royal. He heard her again about five or six years later, but he could only vaguely remember her and her performances.

A showing of the film *Lorna Doone* in the Scala Picture House on O'Connell Street made a bigger impression. Before the film was shown, a tableau was enacted in front of the screen by actors dressed in period costume. Apparently the scene was a wedding in a church, during which a face appeared at a window and either the bride or bridegroom was shot – Cathal was unable to remember the details accurately. What he did remember, though, was that a minuet by Handel was performed.

Even at this age, Cathal was critical of what he saw and heard. He was not at all impressed by a popular musical called *The Arcadians* that was staged in the Gaiety Theatre and to which he was brought by a neighbour; he found it tasteless and lacking in humour.

Apart from music and literature, Cathal still loved the simple pleasures of life. During the summer holidays the Gannons and the Healys often went to the seaside for the day. Sandwiches were made and bottles of milk were packed, and they set off in the morning in the Healys' horse-drawn dairy cart, seated on wooden planks stretched across the sides. They travelled to Merrion Strand, where they swam in crystal-clear water or romped about on the beach. The children also loved to play at the baths on Sandymount beach, running across the bridge to them. The fun over, they generally left at about five o'clock and returned home in the horse and cart.

Another excursion enjoyed by Cathal was a journey by tram to Rathfarnham with his father and brothers. From there they used to walk to a field by the foot of the mountain at the Hell Fire Club and fill tin cans with masses of blackberries that were there for anyone to pick. They were then brought home and made into jam by Mr Gannon or else used for pies.

In October of 1922 Mrs Gannon gave birth to her last child, who was Cathal's youngest sister: Ethna. In November of the following year, Mrs Gannon's mother, Susan Mary Kelly, died.

Eight

L ife can be full of surprises; one thing can lead to another in a most unexpected way and a chance happening can often alter a person's life. Something happened to Cathal at about the age of fourteen that was to steer him in a certain direction for the rest of his life.

For some unexplained reason Mr Leo Dunphy, a man who lived next door to the Gannons, lent Cathal a book about Tibet and Nepal, which was illustrated with reproductions of watercolour sketches. Cathal read it carefully and it made a big impression on him. From this introduction he developed a great interest in Tibet, and read any book he could lay his hands on about the country. Two Penguin books purchased at a later date were *My Journey to Lhasa* and *Magic and Mystery in Tibet*, by Alexandra David-Neel, first published in 1927 and 1931 respectively. They are still amongst Cathal's collection of books.

In 1924 there was a failed attempt to climb Mount Everest, during which the mountaineers George Leigh-Mallory and Andrew Irvine disappeared from view and were never seen again. A film had been made about the heroic expedition and was shown later that year in the Corinthian cinema on the quays, in Dublin city centre. During the interval six Tibetan monks, who had been brought to Ireland for the occasion, appeared on the stage to entertain the audience. Cathal was fascinated by the strange masked dancing, the grotesque costumes and the unearthly groans of the *dong* (long trumpets, generally played in pairs). The dancing may also have been accompanied by wailing *gyaling* (shawms), rattling *damaru* (prayer drums, sometimes made from two human skulls) and clashing cymbals. The effect must have been electrifying. A hermit who had been living in seclusion for some years in a cave, and who would be returning to this austere lifestyle once again in Tibet, gave the audience his blessing.

The money for the cinema had undoubtedly been given to him by one of his aunts, Cissie or Peggy. They would have been willing to finance such an adventure in an effort to encourage Cathal; his parents, in contrast, would probably have discouraged him.

Cathal was so taken with the novelty of seeing real Tibetan monks dressed in their robes and unusual headgear that he followed them on his new bicycle when they toured the city in an open carriage, probably when they first arrived. They were brought to see all the important public buildings. At the back of Dáil Éireann, Cathal saw one of the monks sketching the cenotaph.

The bicycle had been given to Cathal as a present by the Gannons' neighbour Mrs Sidney Ball when she left the country. He had learned to ride it by cycling up and down the Crumlin Road and had finally mastered it on 21 March of that year – a date he would never forget.

At around the same time, whilst reading a series of articles about Tibet (which he always believed to have been in *The Children's Newspaper*, though this cannot be the case), he stumbled across an article written by the brilliant English performer of the piano, harpsichord and clavichord, Violet Gordon Woodhouse. Violet, whose musical talent had begun at the age of seven and who at that stage was known by almost every musician of note in Europe, was the first musician to record on the harpsichord in 1920 and was hailed as the most significant interpreter of early music at the time.

Violet Gordon Woodhouse's illuminating article dealt with the revival of the harpsichord. Included was a picture of her playing a double-manual (two-keyboard) instrument made in the reign of Charles II. According to Cathal, the key points of her article were that music of a certain period should be played on the correct instruments of the period, that harpsichords could be restored and used, and that a large proportion of piano music available at the time had been originally composed for the harpsichord.

At that time Cathal knew what a harpsichord was – the precursor of the piano – and knew that the strings were plucked by plectra made of quill rather than hit by hammers. He had seen harpsichords in the National Museum in Kildare Street, Dublin and in particular had admired an early Italian instrument that was kept in a glass case on its own; as it was displayed without a lid, the strings and soundboard could be seen. The other instruments, including one made by Weber of Dublin, were permanently locked.

Fired with enthusiasm, Cathal went hotfoot to the museum and asked to see the mechanism of one of the harpsichords. Apparently the attendant was not impressed by his appearance – a young boy wearing short trousers, a cap and boots – and promptly told him to get lost; according to Cathal, he was 'thrown out of the place'. Despite this setback, Cathal's interest remained, though he formed a negative opinion of the museum and thought that the authorities showed a woeful lack of interest in the musical instruments.

When, many years later, he was approached by the museum and asked to restore the harpsichords, he refused. He advised them to leave them as they were, especially as they did not want them to be played. His argument was that future historians or instrument builders would be able to learn more from the instruments in their original poor condition; if restored, it would be more difficult to know how the original instrument looked and sounded. Cathal was also critical of how the instruments were being kept; the ambient temperature was too high and the wood was drying out.

It is difficult to ascertain when exactly the harpsichord as we know it came into being. Harpsichord-like instruments were around in the 1400s. Early Italian instruments were highly decorated and beautiful to behold. A motto painted on one of the oldest preserved harpsichords, made in 1560, reads *Rendo lieti in un tempo gli occhi el core* ('I give pleasure at once to the eyes and to the heart').

In the sixteenth century, harpsichords were almost exclusively made in Italy, especially in Venice. Manufacture of the instruments quickly spread to other European countries such as Germany, France, the Low Countries and England. They were either used as solo or accompanying instruments. In ensemble playing, *basso continuo* was employed: a harpsichord with a cello doubling the harpsichordist's left hand or bass line.

By the late 1790s, the harpsichord was being ousted by the piano. The last English harpsichord was made in 1809 by the firm of a German maker, Jacob Kirckman (or Kirkman), who had moved to England in the early 1730s. Ferdinand Weber, also German, had settled in Dublin by 1749 and he made the instrument housed in the National Museum in about 1768 or 1769. He died in 1784.

It is interesting to note that harpsichords were known to composers not normally associated with the instrument: Mozart, Haydn and even Beethoven. Indeed, the original editions of almost all the Beethoven sonatas up to Opus 27 bore the inscription *Pour le Clavecin ou Pianoforte* ('For the harpsichord or piano').

Arnold Dolmetsch, who, with his family, was actively involved in performing and promoting early music in England, built his first harpsichord in the 1890s. By the 1920s, therefore, the revival of the harpsichord and related instruments was under way. There was a certain amount of scholarship at the time, but by today's standards it was limited. Apart from the article that Cathal had read, there was no other literature on the subject available in Ireland.

What Cathal did not realize at the time was that, despite Violet Gordon Woodhouse's legendary capabilities of phrasing and her sensitive performances on the clavichord (a small and very delicate instrument in which the strings are simply touched by pieces of metal), many of the performers of the 1920s knew little about the technique of playing harpsichords in a thoroughly authentic manner. The instrument builders, rather than making faithful copies of old harpsichords, endeavoured to 'improve' them and in doing so created heavy instruments with an insipid and altogether incorrect sound.

Although Cathal developed a sudden interest in these old, half-forgotten instruments, his main love was (and continued to be) the piano. As we have seen, he was familiar with antique square pianos from a very young age. His father's mother had a Broadwood square piano dating from about 1840, which he liked to play whenever he had the opportunity. He loved the light sound of these instruments and, because they were beautiful to look at, he was enchanted by the craftsmanship. The reason for Cathal's preference for the piano was that he was aware of the shortcomings of the harpsichord. Like the violin, it had reached maturity in a relatively short time and thus harpsichords of the 1600s were very similar to those made in the following century. Variety in sound and volume was achieved by adding extra strings and switching between them by means of stops, like an organ. On the other hand, the piano was a more expressive instrument; the volume could be controlled directly from the keyboard by striking the notes lightly or heavily, and it possessed a sustaining pedal. It had also developed considerably over the years, becoming louder, more robust and sophisticated.

The Gannons finally bought a piano in 1924. During Christmas week, Mrs Gannon put £2 into her purse and went into the city centre to buy the boys some jerseys. On the way, she ambled into one of the auction rooms on the quays, where she found a good English overstrung Witton and Witton upright piano. As it seemed to be in such good condition, she ran her fingers over it. She was then approached by a distant cousin of her husband, probably Robert William Gannon, who was in the antique business and worked in Jackson's, the furniture shop in Grafton Street. He said, 'Are you thinking of buying that piano?'

'I wish I could buy it for the young fellow at home – he's playing the piano and he'd like to have one to practise on,' said Mrs Gannon.

'Well now,' said Robert, 'it's a good English-made piano. It's only a couple of years old and I'm down here to bid for it. I'm going to go £45 for it, for my employer. If you could buy that piano for £50, you'd be getting a bargain.'

It was expensive, but as she had often deplored the fact that they had no piano in the house, she was inclined to buy it. She walked around the shops until it was time for the auction. She secured it for £48, returned home and met Cathal. She said, 'Come on down to Guinness's Brewery quick – your daddy will murder me!'

'Why?' asked Cathal.

'I've bought a piano for you and there'll be terrible trouble over it!'

As they walked to the Brewery, Cathal asked her what colour the piano was. She thought that it was black, though she was not sure. They waited outside the front gate until Mr Gannon appeared at five o'clock, pushing his bicycle and talking to a colleague. He was surprised to see them and said, 'What brought you down here?'

'I've bought a piano!' Mrs Gannon replied.

'And where did you get the money to buy it?'

'I had no money – I had £2 in my purse and I paid a deposit, and if you don't like it, we'll have to lose the £2!'

Mr Gannon naturally asked how much it would cost. Mrs Gannon told him the price, which then amounted to eight weeks' wages.

Cathal remembered that his parents had very little to say as they walked to the quays. When they reached the auction rooms and found the shiny black piano, a stool was fetched and Cathal sat down to play it. Delighted with himself, he performed Chopin's 'Minute' Waltz. Cathal thought it a wonderful piano and ably showed off its good points. His father scrutinized it carefully; he got down on his knees to examine the lower section and then opened the lid on the top to look inside. After a while he said, in his usual terse manner, 'That's all right. We'll get it home tomorrow.' Cathal was beside himself with joy.

On the following day, at about six o'clock, the piano was delivered by horse and cart, courtesy of a gang of strong men from Guinness's Brewery. It was lifted into the best room of the house – the sitting room – and a musical evening ensued. For Cathal it was one of the greatest treats of his life. The family was very proud of the piano. As Cathal reckoned that it had probably cost about £84 new, it had been a good buy. The instrument remained in the family; for many years it was kept in Mr Gannon's subsequent home in Dundrum. It then found its way back to Cathal's house. Afterwards it was given to our next-door neighbour.

It may seem strange that this seemingly happy period of Cathal's life coincided with the two years of cruelty to which he was subjected by Brother B— in Synge Street; the Brother's reign of terror lasted from 1923 to 1925.

Now that the Gannons had a piano of their own, the next step was to send Cathal to a good teacher for more music lessons. Early in 1925 he was sent to the Read Pianoforte School in Harcourt Street, near St Stephen's Green, and he had the good fortune to be taught by an excellent teacher, Miss Helen Yates, who was also a painter and sculptor. She had been educated at home by her father, a barrister. Although only five years older than Cathal, she had a 'most wonderful' influence on him. Cathal was under a great debt of gratitude to her because she influenced his taste in music at a time when he needed guidance, for he had been brought up listening to Victorian drawing-room music. Thanks to Miss Yates he came into contact with what he called 'really good music'. Through her he developed a taste for Baroque music, which he enjoyed listening to at a period when it was not very popular. She introduced Cathal to Bach and to some of the sonatas by Scarlatti, mentioning that they were written specially for the harpsichord. Cathal was aware of the fact that they did not sound quite right on the piano and often wished that he could play the pieces on the correct instrument.

Miss Yates also introduced Cathal to the works of John Field, the Irish composer who invented the nocturne and who died in Moscow. Cathal took to this melodic Romantic music immediately; no doubt it offered an escape from the tedium of school. Whenever Cathal sat down at a piano in later life, he invariably played a piece by Chopin or Field; the latter's Nocturne No. 5 in B flat was his favourite and became his 'signature tune'. I have heard him play this and other pieces over the years, right from my childhood. Some years ago, I came across a manuscript book with a youthful composition written in it in the unmistakeable style of a Field nocturne. I practised it in my father's absence and played it for him when he returned. He had forgotten all about it and was quite surprised.

Cathal had no ambitions to be a performer; he just enjoyed the music and was content to play it moderately well. Because of circumstances, as we shall see, he did not take any of the examinations.

Whilst studying at the Read Pianoforte School (run by Miss Patricia Read, also a teacher), Helen Yates brought Cathal to a concert at which he heard a piano concerto for the first time in his life. He remembered Miss Yates explaining the structure of the concerto to him whilst walking in St Stephen's Green on the way to the music school. He, and possibly his mother, went to the concert that evening. The work was the Fourth Piano Concerto by the French composer Camille Saint-Saëns; Freddie Stone was the soloist and Rhoda Coghill played an arrangement of the orchestral part on another piano. Rhoda, seven years older than Cathal, had studied under Patricia Read before proceeding to Trinity College, where she studied and obtained a B.Mus. in 1922. Cathal was fascinated with the music; he enjoyed the 'fireworks' in the first part of the second movement and the striking melody in the final section of the work.

Cathal was also introduced, albeit indirectly, to the eighteenth-century French composer Jean-Philippe Rameau one day at the Read Pianoforte School when he came downstairs after his piano lesson. He stopped at a door to listen to a pupil attempting to play a piece from the opera *Dardanus* by Rameau; the teacher was counting the time aloud and beating it with her foot on the floor. Cathal was enchanted by the music, though at the time he did not know who the composer was.

During this year, the family bought a gramophone player. His father ordered the motor and the parts, which were sent to him from England, and he made himself a tall wooden case in the style of the period. Mr Gannon then assembled the gramophone, following the plans. Cathal found the motor rather noisy.

From this stage onwards, Cathal bought many Red Label HMV records, mostly of piano solo music and songs. The piano music was normally performed by Paderewski or Cortot. Cathal's favourite composers were Field, Chopin and Beethoven. He bought the records in Moiselle's shop in Johnson's Court, Pigott's, McCullough's and May's, all in Dublin's city centre. Four minutes of music cost 7s. 6d.

The popular singers of the time were John McCormack and Caruso. The special Plum-label recording of Galli-Curci, McCormack and others singing the famous quartet from *Rigoletto* cost £1. The Gannons did not rise to the cost of this recording of 'singers bellowing at each other', as Cathal described them. He was never very fond of opera.

For 6d., one could pick up old 78 rpm records in a second-hand shop in Richmond Street. Dating from the early 1900s, they were almost a quarter of an inch thick and had one side only. As Cathal commented, 'You'd be weighed down with them.' The records were all kept in special albums, which were also bought in the record shops.

Cathal continued with his piano lessons throughout 1925 but, sadly, they were not destined to last for long. Another dramatic change in direction was now forced upon him.

Nine

Cathal's ambition was to be a surgeon. His aunt Peggy, who had studied to be a nurse, had noticed how neat and accurate he was and often told him that he would make a good surgeon if he studied as she had done. However, this was not to be. He was unhappy at school and his parents could not afford to send him to a better one, let alone to university. Such an ambitious scheme was simply out of the question.

Eventually his father said to him, 'Look, you're not putting your shoulder to the wheel and you'll have to work at something. I'll get you into the Brewery and you'll serve your apprenticeship as a carpenter.' At that time, Cathal had no interest in carpentry whatsoever, but the prospect of working at anything was better than school.

Cathal left Synge Street in June 1925, at the end of the school year. He was relieved to be rid of the Christian Brothers. At the beginning of September his father arranged for him to be interviewed at Guinness's Brewery by a Mr E.H. Hill, an engineer. Evidently Cathal made a good impression on him, for he was sent to the doctor for a medical examination. On the day of his medical, Cathal's father showed him around the Brewery in order to let him see what it was like. Cathal was duly impressed by all the machinery, the steam engines and the generating station, and looked forward to starting work.

Cathal passed the medical test, though he noticed that he was underweight. Non-tradesmen were expected to be a certain height and weight ('like a bullock', as Cathal often remarked afterwards). According to the medical report, he weighed 6 st 4 lb and was 4 ft 11 in tall. The words 'teeth satisfactory' were written after the heading 'remarks'.

A little over a week later, on 14 September, Cathal was subjected to

Brewery bureaucracy and sent with forms from one office to another. An officious individual rated him soundly about something trivial and nearly brought him to tears. Mr Hill came to the rescue and said to the man, 'You shouldn't speak to that little boy in the way you have spoken to him.'

He was finally sent over to the registry office where he was signed on and, like all employees, was given a number: 18507. Having signed a document known as the Truck Act of 1896, which stipulated that employees could be subjected to fines or dismissal for drunkenness, absence from duty without leave, late attendance, carelessness or wilful neglect, smoking, insubordination and idleness, he was told that he could begin the process of learning his trade the following week.

Cathal started work in Guinness's Brewery as an apprentice carpenter at eight o'clock on Monday morning, 21 September 1925, aged fifteen, his education abruptly brought to a close. He hated the place right from the very start. He had suddenly been wrenched from the cultural atmosphere of Priestfield House and thrown amongst rough workmen in bleak and dreary surroundings. It was not what he had envisaged.

In Guinness's Brewery there were two carpenters' workshops. The Mill or 'lower' workshop in Cooke's Lane was where rough baulks of wood were cut using large saws and then planed. The 'upper' or 'top' workshop in James's Street, adjacent to the main entrance and beside the old Guinness family home, was where all the neat work was done. Originally it had been a malt house; it had been converted into a temporary workshop in the 1890s. Cathal found it an ugly, 'barracky' building. It consisted of two floors; the bottom floor contained a machine called a general joiner, purchased in about 1870, with which one could saw, plane, and make mortises and tenons. A few workbenches were on this floor and more on the next. Cathal was put at a little bench upstairs, where he was taught his trade.

At the time, Bill Lycet was the foreman of this 'top shop' and Cathal's father was the assistant foreman, though Mr Gannon really ran the place. Cathal was amazed to discover how much authority his father wielded and how much he was held in awe by the carpenters. As we have seen, Mr Gannon had been a woodworker in his young days and so had his father – it was in the family's blood. Whilst Mr Lycet was somewhat indecisive, being of a gentlemanly disposition, Mr Gannon was down to earth and spoke with an air of authority. Eighty men worked under him; among them were thirty carpenters. Four or five worked at machines, there were a couple of glaziers, and a 'heavy gang' of men moved furniture and erected scaffolding. There were also helpers for the carpenters. Nothing escaped Mr Gannon's attention; he was very alert. The discipline was very strict and things had to be done properly. When a job was not done to his satisfaction, he used to say, 'Break it up, make it again – that's not right!' No one dared lie to him; it was safer to come clean and tell him the truth. His usual rebuke was, 'That's all right – don't do it again. Be more careful in the future.'

Cathal could not remember his father being unreasonable to anyone or being unduly harsh. Cathal often used to cycle into work with him in the mornings, or else he followed him, arriving maybe five minutes later.

Although Cathal had always seen neat craftsmanship at home, handling woodworking tools did not come naturally to him and at first he was hamfisted. He was fortunate enough to inherit many good tools from various members of the family.

Cathal was apprenticed to a man by the name of Seán O'Neill, one of the best woodworkers in the Brewery. Seán came from Dunmanway, County Cork and had been in America. He had been a footballer in his young days, was a great GAA man and refereed matches up to nearly the end of his life. His work was very neat and Cathal learned a great deal from him. Looking back from an advanced age, Cathal came to the conclusion that he had enjoyed his apprenticeship.

Cathal remembered receiving his first week's wages: 16s. Like a good boy, he brought it straight home and surrendered it to his mother, though he was allowed to keep a few shillings for himself. Being the eldest of five children, money was not that plentiful and every little bit helped.

After a couple of weeks in the carpenters' workshop, Cathal realized that he was never going to like working there. Conditions were appalling; a glazed roof and a few miserable electric lights supplied barely adequate illumination. The place was ghastly cold, especially in winter, and heating was not installed until many years later. During the winter snow blew in through the louvres of the glass roof. The only way of keeping warm was to wait for the foreman to leave, post a sentry on the door, fetch a carefully hidden skipping rope and skip until one felt warmer. At other times the men kicked a ball around.

The only source of heat was a steam radiator in a small storeroom that was used by workmen when applying French polish to a finished piece, as it was imperative to do this type of work in a warm environment. Although this room was supposed to be locked, Cathal and his colleagues were often caught in it trying to warm themselves.

As can be imagined, the toilets were just as cold. These miserable places were situated underground and were controlled by timekeepers, better known amongst the workers as 'shite-house clerks'. These individuals were posted at the entrances of the toilets. Their job was to ensure that the men were not wasting company time, though it was unlikely that any sensible man would want to while away time in such a place in the depths of winter.

No washing facilities were supplied – carpentry was supposed to be a 'clean' trade. However, a blind eye was turned to the illegal practice of fetching a bucket of hot water from the adjacent brewery at lunchtime and knocking-off time. Twenty or thirty men proceeded to wash their hands in the one bucket. More often than not it was necessary to break through a scum of dirt on the top of the water. The men were expected to go to their meals with dirty hands, for technically they were clean. Complaints were met with the argument that if one worked for an outside builder, such good conditions would not be encountered. Consequently the dreadful conditions of the workshop were accepted. Even Mr Gannon conceded that the workshop was cold, but there was little that he could do about it. Higher members of the staff were unapproachable; they enjoyed steam heaters and coal fires in their offices.

Some of the female members of the staff, many of whom had been educated in Alexandra College, were particularly snooty and took scant notice of the working men. However, Cathal did manage to befriend a few of them over the years, especially when he was involved in harpsichord making. They then realized that he was a little out of the ordinary. At a later period, when Cathal was put in charge of keys and locks, he would meet more members of the staff, many of whom became friendly towards him. At the time, Guinness's Brewery was a Protestant establishment that employed Catholics only as working men.

The regime in Guinness's Brewery was strict. If a worker arrived late, he could get away with it for the first couple of times. If his lateness persisted, he would be warned that on the next occasion he would be sacked.

Cathal eventually got used to his new environment, though he would have preferred a more respectable profession in an office. At school in Synge Street, the boys had been directed towards safe jobs in the Civil Service or Post Office; tradesmen were considered to be 'the dregs of humanity'.

It can be safely assumed that at this stage Cathal was able to regain confidence in himself and become more assertive. He certainly inherited his father's strictness and indeed became strict with himself, as evidenced by his meticulous craftsmanship.

Cathal spent most of his time at the bench in the top shop, where he learned joinery and cabinetmaking. He passed his three months' probationary period without any problem. A memorandum forwarded to the Registry Department by Mr E.H. Hill in December 1925 contained a handwritten addendum: 'Cathal Gannon has given every satisfaction and I recommend that he be retained.'

Having mastered the requisite skills, he went on to make furniture and fittings for the directors' offices. For him this was rather interesting. He also framed pictures that were hung in various parts of the Brewery. Occasionally he was given outdoor work to do, such as working on roofs. At the beginning, Cathal remembered crying with the cold when working on roofs in the winter, but he did not dare complain.

Unfortunately, Cathal soon discovered that working with carpenter's tools and playing the piano were not compatible. Finding time to attend lessons also proved to be a problem and he eventually gave up going to Helen Yates and just played the piano, as best as he could, in his spare time. He returned for lessons some years later but found that his hands had become stiff and impaired from so much hammering and sawing. However, his interest in music remained.

Cathal got on fairly well with his colleagues, but he never made friends with any of them. They had a good sense of humour and enjoyed a certain amount of horseplay. In the foreman's absence, they sometimes used to play golf. One of the carpenters had made wooden golf sticks, which, together with the balls and other equipment, were hidden under various benches. These were whipped out and played with for about ten or fifteen minutes when the coast was clear.

At other times, the men chased around and threw dirty, dusty sacks at each other. They also threw sawdust at each other by way of amusement.

Tea breaks were not allowed; a mid-morning break for tea or beer was not introduced until 1953. However, the men managed to make tea surreptitiously in an old glue pot. The tea was made on a steam heater that was used for boiling glue; anyone who drank the resulting brew deserved a medal as the taste was so disgusting.

As soon as Cathal settled into his new career as apprentice carpenter, he started his life-long career in playing pranks, much to the annoyance and often discomfort of his colleagues. The various pranks that he devised helped relieve the monotony of work in the Brewery.

The carpenters' workshop in which he toiled had been made of second-hand timber and quite a number of the flooring boards upstairs had holes of about an inch in diameter. These had been stopped with wooden plugs, but some had fallen out and others had been removed by the workmen. It was therefore possible to look down and see people moving around in the work-shop below.

From 1926 onwards, crystal radio sets became popular and because of the nature of these radios, which used no electricity, a strong enough signal from the Dublin transmitter could only be received within a radius of about thirty miles. Some of the radio shops issued small cardboard maps of Ireland with a strip of celluloid that could be swivelled around Dublin. Miles were marked on the celluloid and thus one was able to discover whether one was within the thirty-mile radius or not.

One of Cathal's tricks was to place such a map on a bench and get his colleagues to invite some unwary workman to guess the distance, as the crow flies, of a certain part of the country from Dublin. Cathal, who was observing the scene from above through one of the holes in the floor, would wait until all the heads were bent towards the map and then would pour a jug of water through a funnel and drench the unfortunate individual who was being challenged. The reader may imagine the reaction and the strong language that followed.

Cathal clearly remembered one victim of this prank: a well-dressed man, in the height of fashion, who sported a starched butterfly collar. He was adamant that a certain place was fifty miles from Dublin and no more, despite the protestations of the others. The map was duly fetched and his error was pointed out to him. As he leaned over to check the distance, Cathal squirted him with water from a brass garden syringe that he had pro-cured. It came down with such force that it took the starch out of the man's collar; when he stood up, the collar had collapsed around his neck. The poor man was in a terrible state.

The workshop was quite noisy with the din of hammering and the sounds of a circular saw or planing machine running for most of the day. On top of this was general hubbub: people talking, coming and going, and tim-ber being moved about.

From next door could be heard the sounds of machinery grinding in the old Number One Brewery. On the top floor of the building in which the carpenters' workshops were situated was a vertical conveyor belt or elevator, which was used for moving barley to the brewery; the noise of this continued until about half past four in the afternoon. When it stopped, one was aware of a certain amount of quietness.

From the street below came the sounds of iron-rimmed cart wheels bumping along cobblestones, motor car horns and rattling trams on their way to Inchicore.

Then, as now, the pervasive smell of hops permeated the entire Brewery and spread around the surrounding area. This never bothered Cathal; indeed, he hardly noticed it. What did bother him were the long hours, especially when he had to work at something that was relatively uninteresting. Work started at eight o'clock in the mornings and finished at five in the evenings. On Saturdays, they worked from eight to twelve.

Cathal was always interested in the machinery in the old Number One Brewery, which was demolished in around 1940. Whenever he had an opportunity, he used to slip away from his work, unseen, and walk around the place, admiring the old coppers, kieves and steam engines. He befriended all the engine men and one of them allowed him to switch off an engine when it needed to be stopped. He explored the basement and loved to go to the top of the malt elevator, from which a wonderful view of the city could be seen. Cathal quickly developed a liking for roofs and high vantage points.

One of the perks accorded to workers in Guinness's Brewery was permission to drink Guinness in the 'taps' or distribution points dotted around the complex. Every man was entitled to drink two pints of Guinness a day. Those who did not wish to drink, like Cathal, were given 'beer money allowance', which amounted to twopence per day.

The men who availed of the free drink were supposed to take it in their own time, for example during their lunch break or after five o'clock. Most of them, however, flouted this rule and drank whenever they had the opportunity to do so. In order to obtain more drink, they did errands and favours for senior members of the staff, who used to issue them with beer dockets for a given number of pints. They even 'touched' or scrounged for free beer. It was no uncommon thing for men to spend far more time than they were allowed in the taps, drinking; by five o'clock they were 'well oiled'.

Cathal was often given beer dockets for 'obligements', as he called them, but he always passed them on to his colleagues, who, needless to say, were very grateful to receive them.

Pillaging beer was a common occurrence in the Brewery; Cathal either heard about or saw men being sacked because of it. He remembered walking to work one morning with a man from Dolphin's Barn who talked about music and who asked him about the difference between a sonata and a concerto. Cathal explained the difference and they parted at eight o'clock when they reached the Brewery. Cathal met him again outside the gate at ten o'clock; he was on his way home, having been dismissed for pillaging beer. Cathal never saw him again.

The man in question had no reputation for being a thief or a drunkard. He had just seen a container of beer, had helped himself and was caught by a Brewery policeman, who may have been trying to catch somebody else. The unfortunate man just happened to be in the wrong place at the wrong time.

Guinness's Brewery had many unique features, including the fleet of steam trains that were used for transporting barley from the Robert Street stores to the Brewhouse, where it was poured into hoppers, brought up in elevators, ground in a mill and soaked in a kieve to produce malt. They were also used to transport wooden kegs around the Victoria Quay yard. There were eighteen trains in operation – numbers 6 to 24 – when Cathal started work. Numbers 1 to 5 had been scrapped before his time, though he had a vague recollection of seeing one of them in a fitters' workshop. As it was decided that it was no longer an economic proposition to save it, it was destroyed.

The trains were also used for taking visitors around the complex. Six or eight people could sit, facing either side, in one of the small carriages; over them was stretched a coloured canopy. A special guide drove the engine and explained all the interesting points to the visitors. The Brewery was built on two levels: the upper level being James's Street and the lower being by the river Liffey. To get from the upper level to the lower, the trains had to go down a corkscrew tunnel, built in the 1870s, which was always of great interest to railway enthusiasts.

Cathal had little contact with the lower level, for, as we have seen, most of his work took place in the carpenter's shop, which was situated on the upper level.

Cathal was always fascinated by the underground tunnels in the Brewery, which linked all areas of the premises. Cathal loved to walk from one to another and travel the entire length of the Brewery underground. The tunnels were always damp and had a peculiar musty smell.

A relic of the past was an old speaking tube that Cathal remembered seeing when he first joined the company. Speaking tubes had been used for communication before telephones were installed; this one example had been left *in situ*. As in a ship, the tube connected two working areas and had a whistle at both ends. In order to call someone, one removed one's own whistle and blew up or down the tube to sound the whistle at the other end. The person at the other end then removed his whistle and the two parties communicated by speaking into the tube.

Those who did not live near the Brewery had their meals in what were known as the workmen's rooms, which had a canteen. A bell summoned the workers at twelve o'clock. When Cathal joined, the men sat at long deal tables and ate from enamel plates. A hot dinner, served at lunchtime, cost about 7d. The meals were rough and ready, though the food was good, solid fare. Ex-labouring men were given the job of serving the food. They carried out the plates of food one on top of another, so that there was always a strong possibility of finding part of one's neighbour's meal at the bottom of one's plate.

Cathal did not avail of the canteen, as five or seven minutes on the bicycle (or fifteen minutes on foot) brought him home to a good meal cooked by his mother. This was the one break in the day that gave him fresh impetus for the afternoon.

Ten

*W*hen Cathal started work in the Brewery, the chairman – Edward Cecil Guinness, the first Lord Iveagh – was pointed out to him. Lord Iveagh was liable to become very upset if anything in the Brewery was changed. Some machinery that had been taken away had to be reinstated because he had remembered it being there as a young man. When he died two years later, it was removed again. One man bragged that he had held a door open for the first Lord Iveagh and that he had said 'thank you'; it was all he could talk about for a long time afterwards.

Despite the fact that Cathal made furniture and fittings for the directors' offices, he rarely met any of the directors; they were far above his station in life. Built in the 1870s and 1880s, the decor of these offices was very dated; the doors were drab and were either oak-grained or painted brown or green. The offices contained Victorian mahogany furniture, such as balloon-backed chairs and fire screens with ugly-looking red poplin insets. Some directors had screens for shielding themselves from draughts. In fact, the screens were often used for another purpose: as certain directors were too proud to use the lavatories, which had to be shared with lesser mortals, they preferred to use chamber pots behind their screens.

If Cathal needed to do any work in one of these offices, it had to be finished before ten o'clock in the morning. Cathal remembered a small staircase across which a silk cord was stretched at about a quarter to ten each morning; only people of a certain class were allowed up the stairs. Outside the directors' offices were men who waited on them and announced visitors. Major work in the offices was done by special office carpenters who started work at six o'clock in the morning. There was a strict hierarchy of staff in

Guinness's Brewery; the upper echelons were Protestants and graduates from Oxford and Cambridge.

The office cleaners were Brewery widows. They also arrived at six o'clock and left at nine, though some worked until ten or eleven o'clock, but well out of the way of the directors. Some of these unfortunate women had to come from as far away as Clontarf and had to walk a considerable distance. However, there were workers' trams that ran between half past five and six o'clock in the mornings and the widows availed of these. Many of the women had children to rear and be educated. Although they led a hard life, the Brewery provided them with many support services that were quite unique in Dublin at the time. The Brewery employed widows or spouses of pensioners in order to provide them with a source of extra income. Meals were provided to widows and even sons of Brewery pensioners on the condition that they attended school, and special allowances were provided to Brewery widows for every child up to the age of fourteen – the standard working age at the time.

Cathal often came in contact with junior, senior and head engineers. Some of them were quite pleasant. The head engineers, like the directors, had a number of offices to the right of the main entrance. There were three types of engineers working in the Brewery: civil, mechanical and electrical. The civil engineers looked after the buildings, roadways, yards, walls and drainage systems. The mechanical engineers maintained the vessels, pipe systems, pumps, and the heating and cooling systems. The electrical engineers specialized in lighting, power, the internal telephone system and, at a later stage, electronic systems and automation. Cathal often had to consult a head or chief engineer about some matter or other.

During Cathal's apprenticeship, which lasted from 1925 to 1931, his wages rose from 16s. to 63s. per week. Wages were paid every Friday. The workers lined up at a small office near the workshop and were organized by a man who roared, 'Come on now, one to fifty, one to fifty,' and then 'Fifty to a hundred, line up here!' The men were therefore able to calculate the time at which they should go down and join the queue. One man was heard to say, by way of encouragement, 'Hurry up men, the wages is about to be gettin' gev out!'

When a worker reached the little office, he shouted his number and was handed a small aluminium container with the money in coins inside. If the amount of money was not correct or if there was a complaint, an official was there to make a note of it. If, however, everything was in order, the tin was thrown into a basket so that it could be used again. It was not until much later that cheques were issued in envelopes.

One old fellow who joined the queue for his wages was known for his propensity for cursing. Cathal and his colleagues used to tease him, which would result in an outpouring of foul language, his getting out of line and becoming confused. He was regularly ticked off for losing his place in the queue. By the time he reached the lady behind the window, he was shouting at the top of his voice. The lady, who was not at all amused, used to throw his wages at him.

Some workers who did shift work often had to come into the Brewery very early in the mornings. The most thankless employment was done by those who worked on the boats on the Liffey or in the racking shed, where the beer was put into barrels. The men arrived at work at around six o'clock in the morning only to be told that they were not needed for the rest of the day and that they could go home. Their foremen probably could have told them the day before, but did not. Rather than walk all the way home again, many of the men spent the day in a public house.

Apprentices were allowed a one-week holiday every year. However, at that time, fully-fledged tradesmen were only given three days' holidays, or more precisely, three separate days off in the year. This consisted of one day called the annual holiday, another one called Queen's Day (in honour of Queen Victoria who had visited the Brewery on 4 April 1900 and expressed the wish that the men should have a day off to celebrate her visit) and an excursion day, on which one was entitled to free vouchers for a day's excursion by train or boat. A worker could take his wife and any children under the age of sixteen with him. The vouchers enabled them to travel as far as the Isle of Man, Holyhead or Liverpool by boat, or as far as Belfast by train.

Theoretically these three days were supposed to be taken separately, but in practice the workers managed to take them together. There was consternation every year coming up to the first week of August when the older men claimed the privilege of taking their three days off along with the bank holiday, so that they might have four days' leave. If a worker could be spared, he could take a day and a half off at his own expense and thus have a five-and-a-half-day holiday – in effect, one week.

This situation lasted until 1936, when the de Valera government finally decreed that workers should have a one-week holiday every year. Some of the older men, who had never enjoyed such a long break from work, found this new arrangement rather perplexing as they had no idea of what they might do for seven whole days.

Cathal was able to enjoy a two-week holiday for most of the years of his apprenticeship, for he attended Bolton Street technical college and passed his examinations, which earned him an extra week of holidays and 1 5s. for each exam. This helped pay for his holidays.

Cathal took a fortnight's holiday during the summer of 1926 with his aunt Cissie, who went to Dingle in County Kerry to attend an Irish course. A photograph of them together in Killarney indicates that they must have travelled around the county. This was Cathal's first holiday taken outside the Dublin area. He enjoyed it; no doubt Cissie would have encouraged him to try speaking to the locals in their native tongue. It was she who encouraged him to think again about the Irish language and the culture of his country after he had been turned against it by the Christian Brothers. He gradually began to appreciate what Ireland had to offer, though he preferred to surround himself with the relics of Anglo-Irish culture; he looked eastwards rather than westwards.

As study at a technical college was part of his apprenticeship, the Brewery paid the fees for Bolton Street college, which he attended four evenings a week after work; a special registry office at Guinness's also supplied the necessary books, pencils and drawing equipment. At Bolton Street he studied carpentry, joinery, building construction and planned drawing – subjects that interested him. Five or six other apprentices from Guinness's Brewery also attended college at the same time as Cathal.

Cathal also attended classes at Kevin Street technical college and the City of Dublin Technical School in Parnell Square. The subjects he studied included English, Irish, history and geography. He was therefore able to continue his education in a more pleasant and relaxed atmosphere than in his experience of school. There were two incentives to spur him on: the aforementioned promise of extra time off work, and the threat of having his apprenticeship terminated and his career destroyed if he failed to attend college and abide by the rules. Undoubtedly at this stage Cathal developed the strong thirst for knowledge that would remain with him for the rest of his life.

He always walked to the colleges – they were a fair distance from the Crumlin Road – often accompanied by some of his classmates. Later he was joined by his brother Jack, who was following the same career in the Brewery. The distance from Cathal's home to Bolton Street was a little over two and a half miles or four kilometres. The reader must be reminded that on the same day Cathal had cycled a distance of about one and a quarter miles (two kilometres) into work in the morning, cycled home for lunch, cycled back to work, cycled home at five o'clock and had spent the day doing hard, physical work. It was no wonder that he developed into a vigorous and physically strong person, and was capable of walking very long distances.

Nevertheless, Cathal did manage to succumb to a dose of rheumatic fever in his mid-twenties. It incapacitated him for a while and left him with a heart murmur. This, regrettably, had a dramatic effect on his health when he reached his eighties.

Despite Cathal's busy schedule of work and study at this period, he did manage to find time to look around Dublin city and see what was going on.

At midday on Saturdays, when Cathal finished work, he often visited the Iveagh Market in Francis Street and then made his way down to Aston Quay, where he examined the contents of the six to twelve odd bookstalls on both sides of the road outside McBirney's shop, near O'Connell Bridge. There were more book barrows lining the side streets leading to Fleet Street. He found this most rewarding and often went home with a few fine morocco leather-bound eighteenth-century books, costing 2d. or 3d. apiece. More often than not, however, he was tempted to buy as many books as possible, for a shilling or two, and relieve the vendor of his load. It was easy enough to carry a pile of books and take the tram home. Cathal must have destroyed quite a number of eighteenth-century books for the *ex libris* plates, the collecting of which was a craze at the time. He also bought back numbers of *The Connoisseur* magazine for 3d. to 6d. each.

Cathal always made for one man in particular, Joe Clarke, who used to set up his bookstall by the gents' toilet (now gone) near the Corinthian Cinema. He erected shelves against the brick wall of an ESB substation and placed all his best books on them. Books of lesser importance were left in a barrow. A set of books were sold as such and not individually. The price of a book ranged from 2d. to approximately 5s.

Cathal always had his nose stuck in a book – mostly at mealtimes. It was no wonder that Professor Kevin B. Nowlan told the Hon. Desmond Guinness many years later that Cathal was always full of 'out-of-the-way information'.

Cathal also became interested in old engravings at this period and bought many in the Iveagh Market and at various auction rooms on the quays. He often bumped into a couple of elderly men who always voiced their concern as to whether the engravings were genuine or not. Cathal always managed to buy the engravings he liked before they found them or else when they were examining and hesitating over them. He mounted the engravings and hung them on the walls of the rooms in Longford Terrace. The house soon turned into a miniature art gallery. Fortunately his parents did not object to these purchases and adornments to their home. Soon the walls of Cathal's bedroom were covered with pictures. When it was time to redecorate or re-paper the room, he took them all down and then put up new ones.

Cathal also bought engravings at the bookstalls. From Joe Clarke he bought four etchings of trees by Antonio Waterloo at 2d. each and a mezzo-tint of the Duchess of Manchester as Diana disarming Cupid.

Despite the general lack of motorized traffic, especially on a Saturday afternoon, the city was noisy enough. In the 1920s one could hear the constant rattling of iron-shod cart wheels and carriages over cobblestones, which were treacherous in icy weather. Horses clip-clopped around the city and tradesmen shouted to one another. At street corners one often heard the sound of a barrel organ or piano. Other sounds of old Dublin were the clanging of church bells and the wailing of factory sirens, which served as reliable guides for timekeeping. At that period it was not usual to wear wristwatches, especially at work; one only wore them on a Sunday. In Dolphin's Barn the church bells rang the angelus at six o'clock in the morning; they rang again at seven o'clock for Mass. People found the church bells more accurate than their alarm clocks, which were often kept lying on their faces. The hooter of the local brickworks sounded at ten to eight.

Cathal always gave himself seven minutes to cycle to work or fifteen minutes to walk. The whistle of the Wills tobacco factory in Marrowbone Lane served as a guide to the time; it went off at around five minutes to eight. If he was late, he jogged to work. It was not uncommon to see men jogging to their work places, though at that time it had nothing to do with fitness – the workmen, like Cathal, were in a hurry.

Cathal heard a radio (or wireless, as it was called then) for the first time when he was fifteen; a friend let him hear a 2LO (BBC) broadcast on a crystal radio set. Part of the programme consisted of South African folk music. For him it was a wonderful experience.

Soon afterwards, articles began to appear in the national press about the up-and-coming Irish radio station, 2RN (later Radio Éireann), which would be broadcast from Dublin and Athlone, starting in January 1926. People became very excited and rushed out to buy wireless sets – mostly of the crystal variety, which cost about 15s. Cathal's father bought a Gecophone, which consisted of a crystal in a little glass tube, mounted in a mahogany wooden box, the 'cat's whiskers' – a piece of wire with a coil mounted at the end of a handle (this was moved about to make good contact with the crystal) – and earphones.

Cathal took to making his own sets, as they were easy enough to put together. The cost of the materials came to 2s. 11d., and the components could all be fitted into a cigar box. He made the coil himself but bought the crystal.

If one possessed a large 'Daventry' coil, which cost 2s. 9d., one might be very lucky and pick up the BBC; this was everybody's aim. The Daventry coil replaced a U-shaped piece of wire in the radio set. Hearing the BBC was a major achievement, as crystal radio sets could, under normal circumstances, not pick up a station outside a radius of about thirty miles from the transmitter. On rarer occasions, thanks to freak reception, one might receive Belgium. People were known to stay up all night searching for stations; successes were reported to and featured in the newspapers.

In 1928 or 1929, the Gannons acquired one of the new valve radio sets. Their model had two bright emitter valves that lit up the room, enabling them to turn off the gas light. As there was no electricity in the house then, the radio had to be powered by means of glass batteries, which had to be brought to a local garage to be charged. They were left there on one day and collected on the next. The batteries only lasted a few days. Larger batteries, square in shape and the size of a Christmas cake, were called high-tension batteries and lasted longer. One frequently saw people carrying glass batteries along the Crumlin Road; they were either on their way to the garage to have them recharged or returning home with them, charged.

Valve wireless sets were often made in Guinness's Brewery as 'nixers'. Senior members of the staff got the workers to make radios for them. It was fun and something of a challenge for people to buy the parts and make their own sets, rather than buy them assembled, and undoubtedly there was a tremendous sense of achievement for the individual once the radio was completed and working satisfactorily. As soon as one was made, another model became available; the radio was then taken apart and a new one made.

Everyone strove to have a seven-valve, super heterodyne model.

Cathal remembered being at a party in a house by the Grand Canal between Parnell Bridge and Harold's Cross Bridge, opposite the Wellington Barracks. The owner was a wireless enthusiast. At midnight everyone was asked to be quiet so that the chimes of Big Ben could be heard, followed by the news from the BBC. Everyone thought this was wonderful and it was talked about in the neighbourhood.

Cathal's brother Willie was interested in radio from the earliest days. Cathal believed that the first two-valve set that the Gannons owned was bought by him; it was probably old ex-army stock. Needless to say, it was a great novelty when bought, especially as it was capable of picking up the BBC.

As Willie was still at school at this period and had no pocket money, Cathal used to finance his purchases. Willie loved rummaging around the Iveagh Market in Francis Street. He often came home and told Cathal about a wireless set he had seen there, complete though in need of restoration, for 7s. 6d. Cathal gave him the money, Willie restored the radio to working order and sold it at a profit. Soon afterwards he would find another and once again Cathal would help him buy it. Cathal never remembered being paid back, but he received the satisfaction of encouraging his younger brother in doing something that interested him greatly.

Cathal remembered colleagues in the Brewery who had stayed up all night trying to get New York or some American station on their radio. These men came into work in the morning exhausted from lack of sleep, but happy to confide that they had succeeded in hearing a broadcast from the other side of the Atlantic.

During the late 1930s, Cathal often stayed up late at night writing letters to his future wife and listening to the radio. He often heard the best of music coming from Germany at one and two o'clock in the morning. It was during these late-night sessions that he heard all the Beethoven and Brahms symphonies for the first time. In the early 1930s he heard instruments that the Germans referred to as *cembalo*, which he suspected were harpsichords, albeit bad ones. When he subsequently heard them being played on the BBC, he learned that he had guessed correctly – they were indeed harpsichords. By this stage, then, he had read about them, seen them and now heard them. As yet, he had not played one and certainly the idea of making one had not occurred to him.

Eleven

C athal's brother Willie was bright; he shared some of Cathal's interests but directed most of his attention to things electrical and mechanical, as we have seen in the previous chapter. He, like Cathal and Jack, had been sent to the Christian Brothers in Synge Street, which he did not like. However, Willie was more rebellious than his brothers and, when one of the Brothers gave him a 'hiding' sometime between 1926 and 1928, he ran away from school and disappeared for the day. The Civic Guards were alerted and he was found in the brickworks on the Crumlin Road late that night.

Willie refused to return to Synge Street and his father allowed him to continue his education at Rialto National School. He was happy there and did very well.

Willie, like Cathal, was an avid reader. He regularly read books at meal-times and always brought one to bed with him. One night he was reading in bed and fell asleep with a book in his hand. Shortly afterwards the gas went off and his light went out. A shilling was put into the meter; the gas came back on but of course it was not alight in Willie's bedroom. When gas was smelt upstairs, the family remembered that Willie had gone to bed and had probably fallen asleep whilst reading. He was rescued, hauled downstairs and brought out into the fresh air. Fortunately no harm was done.

Cathal distinctly remembered what happened next: his father fetched a hammer and a chisel, went up to the bedroom, cut off the gas fitting and blocked it. That was the end of gas in the bedrooms. From then until 1932, when electricity came to Longford Terrace, the family had to retire to bed with either oil lamps or candles.

Cathal's pleasures at this time were simple; the extent of his extravagance was to go to a film at the Princess or Stella cinema in Rathmines on a Saturday afternoon, when admittance was cheap – 3*d*. or 4*d*., perhaps.

At this stage in his life, he would have started to show an interest in girls. It was a common thing for local teenagers and young men to make a date with a girl for about seven or half past seven in the evening, buy a bag of sweets and walk to the top of the Crumlin Road to sit on a grassy bank, chat and then walk back home. On Friday or Saturday evenings a boy and girl might go to see a film; the total expenditure would be no more than a half-crown.

If no rendezvous had been arranged, young men ambled up and down the South Circular Road eyeing the girls (the 'mots') and stopping to talk to them. Undoubtedly a friendship could be started in this manner, but most of the time each party would separate at the end of a conversation and continue walking. The term used for being out on the prowl, seeking female company, was 'clicking'. A common opening line for fellows and girls walking in opposite directions was, 'You're goin' the wrong way!'

In his early twenties, Cathal had a great mop of wavy hair. One girl, who passed him on the road, greeted him with, 'Hey mister, your waves is makin' me seasick!'

There seemed to be a plentiful supply of girls in their twenties in the locality, especially in the 1930s; every evening there was a constant stream of girls cycling along the Crumlin Road towards Crumlin village, on their way home from working in various factories.

The Dark Lane was a great place for courting couples, but it seemed that nothing untoward happened. The meetings were harmless and in general the young people behaved well. At least there was no talk of scandal; if scandals did occur, they probably were not discussed openly.

The opposite sex had never been discussed at school. Boys who fraternized with girls on the way home from school were reported by their classmates to the Brothers, who ridiculed them. A boy who had been seen smoking and talking to a girl deserved no admiration.

At the age of seventeen, unhappy at the prospect of spending the rest of his life in Guinness's Brewery, Cathal tried to change his career by attending Skerry's College in St Stephen's Green, with the hope of passing the Civil Service examinations, but after a year of study he realized that this path was not for him. He left, resigned to the fact that he would have to continue with carpentry for the rest of his life.

During the following year, whilst studying in Bolton Street technical college, the carpenter Mr Hicks brought in a miniature bookcase that he had made for Titania's Palace, which, as we have recorded, Cathal had seen some years previously. The tiny piece of furniture, which was due to be dispatched to England, was exquisitely made. The scale was one inch to one foot. Mr Hicks explained all the features, including the mouldings. The eighty or ninety glass panes in the little bookcase had cost £4 and the total cost of making this addition to the famous doll's house had come to a staggering £20.

At around this time, Cathal espied what he described as a 'most lovely' Broadwood grand piano dating from about 1790 in a second-hand furniture shop in Charlemont Street, a short street that led to the Grand Canal from Camden Street. Although a semitone below pitch, the piano was in playing condition. A magnificent hand-painted panel above the keyboard bore the inscription, 'John Broadwood, Maker to His Majesty the King'. The asking price was £7. Cathal walked down to the shop every evening and gazed into the window. He did not possess enough money to buy it and his father would not give such a sum to him. Cathal was very disappointed not to have bought the piano; if he had, it would have been worth a considerable amount of money in years to come.

Cathal remembered going to look at two square pianos in an auction room on the quays with his instructor from Guinness's Brewery, Seán O'Neill. The auctioneer asked for 15s. for the two instruments, both of which had magnificent mahogany cases. Seán looked at them and said to the auctioneer, 'I'll give you 15s. for the two lids.'

'Oh, you'll do no such thing,' said the auctioneer, 'you'll take the whole lot or nothing. I want to get them out of the place.'

The typical asking price for square pianos at the time was 15s. or 20s.; they were not sought after. Many of them simply disappeared; they were broken up and occasionally use was made of the wood. Often they were converted into writing tables.

Cathal's interest in music continued; at around this period he heard the pianist Walter Rummel play in Dublin. Whilst he played well and Cathal enjoyed the concert, he became aware later in his life that by modern standards the performance had been 'pretty crude'.

He also heard Ignacy Paderewski play in the Theatre Royal in 1928. The place was packed and he and his mother were lucky to get rather hard seats on the stage, around the piano; they cost 5*s*. each. It was a wonderful experience, for they were looking at a man who not only was considered to be the world's greatest pianist, but who also was a composer and statesman. He had been prime minister of Poland in 1919. Like Liszt, he had tremendous stage presence; he captivated his audience by playing beautifully and performing everything from memory. He received such rapturous applause at the end of the concert that he had to play Debussy's *Minstrels* twice; he also played one of the *Hungarian Dances* by Brahms as an encore.

It turned out that Harry Siberry, a pianist whom Cathal met in later life, was seated near him that night on the stage. Cathal heard Paderewski play again in 1931, the last time the pianist came to Dublin.

Cathal's father purchased a car and learned to drive it secretly. On one summer's afternoon in 1929 he said to Cathal, out of the blue, 'Would you like a drive in a car?'

'Whose car?' asked Cathal.

'My car,' he replied.

'You haven't got a car,' said Cathal.

'I have,' he said. 'Come with me.'

Together they walked along Herberton Lane to Rialto Bridge, continued into Brookfield Road and entered a field beside the Auxiliary Workhouse (now part of St James's Hospital) in which there had been a rope-walk. The long building had been converted into garages and in one of them was a second-hand, two-horsepower, two-seater 1922 Singer with solid disc wheels and a 'dicky'. The dicky was a small enclosed seat at the back, which was accessed by opening what looked like the boot of the car; it was large enough to seat two people. The car had cost Mr Gannon the grand sum of £18 10*s*.; Cathal believed that he had given £20 and had received back 30*s*. 'luck money'. Cathal was fascinated by the car. It was in good condition and had been well maintained.

A man by the name of Jack Higgins, who worked in Guinness's Brewery and who had taught Mr Gannon to drive, was there waiting for them and invited them to get into the car with him. He drove Mr Gannon and Cathal to the Phoenix Park and then Mr Gannon took the wheel. When he drove through the Castleknock gates, Cathal was afraid that he was going to crash, but he did not. He drove all the way out to Navan at an even 27 miles per hour – anything faster made the car rattle and shake. This was the first time Cathal had been in that part of the country and the first time that he had seen the Hill of Tara. He very much wanted to climb it but of course did not have the opportunity.

In Navan they stopped for a drink and then drove home; once again, the journey went smoothly.

Fortunately the cost of running a car at this period was not too high. Insurance was not obligatory, road tax amounted to 15s. per horse power and ROP (Russian Oil Products) petrol cost 1s. per gallon. Cathal paid his share in the running of the vehicle.

The family was very proud of the car. On Sundays, after Mass and after Mr Gannon had bought the newspapers, Cathal and he used to drive to the Phoenix Park and stop on the road overlooking the Furry Glen. They would sit on a bench, read the newspapers and enjoy the beautiful uninterrupted view of Ballyfermot and the Dublin Mountains. At that time Ballyfermot was just a small village. They would stay there until lunchtime and return home at about one o'clock.

A typical Sunday lunch in the Gannon household consisted of roast beef, sometimes served with Yorkshire pudding, roast potatoes and cabbage: a substantial meal that was beautifully cooked by Mrs Gannon.

The family would often pile into the car in the afternoon and set off for the mountains. Another favourite excursion was a drive to Bray, where they used to walk up and down the promenade or climb and walk around Bray Head. They often brought a picnic tea with them. However, if guests had been invited in the evening, they returned home for their meal.

Although Mr Gannon wasn't too fond of entertaining guests – his usual reaction to a suggested musical evening was, 'Oh, I wouldn't be having these people around the house' – various friends did come. However, the Gannons were seldom invited back to their guests' homes. Frequent visitors were Cathal's aunts, Cissie and Peggy, who often came for an evening meal, and Annie and Rita Christopher. Rita was a good violinist and pianist. A typical evening's entertainment consisted of a meal, conversation, music and songs.

Mrs Gannon was a good baker, well able to produce bread and cakes for her visitors, but she liked to order these from Bewley's sometimes. A particular treat was a freshly-baked cherry log delivered to the house on a Saturday afternoon and eaten at teatime. Cathal, who always had a very sweet tooth, considered this to be delicious.

Alternatively they drove to Bewley's shop in Westmoreland Street, near the Ballast Office. As there was little or no traffic, they were able to park the car nearby. Mrs Gannon would then buy whatever she needed for entertaining her guests on Sunday evening.

Often they used to park their car in O'Connell Street – there was always space then – and have lunch in Clerys restaurant, which apparently was quite good.

Seán Dempsey, the noted player of the uilleann pipes who lived in Tallaght and who knew Cathal, wanted Cathal to borrow the car during the Eucharistic Congress in 1932 and to drive him around the city; he wanted to sit in the dicky, playing the pipes to entertain the people. Mr Gannon firmly refused permission, saving Cathal the ordeal. Soon afterwards Mr Gannon sold the car for £8 and bought a 1924 bull-nosed Morris Cowley open four-seater.

Twelve

From about 1930 onwards, Cathal began to take a keen interest in antique watches. An old man had once told him about verge watches and, as Cathal had never heard the term 'verge' before, he procured a book on watchmaking from the library and delved into the subject in an effort to educate himself. He discovered that the term refers to a certain type of escapement used in the mechanism of antique watches.

Cathal acquired his first antique watch in an unusual manner. Tom Ohle was a school pal of Cathal's and the two of them often went out cycling together. Whilst waiting for Tom at his house in Kimmage Road one day, he watched his younger brother, aged about three or four, romping around on the floor and was surprised to see a silver verge watch made in about 1810 by Stroud of London hanging on a cord around his neck. The watch was not particularly interesting, but Cathal could not refrain from remarking that he thought it a shame to see a child playing with it. When Tom's father said, 'That watch will never go any more,' Cathal expressed his wish to try to fix it. Mr Ohle replied, 'Well, take it home and if you can get it going, you can keep it.'

Cathal did succeed in making it work again – he simply cleaned it and replaced the minute hand. He then offered to return the watch to Mr Ohle but Tom's father refused to take it back. Cathal thanked him and kept it for a number of years.

Soon afterwards, Cathal bought his first silver 'pair-cased' verge watch – a watch with inner and outer silver cases – for 7s. 6d. at a shop in the Coombe owned by a Mr O'Shea. It was made by George Allen of London in 1765. From that time onwards, he bought watches whenever he found them. His next purchase was a more interesting eighteenth-century watch movement by Charles Craig of Dublin.

In 1931, England went off the gold standard and people began to sell their gold and silver due to the resulting recession. There were at least five smelting shops in Dublin in the early 1930s: two on the west side of St Stephen's Green, two in Grafton Street and one on the quays. According to Cathal, they seemed to be open day and night. Advertisements proclaimed, 'Sell your sovereigns for 39s. 6d.'. A common sight in the antique shops during this period were china dishes and Benares trays piled high with silver and gold watches. Cathal often rummaged through them and alighted on something of interest. Hundreds of watch movements were ripped out of their cases and displayed in shop windows. The average price of a silver watch ranged between 8s. and 15s.; a normal asking price was 10s. A movement cost 1s.

Cathal occasionally attended the Thursday evening auctions at Garland's on Merchant's Quay, which adjoined the church popularly known as Adam and Eve's; now and then he bought a watch or watch movement. He was friendly with a watchmaker named Tommy Gardiner, who had a shop in Patrick Street. Tommy used to bring Cathal behind the auctioneer's perch and let him handle the watches and jewellery, enabling him to examine everything in detail. Cathal was intrigued by the fact that most of the good items were bought by a man named Henry O'Kelly, undoubtedly of Barton House, Rathfarnham, whom he often saw sitting at a large green baize-covered table weighing gold with a spring balance and examining objects with an eyeglass. When Cathal regretted not having bought a watch, Mr O'Kelly sometimes sold one back to him for 10s. or 15s., making a small profit. Cathal found him very accommodating.

Cathal often walked with his friend Tommy Gardiner to a nearby pub, where Cathal treated him to a pint. From here they went to Tommy's shop, where Tommy showed Cathal a watch that he was currently working on and gave him a few tips.

Another person from whom Cathal bought watches was George Collier, a labourer in Guinness's Brewery. George, a genial Welshman, also used to attend the watch auctions in Garland's and buy a number of cheap watches. Six silver Geneva watches on a piece of string used to cost him about 10s, which was a ridiculously low figure.

On the following morning he would bring them into the Brewery and approach Cathal, saying, 'Buy a watch, buddy, buy a watch, buddy!' Cathal used to look at what he had and often bought one. In this way Cathal bought a fine Omega pocket watch for 4s. One of the winding wheels was missing, but a replacement was supplied by Lorcan McNally, a former schoolmate of Cathal's, whose watch and clock premises were located on the South Circular Road, near Synge Street. Cathal paid Lorcan 6s. for work done on the watch. Cathal's father subsequently bought it and had it until the day he died.

George Collier also sold Cathal a lovely Longinis miniature pocket watch for about 2s. – it was like a nun's watch. At another time, Cathal purchased a handsome Swiss cylinder watch of about 1840 with a magnificent dial for 4s. or 5s.

Whilst George was an honest man, a pal of his nicknamed 'Sailor' Reilly was capable of sharp practice. 'Sailor' had been in the Navy during World War I and hence the nickname. Cathal bought a few watches and clock movements from him. Nobody knew where he picked up his goods and no questions were ever asked. He was capable of fixing clocks and was good at locating clock or watch movements. Apparently he was supposed to give some antique verge watches to Cathal as a gift from somebody, but charged him a few shillings for them. Cathal did not mind too much as he thought that the watches were worth the money.

Work in the Brewery continued as usual throughout 1930. By September Cathal had completed five years' service and was transferred to the 'Improver's List'. His wages were raised from 60s. to 63s. per week.

Cathal completed his six-year apprenticeship in September 1931 and was 'discharged' on the 26th. The rule then was that apprentices had to leave and work elsewhere in order to gain experience; if a vacancy in the Brewery arose they would be invited to apply and, if successful, they would be taken back by the firm. It was a strange way of doing things, but rules were rules and they applied to Cathal as much as to anyone else, despite his competency and good reputation. However, on the confidential notice informing the authorities of the cessation of his work, his character was described as simply 'good', his efficiency 'about average' and his attendance 'regular'.

Cathal remembered thanking the engineer Mr E.H. Hill, the man who had given him his job in the Brewery. Mr Hill commented that it was rare for a worker to thank an engineer in this manner and immediately rang a builder to see if there might be a vacancy for Cathal. Cathal was touched by the man's kindness.

Two weeks later, Cathal was employed by McLaughlin and Harvey's for the rebuilding of 1 Thomas Street, the ruined Georgian house belonging to the Guinness family to the left of St James's Gate and beside the carpenter's workshop. One of his workmates was Tom Ohle.

Cathal worked, probably in 1932, for two weeks at the construction of a new building containing dormitories and classrooms at Clongowes Wood College in Clane, County Kildare. He found it a depressing place and was unhappy there.

Afterwards, Cathal found occasional work and was sometimes employed by a friend of his, Fergus Morgan, who was a small contractor with a base in South Richmond Street. Under his direction, Cathal made furniture either in Fergie's workshop or the workshop at home, and fitted kitchens and bathrooms in various people's houses.

For most of the time, however, Cathal was on the dole throughout this lean period known as the Depression or the Hungry Thirties, and he was not employed full-time by the Brewery again until 1937. He was obliged to sign the register every Monday, Wednesday and Friday. The dole payment, which he received every Friday, was 15s. per week and the amount paid to him by the Amalgamated Society of Woodworkers was 10s., totalling £1 5s. Of this he gave £1 to his mother (a fair amount of money then), leaving 5s. for himself.

As Cathal did not smoke and rarely drank, his 5s. went a long way. He was now free to indulge himself in buying as many books, watches and antiques as he wanted. His interest in pictures developed and he bought his first piece of porcelain in Mr Harford's second-hand shop on Essex Quay: a blue and white Chinese cylindrical brush holder, for which he paid 5s. This he considered to be a substantial amount of money.

Some time later he purchased a fine blue and white bowl made of eggshell porcelain, which he at first thought was Chinese, but which he later realized was Dutch. This he bought for 5s. in Jackson's china repair shop in Crampton Court, off Dame Street. When Cathal called back to the shop on the following day, Mr Jackson wanted to buy the bowl back from him. Anthony Fritz Maude, who lived in Belgarde Castle, Clondalkin, and who was secretary of the Representative Body of the Church of Ireland, was an enthusiastic collector of oriental art and had seen the bowl in the window of the shop when it was closed. When he returned to the shop, Cathal had bought it. Although Mr Jackson very much wanted to sell the bowl to Captain Maude, Cathal wisely refused to part with it.

The Hungry Thirties was therefore a formative period in the development of Cathal's taste in the arts. Through reading, observing, buying bric-a-brac and listening to music, he educated himself and gradually became a connoisseur of eighteenth-century refinement, though at heart he remained a true Dublin craftsman with a ready wit and earthy sense of humour. Cathal's circumstances never allowed him to acquire airs and graces.

A typical Saturday afternoon's journey around the junk and antique shops of Dublin during the 1930s and 1940s, either by bicycle or on foot, started directly after lunch, when he would call to Mrs Alcock's shop in Dolphin's Barn Street. She dealt in second-hand furniture and an occasional longcase (or grandfather) Georgian clock, costing from £2 to £2 10s. Cathal bought some nice pieces of porcelain here and, on one occasion, three oil paintings and four watercolours by Alexander Williams (1846–1930). They were unmounted and painted on millboard; the seven pictures cost 5s. He gave most of them away to Jack, Willie and others, and kept just one depicting wild flowers at Portmarnock, which he later had framed and mounted, and which still hangs on a wall at home.

Next Cathal would make for the Iveagh Market in Francis Street, where a Mr Conlon, a tall ex-policeman, kept an interesting stall full of bric-a-brac, including old gramophone records, which could be tried out on an old hand-wound player with a large horn. The sound was always dreadful. Cathal bought a couple of watches from Mr Conlon.

There were other interesting stalls in the market; at one of them, run by a man who had a stiff leg and walked with a stick, he bought a miniature Vienna clock of about 1880, ten inches high, for 7s. 6d. While Cathal was in the market, his brother Willie came along, looking for him. A woman who recognized him said, 'Your brother's in there – he's just bought a *piano* clock.' Dubliners then often pronounced Vienna as *piano*; a term commonly heard was 'piano roll', meaning a Vienna roll.

Cathal threw out the broken carved wooden case, shaped like a cottage, and made his own neat and elegant case of fine walnut with glass in the front and sides. This was kept in good working condition for many years afterwards.

From the Iveagh Market, Cathal proceeded to the quays via Winetavern Street, where he would look in the window of Gorman's pawnbroker shop. From here it was a short hop to Essex Quay, the one-time home of the watch industry. Number 9 was Mr Harford's second-hand shop, where Cathal had bought his first piece of porcelain. Cathal also bought a Black Forest clock from Mr Harford for 15*s*., which he later gave to his brother Jack.

At number 13 was the gold- and silver-leaf manufacturing premises of Henry Phillips and his brother; the two men could be seen beating gold and silver and putting the thin leaves into books. At number 23, Albert Ledbetter worked as a jeweller, watch and clockmaker. Here Cathal bought a couple of verge watches at 10*s*. each. Mr Ledbetter later moved his shop to Nassau Street. Another watchmaker and jeweller, William Donohoe, had his premises next door at number 24.

Cathal found Wellington Quay rather uninteresting; the shops there dealt mostly in religious art. An exception was Mrs Goyer's antique shop, which stocked porcelain and reproductions of coloured prints.

Mrs Higgins had an antique shop at 1 Aston Quay. Her shop was packed with antiques and she was a very talkative person. At number 6 was Edward Massey's bookshop. Either he carried the same stock all the time or never sold it. He had a branch in St Patrick's Street, Cork, which was identical to his shop in Dublin – stock and all.

As stated previously, bookstalls lined both sides of the street at Aston Quay. After Cathal had browsed amongst them, he crossed over by O'Connell Bridge to Bachelor's Walk to take a look in Hill's auction rooms. Cathal could remember seven auction rooms along Bachelor's Walk at one time; Thom's Dublin Street Directory for 1935 lists Scannell's, Davis's, the Arcade Auction Rooms, Jackson's, Tormey's, Cox's and McMullen's.

Turning into Lower Liffey Street, Cathal always headed for Tom Delaney's furniture store at numbers 32–4. The premises is now demolished but for many years was used as a store by Hector Grey. Tom was a most helpful man and always made Cathal welcome at his shop. Several times, at Tom's suggestion, Cathal met him on Sunday afternoons in the National Museum, where Tom pointed out and discussed the various articles of furniture that he had sold to the museum over the years.

In Upper Liffey Street was Mrs Fallon's furniture shop at number 6. Many years later, in 1955, Cathal purchased two single-hand longcase clock movements with brass dials here for £4. Both had been made in Sussex in about 1760; one in a place named Bramber and the other in Lewes Cliff, just five miles away. Cathal gave away the former and kept the latter, making a handsome wooden case for it many years later.

Henry Naylor's antique shop was at number 8. This was a very expensive place and well beyond Cathal's means.

From Upper Liffey Street, Cathal usually made his way to Mrs Conlon's antique shop at 1 Jervis Street. She usually stocked a large selection of porcelain and occasionally a watch. Mrs Conlon was a pleasant elderly lady and could be found, weather permitting, sitting outside her shop saying her prayers.

From Jervis Street, Cathal moved to Upper Ormond Quay and stopped at Charlie Morisy's shop at number 28A, at the corner of Ormond Place. His shop was packed to the roof with books and he had a selection of antiques displayed in the window. Ormond Quay was the home of solicitors and several times Cathal met and chatted to Reuben J. Dodd, who practised in 12 Upper Ormond Quay. As we shall see, Reuben Dodd sat beside Cathal at the meetings of the Old Dublin Society from 1934 onwards.

Having finished his journey along the quays, Cathal then went to 46 High Street, where two elderly sisters ran a watchmaker's shop owned by their father, who had died some years previously. The shop fascinated Cathal; it was full of odds and ends such as longcase and mantle clocks, broken lever watches and even books. Apart from a small premises opposite Kevin Street Library, Cathal believed it to be the last Georgian bow-fronted shop in Dublin. Cathal could not remember having purchased anything from the two sisters.

Having covered such a large area, it was time to either cycle home or catch the number 50 bus, which left Cathal almost to his hall door on the Crumlin Road. By this stage he was in good form for his evening meal. Cathal rarely arrived home empty-handed; he normally had bought a watch, a couple of books or perhaps a print or two. On Saturday evening he often went out to see a film.

Cathal often varied his Saturday afternoon peregrinations by taking a tram along the South Circular Road to Lorcan McNally's watch and clock shop near Synge Street. Cathal found him very helpful, especially if he was in need of something like hands or glass for a recently purchased watch. Whilst quite willing to assist Cathal, Lorcan never showed any real interest in antique watches or clocks.

In nearby Rathmines was Thomas W. Cooke's shop beside the fire station, where Cathal bought a silver antique watch for 10s. The shop closed down a few years later and at the final sale Cathal bought a banjo-shaped barometer for 6s.

Cathal often took the tram to St Stephen's Green, where he had a look in the smelting shops, one near the Unitarian Church and the other beside the Green Cinema. Here Cathal frequently purchased a watch or a couple of movements at a shilling each. When buying a silver watch, he was always reminded that the case contained 4s 6d worth of silver. If he asked for just part of a movement, he was invariably handed a complete one.

Whilst in this general area, Cathal often called to Mr McGrath's antique jewellery shop at 51 Stephen Street, off South Great George's Street. Mr McGrath dealt exclusively in silver; his large shop window was packed with silver salvers, tea sets, trays, candelabras and so forth – all badly in need of cleaning. He usually had between six and a dozen silver watches displayed under his glass-topped counter. Cathal bought several verge watches from him, for between 6s. and 10s. After Cathal had made his pick, Mr McGrath would say to him, 'You have chosen a good fresh one!'

As the shops in Grafton Street were too expensive for Cathal, he took himself to 18 Nassau Street, the premises of David Cherrick, a pleasant, elderly man with a white moustache, who was always neatly dressed in a dark suit, a butterfly collar and homburg hat. He was always ready for a chat. Cathal bought several watches from him and years later he advised Cathal to keep them as he would live to see the day when he would be able to ask £5 each for them.

The watch that Cathal cherished most was bought in Hessel Wine's antique shop in 23A Dawson Street. It was made by John Crosthwaite of Dublin in 1788. Crosthwaite was an important maker; he was born in 1745 and died in 1829. In 1788 he worked in Grafton Street.

Cathal bought this watch in 1933 having just collected his 15s. dole money. He stopped to take look inside Mr Wine's shop and discovered this beautiful pair-cased watch. He asked Mr Wine for the price and was told that it would cost him 15s. Mr Wine offered him another Dublin-made watch and told him that the price for the two would be 25s. As Cathal could only afford one watch and liked the Crosthwaite so much, he handed Mr Wine the money he had just collected. When he commented on the excellent condition of the watch, Mr Wine told him that it had been found in a secret compartment of an eighteenth-century writing desk, where it had probably lain for many years.

Another happy hunting ground was an area known as Moore Street Market, which took place in Cole's Lane (now gone), Sampson's Lane and Anglesea Market (also gone). This area always reminded Cathal of a market in Morocco. Here he bought two nineteenth-century clock movements, which he removed from damaged cases.

Despite the large number of clocks, watches and watch movements that Cathal bought during this period, only a small collection survives. He either sold them at approximately the same price that he had paid or gave many of them to other people. This was typical of Cathal — buying things that he liked and then giving them to others when he tired of them; he rarely sold anything that he possessed. He certainly was not a businessman. All in all, he was content with his lot and had no driving ambition; he worked hard, developed an interest in many things and lived life as fully as he could. He was both conscious of the poverty that surrounded him and aware that money could not buy happiness. His nature was to be generous. Having been brought up when times were hard, he was happy to have enough money to survive on.

Interestingly, Cathal never claimed to know much about clocks or watches. He felt that his knowledge was limited but his appreciation for fine craftsmanship was unlimited. Fortunately he was ahead of his time and bought antiques when they were not very fashionable; as a result they were affordable.

Thirteen

*E*very day Cathal went off in search of work on his lightweight three-speed Saxon de Luxe bicycle, but due to lack of interest he never over-exerted himself. Instead, he spent most of the time out and about, enjoying himself and visiting the public libraries. During the summer, he cycled to Seapoint at Blackrock in the morning for a swim and returned home for lunch. He would often return in the afternoon and swim again. On the whole he had a 'whale of a good time' and 'enjoyed every moment' of this period.

Cathal had acquired the Saxon bicycle from his friend, Jim O'Dea, who was a keen cyclist. Jim had bought it on the instalment system and then had had another bicycle made. He asked Cathal if he would continue the payments and Cathal agreed. The total cost of this fine hand-built bicycle with its 'electric bronze' finish came to twelve guineas. Cathal kept it for many years and used it for cycling to the Brewery. I can remember, when I was very young, being perched on a little seat mounted on the crossbar of this bicycle.

Cathal and Jim O'Dea often went cycling together in the summer. A favourite trip was out to Jacob's pub in Saggart, where they relaxed over a pint of beer. At the very most, Cathal drank two pints. O'Dea belonged to the Cyclists' Touring Club and regularly went off with a gang of people to cycle about fifty miles a day. Cathal remembered the Navan Road 'teeming with backsides and bicycle wheels'. The cyclists wore black clothing in an effort to be inconspicuous. Cathal joined the club for a short while but did not share the degree of dedication shown by the members. Instead, Cathal teamed up regularly with his old school pal Kevin Cregan and set off with him on a more leisurely journey to the Step Inn at Stepaside in south County Dublin. The owner, whose name was also Cregan, had a good piano and Cathal was happy to play some music or accompany anyone who chose to sing a song. After they were 'thrown out' at midnight, they made their way homewards.

As well as cycling, Cathal also enjoyed long walks. He and Jim O'Dea usually went walking together two or three times a week. Cathal enjoyed Jim's company; like Cathal, Jim was interested in many different subjects and conversation came easily. Either Cathal called at Jim's house in Dolphin's Barn at half past seven in the evening or Jim called for him at his home in Crumlin Road, depending on which direction they were going. Together they footed it to Molloy's pub in Tallaght, where they drank a bottle of stout, ate a sandwich, talked to the locals and often listened to an argument about politics. The return journey took them through Greenhills, which was then completely unspoiled. The walk there and back was exactly ten miles long.

On other days they travelled by bus to Blanchardstown in north County Dublin. From here they walked, via Corduff, Ballycoolin and Cappagh, to the small village of Finglas, which was then in the middle of nowhere. There were two pubs there: Top Flood's and Bottom Flood's. If the boys were in the mood, they stopped for a bottle of ale or stout. Afterwards they waited for a single-decker bus at the triangular village green and travelled to O'Connell Street in the city centre. From there they walked a short distance to the Red Bank Restaurant in D'Olier Street, which had a bar and grill room. Cathal and Jim always made for a quiet corner of the bar. Behind the counter was a fine, fresh middle-aged man with white hair, perhaps in his sixties, who was extremely friendly and always delighted to see them. He liked to talk to Cathal about traditional Irish music. They had a friend in common: the piper Seán Dempsey. Apparently the man's greatest pleasure was to hear Seán perform a piece called 'The Rights of Man'.

Ensconced in this establishment, Cathal and Jim always ate delicious prawn and tomato sandwiches, washed down with a pint of beer, which at that time cost 7d. They conversed with the white-haired man for about half an hour or so, then 'hit the road', making their way back to Dolphin's Barn, which they reached at about eleven in the evening. The ten-mile 'ramble' completed, Cathal fell into bed and slept like a log.

Cathal also went walking with other friends. He regularly 'palled up' with his Synge Street schoolmate Michael Wall and a young solicitor named Dan White, who lived in Lower Clanbrassil Street. Dan originally came from Dolphin's Barn; Cathal had met him on a Mount Argus excursion and had fallen into conversation with him.

The three of them regularly took the tram to Rathfarnham and walked, via the Featherbed, to Enniskerry, where they had a 'knife-and-fork tea' of sausages, rashers, eggs and bread dipped in the frying pan at Mrs Windsor's restaurant. Cathal played the piano, they had a 'sing-song' and afterwards they walked to Bray and travelled home by train. In summer they went for picnics with a group of girls.

On Sunday afternoons the three of them caught the train from Westland Row station and travelled to Dun Laoghaire, Killiney or Dalkey. Alternatively they took a train from Harcourt Street station to Bray; the cost for this journey was 1s. 6d. for first class or 1s. for third class. Having arrived at their destination, they set out for a walk – for example, around Bray Head – and then they returned home.

From about 1928 onwards, Cathal had been going on regular train excursions, usually on Sundays during the summer, with Jim O'Dea. Prices were affordable: a return journey to Cork, for example, cost 7s. 6d. and a trip to Killarney cost 10s. They went everywhere: Cork, Killarney, Bundoran, Waterford and Tramore were regular destinations. It was usual for them to bring packed lunches.

On these trips it was a regular occurrence for a gang of fellows to meet up with a group of girls and treat them to tea. Then, on coming home, five fellows and five girls would occupy a section of a carriage and lock the door with a key that one of them had acquired somehow. One of the girls' berets was forced over the light in the carriage and the place was plunged into darkness. The fellows and girls then indulged in some 'innocent' fun and games all the way home while others tried to open the door.

A cheaper option was to go on one of the mystery tours that set off from Amiens Street Station on a Saturday or Sunday afternoon. These cost about 2s. 9d. and a trip of at least fifty miles was guaranteed. Thanks to Jim's contacts amongst the railway personnel, he and Cathal always knew where the train would be going. The journeys started at two or three o'clock in the afternoon and returned at seven in the evening. Cathal could remember going to places such as Cashel and Athlone.

The excursions with Jim O'Dea lasted until about 1939, when Jim got married and the war years began.

Cathal finally managed to take a proper look at the harpsichords in the National Museum in 1931, when he was twenty-one years of age. A Mr

Doyle, who lived on the Crumlin Road, worked as an attendant in the museum and was able to lock Cathal into the music department on a Sunday afternoon so that he could look at the instruments in peace. All the instruments were opened for him and so Cathal was able to examine them carefully. The harpsichords were in poor condition; they were dusty and unplayable. Cathal was shocked by the complexity of their structure; he realized that making such instruments was beyond his capabilities. At least he was satisfied that he had got this out of his system – or so he thought.

Nonetheless, his interest in harpsichords remained and he continued to listen to them on the radio or on records. During the 1930s, Cathal bought a record of Handel's 'Harmonious Blacksmith' played on a harpsichord; on the other side was Mozart's *Rondo alla Turca*. These pieces were probably played by the famous harpsichordist of the period, Wanda Landowska.

Born in Poland in 1877, Wanda Landowska was Violet Gordon Woodhouse's most formidable rival, though many found her technique rather mechanical. Landowska was supplied on a regular basis with harpsichords made by the Parisian firm Pleyel. Indeed, her name became synonymous with Pleyel; this was to the manufacturer's advantage when it came to selling instruments. Whilst Gordon Woodhouse tended to retreat from the public eye, Landowska did exactly the opposite and became a well-known virtuoso on the Pleyel harpsichord (described by some as a 'plucked piano' owing to its heavy construction. Cathal had also heard it referred to as a 'fortification'). Authenticity was not a priority with Landowska or Pleyel.

Wanda Landowska made many twelve-inch 78 rpm recordings and Cathal bought some of them at Moiselle's gramophone shop in Johnson's Court – he was probably one of the first people to buy them in Dublin. These records had to be specially ordered from London as they were never in stock. As the assistants knew nothing about harpsichords, Cathal generally had difficulty in making himself understood. On one occasion, when Cathal was ordering a record of music that he had heard on the radio, the young lady asked if the harpsichord was some type of religious instrument. When Cathal spelled the word and began to explain that it was the forerunner of the piano, she excused herself and said, 'Oh – I thought you said "harps of God"!'

If Cathal had decided that he could not make one of these instruments, he certainly knew that he could not afford to buy one. Since starting work he had bought back numbers of *The Connoisseur* magazine. Now and then he saw photographs of harpsichords, which often fetched around £50 at auctions –

a fantastic sum of money at the time. Cathal regularly looked in the Dublin auction rooms but never once found a harpsichord.

One of Cathal's friends, Matt McNamara, who worked initially in Butler's antique and fine art shop on Lower Ormond Quay and then in Millar and Beatty's store, Grafton Street, where he was in charge of the antique section, used to go around the auction rooms buying furniture for his employers. Butler's gave him permission to buy any square piano he could lay his hands on at 3s. 6d. each. If, on the other hand, they were ornate and richly inlaid, he was allowed to pay up to 5s. These instruments were then taken into the company workshop and converted into writing desks, which were sold at inflated prices. This type of work kept the cabinetmakers busy during slack periods. They usually had a room full of square pianos, one stacked on top of another.

As we have noted earlier, this was how so many elegant square pianos disappeared off the scene. As with so many other things, fashion took its toll on musical instruments. When harpsichords went out of vogue, people traded them in for square pianos and received a £5 allowance; such was the enthusiasm for these instruments that one music publisher was willing to 'throw in' a square piano free of charge if one ordered a certain amount of music over a given period. Later, the square piano, which could not stay in tune for very long, was ousted in favour of the more dependable and popular upright piano. By this time, however, the middle classes could afford to buy upright pianos, thanks to mass production and higher wages.

Nonetheless, cultured people tended to hold on to their square pianos. Regency paintings depicted people of quality sitting at square pianos. Auctions of big houses invariably included such instruments. At some stage, Cathal read the book *Seventy Years Young* by Elizabeth, Countess of Fingall, in which she mentioned a 'spinet' being discovered in the servants' hall of Killeen Castle, County Meath, by Hugh Lane and herself. Cathal realized that, like many people, the Countess had used the term 'spinet' incorrectly to describe a square piano – the misuse of this word still persists. He went to the auction of Killeen Castle in the 1950s and saw the elegant instrument, which he failed to buy because it was sold at a very high price.

The 31st Eucharistic Congress was held between 21 and 26 June 1932, in Dublin. An international event, people from all over the world flocked to the city. The Solemn Opening of the Congress took place at the Pro-Cathedral in Marlborough Street and was attended by a large number of visiting priests and bishops. Masses and various ceremonies were held throughout the city; it was even possible to attend an Orthodox service. The whole of Dublin was bedecked with banners, decorations and coloured lights (then a novelty owing to the recent introduction of a national electrical supply). In tenement houses, fanlights over hall doors were filled with candles, holy pictures or portraits of former popes. In poor areas of the city, altars, complete with 'all the trimmings', were erected everywhere. An altar, erected against the wall of an ESB substation in a square at Newmarket, bore a banner proclaiming that 'this altar has been blessed by the Bisshep'. A banner elsewhere in the city read 'God bless the Pope and his Papal Sea'.

The events over the six days included many religious processions. One such procession was to start at Dolphin's Barn Church and go along the South Circular Road. A row blew up at home when Cathal refused point-blank to join it, despite threats and protestations from his father. Cathal said that he had no desire to go about 'airing his religion' in what was then a respectable area inhabited mostly by Protestants. When the rest of the family went off to join the procession, Cathal went out for a walk.

It could be said that at this period Cathal's faith was lukewarm and that such incidents made him feel inclined to turn away from the Church, but he and some of his companions did walk to the Phoenix Park for a special Mass that was attended by a huge crowd. By all accounts, it was a great occasion.

As usual, Cathal was quick to see the funny side of things. As well as observing the misspellings noted above, he remembered a large painting executed on the blank side wall of a house in Bride Street, facing Peter Street. Some local artist had done his best to depict Saint Patrick banishing the snakes from Ireland. Obviously he had never stepped back to examine his progress, for the proportions were awry. The higher up he had painted, the smaller the details had become. Consequently, Saint Patrick's head was comically tiny. When he had been painting the picture, everybody passing by had stopped to admire the work in progress and had encouraged him. It remained on the wall for many years afterwards until the building was finally pulled down.

Electricity came to the Crumlin Road in 1932. Mr Gannon, who was strict about bedtime, put a master switch in his own bedroom and so, when he retired for the night, it was lights out. Anyone who returned after that time had to grope in the dark or use a candle.

Some years previously, the violinist and traditional musician Arthur Darley, who had been in Trinity College, had died. In order to entertain his son, who also showed an interest in traditional Irish music, a musical evening in his memory was arranged some time in 1932 by the piper Seán Dempsey at his home, Airton Cottage, in Tallaght. Cathal was invited.

To the best of Cathal's memory, a total of six uilleann pipers, a flautist and a number of other guests were squeezed into the two-roomed cottage. Once they were in, there was not much chance of getting out, which made it awkward for those who needed to relieve themselves outside the cottage. Amongst the pipers were Leo Rowsem and Ned Potts. The music – 'such as it was', as Cathal said – went on until the small hours of the morning. It nearly demented Cathal, but he stuck it out to the bitter end simply because he relished the novelty of the night's entertainment and believed it to be so bad as to be funny. Jigs, reels, hornpipes and even hymns were played: Cathal remembered Seán's solo rendering of 'Sweet Sacrament Divine'.

Refreshment consisted of tea, hot home-made bread, baked over the fire by Seán's mother, and butter. Seán was ecstatic and frequently commented, 'Be Jaysus mother, that's great music – that's great music!'

He then went on to praise the uilleann pipes by saying, 'You know mother, it's the most naa-tur-al music in the world!'

'How do you make that out, Seán?' Mrs Dempsey asked.

'Well,' he said, 'the pipes is all nature. The chanter is made out of ebony, it's mounted with ivory out of an elephant's tusk, and the keys are made out of brass, which is dug out of the earth!'

Ned Potts's father lived in a small two-bedroomed house in the Coombe, near Francis Street. Ned, who worked in Guinness's Brewery, told Cathal that about a dozen people, some of them up from the country, frequently dropped into the house and held a musical evening. How they all fitted in, Ned never knew. He could remember being put to bed with the other children while the adults downstairs played or discussed music. Ned gave up playing the uilleann pipes later and took up playing a saxophone in a dance band, much to his father's disgust. His father always referred to Ned's saxophone as his 'Japanese bugle'.

The father, who not only played the pipes but also made them, was something of a character. He worked in the Brewery as a drayman. When in 1922 Pope Pius XI was elected in Rome, Mr Potts heard a newspaper vendor shouting 'Stop press!' He pulled up and asked the boy, 'What's the news?'

'The election of the new pope,' replied the young fellow.

'Oh good!' he said. 'That's one up their arse in Belfast! Yup!' – and off he went in the horse and cart.

Cathal bought his first painting in 1933 in a small antique shop in Kildare Street, opposite the entrance to the National Museum. It was a small, delicate study of cattle in a meadow under a cloudy sky by the Irish artist Alfred Grey, done in either oil or gouache on millboard. This painting is still part of Cathal's collection. At the same time he bought two prints at 3*d*. each by Thomas Milton: one of Belan House, County Kildare and the other of the Casino at Marino. These also remain at home. He also bought several antique prints in this shop for his aunt Cissie's house, but they were all dispersed later.

At around this time, Cathal bought, for the grand sum of 6*d*., a rather primitive-looking picture of Westport Quay painted on a wooden panel. As he intended to have it cleaned and varnished, Cathal removed it from its frame and discovered the name J.A. O'Connor on the back. O'Connor was one of the most important Irish painters of the nineteenth century but unfortunately his name meant nothing to Cathal at this period. The picture could have been a preliminary sketch for a painting that now hangs in Westport House. Cathal put it to one side and his father, thinking that he had thrown it out, promptly chopped it into pieces. As Cathal casually remarked, 'That's the sort of thing he did.'

Thanks to Cathal's observation and good taste, he was the first to introduce the use of picture-mounting board in Guinness's Brewery. Up until then, the tendency had been to put a painting straight into a frame adorned with heavy Victorian or Edwardian mouldings, cover it with glass and place a wooden board at the back. Cathal had noticed, in the late twenties and early thirties, the new trend of using a very narrow frame and a wide mounting board, often cream in colour. When asked to frame pictures in the Brewery, Cathal adopted this new fashion, making the frames and cutting the mounting board himself. The new style soon caught on.

Indeed, Cathal was kept quite busy framing pictures in Guinness's Brewery. In the late 1930s and before World War II, many people asked him to frame colour reproductions of famous works of art that they had taken out of calendars, which they had probably been given free. There was often a glut of these pictures in January, when new calendars were issued. These minor jobs came under the heading of 'nixers'. As a consequence, Cathal often encountered pictures that he had framed when visiting friends and colleagues at home.

It seems that Cathal was employed by Guinness's Brewery on a temporary contract for one year in November 1933, after which he worked with Fergus Morgan on and off until January 1937.

An event that occurred in June 1933 was the successful passing of the junior grade piano examination by Cathal's ten-year-old sister, Ethna, at the Read Pianoforte School in Harcourt Street. A bright, cheerful and attractive girl, whose brown hair was usually styled into ringlets, Ethna shared many of Cathal's interests and had become his favourite sister – indeed, his favourite person in the whole family. She probably understood him better than anyone else. She was highly intelligent, was musical and read a lot; Cathal liked to encourage her. She and Cathal used to go out for walks together. She was always interested in observing Cathal repair antique watches. She knew the names of all the parts and the order in which they would have to be reassembled. Cathal remembered how she had assisted him when he was cleaning some eighteenth-century prints.

Sadly, little Ethna did not live long. She and Cathal's other sister, Maureen, attended the Cross and Passion College in Kilcullen (though both had started their education at Warrenmount Convent). During the summer of 1934, Ethna had felt a little unwell. She and Maureen were due to go back to school in September. Cathal distinctly remembered how Ethna had asked to go out for a drive in the car the evening before returning to school. Mr Gannon was not in favour of stirring out, but Cathal invited everyone to come. Cathal, Ethna, Mrs Gannon and possibly Maureen set off in the car at about half past seven and Cathal drove them to the Featherbed Mountain, from which they walked towards Killakee. Ethna and Cathal sat on a wall and watched the city light up as night fell. This was to be the last time that Ethna came out in the car with them.

The girls returned to school the following day and a little over a week later, Mr and Mrs Gannon drove to Kilcullen to see them. They found that little Ethna was ill. The nuns had noticed that her concentration had been poor and that she was inclined to be sleepy all the time. As the local doctor could not discover what was wrong with her, Mr and Mrs Gannon decided to bring her home. She was put to bed and from that time onwards she gradually sank into a coma. Sir John Lumsden examined her but had little idea of what was wrong. Mrs Gannon decided to procure the services of a Dr Foster, who lived

in Rathmines Road. Straight away he diagnosed meningitis and said that Ethna would only live for another couple of days, which indeed was the case.

She died on 1 October 1934, a little less than a month short of her twelfth birthday. Cathal was greatly saddened by the loss of his sister and Mr Gannon was heartbroken. For her burial in Mount Jerome cemetery, Mr Gannon donned a black tie and wore it for the rest of his life.

Coming home from the funeral, Cathal remarked to his mother, 'It's a great pity we didn't get a nice photograph of Ethna taken before she got sick.'

His mother said, 'Well, fortunately I did get one taken during the holidays, and we should be getting it any time.'

They soon received a lovely photograph of her and another that had been taken of her and Maureen together. Several copies had been supplied. Unfortunately, poor Ethna never saw them as they had not been ready in time.

Fourteen

*O*f all the anecdotes in Cathal's repertoire, his one about Jem Lawlor was perhaps his favourite – he repeated it many times during his life for the amusement of his friends. The reader has read of Cathal's friendship with Jim O'Dea and their walks to Finglas in north County Dublin. Jim was friendly with the Kennys, a family who lived in a somewhat derelict Georgian house some two or three miles outside Finglas village called Huntstown House. Whilst both Joe Kenny and his brother Charlie ran the large dairy farm, only Joe lived in the house all the time.

Joe lived in just two rooms: a big old kitchen in the basement and a bedroom that contained a not particularly clean bed. Charlie, Joe's brother, lived and worked with his sister at the family dairy shop in Blackpitts; he was a farmer and sold cattle. He was a more respectable individual and only stayed occasionally at Joe's house.

Despite their wealth, the two brothers lived without comfort. Whenever they wanted milk, one of them used to milk a cow and plonk the milk, with the froth and dirt still floating on the top, on the kitchen table.

In 1934, Jim O'Dea told Cathal that the Kennys had a dairy boy, named Jem Lawlor, working on the farm. He was a bit 'touched' or simple and believed that he was one of the finest singers in the country. In order to humour him and entertain themselves, the Gardaí in Finglas village encouraged him to sing into a broken radio set that had been rigged up in the station, convincing him that he was in fact broadcasting and could be heard all over the world.

Jim brought Cathal out to meet this old fellow with the aim of informing him that they were from Radio Éireann and that they wished to start a 'pirate' radio station in Huntstown House and employ him. They were supposed to be dissatisfied with the way Radio Éireann was being run. Cathal was introduced to him as James Clandillon, the son of the director of Radio Éireann, and O'Dea was introduced as Dr O'Donovan – the idea being that if somebody forgot and called him 'O'D.', it was merely a shortened form of O'Donovan. Cathal and Jim were entertained by a selection of comic songs and ballads in the kitchen of Huntstown House; they found it great fun. They elaborated their plan to set up the clandestine radio station and encouraged Jem, who was a veteran of World War I, to air his views on the present government. Cathal said that he would make the necessary arrangements and bring out equipment the next time they came.

Cathal procured a load of old electrical equipment from his brother Willie – a broken telephone, switches and lengths of cables – which he mounted on a wall in one of the rooms in Huntstown House. When all was ready, a switch was thrown to put the new station 'on the air', an announcement was made and Jem stepped forward to what he believed was a microphone in order to make a political speech. He attacked de Valera and the government, and was egged on by Cathal, Jim and Joe Kenny, who whispered to him what to say and what not to say. Jem's arch enemy was Count John McCormack. The others pretended to listen to the audience's reaction by holding up another broken telephone to their ears and annoyed Jem by telling him that McCormack was listening and cursing him. Jem responded by losing the run of himself and using strong language. He then sang some songs and they broke for a cup of tea, resuming the broadcast later.

From then on, Cathal and Jim made regular visits to Huntstown House, sometimes by bicycle and other times in the family-business van borrowed by Jim from Gleeson, O'Dea & Co., the house-furnishing and ironmongery shop in Christchurch Place, Dublin. It did not appear strange to Jem that they should arrive in such a van. Some of the other dairy boys on the farm were invited in for the regular 'broadcasts', which they took very seriously and believed to be genuine. Cathal, Jim and Joe managed to fool not just old Jem but many of the local people.

As the reader may have gathered, Jem Lawlor was a loyalist. According to him, nothing was good in Ireland. Probably due to the success of his broadcasting career and the praise that was lavished upon him, he took it into his head that he should be awarded a title. As we shall see a little later, circumstances were to bring Cathal on a short holiday to England. Consequently,

Cathal was able to offer his services and told Jem that he would make it his business to see the Lord Privy Seal and the Lord Chancellor whilst in London.

From London he sent postcards, which he had prepared at home in Dublin, to Jem. Included was one written from Buckingham Palace, stating that he had had an audience with King George V, who had been informed of what Jem Lawlor had been doing for the British in Ireland, and that it was certain that he would receive good news soon. Another postcard indicated that Cathal had been to see the Lord Chancellor, who had said that serious consideration was being given to making him a knight bachelor or baronet.

When Cathal returned home he met Jem at Huntstown House and asked him, 'Did you get any news?' Jem showed him all the letters and postcards. Cathal advised him to keep his fingers crossed; he told him that he was not at liberty to say a great deal, but that something would happen soon.

Shortly afterwards, Cathal succeeded in obtaining a sheet of parchment and he and Jim O'Dea sat down one evening in the shop at Christchurch Place. Writing in his best copperplate handwriting, Cathal began a bogus document, declaring Jem a knight bachelor:

'Greetings to all whom it may concern. I, George V, King of Great Britain, Emperor of India and dominions beyond the sea, [etc.,] do hereby enact that James J. Lawlor of Dubber, Finglas, County Dublin, shall hence-forth be known to all and sundry as Sir James J. Lawlor, Baronet ...'

This was not all; Sir James would also be Seneschal of Kilshane, Recorder of Knocksedan, Lord Privy Seal of Jamestown and Commander of the Fleet of Pass If You Can Quarry (a small pool of water near St Margaret's, now filled in).

At the end of the wordy document, a piece of red ribbon was attached and a half-crown was pressed into a blob of sealing wax, leaving a back-to-front impression, which was never noticed. The document was then rolled up and placed inside a cardboard cylinder. Surreptitious arrangements were made for the delivery of the package on a certain day when they would all be gathered in the kitchen of Huntstown House.

On the appointed day, Jem was asked whether he had received any news or not. He said that he had not, but was still hoping. At this point there was a knock on the door and Jim O'Dea went upstairs to answer it. He came down with the cardboard cylinder and, handing it to Jem, said that a special messenger had delivered it.

On opening the document, old Jem began to tremble with excitement.

He produced a sixpenny pair of reading glasses, bought in Woolworths, and began to read it. When he finished, he was congratulated and addressed as Sir James. He was delighted with himself. The other dairy boys were fetched and shown the document. They were completely taken in, and from then on Jem was known as Sir James until the day he died.

Cathal and Jim O'Dea put on a show of wondering how King George V knew all about Jem and the localities mentioned in his title. 'Well,' said Sir James, 'his grandmother Queen Victoria travelled along the Ashbourne Road down to Slane Castle and she passed by the head of the road there — so that's how the royal family know where I came from.'

Sir James now began to dress in a shirt with a 'butterfly' collar, a white waistcoat and an old long-tailed coachman's coat that Cathal had obtained from a castle in Dalkey. Although the latter was several sizes too big and stuck out in front of him, Sir James wore it on all 'official' occasions.

Cathal kept a photograph of him in this 'regalia'. In April 1936 Sir James walked all the way to Henry Street in Dublin city centre and had himself officially photographed in a studio. According to Sir James, the photographer 'was amazed — he never saw the like of me coming into the place before!' Apparently the photograph cost 6d.

Much to the annoyance of Father Russell, the parish priest, Sir James was wont to make his appearance in Finglas Church dressed in this rig-out. Father Russell announced from the pulpit that it would answer the people better if they paid more attention to the holy sacrifice of the Mass than look at Sir James J. Lawlor coming and going.

As if this were not enough, Cathal supplied him with two medals, which he made in the Brewery from pieces of old aluminium. One, in the shape of a swastika, bore the inscription, 'To my friend Sir James J. Lawlor from Herr Hitler'. Another, in the shape of a Maltese cross, read, 'From Signor Mussolini to Sir James J. Lawlor'. These two medals, both about two inches in diameter, were attached to his cheap nickel watch chain. Whenever he danced, they jangled like a pair of gongs.

Because the 'broadcasting' sessions were somewhat repetitive, they soon became a little tedious; a change of routine or venue was imperative. Fortunately Jim O'Dea knew a publican in Moynalvey, near Summerhill in County Meath. The man was in his seventies, was a bachelor, lived alone and owned a very neat pub-cum-grocer's shop that also dealt in hardware. At the back of the shop was a small room lined with shelves containing many good books, including the latest Penguin editions. The man had converted some comfortable old motor-car seats into domestic use. A cheerful fire made the room snug and welcoming. It was to this room that the man retreated during quiet periods of the day when no customers were around. At the back of the shop he had built a tennis court, where he and the parish priest played.

Cathal and Jim often visited this well-preserved man, travelling to his place either in Mr Gannon's car or in a car that O'Dea had borrowed. They told him about Sir James and he said, 'Bring him down here some night and we'll have a bit of fun with him.'

At the next available opportunity, Cathal and Jim drove Sir James to Moynalvey. He was brought into the pub and formally introduced to the publican, who produced drinks on the house. After some polite talk, a 'microphone' was rigged up in a conspicuous place and a 'broadcast' was begun. Sir James launched into his usual political speeches and songs. The publican was fascinated by the performance. What amused Cathal, though, was how the local people took it so seriously and gathered in the pub, so much so that, before the night was finished, it was packed. Many of the people were Irish speakers from the West of Ireland who had settled in Meath. Whenever Cathal or Jim needed to relieve themselves outside, the locals stood to one side to let them out and treated them with great respect.

As usual, throughout the evening Cathal or Jim received bogus telephone calls from around the world. Holding a broken telephone to their ear they said, 'It's going down very well! The Opera House in Madrid is packed with people – they're clamouring for more – they want that song again!' Sir James would oblige with:

A proud boy was Barney to wed Nora Kearney,
The purtiest girl in the town …

or 'The Day Delaney's Donkey ran the Half Mile Race'.

It was normal practice for Jem to finish a session by singing 'God Save the King'. On hearing this, Joe Kenny pretended to get upset and shouted, 'F— the King!' The switches were quickly turned off, a row invariably started and the two men had to be placated.

On one occasion Jem, Joe Kenny and Jim O'Dea were arguing in the car whilst driving back to Finglas from Moynalvey. Sir James shouted to Jim, 'Dr O'Donovan, stop the car, stop the car!' He had been trying to get out and was threatening to walk home as a protest against Joe Kenny's abuse; the disagreement had started after he had sung the British National Anthem yet again. Patching up the row proved to be a difficult task, but peace was restored. Soon after this he wrote a letter, which Cathal kept.

3 July 1939

Dear Sir, I wish To Announce To You That Im Not coming up To Hunts[town] House To Brad Cast Any More If You want Me To Brad Cast I will Go To Moy[nalvey] Natuly But I will Protest Againt Bringing Joseph Kenny. This Is To Certify That You Carry This Promis of Mine out I want Dress Suit The Next Time I Go up So Please Let Me Know If You Can Get A Car I'm Cutting All Radio Programmes out In Huntstown House You Can Tell Mr Clandillon If You Have Any Letter Please Post To My own Adress I Must Defend My Title Because Im Not Going To Be Assualted Any More I will Not Allow Any More Intrruptions one The Radio Send Me A Answer To This Letter As Soon As Possiple

I Remain Your obident Servant Sir James J [Lawlor] Bt Little James Town Finglas C[ounty] D[ublin]

Because of the amount of respect accorded to him and his growing sense of importance, Sir James became hungry for titles and in time asked if it were possible for him to become a lord. Cathal indicated that, as he was due to go to England again, he might talk to the Lord Chancellor to see if he could be made a peer of the realm. However, to further Sir James's cause, various forms would have to be filled in. Included was his war record, a form that Jim O'Dea created, using the company typewriter. This began, 'Please state battles you were involved in.' Joe Kenny urged him to include the Battle of Cairo, but Sir James hesitated.

'I don't think there was a Battle of Cairo,' he said.

'It doesn't matter a damn,' said Joe. 'You fill it in – they won't know to the difference!' So Sir James obligingly wrote down 'the Battle of Kairo'.

It was then deemed necessary that Sir James become a member of the Incorporated Society of Broadcasting Artists. He showed interest in this but complained that he had no papers to prove his competence. He was duly furnished with a typewritten piece of paper proving that he was a seasoned broadcaster. He was finally awarded a certificate stating that he had been elected a member of the 'Incorporated Society of Broadcasting Artists, incorporated by Act of Parliament in 1793'. Sir James kept this certificate by him on every occasion and, needless to say, never queried the date.

Cathal collected the completed forms and a copy of the certificate and set off again for London, where he was supposed to deliver them at White-hall. Cathal sent him a postcard on the following day to say that the papers had been successfully delivered. Once again, Sir James was put into a state of agitation as he waited for news.

After a while, another scroll was delivered to Huntstown House in exactly the same manner as before (Sir James heard the knock on the door but did not see the messenger), and there was great rejoicing when he learned that he had been created Lord Skephubble. As before, everyone wondered how the King knew about this out-of-the-way village in north County Dublin, but his lordship had a ready answer: 'Ah, it's quite easy – sure, they have maps over there!'

Some time afterwards he was made Duke of Saucerstown, but he pre-ferred the original Sir James, the title by which everyone knew him.

When World War II began in 1939, cars went off the road, transport became more difficult and Cathal and Jim no longer made the journey out to Huntstown House. Joe Kenny died as a result of an accident: the tractor that he was driving keeled over when he was turning a corner.

Cathal saw Sir James again many years later at the Boot Inn in Ballymun, where Sir James was employed as a doorman. It was the last time that they were to meet, for the unfortunate man came to a sad end; some time later he was found drowned in a ditch in north County Dublin.

Fifteen

*M*ention has been made of Matt McNamara, who worked in Butler's antique shop on Ormond Quay and then Millar and Beatty's in Grafton Street. Matt and his wife lived in a house on Rathfarnham Road. Cathal was invited there, became a regular visitor and befriended the two spinster daughters, Lil and Eva, who were around Cathal's age, though he never discovered exactly how old they were. Lil, whose proper name was Delia, had a lively mind and was interested in literature; her younger sister was a little more retiring. The friendship was to last for more than sixty years.

One Sunday afternoon in 1934, Cathal met Grace Plunkett at the McNamaras' home. Cathal had heard about this lady; born Grace Gifford, she had married Joseph Mary Plunkett a few hours before his execution at Kilmainham Jail in 1916. Grace was friendly with the McNamara girls' aunt, Mary Perolz, who was of Huguenot origin and a well-known member of the Cumann na mBan, the female branch of the IRA. Another of Grace's acquaintances was Constance Markievicz.

Cathal also met Grace Plunkett at the meetings of the Old Dublin Society, which he attended with the McNamara sisters. Cathal joined this society at around the time it was founded in 1934 and remained a member for about five years. The Old Dublin Society held its meetings in the Lord Mayor's Court of the City Assembly House, now the Civic Museum, in South William Street. Alderman Tom Kelly, who had chaired a committee that supported the founding of the Hugh Lane Municipal Gallery of Modern Art in 1907, was the first president. Cathal found him a very pleasant man and enjoyed the lectures that he gave. As Alderman Kelly lived on the South Circular Road, Cathal often walked home with him. Alderman Kelly had a second-hand bookshop in Trinity Street, where he often sat reading. He sold quality books and displayed choice editions in the window, which he was reluctant to sell. He often loaned books to Cathal. Many years later Cathal met his granddaughter, Kathleen Kelly, who worked as an accountant in Guinness's Brewery.

Cathal met many interesting people in the society. Reuben Dodd, the elderly Jewish solicitor who practised in 12 Upper Ormond Quay, often sat beside Cathal. He was a swarthy individual who always smelled of cigars. Cathal found him very pleasant and got on well with him. A story in James Joyce's *Ulysses* relates how his son fell into the Liffey and was rescued by a boatman. It was rumoured that Reuben had paid the boatman just 2*s*. for saving his son's life.

Other members of the society were Hanna Sheehy Skeffington, widow of Francis Sheehy Skeffington (who had been shot in 1916), Professor Mary Hayden, who taught history in University College Dublin, and Grace Plunkett's sisters Katie Wilson and Nellie Donnelly. Another sister of Grace's, Sidney Czira, who used the pen name John Brennan, and Miss Boydell, an aunt of the late Professor of Music at Trinity College, Dublin, Dr Brian Boydell, attended the meetings. Miss Boydell always arrived in an elegant chauffeur-driven motor car. The driver waited outside and drove her home when the meetings were over.

Cathal became quite an active member of the Old Dublin Society and read two papers to its members: 'Saint Patrick's Cathedral' (9 November 1935) and 'Dame Street and its associations' (6 April 1936).

The society also organized outings. Cathal remembered visiting Maynooth College with a group that included Grace Plunkett. They also went to Malahide Castle, where Cathal encountered Kevin B. Nowlan for the first time. Kevin, who was only about fifteen years of age then, gave a talk on the castle and the medieval church in the grounds; the group was amazed that such a young man could speak with such authority. Later, Kevin and Cathal were to become good friends.

The society members also went on walking tours of Dublin, especially around the narrow back streets of the Liberties before many of the old buildings were demolished. They also visited St Patrick's Cathedral; afterwards, Grace and Lil McNamara went with Cathal to a place that they had never seen before: the Iveagh Market in Francis Street, where the local tenement dwellers bought second-hand clothes. They thought it great fun to look at the various stalls and hear the vendors calling out their wares.

In 1935 Cathal met Maeve Cavanagh MacDowell at another gathering in the McNamara household. She wrote contemporary plays and, in Cathal's estimation, indifferent poetry. Cathal considered her to be a pleasant woman and in time came to know her very well. He often visited her at her house in Larkfield Grove, near Harold's Cross. She used to speak about her late husband, Cathal MacDowell, who had been an artist and a highly intelligent man. Maeve owned a small three-roomed wooden house on Kilmashogue Mountain, behind St Columba's College, and encouraged Cathal to use it as she rarely went there. At the time it was in a lovely, unspoiled spot.

Cathal's friendship with Grace Plunkett lasted a long time. Cathal enjoyed her company – she was 'one of the great eccentrics', as he put it. After the Old Dublin Society's weekly meetings, Cathal, the McNamara sisters and Grace walked the short distance to her flat at the top of 11 Nassau Street, a building given over mostly to offices. Situated where the Kilkenny Design Centre now stands, it has long since been demolished. The flat had a balcony, which was an extension of a bow window beneath it, and there they would sit on summer evenings, overlooking the grounds of Trinity College where they could see students running, jumping, playing cricket and rugby. At that time there was very little traffic, especially in the evenings.

Grace had been arrested in February 1923, during the Civil War, and had been detained in Kilmainham Jail for about three months. With her, apparently, was Helena Molony, whom Cathal also knew. In order to occupy herself Grace painted a Madonna and Child on one wall of her cell, and on another either a Spanish dancer or a depiction of Irish saints – accounts vary.

When she left the jail, she succeeded in taking a wooden stool with her. She kept this in her flat and used it as a stand for her Singer sewing machine. She was always sewing and making her own clothes; every time Cathal visited her, she was either trying to make a skirt or a blouse. She always had trouble making collars; they never seemed to sit properly for her. As Sunday was her sewing day, she did not welcome visitors.

Cathal was travelling on a tram with Grace when she opened a little case that she carried with her. Much to his embarrassment, he noticed a cell number stamped on the inside. The case had obviously been issued to her whilst in prison and she had kept it.

Grace had lived for several years in poverty; she had lived in a bleak top flat, a very small affair of probably only one room, in a building in

Westmoreland Street, most of which, like the one in Nassau Street, contained offices. One Christmas Day, soon after the 1916 Easter Rising, she had eaten nothing more than bread and dripping, and her only company was a little mouse that came out of its hole to join her. Before living in Nassau Street, she had lived in Parnell Square. In 1932 she was given a pension by the Fianna Fáil government. The pension was not index-linked and soon lost its value, leaving Grace in an impecunious state.

Grace was independent in her ways and was forthright in her views. She once said of opera: 'Instead of saying "let's have a game of cards", you *sing* it.' When she received a postcard from somebody in which the person had written 'having a great time *laying* in the sun', she dismissed it by calling it 'a servant's letter'. She referred to George Moore, the famous writer and artist, as 'that man with the fishy eyes'.

Grace was also an artist and a well-known caricaturist who portrayed prominent Abbey actors. Two books of caricatures, *Twelve Nights at the Abbey Theatre* and *Doctors Recommend It*, were published in 1929 and 1930 respectively. She used her own copy of the former as a writing pad. Cathal often saw her with this ink-stained book on her knee when she was writing, and one day said that he thought it was a pity that she should be using it in such a fashion.

'That's all the use I find for it,' she said. 'If you can give me a nice level piece of timber the same size, I'll let you have the book.'

Cathal procured a piece of plywood, removed the sharp corners and presented it to her. Happy with this, she gave him the book of caricatures and also the other volume.

At a later date, when Cathal was helping her move her belongings to a new flat in the Nassau Street area, he came across the love letters that Joseph Mary Plunkett had written to her before he was executed. At this time Grace had lived at 8 Temple Villas, on Palmerston Road, but Joe, who always got the numbers mixed up, continually posted them to number 9, where an out-and-out Unionist family used to live. The arrival of these letters and the inevitable handing over of them to Grace drew much attention to them.

Grace, who had kept the letters for so long, now wanted to throw them out. Cathal, however, talked her into donating them to the National Library, which she eventually did. Just as she had parcelled them up and was about to seal them, she asked Cathal to read them to her. Cathal, therefore, was the only other person at that stage to read the letters. For some reason, Cathal's reaction to them was not favourable.

In January 1936 Cathal worked in Guinness's Brewery on a temporary contract, but was employed by McLaughlin and Harvey's, who supplied tradesmen to the Brewery when needed. In the same year he joined four more societies.

At a general meeting held on 21 April Cathal was elected a member of the Royal Society of Antiquaries of Ireland, which had its headquarters in Merrion Square. Cathal remained a member for four or five years. He met a number of interesting people at the meetings and excursions: the Jesuit priests Fr John Ryan, Professor of Early (Medieval) History at UCD, and Fr Charles Scantelbury, member of the Belvederian Community and editor of various Jesuit publications. He also met Charles McNeill, who was a great expert on medieval documents and was the Leinster vice-president of the society. Cathal remembered the ease with which he read and translated medieval documents written in Latin. Cathal also met Seán P. Ó Riordáin, Professor of Archaeology at UCD, who gave a lecture in May 1936. Cathal remembered him, presumably on another occasion, bringing in a set of bronze axes and knives that had been excavated that morning in the hills by Lough Crew in County Meath. There was great excitement when the members examined the artefacts, which were between 2500 and 3000 years old.

Cathal was now moving a little upwards in society, hobnobbing with the likes of T.P. Le Fanu, CB, MRIA, the president of the society, and Lady Dorothy Lowry-Corry, who was the Ulster vice-president and who gave a lecture in October 1936. However, he never befriended such people; in all probability he held them in awe.

In 1936, Cathal also joined the Academy of Christian Art; the meetings were held in 42 Upper Mount Street. Grace Plunkett's father-in-law, Count George Plunkett, was one of the leading lights and gave several interesting talks on the early Florentine and Italian painters, which was his speciality. Seán Keating, the artist, gave lectures; Cathal found him very refreshing as he always had some innovative take on art or something interesting to say. Two other men who were involved in this society were Liam Gogan of the National Museum and the writer and gaeilgeoir J.J. O'Kelly, who used the pseudonym Sceilg (Rock). O'Kelly had been involved in the Sinn Féin party and at one time had hit the headlines for refusing to pay his rates because his notice was not printed in Irish.

In addition, Cathal joined the Dublin Shakespeare Society, which met in a hall in Rathmines. Cathal attended play readings and the occasional play but he never became actively involved.

Finally, in the same year, he joined the Dublin Gramophone Society, which met in a back room of Mitchell's high-class restaurant and tearooms in Grafton Street, opposite Wicklow Street. Cathal remembered the pianist Charles Lynch giving a talk on Beethoven's Fifth Piano Concerto, (the 'Emperor'), and illustrating it by means of scratchy 78 rpm records, which needed to be changed every few minutes, often in the middle of a movement.

It was at one of these meetings that Cathal heard Antonín Dvořák's Symphony No. 9, *From The New World*, played for the first time. The year 1937 was the fortieth anniversary of Brahms's death and so music by the composer, including some of his *Lieder*, was played. The one hundred and tenth anniversary of Schubert's death was celebrated in 1938 by listening to music written by him.

During this period, Cathal became a frequent visitor to Dublin's art galleries and museums, where undoubtedly he met more interesting people.

An all-night party was given on a Saturday evening in 1936 by Ned Sheehy and his wife, the artist known as Anna Kelly. She was quite a good artist; Cathal once owned some framed linocuts by her, which he later gave to a sale-of-work. The party took place in their cottage in Glencree Valley, below the Reformatory. The cottage was beautifully situated and one approached it along a path facing the former youth hostel. Cathal drove Grace Plunkett and his brother Willie there in his father's car.

The party started sometime in the evening with a meal; Cathal remembered eating cakes and drinking lemon tea. A number of well-known people were present, including one or two members of an IRA family, the Gilmores. Cathal remembered that the cottage was 'beautifully whitewashed' inside and had a wide border of whitewash on the floor. Mr Sheehy was dressed in an embroidered Hungarian blouse. A girl danced barefoot to the accompaniment of Debussy's *Prélude à l'Après Midi d'un faune*, which was played on an old horn gramophone. Everyone was 'in and out of the house, courting and doing all sorts of things'. More tea was served and they sat talking around a huge fire. Grace Plunkett had brought a parcel of kippers, which were cooked, and she and the guests ate them with their fingers. The sight of day breaking above Lough Bray was a memorable experience.

Cathal and Willie then drove homewards, stopping for six or seven o'clock Mass in Mount Argus, and retired to bed, no doubt exhausted but happy.

At around this time, Grace Plunkett introduced Cathal to her solicitor friend John Burke, who lived in Rostrevor Terrace on Orwell Road, Rathgar.

John was a picture expert; as well as being a collector, he did a certain amount of dealing and he was one of the governors of the National Gallery in Dublin. He owned a wonderful collection of paintings, including the finest works by Sir Walter Osborne that Cathal had ever seen. As a child, I can remember being brought to his house and noting all the pictures, especially those stacked on the floor against the walls.

John used to commission Seán O'Sullivan to draw portraits of various important people. Cathal remembered how he persuaded Seán to draw the actress Ruth Draper, who had come to Dublin. Many of Seán's drawings may now be seen in the National Gallery, Dublin.

John could be a little odd at times. In the early 1950s he had a seventeenth-century Spanish still life that he was trying to sell for a parish priest. He showed it to Cathal, who was very taken with it; it contained a flower arrangement, a book and an antique watch.

'I'm doing my best to try and get £40 for this painting for this priest, if I can get that I'll be happy,' said John.

'Well,' Cathal said, 'I'll offer you £40 for it right now.'

For some unknown reason, John refused to discuss the matter any further and proceeded to tell Cathal a funny story that John McCormack had told him. Cathal tried to steer him back to the subject of selling him the painting, but in vain.

John also owned a magnificent painting by Sir Gerald Kelly of a Burmese dancing girl, which he purchased for £50 at an auction. Cathal was willing to give him three times that amount for it, but he would not part with it.

In 1936, Cathal went to the Theatre Royal to hear the first complete performance of Beethoven's Ninth Symphony, only parts of which had been heard before, although he had heard the entire symphony on the radio from Germany. This was a mammoth undertaking at the time and was organized by the Prussian conductor Fritz Braze, who came to Ireland in 1922 and became the director of the Army School of Music in Dublin. He remained at this post until about 1940. He arranged many Irish airs, such as those by the blind harpist, Carolan, as marches for the Army band.

When Cathal's sister Ethna had won a certificate at the Read Pianoforte School in 1931 or 1932, it had been presented to her by Fritz Braze. As he was so tall and she so small, he had lifted her up into the air.

During the 1930s, Cathal made two failed attempts to join the Royal

Dublin Society, which still has its headquarters in Ballsbridge, south Dublin. Dick Davis, a well-read colleague of Cathal's in Guinness's Brewery, encouraged Cathal to join, but it was no use. Cathal was obliged to write down his trade on the application form and this did not help matters. Obviously working-class Roman Catholics were not made welcome. Understandably, Cathal was rather disappointed.

Nonetheless, Cathal could have attended some of the events without being a member. Unfortunately nobody thought to tell him about a lecture given by the famous Dolmetsch family, who demonstrated their early musical instruments. Cathal heard all about it the following day, but of course that was of no use to him. Cathal realized the difference it might have made to him if he had attended this lecture; he felt that he was just unlucky.

The year 1936 was a fruitful one for Cathal. In October he acquired his first antique piano: a fine Regency grand made in London by Round, Jones and Co. in about 1810. He bought this for £3 in M. & W. Jackson's furniture shop in Grafton Street. The piano had six octaves, a mahogany case, four reeded legs and a satinwood nameboard that incorporated the coloured plumes of the Prince of Wales. It was in good condition and had a good tone; Cathal restrung it and put new coverings on the hammers. He kept the piano in the conservatory at the back of the house in Crumlin Road.

Unfortunately, this fine instrument took up too much space in the small Gannon household and began to suffer from dampness. Cathal was obliged to sell it, at the same price that he had paid for it, to Mrs Alcock who owned the second-hand shop in Dolphin's Barn Street. Cathal had no regrets parting with it as his heart was still set on obtaining a harpsichord if at all possible. Indeed, he had toyed with the idea of converting the piano into a harpsichord; nobody wanted such a piano in the 1930s and harpsichords were simply not available.

This then was the start of Cathal's career in restoring old instruments – a job that he found most satisfying. One may wonder how he acquired the knowledge to tackle such a job; unfortunately he was always silent on this point. Obviously the combination of his skill at fine cabinetmaking and his interest in music helped. He was also lucky that this first piano was in such good condition; if the piano had been badly damaged or in poor shape he may not have had the courage to restore it. He was aware that a great deal of music had been written for this type of piano and that such an instrument should be used to perform it. Restoring it convinced him that pianos of this type could be used successfully on the concert platform. Cathal indeed was ahead of his time in this regard; nowadays it is common practice to use pianos of the same period as the music that is performed on them.

In time, Cathal was to find the restoration of early pianos, even those in a deplorable state, the most rewarding of jobs. Seeing an instrument come back to life after people had declared that it could never be made play again, was, for him, immensely satisfying and more of a challenge than making an instrument from scratch. Restoration also spared him the drudgery of construction. Cathal was aware of his shortcomings and relative inexperience at building an instrument as against the competence of the old masters who had made the pianos that he aimed to restore; he felt confident that the sound of a properly restored piano was guaranteed to be good – in contrast to his efforts to create an instrument, which could possibly end in failure. Cathal realized that these old masters had their craft 'in their blood', whereas he did not come from a long line of piano or harpsichord makers. By working with an old piano and discovering inscriptions inside it, Cathal felt that he was coming into contact with the original maker and bridging the gap of a century or so between the last instrument of its kind and a whole different generation of craftsmen.

Cathal realized from an early stage that altering an old piano during restoration was not permissible and thus he became a sensitive and sympathetic restorer.

At around this time, Cathal's father bought his third car: a magnificent twelve-horsepower 1928 Singer Saloon with an aluminium body painted brown, which cost £28. It was positively luxurious; it had four doors, the fascia board was made of beautiful polished mahogany, there were green silk blinds with tassels on the windows and at the back there were cut-glass lights for reading. The seats were inflatable and extremely comfortable. The car had servo-assisted brakes on all four wheels; in order to warn the traffic behind that the car could stop suddenly, a red triangle, a caption and a red light were affixed to the rear.

It was in this car that Cathal rather unwillingly travelled with his brother Willie, his sister Maureen and his parents to Glengarriff, County Cork, for a holiday in August 1936. As we have noted earlier in this chapter, Cathal was then working in Guinness's Brewery on a temporary contract. Until this point, he and other tradesmen had only enjoyed three days' annual leave per year. In 1936 the de Valera government announced that workers in the building trade were henceforth entitled to have a full week's holidays. With little or no warning, Cathal found himself with a week off and nothing planned. He consequently accompanied his sister and parents on their journey rather than stay at home on his own.

They drove to Glengarriff on 1 August, Cathal's twenty-sixth birthday and checked into the Poulgorm Hotel, which was run by the Harvey family. During the evening they had a little bit of music and Cathal was persuaded to play a Mozart sonata on the lovely Schiedmayer piano in the drawing room. A gentleman from Belfast, a Mr Lindop, sang and Cathal played his accompaniment. On the following day, Cathal was introduced to one of two young English ladies, a pleasant, fresh-looking, 24-year-old, brown-haired and round-faced girl of medium build named Margaret Key, and fell easily into conversation with her. Margaret's friend, Kathleen Reynolds, who worked in the office of a railway company in London, had decided to attach herself to Cathal's brother Willie and was anxious to introduce Margaret to Cathal.

Without realizing it, both brothers had met their future wives. For Cathal, it must have been a fitting culmination to such a rewarding year and the best birthday present that he could ever be given.

Sixteen

Margaret Key, an only child, was born on 15 November 1911 in Holloway, London. Her father was Joseph Key, a glass cutter who worked in Holloway Road, and her mother, Alice Amy Hoadley, was a dressmaker. Joseph and Alice, who were of good Church of England stock, had married sometime around 1908 and lived in rented rooms on the first floor of an old house in Yerbury Road; the owners, Mr and Mrs Woodgate, who were very kind to young Margaret, lived on the ground floor.

Sadly, Margaret's father was a diabetic and died suddenly from his condition at the age of forty-three. Margaret, who was eleven years of age at the time and who was a carefree, fun-loving girl, really did not understand what a catastrophe this was. She was sent to stay with friends, the Stuarts, who lived near Finsbury Park, and did not attend the funeral. Her father simply passed out of her life.

Her mother, on the other hand, was devastated and suffered a nervous breakdown. Margaret supposed that she received some type of medical care. As money was in short supply, Mrs Key had to take up dressmaking once again in order to make ends meet.

When Margaret was fourteen, her mother married again. The Woodgates had some time previously told Mrs Key about a gentleman by the name of William Lewis Clench who worked in the London, Midland and Scottish (LMS) railway company. He had been transferred from Coventry to London and had nowhere to stay. The Woodgates managed to persuade Mrs Key to take him as a lodger; as they pointed out, it would bring her some much needed extra income. Margaret's mother looked after him, cooked meals for him, did his washing and in the end they decided to marry.

Margaret attended the low-key wedding and was happy for her mother. Mrs Key, now Mrs Clench, was a relatively young woman and had a long life ahead of her; it would have been a bleak prospect to live it on her own. Soon afterwards, the rented house in Yerbury Road went up for sale, and as Mrs Clench had no real desire to buy it, she decided to look elsewhere for one. She and Mr Clench finally bought a new semi-detached house in Spencer Road in Wealdstone, Harrow (now in the Greater London Area).

At the age of sixteen Margaret sent off an application for a job in the railway company accompanied by a note written by Mr Clench, in which he stated his preference for her to be employed at the headquarters at Euston Station. Margaret was lucky. She was called for an interview and asked to sit a little examination, which she passed. She started work on 17 April 1928 not at Euston Station, but at another LMS base in Carlow Street, about ten minutes' walk away.

Once Margaret had started working with the railway company she was entitled to free passes and cheap travel, enabling her to take off on holidays. She was given four passes a year; three of these she could use on the LMS and one on a 'foreign' railway, such as the Great Western or the London North Eastern. Margaret was also given a free season ticket, which paid for her fare into work every day, from Harrow to Euston Station.

The places she went to for her two-week summer holidays included Scarborough, Devon, Cornwall, Colwyn Bay and Barmouth in Wales, Dunoon in Scotland, Stratford-upon-Avon, Southsea, the Wye Valley, the Isle of Wight and the Isle of Man. Generally Margaret travelled alone or with a friend – her parents had no objections to her setting off on her own. The fact that she looked older than her age was an advantage to her. She and her parents often went to Dartmouth in Devon at Christmas, where they stayed with the Huttons, who ran a shoe shop downstairs in their home and a guest house upstairs. Margaret and her parents found them extremely pleasant people. Old Mr Hutton had two daughters, neither of whom were married.

Margaret had been to Ireland once before, sometime in the late 1920s. She had travelled with her mother and stepfather by train to Holyhead and by mail boat to Dun Laoghaire, which they reached by early morning. They went to Dublin and were shocked at the state of the city, which had been left in ruins after the Civil War. It was wet and they were disturbed at the sight of old women in shawls rummaging in dustbins. As Mr Clench's sister had once worked in the Bray Head Hotel, he suggested that they go to Bray. They made the journey, but in the end Mrs Clench decided that she did not like Ireland and they decided to take the night boat back to Holyhead.

Undeterred by this, Margaret was enticed back to Ireland in 1936 when she noticed the photographs of Glengarriff in County Cork that adorned the long-distance trains in England – to her it looked beautiful and well worth visiting.

A frequent traveller on the train from Harrow into London every day was a colleague of Margaret's, Kathleen Reynolds, who lived near Spencer Road and who worked in an LMS office at Euston Station. Margaret told her of her desire to visit Glengarriff and asked her if she might be free to join her. Kathleen replied that she would.

The two girls set off either late in the evening on Friday, 24 July, or early the following morning. They took the train from Harrow into London and from there to Fishguard in Wales, then boarded the ship bound for Rosslare. Kathleen proved to be a poor sailor and became violently seasick. Thanks to the excellent network of railways criss-crossing Ireland at that time, they undoubtedly made their way from Rosslare to Kenmare entirely by rail; Margaret had long forgotten the details. Because they travelled on the Great Southern Railway, which extended the same privileges to employees of other railway systems, they travelled free of charge, thanks to their special passes. Indeed, if it were not for the passes, the price of the journey would have been prohibitive.

They finally arrived at the Poulgorm Hotel in Glengarriff sometime on the Saturday, exhausted after the long, tedious journey. The hotel proved to be agreeable and comfortable, but Kathleen, who was badly out of sorts, embarrassed Margaret by grumbling about the state of the bedroom. The maid was ordered to fetch the owner, Mrs Harvey, and Kathleen complained that the sheets had not been washed and the water in the jug had not been changed. 'You must remember we live in the country,' Mrs Harvey explained, 'and we have to rely on drying the clothes outside.' Despite Margaret's attempt to placate the owner, news of the incident travelled amongst the guests and nobody spoke to them. Margaret felt miserable and wished that she had not come.

Nevertheless, the weather was good and the scenery around Glengarriff lived up to Margaret's expectations. She was fascinated by the crossroad dancing that she and Kathleen watched in the evenings – she had never seen anything like it before.

Things brightened up considerably on the arrival of two gentlemen from Belfast: Jimmy Kirkpatrick and Mr Charles Lindop, who took a lively interest in the two girls. Now Margaret and Kathleen had someone to talk to. Jimmy and Mr Lindop were touring the country by car and were to stay in Glengarriff for three days until the following Sunday before proceeding to Cork. From there they planned to go to Dublin for the Horse Show. Jimmy worked in a linen factory and was about thirty years of age; Mr Lindop, who taught music, was in his fifties. The latter entertained the guests in the hotel by singing. Both were well educated. Jimmy, whose catchphrase appeared to be 'Do you see now?', became infatuated with Margaret and subsequently wrote her five impassioned letters, which she kept in the chest of drawers beside her bed until her dying day; no doubt she re-read them from time to time. 'I need hardly say that I was rather struck on you,' Jimmy wrote in his impeccable handwriting, 'and I think that you are one of the finest and nicest persons that I have ever met.' He requested a photograph to remind him of 'the three happiest days that I have spent for years ... You were really wonderful and I think the chap that gets you to look after is going to be a jolly lucky fellow.' Mr Lindop wrote her just one letter, in which he described Jimmy as 'as daft as any one' and made mention of Kathleen's 'funny little idiosyncrasy about drinking nothing but water'.

The two gentlemen brought Margaret and Kathleen out in their smart car, driving them to the local scenic spots such as Bantry Bay, the Healy Pass and Gougane Barra. Together they took the boat out to Garinish Island to admire the Italianate gardens and flora. All in all, they had a great time together. Kathleen's nose was put out of joint when Margaret was placed in the front seat beside Jimmy and presented with a box of chocolates. The two men would gladly have stayed longer in Glengarriff if it were not for the fact that they were obliged to meet friends in Cork. Indeed, they invited Margaret to come with them, without Kathleen, and proposed leaving her to the boat at Rosslare. However, she declined the offer, saying that as she had come with Kathleen, she would not abandon her and would go home with her.

By and by, some new guests – the Gannons – arrived on Saturday, 1 August. According to Margaret, Kathleen, who had tired of Jimmy and Mr Lindop, came into the dining room and announced, 'There's either going to be two or four of us for the next week.'

Margaret merely replied, 'Oh.'

'Yes,' Kathleen continued. 'I've just met a young man in the hall and he's got his brother with him. Would you like to be introduced to him?'

Margaret said that she would and so she was introduced to Cathal. Margaret found this 26-year-old man with a fine head of wavy brown hair and grey-blue eyes, dressed simply but smartly in a sports jacket and trousers, very pleasant, polite, interesting and good-looking. There was no trace of roughness or roguishness in his character; he told Margaret about his interests and produced photographs of his collection of antique watches. Margaret detected a romantic streak in him and obviously decided that she liked him. Although less experienced than Cathal in consorting with the opposite sex, Margaret had known two or three young men before she met Cathal, though none of them had been thought of as boyfriends. Interestingly, Cathal thought that Margaret and Jimmy were engaged ('no such luck for me', Jimmy wrote) as they had been so much together during the preceding days. Margaret, for her part, had a sneaking suspicion that Jimmy was either married or had been married, though she was very uncertain about this.

In the evening, Mr Lindop found that he had a new accompanist for his songs. Margaret, as usual, enjoyed the singing and thought that Cathal played the piano very well. Jimmy had noticed Margaret's admiration for Cathal, for in the first of his letters to her, written on 11 August, he wrote, 'I hope that you did not fall too hard for the pianist'. He did have a good opinion about Cathal, however, for later he wrote, 'I rather thought that Charles [sic] would be quite a good sort. He looked to be rather intelligent and not quite so gay as the other boy.'

On the following day, Jimmy and Mr Lindop left. Margaret went outside to bid a tearful goodbye to them both, but Kathleen refused to say farewell. Before leaving, Margaret and the two men exchanged addresses. Jimmy was worried about the tears; he wondered if Margaret were unhappy or if he had offended her in some way.

Cathal and Willie now proposed that they go off for a drive somewhere and the two girls happily joined them. As Kathleen had already latched on to Willie, she left Margaret with no choice but to stick with Cathal. At least they were all better matched as regards age. For the rest of the holiday, the girls went out touring around the area with the two boys in their father's car; Mr and Mrs Gannon and Maureen were obviously content to stay put in the hotel at Glengarriff. The girls saw little of the boys' parents and sister, though they had, of course, been introduced. Mr Gannon had greeted Margaret cordially and decided that he liked her; Mrs Gannon, however, treated her a little more cautiously. Margaret liked Mr Gannon, but found his Dublin accent and colloquialisms a little difficult to understand at times. She subsequently discovered Mrs Gannon to be 'a little coarse' and inclined to say inappropriate things – Mr Gannon often had to silence her.

Because of the girls' welcome presence, Cathal's plan to join a friend somewhere nearby if the holiday proved to be boring was now unnecessary. Fortunately, there were no more hitches during the final week of the holiday; Kathleen was happy with her new companion and gave no further trouble. Margaret relished her time in Glengarriff and declared that it was the nicest holiday that she had ever had.

Seventeen

_F_ortunately Margaret's parents were not too upset to hear that their daughter had met an Irish Catholic whilst on holidays; they probably thought that letters and photographs would be exchanged for a while and that the holiday romance would soon end. Consequently they never tried to put a stop to the friendship. As regards marriage, however, they had their mind set on a young man whom Margaret had met at night school when she was sixteen. Margaret, on the other hand, was not very keen on the young man in question.

Meanwhile, Cathal began corresponding with her, often sitting up until late at night to write long letters containing news of his activities and the various societies to which he belonged. It was not unusual for him to write fifteen to twenty pages. As soon as she received a letter, which was normally on the following day, she answered immediately, though she had relatively little to say. Margaret often received two or three letters from him every week.

At a later stage in their friendship, Cathal used Grace Plunkett's telephone to speak to Margaret about once a week; as Mrs Clench disliked telephones and did not possess one, Margaret went to a friend's house to receive Cathal's calls.

Jimmy Kirkpatrick corresponded with Margaret until September 1936 and invited her on a weekend visit to Blackpool in order to see the illuminations, but Margaret declined his offer. Towards the end of August he wrote to her, telling her that he hoped that she would not be offended if he sent her a 'sample' of the fabric made at the factory where he worked. He invited her to choose a colour. Not knowing what she was about to receive, Margaret played safe and asked for blue, her favourite colour. She was sent a beautiful tablecloth, a 'mixture of silk' that seemed 'to be all the rage' at the time, and which is still in regular use seventy years later.

It is evident that Jimmy was still infatuated with Margaret. In his letters, he described how cruel it was of her to have left 'two broken-hearted Irishmen' (he and Mr Lindop, who also had a good opinion of her) behind. 'However, it is nice to know that I have a companion in my misery. I do not think that I had the chance to overwhelm you.' One of Margaret's letters ended with an X, signifying a kiss. 'I am sorry that I am not able to get that X,' Jimmy wrote to her, 'but I suppose I shall have to cut it out of your letter. I think that it would be a lot more valuable than the cloth.' He also referred to a quarrel between Margaret and 'her boyfriend at home', which may have been occasioned by her 'trip to Ireland'. Is this 'boyfriend' the young man whom her parents wished her to marry? In the last surviving letter, Jimmy asks: 'What about your friend – have you made it up with him yet? and does he realize that you are worth caring for and worth looking after?'

Having gone on a short holiday to the Trossachs in Scotland after her trip to Ireland, Margaret paid Cathal a weekend visit in October 1936; her parents had allowed her to make the journey on condition that she travelled once again with Kathleen Reynolds. Needless to say, Margaret was old enough to make her own decisions, but she had become accustomed to being under her parents' control. The visit was made possible by the LMS company's method of paying for overtime. Margaret and her colleagues were expected to work overtime once a month; there was an option of being paid 1s. 3d. per hour or being allowed to take a Saturday morning off now and then. Margaret worked the overtime and chose the latter.

Cathal was also able to take the Saturday morning off work and he and Willie managed to borrow their father's car. They collected Margaret and Kathleen at Dun Laoghaire in the morning and brought them to the Lenehan Hotel in Harcourt Street, where they were to stay the night.

The four of them spent a pleasant couple of days visiting the Phoenix Park, the Dublin and Wicklow Mountains, Glencree Valley and Glendalough. They had a meal in the Fox Farm restaurant, near Powerscourt Waterfall, Enniskerry. They even travelled to Clongowes Wood College in Clane, County Kildare. Fortunately they were blessed with good weather and thus the girls formed a good impression of Dublin and its environs.

Margaret came again, though this time on her own, in the middle of November and stayed, as before, at the hotel in Harcourt Street. Neither she nor Cathal remembered exactly where they went on this visit, but Margaret can recollect being brought to the Boyne Valley on one such occasion.

These weekend visits, which were to be repeated for the next couple of years, were arduous; they necessitated travelling overnight on Fridays by rail from London to Holyhead and by mail boat from there to Dun Laoghaire, and travelling back overnight in the opposite direction on Sundays so that Margaret could return to work on Monday morning. Cathal made weekend journeys to Margaret in Harrow in a similar manner.

Margaret invited Cathal to England for Christmas in 1936; this was the first time Cathal had ever ventured outside the country. To make this journey of just a few days, he had to take some time off at his own expense. It cost him £2 10s. for the return journey to London – no doubt he borrowed the money from one of his aunts as he was not in the habit of saving. Cathal was a poor sailor and travelling by sea could be rough, due to the small size of the ships. He sailed overnight, taking the nine o'clock mail boat from Dun Laoghaire to Holyhead and then went by train to London, which he reached at about six o'clock on the following morning. He then took the train to Harrow railway station, where he was met by Margaret and brought to the family home in Spencer Road. Cathal immediately realized that he was no longer on his native turf; by comparison with his Irish friends, the Clenches seemed a shade formal and serious. In Cathal's opinion, conversation dealt with trivial matters; privately he noted, with some apprehension, the inordinate amount of time they spent discussing the bin-collection times. He probably felt that he and the Clenches had little in common – and doubtless the feeling was mutual. The Clenches never told Margaret what they really thought of Cathal.

Nevertheless, the holiday proved to be quite agreeable. After Cathal had rested and spruced himself up, Margaret, her parents and he travelled back to Euston station in London, took the underground railway to Paddington Station and set off for Dartmouth in Devonshire at about midday. The journey, which cost 35s., was Margaret's Christmas present to Cathal. At a time when she earned about £2 10s. per week, this was quite a substantial sum of money. They eventually reached their destination by about five or six o'clock in the evening.

Cathal was delighted with the unspoiled little town and enjoyed staying with the Clenches' friends, the Huttons. He was pleasantly surprised to find a piano in the house.

On Christmas Eve, Cathal took himself off to the local Catholic church for midnight Mass. Christmas Day was spent with the Huttons, eating traditional fare and making merry. Cathal undoubtedly played the piano and he and Margaret walked by the river Dart.

Cathal, Margaret and the Clenches probably journeyed back to London on Sunday and Cathal repeated his long, tedious journey back to Dublin, returning to work on Monday morning.

Cathal's parents were not pleased by the fact that Cathal did not stay at home for Christmas, but Cathal was not bothered by this. It had never dawned on Margaret that his parents might object. Cathal joined her and the Clenches in Dartmouth again in Christmas of 1937 and 1938; despite the gruelling journey, he obviously loved the holidays.

Margaret visited Cathal in Dublin several times during 1937 and 1938 and on a couple of occasions stayed in Grace Plunkett's comfortable flat in Nassau Street. Grace was very kind to her and treated her very well. Margaret only slept in the flat on Saturday nights and ate breakfast with Grace on Sunday morning, after which she was collected by Cathal. Margaret found her pleasant but a little eccentric; according to her, she did not dress particularly well and wore a collection of home-made blouses, all made to the same pattern but of different materials.

In January of 1937, Cathal's father told him that the doctor in Guinness's Brewery wanted to see him; Cathal was given a brief medical check-up, put 'on the books' and was finally employed by the firm on a permanent basis, earning a little over £4 a week. Although it was a fairly good wage at the time, Cathal envied anyone who earned £5. He was given his own special bench in the top shop.

At the same time, he resumed attending the City of Dublin Technical School, Parnell Square, in order to gain a few extra days of holidays. He attended classes just one day a week, studying English, history and geography between half past six and half past nine.

In the Brewery, Cathal was producing neat woodwork as he had done before: fine mahogany cupboards for the directors' offices, in and out trays, stands for telephones and a desk for the head chemist. Despite the gulf that existed between the workers and the authorities, Cathal managed to become acquainted with many of the latter, though his relationship with them was to improve at a later stage of his career. Cathal made up his mind to enjoy his work and sought amusement by playing pranks on the scores of semi-literate men employed by the firm, many of whom were veterans of World War I and the Boer War. Such men had quaint turns of phrase and many funny stories to relate.

Cathal's brother Jack, who was working in McLaughlin and Harvey's as a carpenter at this time, was eventually put on the Brewery's books and employed by Guinness's, even though he had not served his apprenticeship with the firm. He was put in charge of the wooden vats.

The workshop in which Cathal worked was still ghastly cold in winter. Cathal procured a thermometer and hung it on the wall, where it registered 42°F. As the Board of Trade regulations stipulated that no workshop be under 50°F, Cathal complained to the head engineer, who took the thermometer away to be tested. He returned shortly afterwards and said, 'Your thermometer is wrong; it's reading two degrees too high, so the temperature is 40°F.' Within a matter of weeks, steam heaters were installed and the place was too hot. At least it was better than brushing frost off the benches in the mornings or handling frozen tools.

A by-product that was made in the Brewery in the late 1930s and exported to England was GYE — Guinness Yeast Extract. Cathal managed to buy jars of this on a regular basis. Dark brown in colour, almost black, it was a thick, treacly substance with a very strong savoury taste. Spread thinly over bread and butter, it was quite delicious and no doubt very healthy. However, as it was only a small industry, it was always expensive. When one of the centrifuges used in the manufacturing process smashed to pieces in the late 1960s, it was discontinued as it would have cost too much money to replace the equipment. Cathal regretted that he had not bought a few dozen jars before its demise.

Around the mid to late 1930s Cathal became acquainted with David Owen Williams, better known as Owen Williams — though Cathal always referred to him as D.O. Williams. He was a brewer in charge of the Experimental Laboratory; he later became head brewer and then assistant managing director. Cathal believed that he first met him through an engineer named Dickie Burgess, a friend of his. Mr Williams owned a Georgian chest of drawers, one of the locks of which was faulty. Cathal went to his house, a mews in Adelaide Road, to fix it for him. From then on they became friends. He was a very generous man and usually gave Cathal a present of a book for any little turn done for him. Mr Williams was also musical and played the piano.

In the mid-1930s Cathal also met and befriended Dr Arthur H. Hughes, who became a managing director. Cathal remembered chatting to him when he was still a junior brewer. Cathal was given the job of constructing a bookcase with sliding doors for his office, which meant that he was frequently in contact with him during the installation. Cathal found him an extremely nice man.

It was refreshing to encounter such well-mannered individuals amongst the authorities at a time when such people generally adopted a domineering manner to their 'inferiors', so much so that the simple workmen were terrified by them. It was not uncommon for Cathal to be summoned by a command such as, 'Gannon, come here,' or 'Gannon, I want you to do this.' One obnoxious individual, who was in charge of the Watling Street Laboratory, examined a record of the workmen who had been in the laboratory and said to the young lad who had written it, 'What do you mean by this? *Mr* Mac-Donnell and *Mr* Lycet? They're not members of the staff. Put down "Lycet and MacDonnell".' The young lad, John Byrne, was obliged to rub out the offending titles and reduce the names to surnames only.

Cathal and his colleagues derived a certain amount of amusement out of a rather 'light-fingered' carpenter named Dick. Dick stole everything he could lay his hands on. On one occasion he found a handsome second-hand brass knocker in the Brewery and, when the coast was clear, he removed it. When the knocker was discovered to be missing, an effort was made to find the thief, but in vain.

When things had quietened down, Dick casually fitted it to the hall door of his house, which was in Thomas Street, near the Brewery. It was recognized and talked about, but nobody embarrassed Dick or accused him of stealing it.

Shortly afterwards, Dick went to the Isle of Man for a holiday. Knowing that brass knockers were often stolen from hall doors, he took the precaution of removing it before he left. When he returned a week or two later, he replaced it, but was observed by a Brewery colleague from across the road. Dick went to the back of the house to fetch a tool and in the short space of time he was absent, his colleague walked over to the door, unscrewed the knocker and put it into his pocket.

A doctor who lived nearby happened to be looking out of his window and saw what happened. He telephoned the police, but by the time they came the knocker was safely back in Guinness's Brewery. It was given to a carpenter who looked after the furniture in the directors' offices and who started work at 6 am. He affixed it to the door of the carpenters' workshop and it was there by eight o'clock the following morning, when all the men started work. There was great merriment when each man tried out the knocker, including Dick, who looked at the knocker as if he had never seen it before. Wisely, he never made any comment.

In Easter 1937 Cathal travelled to Colwyn Bay in Wales, where he met Margaret for a short holiday. They stayed in a guest house there. By chance, Cathal's aunt and uncle, Mai and Billy Gannon, who lived in Leinster Square, Rathmines, were staying in nearby Llandudno and invited Cathal and Margaret to join them for a few hours. Margaret had met the couple previously in Dublin. Cathal was not accustomed to seeing his aunt and uncle very frequently. Whilst in Wales, Margaret and Cathal visited Chester.

In the summer of 1937 Cathal joined Margaret and went to Dartmouth for a holiday, staying once again with the Huttons. On this occasion they had the time to visit Dartmoor, Totnes and Goodrington Sands.

Between 20 September and 2 October 1937, the Dublin Loan Exhibition was staged by the Old Dublin Society in the Municipal Gallery of Modern Art, by now housed in Charlemont House, Parnell Square. Cathal loaned a picture and some watches and was employed as a steward for the thirteen-day period. The exhibition, which was 'intended to illustrate some phases of the chequered history of Dublin', was officially opened at 8.30 pm on Monday, 20 September by Seán T. O'Kelly, TD, Minister for Local Government. It was attended by more than 160 people per hour and was hailed as a tremendous success. Several detailed articles about the exhibition and the history of Dublin appeared in *The Irish Times*.

Official photographs show the familiar exhibition rooms of the gallery bedecked with numerous prints, paintings, portraits, photographs, maps and plaques. Large faded areas of wallpaper where the original paintings had hung are prominent. Various other artefacts were on view. Many of the portraits were loaned by the National Gallery; some pictures belonged to Alderman Tom Kelly. A wash drawing of Wormwood Gate, *c.* 1855, by Alexander Williams, RHA, which Cathal owned, adorned one of the walls. Cathal also loaned six of his Dublin-made antique watches and watch movements.

One evening when Cathal was on duty in the gallery, dressed in what he considered to be a rather smart check sports jacket, Grace Plunkett introduced him to a lady as an expert in art of the French school. He was momentarily taken aback by Grace's wildly exaggerated introduction but quickly regained his composure and acted the part. Apparently the lady remarked to Grace afterwards, 'He may be a great expert on French art, but he looks more like Al Capone!'

Cathal met many interesting people at the exhibition. He remembered having an argument with the priest and republican Father Michael O'Flanagan, who had been silenced and suspended several times for meddling in politics. Father O'Flanagan had become vice-chairman of Sinn Féin and had said the prayers when the first Dáil was opened in the Mansion House in 1919.

Cathal also met Kevin B. Nowlan, now almost sixteen years of age, and struck up a great friendship with him. Kevin was at that time a student in Belvedere College where, interestingly he was nicknamed 'the professor'. He received great encouragement from Father Charles Scantelbury and Professor John Ryan SJ. Indeed, Kevin believes that he learned more from Father Scantelbury than he did from any of the other priests. Both Cathal and Kevin attended the meetings of the Old Dublin Society, which Kevin joined at the behest of William Sheehan; like Cathal, Kevin read some papers to the members. These talks were often summarized in the newspapers. Cathal introduced him to the Academy of Christian Art. Father Scantelbury got Kevin into the Royal Society of Antiquaries of Ireland – as we have seen, Cathal was already a member.

After the meetings, Cathal often walked with Kevin to his home in Rathfarnham; once or twice he visited the house and met Kevin's parents. Kevin's father, John Nowlan, was a fine baritone singer and had imbued his son with a love of opera.

Cathal and Kevin went out for walks together, often covering long distances. On one occasion, during the war years when Kevin had acquired a bicycle due to the curtailment of public transport, he and Cathal cycled all the way to Jigginstown House in County Kildare. Having admired this huge seventeenth-century mansion, built by the Earl of Strafford and by then in ruins, they cycled home again; towards the end of the journey, Kevin fell off his bicycle from sheer exhaustion. On other occasions they walked for miles through north County Dublin or up the mountains, talking about everything under the sun.

Kevin always spoke very precisely. At that period, one was entitled to enter a public house outside opening hours if one was travelling. This entitlement was known as '*bona fide*', which Kevin insisted on pronouncing in the Latin manner, as distinct from the Anglicized version commonly used.

One night he knocked on a pub door and the owner cautiously opened it a few inches.

'*Bona fee-day*,' articulated Kevin carefully.

'Wha'?' grunted the owner, staring at him blankly.

'*Bona fee-day*,' repeated Kevin, unperturbed.

'Oh – *bonafied*!' exclaimed the owner after some moments' hesitation. 'Come in, come in!'

Cathal found his new companion very interesting and entertaining. Kevin, for his part, found Cathal's company delightful. Cathal struck him as being well-spoken and a 'better educated sort of man than one might have expected from a Dubliner of the time'. He was also 'very impressed always by his sense of gentility'. He always 'got an impression that he was a very gentlemanly man – that old-fashioned style, which I think is something which is well worth remembering'. For Kevin, the term 'well bred' summed up his impression of Cathal. He noticed that Cathal always had his nose in a book, 'indeed more than most people in the Old Dublin Society – I got that impression'.

Cathal and Kevin left the Old Dublin Society after a disagreement between Kevin and the authorities over a paper that he had read concerning the age of Dublin. In it, Kevin had advanced the theory that the city was a Norse foundation and that there was an earlier or contemporary Celtic monastic settlement by the Liffey.

At about the same time, the City Manager thought that it might be a good idea to celebrate the Norse foundation of Dublin and approached Paddy Meehan and possibly Alderman Tom Kelly. They would not countenance the idea, being convinced that Dublin was much older and known as a port by the ancient Greeks. When Kevin read his paper, they realized that what they had said to the City Manager was being challenged. They asked Kevin to withdraw what he had said, but he refused to and received encouragement from Professor Ryan of University College Dublin. The incident was reported in *The Irish Times* and Kevin did not return to the society until many years later.

Cathal and Kevin also attended the theatre together; they frequently went to the Gate Theatre, which had been founded in 1928 by Micheál MacLiammóir and Hilton Edwards, under the patronage of Lord Longford.

At the time, Kevin remembers, Cathal was 'very keen on the theatre'. Cathal remembered attending performances of *Night Must Fall*, the chilling murder mystery by the Welsh playwright Emlyn Williams and *Mourning Becomes Electra* by the great American writer Eugene O'Neill. Although originally billed as 'a moral domestic drama in five acts' and written as an aid to the temperance movement in America during the 1840s, *The Drunkard* (or *The Fallen Saved*) by an anonymous writer proved to be very funny as it was grossly over-acted. Cathal and Kevin often saw Lord and Lady Longford standing at the door collecting money for the theatre's funds.

Jim O'Dea often brought Cathal to the Olympia Theatre to see his uncle on stage. They entered by a side door and watched Jimmy O'Dea's performances from the wings. Whilst Cathal enjoyed the sketches, he found the famous actor's asides even funnier; while the audience laughed at the jokes, Jimmy made remarks – many of them unprintable – to the people in the front rows, who responded with redoubled laughter. As soon as the dancing and comic songs began, Jim and Cathal left. Nevertheless, Cathal did enjoy listening to Jimmy's recorded songs, such as 'Biddy Mulligan, the Pride of the Coombe'.

Although Cathal was amused by such rough-and-ready music, he was rather intolerant of 'light' music – the 'popular' classics made him cringe. Opera, operetta and Gilbert and Sullivan's humour left him cold, and he disliked ballet. It seemed that, in general, he was only prepared to listen to 'serious' music – any type of visual distraction was unwelcome. Whilst he did listen to some of Mozart's operas on the radio from time to time, he never took any interest in the complicated (and, to him, nonsensical) plots. Later composers of opera, such as Verdi or Puccini, made him grimace.

Cathal and his friends continued to go the picture houses, as cinemas were usually called. Cathal remembered being in one cinema where some lads, who sat up near the front, were smoking pipes into which they had put turf (peat) instead of tobacco. The resulting cloud of smoke was so thick that the film could be seen both on the screen and on the smoke; to Cathal, who relished the prank, it looked quite bizarre.

Cathal and his companions usually opted for the 'cushioners' (the comfortable seats), which cost 9*d*.; the 'woodeners' cost 4*d*. They watched films starring Charlie Chaplin, Laurel and Hardy, the Marx Brothers, Wheeler and Woolsey, Shirley Temple and even Popeye. Laurel and Hardy were undoubtedly Cathal's favourite comic actors; he loved their sense of the ridiculous and never failed to laugh at Stan Laurel's crying. Two local cinemas appeared at this period: the Rialto, known as the 'Ri', and the Leinster in Dolphin's Barn.

On Sunday nights Cathal often went to the Mansion House with Michael Wall and Dan White for the céilís – evenings of traditional Irish music and dancing; they merely went for the fun. Admission cost a shilling. The céilís were very well organized and neither drinking nor 'fool-acting' were tolerated. According to Cathal, the people always danced very well.

Drunkenness was as common a problem then as it is now. Every Saturday night drunken men were brought home and rows were seen at street corners. Cathal always enjoyed a good row; if he ever became involved, he encouraged the people or threw in a few words to raise tempers and walked away, leaving them to fight amongst themselves. He also put this technique to good use in Guinness's Brewery.

Everybody seemed to be drunk on Christmas Eve. Cathal and Jim O'Dea often rambled around the slums in Francis Street, the Coombe and Kevin Street during the 1930s, observing rows and fights erupting from public houses into the streets. Such fisticuffs or 'dust-ups' provided welcome 'entertainment' for the denizens of the tenement houses who came running out into the street to watch the free shows. Whilst Cathal could see the funny side of it, he also realized how pathetic and depressing such scenes really were – especially when children were heard crying because of the drunken state of their parents. Cathal was not blind to the poverty and poor conditions to be found in Dublin's depressing slums; far from avoiding them, he constantly passed through them on his way to work. However, like many of his generation he tended to speak little of them, regarding them simply as being an integral part of the city in which he had grown up. He, like his aunt Cissie, enjoyed talking and laughing with the poor people and felt at ease amongst them. He relished the humour found in the plays of Seán O'Casey and laughed heartily at Jimmy O'Dea's famous interpretation of a typical Dublin fishwife.

The inhabitants of the tenement houses, who had a naturally wry sense of humour, could also be funny without realizing it; Cathal heard many amusing turns of phrase. He once encountered a woman holding the hand of a child whose head was bandaged. Seeing them, another woman remarked, 'Missus, if you had 'a' bringin' that child to me, I would 'a' curin' him. Mister Nolan the chemist sells an ointment that opens, draws and shuts.'

Cathal overheard many remarks like this and picked up the colourful vernacular of these 'characters', incorporating it into his own everyday speech. We have noted in an earlier chapter how Cathal spoke with an English accent when a child; school and then work eliminated that and replaced it with a typical Dublin working-class accent, complete with its unique phraseology, now sadly disappearing. His own father, although precise about his written English, spoke in this manner; whilst he always said 'I *done* that', he would never write it. Cathal's language became full of lively expressions and idiosyncrasies, which he used freely when relating his much-loved funny stories, mainly concerning the happenings in Guinness's Brewery. Despite Cathal's attempt to speak in a learned manner, he frequently used colloquialisms such as 'there was a man lived in Thomas Street' and the very Irish 'he was reading the newspaper and he eating his dinner'. However, he always studiously avoided the Irish language-based construction 'he's after coming in'. For him, the past tense of the verb 'to eat' was always the older form 'eat' – rarely 'ate'. Bad grammar was inadmissible.

Cathal did make an effort to revert to his original English accent on more formal occasions, though without much success. On such occasions, when speaking to people 'above his station', his language was inclined to be stiff and somewhat forced; in an effort to speak correctly he altered to pronunciation of the word 'and' (a word that he always overused) to something like '*end*'. Cathal's efforts to write in formal English were always a little shaky, despite the fact that he read copiously.

The general misery of life for many in Dublin was enlivened by the presence of many colourful characters at this period; 'Doctor' Rock made a regular appearance in College Green with a machine that gave electric shocks. These were supposed to strengthen an individual's muscles. For the price of a penny, one held a couple of handles while the current was increased. A large dial, numbered from 1 to 360, measured the current. Doctor Rock kept up a running commentary, saying, 'There's a strong man – 280,' and so on. If one managed to endure the current until the indicator reached 300, the penny was refunded.

Beside him was 'Doctor' Mitchell, who was supposed to have worked in Guy's Hospital. He displayed a large photograph of himself and sold a variety of nostrums and patent medicines in bottles for a shilling each. His hair was very long and reached to his waist.

A colourful individual who hung out of the railings of the High School in Harcourt Street making semi-political speeches was 'O.K.' President Kealy.

He was either a veteran of World War I or the Boer War. Cathal never knew why his title was prefixed with the 'O.K.' — maybe it was a catchphrase of his. He was called 'President' because the crowds who either heckled or encouraged him told him that he would become the next President of Ireland.

On one occasion when Kealy was making a speech outside Harcourt Street railway station, the crowd complained that they could not hear him properly and he was put standing on the top of a taxi. While he was speaking, the owner got into the vehicle and began to drive away, much to Kealy's consternation and indignation.

An aristocratic lady who frequented the Harcourt and Hatch Street areas of Dublin regularly walked around in an Edwardian costume consisting of a grey dress, a coat, a feather boa and a large hat that would have been fashionable in the 1890s or 1900s. Cathal's mother told him that she was a doctor's widow and that she probably lived in Hatch Street. Apparently she carried herself magnificently.

Another lady, who was quite eccentric, lived either in Terenure or Rathgar. She wore sandals and a Chinese coolie hat. She rouged her cheeks and was always smiling. Although wealthy, she slept in a small summer house in the front garden of her house. Cathal was told that she was quite artistic.

Another feature of Dublin at that time were the barrel pianos, which were pushed around on wheels and played by turning a handle. Hanging from each one was a cage containing a budgie, who for a fee of a penny or twopence would hop onto a stick and pick out a small envelope from a drawer, in which one's fortune was to be found printed on a piece of paper.

Eighteen

An interesting person whom Cathal met in 1939 was the blind musician and arranger of Irish music Carl Hardebeck. He was introduced to him at his house in Synnot Place, off Dorset Street, by his brother Willie.

Carl Hardebeck, whose father was German and mother was Welsh, was born in Clerkenwell, London in 1870. He lost his sight when he was a baby. He was educated in London and showed a marked aptitude for music. At the age of twenty-four he moved to Belfast where he opened a music store, but the venture failed. Despite this, he remained in Ireland for the rest of his life, studying the Irish language and collecting folk songs from around the country. He lived and worked in Cork for a while, returned to Belfast and finally settled in Dublin in 1932, where he taught Irish and traditional music in the Dublin Municipal School for two years. He secured prizes at the Feis Ceoil and on many occasions acted as adjudicator in singing and musical competitions.

Although a huge, well-built man, he was shy and retiring by nature. If it were not for his bald head and the forbidding, round dark glasses that he always wore, he could have been described as a handsome man. In later life, when Cathal knew him, he suffered from bronchitis and the present of a bottle of whiskey, which would 'loosen him out', was always welcome. He spoke with a distinct Northern Ireland accent and addressed everyone as 'boss'. 'If I had my sight, boss,' he would say, 'I'd be conducting an orchestra on a cruiser.' At one time he played the organ in St Mathew's Church, Belfast. As there was an icy draught in the church, his bald head felt cold. Carl asked for and received permission to wear a priest's black biretta, which confused everyone.

Cathal mostly visited him at his house on Monday evenings, from half

Cathal as a baby, aged ten or eleven months.

The Gannon family in the back garden of 20 Longford Terrace, 1931.
Back row, left to right: Cathal, his brothers Jack and Willie, Mr Gannon.
Front row: Mrs Gannon, Mr Gannon's mother Catherine Gannon (née Beggs),
Mr Gannon's sister Alice (Sister Flora), Cathal's sister Maureen.
Seated on ground: Cathal's youngest sister, Ethna.

Cathal as a boy in the back garden of Priestfield House.

Esther Kelly (Cathal's Aunt Cissy).

Margaret Kelly (Aunt Peggy), aged thirty-two.

Cathal's future wife, Margaret Key, aged twenty-three.

Cathal in the back garden of 82 Crumlin Road, mid-1930s.

Sketch of Cathal by Grace
Plunkett, *c.* 1940.

Cathal's friend Kevin Cregan.

Professor Kevin B. Nowlan (Associate Professor of Modern History,
UCD), photographed in October 1971 for the RTÉ programme 'The
Treaty Debates'. *(© RTÉ Stills Library.)*

Cathal seated at his first harpsichord,
completed in 1952. Photographed in the
sitting room at Herberton Road, Rialto.

The dining room at Herberton Road.

Cathal working on a harpsichord in his workshop at Guinness's Brewery.
(© Guinness & Co.)

Cathal, Mrs Aiken, Lord Moyne, myself aged ten, Mirabel Guinness and
John Beckett at the reception for handing over the first Guinness-Gannon
harpsichord to the Royal Irish Academy of Music, April 1965.
(© Guinness & Co.)

Cathal, Kevin McCourt (Director General of RTÉ) and Lord Iveagh at the
reception for handing over the Guinness-Gannon harpsichord to RTÉ,
September 1966. *(© Guinness & Co.)*

The courtyard at Knockmaroon, Castleknock.

Seated at the restored Longman and Broderip square piano at
Knockmaroon.

Cathal at his harpsichord based on a model by the French maker Pascal
Taskin, at Knockmaroon, 1978. *(Courtesy of* The Irish Times.*)*

Cathal with his honorary MA degree,
Trinity College, July 1978.

With John Beckett in China,
July 1980.

Cathal's best friend, William Stuart, conversing with Mary Dunne, wife
of the singer Frank Dunne. Patrick Horsley in the background.

past seven until ten o'clock. Cathal remembered that he was never offered a cup of tea. The house was small; it had a living room, a bedroom and a kitchen at the back. Carl's third wife, a stout and homely woman, was usually there. After Carl had drunk a glass of whiskey, he would play and sing at the drop of a hat. Cathal loved to listen to him playing his excellent arrangements of Irish melodies on a magnificent Schiedmayer harmonium. The instrument had a 'percussion' stop, which Carl used to great effect. Carl also owned a Knauss piano, but played the harmonium by choice. Cathal considered him to be a 'first class musician'; he could talk about plainchant 'until the cows came home'. He and Cathal often listened to classical music on the radio. Cathal learned a great deal from him and began to share his love of Irish melodies, especially slow airs. Cathal subsequently borrowed the George Petrie *Complete Collection of Irish Music* from the library and played some of the pieces at home. Following Hardebeck's style, he learned to harmonize the melodies in a similar manner. Cathal's fondness was for arranged Irish music; unlike Hardebeck, he was never that much enamoured of the traditional style.

Cathal often brought somebody else with him to Carl's house, such as Kevin B. Nowlan, Margaret, his brother Willie or his sister Maureen, and Carl was always delighted to receive them.

Cathal always felt that not enough attention was given to Hardebeck, who was one the instigators in the revival of Irish music; indeed he was largely forgotten about after his death. This was probably due to his mixed origins and place of birth. Cathal considered Carl's arrangement for orchestra of *The Lark in the Clear Air* to be wonderful; he heard it being played on BBC radio. Carl, however, was content to sell it to the music publishers Boosey and Hawkes for just six guineas.

Sometime early in 1939, Margaret came to Dublin on one of her regular weekend visits. As usual, Cathal met her at the boat on Saturday morning and brought her into Dublin. On this particular occasion he seemed rather distant and surprised Margaret by saying, 'I won't be able to see you until this afternoon because I have to go and see my aunt.' Margaret realized that something must be amiss as he could visit his aunt at any time. She was left on her own that morning and met Cathal again after lunch. Naturally she wondered why, if Cathal did not want to see her, he had not told her in advance and saved her the tiring journey by overnight train and boat to

Dublin. She was disturbed by Cathal's changed attitude to her – he offered no explanation – and the visit was unpleasant. Shocked, she returned to Harrow, wondering if he had met some other young lady.

Cathal himself remained silent on this point, merely commenting that they had broken off their relationship and stopped corresponding because they were 'not in agreement as regards religion and little things like that'. Could it have been possible that his parents or relatives did not favour him befriending an English Protestant or did he have his own personal qualms about the relationship? Margaret's impression was that his parents, especially his father, quite liked her. Mai and Billy, Cathal's aunt and uncle, certainly held her in high regard and told Cathal that she was 'too good' for him.

The fact that he might have tired of her and used religion as an excuse to break off the relationship with her is possible. That summer he, Dan White and Michael Wall took themselves off on holidays to Torquay in Devonshire and had photographs of themselves taken on a beach embracing a couple of well-endowed English girls dressed in swimsuits.

Apart from the girls, one of the thrills during this holiday was a fairground where the three lads spent an evening – and a small fortune – on the roundabouts, swings and chairoplanes. They got into a swingboat together, spent most of the evening in it and swung themselves so high that the man in charge threatened to apply the brake if they would not comply with the safety regulations.

Whilst having a meal with the lads, both of whom were puffing on fags, Cathal was challenged to smoke a cigarette. He had smoked a little in the past but was not interested. He accepted the challenge and afterwards said, 'That's the last cigarette I will ever smoke.' He never touched another one.

Cathal always associated this holiday with Beethoven's Piano Concerto No. 3, which he had heard being played on the radio and which he and the two lads continually lilted or whistled. They also hummed the melody of a mazurka by Chopin.

In September, Margaret went on a holiday to Newquay in Cornwall with a colleague named Marjorie Johnson and stayed in a guest house on the seafront. Towards the end of the holiday, which proved very pleasant, World War II began.

Margaret's friend Kathleen Reynolds left England at this point for the safety of Ireland and married Cathal's brother Willie in Dublin.

In Harrow, on the outskirts of London, life went on as normal for quite some time and one could be forgiven for thinking that no war was taking place. After some time, of course, the German planes did appear and began to bomb the city. Friends of the Clenches were killed in Coventry when a bomb fell on their house; the couple had been hiding under the stairs.

The all-clear signal was given every morning when Margaret set out for work but the air-raid siren sounded in the evenings when she returned home. She was therefore always anxious to be back before six o'clock. From then on, until the all-clear was given on the following morning, one was at the mercy of the German bombers. The low-flying aeroplanes made an alarming noise and bombs could be heard falling and exploding intermittently throughout the night. Several firebombs were dropped on the houses in Spencer Road, setting the roofs alight. Margaret remembers being terrified out of her wits one night when an aeroplane roared very low overhead – she expected the house to be hit at any moment, but fortunately it was not.

Shelters had been erected in the street for those who were afraid to stay in their houses at night. Although the Clenches were as frightened as anyone else, they did not use the shelters; they stayed at home and hoped for the best. Following the example of many other people, Margaret tried to sleep under the table in the dining room for protection but soon gave it up for the comfort of her bed, thinking that if a bomb was destined to fall on the house, there was nothing she could do about it and that she must take some rest. Fortunately the family and the house survived the grim onslaught but neither Margaret nor her parents escaped unscathed; Margaret's constant fear and anxiety undoubtedly contributed to her hair turning grey prematurely.

The effect of the war on the people of Ireland was relatively minor; the main side effects were the lack of basic provisions and cars being forced off the roads due to the unavailability of petrol.

In 1940 Cathal bought a square piano at the Iveagh Market for 30s ; it had been made by John Broadwood and Sons in London in about 1825. As it was not in very good condition, Cathal set about restringing it and putting new leather coverings on the hammers. It had a reasonably good sound and appearance. Cathal kept the instrument upstairs in his bedroom.

At around the same time, Cathal's belief that these instruments were worth keeping was put to the test when he read an article in the *Musical Times* about somebody who was laughed at for declaring that he had played a piano of Liszt's period, the 1820s, and that he had found it satisfactory. The piano was condemned and deemed only to be 'fit for a rubbish heap'. Cathal was inclined to take this seriously but fortunately common sense prevailed and he continued to treasure such old instruments.

In the same year, Cathal bought an Alexandré harmonium with fourteen stops for £2 at Lalor & Briscoe's, the auctioneers on the quays, no doubt having been inspired by Carl Hardebeck's instrument. It was unplayable when he purchased it but he succeeded in restoring it to playing condition. He paid another £2 to have it French-polished. Initially, he was very proud of this instrument and thought it the best of its kind. Like the Broadwood square piano, it was put in his bedroom in the house on Crumlin Road. Cathal acquired a second harmonium some time afterwards.

Cathal's friendship with Grace Plunkett continued throughout the 1940s. She loved going to Paris and went there regularly. She often told Cathal about the various museums and art galleries, and encouraged him to go. However, Cathal never went; the war made things difficult, the journey would have been long and arduous, and maybe his ignorance of the French language put him off. However he must have shown some interest, for Grace drew him a map of the city and gave it to him. On an earlier trip to Paris, Grace had bought two Japanese prints from a vendor on the banks of the Seine, which Cathal framed for her.

At around this time Grace gave Cathal a short note incorporating a sketch, which had been sent to her from the artist William Orpen. The note was written on the official stationery of the 'London and North Western Railway. Holyhead & Dublin Express Steamers. Royal Mail Route', the words of which form the hat of a caricature of Orpen himself. At the bottom is Orpen's monogram supplanted by a small cross, undoubtedly in imitation of the sacred heart. Grace studied art under Orpen at the Dublin School of Art; he regarded her as one of his most talented pupils. She also studied at the Slade School of Fine Art in London. Orpen often sketched her during her student days and painted her in 1907 as one of his subjects for a series on 'Young Ireland'. Grace offered Cathal one of these sketches and also 'This is you and this is me', a quick sketch of a missed appointment at the statue of Eros in London, but Cathal foolishly declined them.

However, Grace did a lightning sketch of Cathal on a small card, initialled G.P. (not too accurate, though capturing his likeness), and wrote a 'diagnosis' of Cathal in pencil on a piece of notepaper. It reads as follows:

DIAGNOSIS (Cathal)
<u>Probable Facts</u>
Spends undue amount of time alone.
Is silent at home where politeness does not compel conversation.
Not a deep or logical thinker – because logic not necessary in art.
Is purely the artistic type – but without the creative faculty. The
creative faculty in artists embodies the need for constantly doing
new things – in a non-creative artist this can be sublimated in two
ways – to buy and sell pictures – or antiques.
<u>Judgement</u>
Cathal therefore will never be happy unless he deals in antiques.

Lacks initiative in forms of amusements and food – could be given
the same things every day and he would not protest.

By and large, Grace's 'diagnosis' was not far off the mark. It is impossible now to know how much time Cathal spent alone or was silent, but he was never a deep thinker; he was content to learn from books or other people, form his own opinions based on what he had learned and to involve himself with antiques, art, literature and the people around him. He loved facts and figures. Whilst he held strong views about certain topics, his conversation was rarely about himself or his feelings and he preferred to talk about others, regaling the listener with anecdotes or endless pieces of unusual information. Whilst he was artistic and appreciated art, he was not a creative artist, as Grace pointed out – yet much of his work was creative and made to be admired.

Grace's last sentence is alarmingly accurate. Because of his circumstances, Cathal's amusements were simple and inexpensive: long walks, long conversations, poking around antique shops, cycling and going to the cinema. He was always a person who ate whatever was put in front of him, no matter how good or bad it was, and, if left to his own devices, he tended to eat an unvarying diet. Meals were often a bothersome interruption to his work or amusements.

In 1941 the twenty-fifth anniversary of the 1916 Easter Rising was celebrated and commemorative medals were made. Such a medal, awarded posthumously to Joseph Plunkett, was sent to Grace. She received it in the post and showed it to Cathal before intending to consign it to the bin. Cathal pleaded with her not to throw it away and she gave it to him.

Professor Kevin B. Nowlan can remember being shown this medal when

Cathal had brought him to meet her for the first time in her flat in Nassau Street. When they arrived, she said, 'There's a danger that Ned de Valera will call this evening.'

'Oh,' said Cathal, 'we'd better go and not stay here.'

'Oh no,' she said, 'you stay here because I told him I mightn't be in.'

Shortly afterwards the door bell rang. They popped their heads over the balcony and saw two cars below. 'That's Dev all right,' she said and did not answer the bell. Eventually they saw him return to his car and off he went. Cathal protested at Grace's treatment of him, but she was adamant and said, 'No – I'd find him too tedious.'

Having shown the medal to Kevin, Grace proceeded to tell him how she had remembered de Valera sitting in his Sinn Féin office, with his head in his hands, saying, 'Gracie, Gracie, what am I going to do?' Having a large family at that time and little or no income from the party, he was finding it hard to make ends meet. Grace said laughingly, 'Within a year Fianna Fáil was on the road,' implying that de Valera's financial needs were instrumental in setting up the Fianna Fáil party.

Either in late 1941 or early 1942, Cathal must have felt a pang of remorse for having distanced himself from Margaret, allowing her to suffer throughout the war in England, and wrote to her out of the blue. It is possible that he was urged to do so by his aunt and uncle, Mai and Billy, who may have thought that Cathal had acted foolishly. Margaret was delighted to receive Cathal's letter, in which he expressed his concern for her, and they began to correspond once again. Cathal now urged her to come to Dublin where she would be safe. Margaret explained how she could not give up her work, drop everything and come to Dublin, especially as British subjects were not allowed to travel outside their country at that time, unless for some specific purpose. Margaret applied for a transfer to the LMS office in Dublin, but there was no vacancy. If she were to come to Dublin, the only solution was for her to marry Cathal. As this would necessitate a change of religion, Margaret's parents were not too pleased, but fortunately they did not object.

Consequently Margaret and Cathal became engaged; Margaret bought her own engagement ring in England and Cathal paid for it. When the paperwork was completed and permission was granted for Margaret to travel to Dublin on account of her decision to marry, she procured a return ticket, in case things did not turn out as expected, packed her bags and the wedding presents that she had been given, and set off during the first week of August 1942. Her mother and stepfather accompanied her by train to Holyhead. Naturally they were both very disappointed that she had decided to go to Dublin; Mrs Clench still pictured the city as she had seen it in the 1920s and found it hard to believe that it had changed dramatically since then. She was understandably upset at the thought that she would not have Margaret at home any more. The thought that a bomb might strike the boat on its journey to Ireland was another worry for her and of course for Margaret.

When they reached Holyhead, Margaret boarded the mail boat and waved to her parents on the quayside. Because the departure was delayed and Mr and Mrs Clench had to travel all the way back to Harrow by train, they were obliged to leave before the boat set sail. Reluctantly – and no doubt tearfully – they waved for the last time and disappeared from Margaret's view. She felt sad and wondered whether she would ever see them again. Mixed with this was a feeling of anxiousness about the dangerous crossing that lay ahead and joy at the prospect of being united with Cathal once again.

Nineteen

With its portholes blackened, the ship slowly zigzagged its way across the Irish Sea in an effort to avoid detection and to make it a little more difficult for it to be bombed or torpedoed by submarines. The journey seemed endless but at last the boat docked safely at around midnight in Dun Laoghaire.

Amongst Margaret's luggage was a large box containing her wedding presents, which had to be carried by a porter. Fortunately the young official at customs was happy to read a list of its contents and not ask Margaret to open it. A large trunk containing all her clothes had been sent in advance along with the key, so that it could be opened and examined. It would be collected from customs later.

Cathal, who had waited anxiously on the quayside from nine o'clock, when the boat was due to arrive, was there to meet Margaret. Although relieved that she had made the journey safely and pleased to see her again, he would have noticed that she looked weary and that her hair had begun to turn grey – she had told him about this in advance.

Apart from being happy to be reunited with Cathal, Margaret was delighted to see the city lit up and people going about their business as she had remembered it before the war had started.

Together they travelled by train to Westland Row station. There they tried to find transport to Mai and Billy's house in Rathmines, where Margaret was to stay. Because the few taxis that existed had stopped running at this late hour, they were lucky to obtain the services of a horse-drawn cab. When they asked to be taken to Rathmines, which was quite a distance away, they were amused when the driver whispered to them, 'Sssh – don't tell the horse or else he won't go!'

They paid the driver 10s. and finally arrived at the house in Leinster Square, where Mai and Billy had kindly stayed up to welcome Margaret. Cathal had to walk home due to the lack of public transport.

Mai and Billy treated Margaret very well. They showed her to a nice bedroom at the front of the house, where she slept soundly. The house was big and comfortable and on a tram route; the journey into town cost 2d. Margaret enjoyed her three-month stay. During that time, she met Mai and Billy's friends and both she and Cathal were invited to participate in occasional musical evenings, which proved to be very pleasant. Mai had a small circle of lady friends, to whom Margaret was introduced.

Two things had to be done before Cathal and Margaret could be married: a house had to be found and Margaret had to convert to Catholicism as mixed marriages were very much frowned upon at that time. In between house-hunting, she went regularly to a convent where a nun gave her instruction. Although there were some points that she found difficult to understand or accept, she found that Catholicism and her former religion had many things in common and did not find the conversion too strange. Despite the fact that the Mass was then said in Latin, Margaret did not learn any of the language, so apart from the common prayers, which were said in English, much of the Mass was incomprehensible to her – as it probably was to many people. The priest who received her into the Catholic church, Father O'Halloran, interviewed her several times during the course of her conversion and she took the opportunity to ask him questions on points of doctrine that she could not understand. She found him very helpful and pleasant.

In the meantime, a colleague of Cathal's in the Brewery, Jim Browne, told him about a small three-bedroomed house that was for sale in Herberton Road, Rialto. Cathal and Margaret went to look at it, but Cathal was hesitant about living in the area, which was not considered to be very chic. Margaret sensibly pointed out that the house was within walking or cycling distance of the Brewery, that the terminus of the 19 bus route to the city centre was just a few steps away and that the area had its own shops.

Cathal brought his father to view the house on 16 September. When Mr Gannon expressed his approval, Cathal decided to waste no more time and bought it on the spot. He paid a £5 deposit and made arrangements for a loan from the Guinness Permanent Building Society. He and Margaret then had to wait for the legal proceedings and handing over of the house, which took much longer than expected as the former owners were slow about leaving and moving to Northern Ireland.

A charming letter from Margaret's mother to Cathal, dated 30 September 1942, reads:

> Dear Cathal,
>
> At last I write to thank you for your very welcome and greatly appreciated lines added to Margaret's letter.
>
> It is a comfort to know you are both so exceedingly happy. I know Margaret is, and she has every confidence that her future life will be all that could be desired. We sincerely hope nothing will ever destroy your faith and happiness in each other.
>
> Naturally I felt rather worried when Margaret left home, she took a risk, but now I know she has so many kind friends and is enjoying life so much, there is little else that matters.
>
> Needless to say we miss her very much, she spent most of her time at home, but it is her life and her happiness that counts; we know the break must come some time, sooner or later.
>
> We are so glad you have found a suitable house, by Margaret's description we think it must be very compact, I am sure you must be very thrilled about it. What a busy time you will have during the next few weeks. Your time will be fully occupied but I can picture you both in your little home, carefully planned and tastefully arranged, how very proud you both will be.
>
> Margaret I am sure will make a perfect housewife, everything will have to be just so in her dream house.
>
> Wishing you all the blessings that life can give, a long and happy future, is the sincere wish of
>
> > Yours affectionately,
> > A Clench.

Along one side of the envelope is a pink sticker bearing the words 'An Scrúdóir d'Oscail – Opened by Censor'. Underneath can be seen the British sticker, 'Opened by Examiner 7516'. When Margaret was in England, the censors had written to her to query Cathal's first name, which was not familiar to them; she had to write back and explain that it was the Irish equivalent of Charles. They probably wondered if it was a German name.

Although the house was in reasonably good condition, Cathal set about redecorating it, furnishing it and laying down good quality pre-war carpets. Some of the furniture was bought in Gorevan's, Camden Street, although there was little available during the war years. Cathal made much of the furniture himself, including a set of six dining chairs (which his father later copied), a hall table and the bedroom furniture. He also repaired the mahogany oval table that his mother had bought for 9s.

During the decoration of the house, Margaret used to walk from Rathmines to the South Circular Road where she caught the 19 bus to Rialto, but as the buses stopped running at 9.30 pm Cathal had to give her a crossbar back on his bicycle. They worked in the new house until midnight on the day before they were married.

Margaret and Cathal were married on Saturday, 28 November 1942 in a small side chapel of the Church of St Andrew, Westland Row. The fashion then was for couples to get married at eight o'clock in the morning and then set off on their honeymoon. Margaret was horrified at the idea of being married so early in the morning and asked for the ceremony to be held at eleven o'clock. She wore a pale mauve dress with blue embroidery; over it she wore a jacket made of the same material. As it was a cool winter's day, she wore a fur coat and a brown hat with a veil. Cathal wore a suit. The wedding was a simple, modest affair and was attended by about ten people, mostly members of Cathal's family. Because of the war, the Clenches could not come until after Margaret was married. Cathal's sister Maureen was maid of honour and his friend Kevin Cregan was best man. Cathal's parents were present, as well as Mai and Billy and his aunt Cissie.

The thought of her parents in wartime Britain did not upset Margaret's happiness, for the air raids, especially in the outlying regions of London, had subsided somewhat and conditions were not quite as dangerous as before.

After the wedding they left in a taxi for Mai and Billy's house in Leinster Square for the reception. Cathal's mother had cooked a turkey and ham; Margaret and Mai had made many of the other dishes. The wedding cake had been bought in a shop. After the meal, which was very tasty and enjoyed by everyone, Cathal played the piano and they spent the afternoon chatting.

In the evening, Margaret and Cathal went to the Abbey Theatre to see George Bernard Shaw's play *In Good King Charles's Golden Days*, which did not make much of an impression on Cathal. The fact that he did not enjoy it much was not too surprising; in the words of a modern reviewer, 'It is, without doubt, one of the worst plays ever written by Bernard Shaw, almost totally devoid of plot, historically suspect and full of endless rounds of speechifying.' (John Coulbourn, *Toronto Sun*.)

That night they returned to the comfort of their new home and the very practical though highly unusual wedding present given to them by Grace Plunkett: two single beds. She had also given them an oil painting on ply-wood entitled 'Parisian Gaieties' by J. Humbert Craig. John Burke had bought this for nine guineas from the artist, though Cathal was not supposed to know this. This picture, along with other simple pictures in the house, would undoubtedly have been hung with a great deal of precision on two nails, using a spirit level; Cathal hated to see pictures hung crookedly.

Another welcome present was a pound of tea, given by a Brewery col-league. Because of the war, tea was quite scarce; only half an ounce was allo-cated per week per person. Consequently, Margaret and Cathal kept their consumption of tea to a minimum and took to drinking cocoa in the evenings.

Cathal had been granted three days' special leave on top of his week's holiday from the Brewery. He and Margaret spent their 'honeymoon' putting down floor covering, decorating and waiting for furniture to arrive by horse and cart from various shops. Because of difficulties with transport, the shops could not guarantee that their goods would be delivered on time.

As the weather was cold and as both Margaret and Cathal were anxious to complete the work in the house, neither minded the lack of a honey-moon. However, Mrs Gannon was a little put out by the fact that they had not gone on one and told those who asked her about their plans that they had gone for the weekend to Enniskerry.

Another very good reason for not going on a honeymoon was Cathal's lack of money. What little he had was spent on decorating the house. Real-izing that Margaret was better qualified to look after day-to-day expenses, Cathal from then on sensibly handed his pay packet, containing £4 12s. 6d., to her every Friday, without complaint. He kept a few shillings for himself and allowed her to pay all the bills and do the shopping.

When the decorating was finished, they had a neat, comfortable and tastefully furnished house to live in – something they could be proud of, as Margaret's mother had correctly predicted. Not many small houses in Dublin had such a pleasing appearance. Many people were to comment on it, including Grace Plunkett, who regarded it as a very refined house. She told John Burke that it was the most tasteful house she had visited in Ireland.

The small gardens at the front and back were made neat and tidy; in the front garden Margaret and Cathal planted roses and lavender bushes.

Following the fashion of the time, Cathal had painted the exterior cream and a pale shade of green. Fine net Sundour curtains with a delicate floral pattern hung in the windows. Inside, the walls of the hall, landing, sitting room and breakfast room were painted plain white. Pictures of Cathal's choosing adorned the walls and a longcase clock was placed at the end of the hall, beside the door into the breakfast room and scullery. Another longcase clock was kept in the front dining room. Grace had given one of the Japanese prints she had bought in Paris to Cathal and he hung it on a wall in the back sitting room. It depicted a man (possibly an actor) holding beads, in front of an elaborate screen or panel. A reproduction of Vermeer's 'View of Delft', which Cathal had bought at Arigho's in Christchurch Place, hung on the opposite wall. Also in the sitting room was Cathal's Alexandré harmonium, the Broadwood square piano and a Pye console model radio, which Margaret had bought. This was later moved to the breakfast room. Plenty of good books were displayed around the house.

One of Cathal's colleagues in the Brewery, Matt Golding, had a look at the house from the outside and told Cathal, 'I didn't like your curtains – they just hang limply. I preferred the house next door where the woman had the curtains gathered back into brass holders.' This was in accordance with the fashion of the time. There was a flowerpot on a stand in the middle of the window with the gathered curtains; Cathal regarded this as being in rather poor taste.

Margaret found her new role as a married woman and housewife a little strange at first, but soon settled into it. It felt unusual not having to go to work every morning. At first she was not much of a cook as she had never prepared a meal before; her mother, who was a good cook, had provided all her meals in England and it had never occurred to her to learn. Because of her sweet tooth, baking cakes presented no problem but now she had to peel potatoes, boil vegetables and prepare meat, a job she hated and continued to hate.

Because she was neat and tidy and spent most of the day at home doing housework, she frequently forgot the time and did not have Cathal's dinner ready when he came home in the middle of the day. Fortunately he was patient and merely said, 'I wish you'd get the dinner ready a little earlier because I like to have a rest after dinner before I go back to work.' Gradually she learned to keep better time.

A constant source of irritation during the war years was the lack of gas for the cooker – it came on at midday and then again at six o'clock. As Cathal usually arrived home from work by ten past five and was craving for a cup of tea, he hit upon a plan. He chopped up some sticks at work and brought them home in his pocket. He put them into a tin and lit them; being dry and thin, they kindled immediately. He then put the tin into the fireplace, placed a kettle on it and within minutes there was boiling water.

At in-between times, just a glimmer of gas was available; it could provide just enough heat to boil a kettle of water if the iron ring on the top of the cooker was removed and the kettle rested on the burner. To make sure that gas was not used during these periods, a 'glimmer man' often called to people's houses at unexpected moments. In order to check if the gas had been used, the glimmer man felt the burner to see if it was hot. If one was caught, one could have the gas supply cut off for a week or two. Cathal, like many other people, kept a basin of cold water ready in the sink. If there was a knock on the door, the kettle was removed, the burner immersed in the water, replaced and the top put back. Although the glimmer man only called once or twice to the house at Herberton Road, Cathal and Margaret were always on the alert.

Cathal used to buy wet turf at Rialto Bridge from an old man who transported it from the countryside by boat. Cathal acted rationally; he bought the turf in the summer and stocked up. He and the boatman became friends and consequently Cathal was given a little extra when it was needed. When Cathal bought turf from him, he placed a sackful within the frame of his bicycle, pushed it home and returned for another, repeating the procedure until he had brought all the turf to the house. The old man constantly grumbled, saying, 'These posh people with their three-piece suites and their pianos – it'd answer them better to buy a hundredweight of turf!'

During these times of fuel shortages, other people were reduced to chopping up their furniture and burning it in order to keep warm in the winter. When a supervisor in the electricians' shop in Guinness's Brewery ran out of fuel, and one of the members of his family lay dying in bed, Cathal's father brought bundles of sticks up to the house at Mount Harold Terrace, Leinster Road.

Because of the various jobs to be done around the house, Margaret was anything but bored; she was constantly busy cleaning, washing, ironing and cooking. There was no pressure from Cathal or from the family to produce a child. Margaret's attitude was that this was a private matter and Mrs Gannon realized that questions about the possibility of having a grandson or granddaughter were not in order.

Fortunately for Margaret, Cathal's attitude towards her did not change much after marriage and he proved to be an ideal, even-tempered husband. His only criticism was that Margaret talked too much about trivial matters. He obviously regarded himself as being more academic than she was and believed that he could talk about more interesting topics. Rather than argue with him, Margaret decided to say less and let him talk more. Apart from this, there was little or no tension, though Margaret was to discover that Cathal could be difficult to live with at times. He tended to be domineering and she felt like a 'little dog running behind him all the time'.

Now that they were married, the Clenches were entitled to visit their daughter. Although they thought they would not meet again until after the war, Mrs Clench wrote to Margaret saying that she wanted to see her. Margaret invited her parents to visit them and they came in June 1943.

When the Clenches arrived at Dun Laoghaire, it was a fine sunny day. In the city centre they were amazed at the plentiful supply of fruit, vegetables, meat and butter that was available in the shops, just as it had been before the war in England. They were delighted to see how much Dublin had improved since they had seen it last and thought it wonderful to be in a city where life went on quite normally.

They were enchanted by the newly painted and decorated house and relieved that Margaret was safe and well looked after. Cathal and Margaret brought them for tram rides, bus runs and walks, and introduced them to their friends, such as the Cregans. Cathal also brought them to meet the various members of his family, and Mai and Billy Gannon invited them to their home in Leinster Square. They therefore received a very favourable impression of Ireland.

They came again for Christmas (1943) and had their Christmas dinner with Margaret and Cathal at the Gannons' house in Crumlin Road. From then on they came to Dublin twice a year, either after Easter or during the summer and around September or December. Because of Margaret and Cathal's tight financial situation and because of the difficulties of travelling to England at the time, they postponed visiting the Clenches in Harrow until 1946, when the war was over. In general, Irish people avoided travelling to England because of the dangers involved.

Because cars were off the road and as Cathal did not possess one, he and Margaret had to use public transport. In order to give themselves more freedom, Cathal bought Margaret a second-hand bicycle from Stephen Moran, the husband of his sister Maureen. The bicycle had belonged to Stephen's former wife, who had died. The government's controlled price for a second-hand bicycle then was £8, which Cathal paid.

Cathal then proceeded to teach Margaret to cycle. After a few weeks she mastered the technique and together they went for picnics to the country-side. They managed to cover many miles. With them they brought a small nickel-plated kettle-cum-teapot with screw tops both on the spout and the top. This they filled with water and placed in a light plywood box containing a little spirit stove, a bottle of methylated spirits, matches, a tea infuser, some milk, sandwiches and cakes. The box, which Cathal had made, was then attached to the carrier of his bicycle. On top of this he placed cycling capes in case of rain.

The couple regularly cycled up the Dublin Mountains or out to Brittas, where they relaxed and had their picnic lunch, washed down with a cups of freshly made tea. On Saturday afternoons they often cycled to Terenure, from where turf lorries set off for the Featherbed Mountain, transporting the men who worked in the bogs there. For 1s. 6d. they could climb up into the back of a lorry with their bicycles and go with the workmen, who some-times brought their wives with them. It was good fun and Margaret and Cathal got to know the people. They were let off either at the Featherbed or the Wicklow Gap. From there it was downhill via Luggala and Enniskerry or Manor Kilbride and Blessington, then homewards.

On other occasions, mainly on Sundays, they cycled through Blessington to Poulaphouca or visited Jim O'Dea and his wife, who lived on the main street in Celbridge. Often Cathal and Jim went for a walk together for old times' sake. They frequently left Celbridge at midnight and did not return to Rialto until one o'clock in the morning. Cathal then woke up on Monday morning at ten to seven, in time to be at work by eight o'clock.

They also made journeys into north County Dublin, to Corduff, Bally-coolin, Huntstown, St Margaret's and Finglas, then still undeveloped. Often they passed Castleknock College and peered through the trees at Knockma-roon House, which was barely visible from the road. Cathal often wondered who lived there. He loved the area and wished he could live in it sometime.

He and Margaret were enchanted by the masses of primroses growing in the hedges along the lanes near Tyrrelstown House, near Mulhuddart. When his uncle Billy Gannon had to have a carbuncle removed in the Whitworth Hospital on North Brunswick Street, Cathal and Margaret visited him and brought bunches of primroses; the nurses loved them so much that they were asked to bring more. They went to the hospital every second day and in the evenings, before they went, they cycled off to pick more primroses. In time, most of the wards were bright with the yellow flowers.

Cathal loved to escape to the countryside in this manner and savour the fresh air. Rialto and the surrounding area had become built-up; during the winter months, one never saw a tree from one end of a week to another.

Twenty

*B*y this time Cathal had given up attending the various meetings of the societies to which he had belonged and also was no longer taking long evening or weekend walks with his pals. Now his priorities were Margaret, the new house and his work in Guinness's Brewery.

Cathal had become acquainted with Sir Haldane Porter, one of the directors, when he was asked to fix a clock belonging to him some time previously. Sir Haldane, who had come from England to work in the Brewery, had lived in Dalkey; he moved to 98 James's Street when commuting in and out of the city became difficult during the war years. The house was elegant and had fine interior plasterwork. The bath had to be repositioned to accommodate Lady Porter, who was crippled.

When Cathal went to this house, he took notice of the beautiful furniture, library of books and collection of clocks that Sir Haldane had brought from England. Cathal was shown a late seventeenth-century longcase clock decorated with marquetry. Fixing it proved to be easy: it was simply a matter of untangling the cords to which the weights were attached and oiling the movement.

From then on, Sir Haldane summoned Cathal when anything needed attention and enjoyed talking to him, mostly about his furniture, which he realized Cathal admired. He wanted to bring Cathal to St Patrick's Hospital (known locally as the 'Number Three Brewery'), to show him Dean Swift's watch, which was kept there. However, Cathal had seen it before, along with a desk and some books that the Dean had used, whilst on a visit organized by the Old Dublin Society.

Sadly, Sir Haldane had a bad heart condition. After he retired from the

Brewery in 1944, arrangements were made for him to go to Portobello Nursing Home. On the day he was to leave, he stopped all the clocks in his house before the assistant managing director, Dr C.K. Mill, came to collect him. At the last moment, he excused himself in order to answer a call of nature. When he failed to reappear, and as Sir Haldane had locked himself into the bathroom, Cathal was telephoned and told that he was needed urgently. Having failed to open the lock, Cathal went outside, broke the window and let himself in. Sadly, he found Sir Haldane dead on the floor.

Naturally the war had an effect on the running of Guinness's Brewery; horses and carts were used for transporting goods around the city and extra barges were built for the canals. Fortunately there was no shortage of timber as, due to an error, a double order had been received and put to one side during the early years of the war. When an official suggested sending back half the timber, Cathal's father said, 'On no account – there's a war on and there'd be a shortage of timber. Hold on to everything you have.'

The Brewery had large stocks of various things that were held in reserve, in case of an emergency. One notable example of this was several thousand tons of coal fashioned into walls with passageways running between them and gates at either end; Cathal often walked through them. The authorities had taken the precaution of whitewashing these 'walls' so that if any coal was stolen, it would immediately be noticed. Nonetheless, some of the men managed to smuggle coal out in small bags hidden under their coats. They could be seen staggering out of the gates looking much fatter than usual.

A person employed by Guinness's Brewery was always envied. It was said that once you got into the Brewery, there was no further need for worry; Cathal was always conscious of this, realizing that he would always be adequately paid and looked after. Any woman who married a Brewery employee also never needed to worry; it was said that the husband was worth money both dead and alive, for after his death she would receive the widow's pension. Employees could rest assured that they would receive a good pension, which was non-contributory, though many did not live long enough to receive it. As we have seen, the Brewery had a building society and a loan scheme, various canteens, a free medical service (including dentistry and later chiropody and massage), a centre for pensioners to relax, free beer and various other perks including red flannel for old widows who might need it during the cold winter months. Cathal came across two large bales of this flannel in a cupboard during the 1960s.

At this period coopers still worked in the Brewery, making wooden barrels for the stout. As they were paid according to piecework, they worked very hard indeed, starting and finishing when they liked, as they did not have to keep regular hours. Cathal remembered seeing them eating their lunches with one hand and wielding a hammer or some other tool with the other. They also drank like fish. When they had finished making a barrel, they rolled a piece of newspaper into a cone, filled it with stout and drank it. They then screwed up the paper and threw it on the floor, destroying the evidence.

As we have noted in an earlier chapter, employees were allowed to drink a certain amount of Guinness in the various 'taps' around the complex, either according to their daily allowance of two pints or on production of a 'scrip' or a beer docket issued by a senior member of staff. The scrips resembled a tram ticket; they were blue, were torn off a roll, had 'One Pint' and a serial number printed on them, and were stamped on the back with the date. Once they were used, they were torn in two and thrown into a bin.

Cathal came across some of these torn scrips and, out of a sheer sense of 'divilment', decided to see if they could be repaired. Matching the two halves and putting one on top of another, Cathal discovered that having cut through them with a sharp knife held against a straight edge at an angle of about twenty degrees, he could glue them back together with Durafix. Once the glue had set, the join was invisible. He erased the date stamp by using a piece of fine sandpaper and stamped them again.

Cathal gave the repaired scrips to his colleagues, who used them successfully in the taps. Some of the tap workers wondered why the repaired scrips did not tear in the same way as the new ones – they tended to break cleanly into two halves. Soon they became suspicious.

A good-humoured member of the staff, who was well known for his generosity when it came to issuing beer dockets to the workers, had an idea that Cathal was somehow responsible for the superabundance of scrips, but never said anything to him. The theory was that somebody must have had a printing press in the Brewery and that the old numbers were being reused. Cathal eventually ceased his experiment when he realized that it might get out of hand.

The aforementioned member of staff told Cathal that when he went out on pension, the authorities, who knew about his generosity, presented him with a beer docket, bearing his signature, for fifty-three pints. He denied ever having issued this docket or having written his signature on it and concluded that somebody must have forged it. Obviously some workers were having a party and had run out of drink; using the forged docket they had managed to get what they wanted. The man laughed at the incident and merely said, 'Good luck to them!'

Cathal, forever up to his tricks, succeeded in obtaining some methyline blue dye from a colleague in the pharmacy and amused himself by placing pinches of it into worker's pints when they were not looking. The unfortunate men received the fright of their lives when they discovered that their urine was blue! Fortunately, the dye was harmless.

Pilfering beer continued unabated, despite measures taken by the authorities to stop it. One method of carrying stolen Guinness was to use a spotlessly clean bucket and mop, into which the stout was poured. The result, of course, looked like genuinely dirty water.

At around this time, Cathal was shown a short section of piping that looked for all the world like a porcupine, for sticking into it were hundreds of little wooden plugs. The pipe, which protruded from a wall, had once carried stout from one building to another. The men had knocked holes in it with a nail, helped themselves and then, when finished, had plugged the holes with thin wedges of timber. As this was effectively hidden in a back alleyway it was not discovered for a long time. When eventually found, the pipe was removed and re-routed, and the holes in the wall were filled with cement.

In the early days of the Brewery, when Guinness was not produced abroad, an extra-strong brew was made for export. Because of its strength, it kept in good condition for months aboard ships en route to other countries. This powerful drink could be sampled and drunk in what was known as the Red Biddy hut, situated in the Brewery. It had acquired its name from the strong cheap wine drunk by down-and-outs. Cathal once tried some of this 'foreign beer' and found it extremely palatable, though he had to be careful going out into the fresh air, for it went to his head immediately. He could remember his legs almost going from under him.

A colleague of Cathal's named Ben, who was 'a great man for the drink', relished this export brew and once spent most of the day in the Red Biddy hut drinking it. By the afternoon, he was so drunk that Cathal and his companions had to steer him to an old storeroom and put him lying on a bottom shelf, where he immediately fell asleep. As it was extremely cold, they wrapped him up well, using mats and coats. They locked him in and he slept soundly until about four o'clock, when they woke him. Another colleague brought him home on the tram.

Ben, who had been in the British Army and had come to work in the Brewery after World War I, was a refined Protestant at heart but he was capable of using very strong language and becoming involved in questionable situations that are best omitted from this account.

Whilst fighting in World War I, Ben came across a dead German. In one of the man's pockets were two Kropp hollow-ground razors, which Ben helped himself to. Kropp was the best brand of razor at the time; indeed, Cathal used this type himself. Ben was very pleased with his find and used the razors frequently.

However, on the day before Armistice Day, somebody rifled his knapsack, stealing both the razors and a figurine that he had found in a ruined French house some four years previously. He was annoyed at the loss of the figurine, as he maintained that it brought him good luck. When Cathal asked him to describe it, he replied, 'It was a little man with his legs crossed and a bare tummy.'

'It sounds to me like a Chinese Buddha,' suggested Cathal.

'That's what it was,' he said, 'it was a Chinese Jaysus! I never had any luck since I lost it – the curse of God on the man that stole it from me!'

Cathal continued to amuse himself by playing pranks, often with the help of his colleagues. In this way he earned the nickname 'ructions Gannon'. He became notorious for either starting an argument or introducing a topic that he knew would not go down well with certain individuals. Often he praised a person who deserved no praise; that was enough to rise tempers. Once he had started or encouraged an argument, he walked away, leaving the men to fight amongst themselves. Cathal's explanation for teasing his colleagues or playing pranks on them was that the working day was long and tedious; the men, who were not given tea breaks, needed some type of escape. Such relatively harmless amusements relieved boredom, provided a certain amount of entertainment and helped release pent-up energy and anger.

During the war years, there was no proper wash room for the carpenters. However, in the workshop was a big sink, about 4 ft by 3, with a supply of hot and cold water. Mounted on the wall was a large tray containing liquid soap. At about ten minutes to five, before they knocked off, the men came in, dipped their hands into the liquid soap and plunged them into the water to wash it off. Sometimes Cathal or his pals washed their hands in a small amount of water a little earlier and, having dirtied the water, filled up the sink with scalding water. By and by the other men came in, talking and laughing. Cathal and his accomplices did their best to distract them by chatting to them whilst drying their hands. Seeing that the water had already been used, they dipped their hands in the soap and, as usual, plunged their arms, up to their elbows, into the boiling water and roared. Needless to say, the language that they used was 'choice', as Cathal described it.

As the holes in the ceiling above the sink were still there from previous years, Cathal often stationed himself upstairs in his workshop with a brass garden syringe full of water, which he aimed at the tray of soap through one of the holes. He waited until a group of men had gathered round the sink, then gave the syringe a quick jab, causing the soap to splash into the men's faces. The water hitting the metal container made a noise like thunder. As can be imagined, Cathal was treated to a volley of curses.

Cathal also aimed his syringe at a hot steam radiator downstairs. When work was slack and the supervisor was out, the men turned up the heat and sat around the radiator, chatting. On one occasion, when Cathal was directly overhead, he carefully poured a bucket of cold water over the radiator, which was turned up full. There was a loud hiss as the water exploded into a great cloud of steam. The workmen all jumped back, including one individual who had just come out of hospital, having undergone a hip operation. Most of them were saturated with the steam and boiling water. They all thought that the radiator had burst, but eventually they realized what had happened. It had taken them all by surprise.

Even colleagues answering the major office of nature were unable to escape from Cathal's pranks. At one stage the workmen's toilets – perhaps they were temporary – consisted of cubicles containing holes in a wooden seat over a common channel of water than flowed from one cubicle to the next. Cathal and his pals conceived a devilish plan to float lighted wads of newspaper in the water, which floated down the channel under the toilet seats, much to the consternation of the men in the cubicles. The roars and shouts could be heard some distance away.

Mice were a constant menace in the Brewery. One time, a workman made a large trap and caught twelve live mice in it. As the men did not know what to do with them, Cathal suggested that they bring them down to the cats, but they did not like the idea. They looked down from a window to James's Street and saw three or four women underneath, talking to one another. Opening the trap, they 'poured' them out of the window. The mice did not fall, but *ran* down the wall and scattered in all directions under the women's feet. The men could hear the women's screams clearly from the window high above.

One man in the Brewery had two hard hats: one that he wore when working and the other that he wore when coming to work and going home. Both of them were old and tattered. One day, Cathal decided to do a job on the man's 'going home' hat. He cut it down in height and made it look like an old-fashioned parson's hat.

Just before the bell went at five o'clock they started an argument with the man and, whilst he was distracted, somebody clapped the hat on his head and urged him to go home. He walked all the way to Rathmines wondering why people were looking at him strangely. When his wife opened the hall door, she said, 'What's wrong with your hat?'

The poor man was in a terrible state. He had felt the top of his hat touching his head and had thought that his hair was brushed the wrong way.

An engineer by the name of Mr Hiscock discovered hard hats at a sale in Frawley's of Thomas Street for 3s. 11d.; as they were too good to be missed, he went in to look at them and discovered that they were of quite good quality. He tried one on and as it suited him, he bought it. He returned with it to his office, put it on a peg and used it as a second hat.

Proud of his new bargain – hats of that calibre cost about 21s. at that time – he showed it to everyone, advising them to purchase one before the sale finished.

Dickie Burgess, who shared an office with Mr Hiscock, decided to play a trick on him and took himself off to Frawley's, where he bought a similar but cheaper hat. During Hiscock's absence, he exchanged the 'bargain' hat with the cheaper one, placing it on the same peg. When Mr Hiscock returned, Dickie and a few of his workmates went into his office, started a row with him and in the course of it, Dickie threw the hat on the floor and put his foot through it. As the reader can imagine, Mr Hiscock was anything but amused!

Although he was liked by everyone, the unfortunate Mr Hiscock was frequently the butt of jokes. He was wont to carry an umbrella on his arm, though he seldom used it. However, when it began to rain one day whilst he was in College Green, he opened it and out fell a pound of confetti that his Brewery colleagues had placed in it some days previously.

When he was out sick for a few weeks, everyone enquired about him.

When it was discovered that he was due back to work on the following Monday, Dickie Burgess went to the visitors' waiting room and obtained three dozen postcards of the famous advertisement for Guinness, depicting a man pulling a cart with a horse in it. He then bought three dozen stamps, stuck them on the cards and invited everyone who came into the office to write 'get well soon' or some similar set message on them. Dickie then posted them all, in one go, to Mr Hiscock's address in Mount Merrion Avenue.

Poor Mr Hiscock was woken either on the Friday or Saturday morning by a noise in the hall. The postman had become so fed up putting the thirty-six postcards through the letter box that he placed wads of them in it and banged them with the palm of his hand, so that some of them shot up the stairs towards the bedrooms and others down the short flight of steps to the kitchen. The hall was littered with them. Mr Hiscock was not a very happy man when he returned to work on the following Monday morning; he entered his office cursing 'the bloody eejit' who had thought of the idea.

When Cathal and some helpers had to remove a desk from Mr Hiscock's office, they were obliged to turn it sideways as it was too wide to go out through the door. As they did, Mr Hiscock exclaimed, 'Ah – now, *that* accounts for it!' As Cathal and the lads did not know what he was talking about, they asked, 'What is it, Mr Hiscock?'

'Look,' he said. Tacked to the underneath portion of the desk by means of a couple of rusty drawing pins was the skeleton of an old fish. The odour had bothered Mr Hiscock for a long time; he had been opening windows and blaming men with smelly feet. He could never discover the source of the smell. It transpired that his colleague Dickie Burgess had affixed the offending fish to the underside of his desk some years previously over a bank holiday weekend when Mr Hiscock was absent.

Dickie Burgess, who was a prankster like Cathal, seemed to have a propensity for placing smelly fish in out-of-the-way places. He wired a herring to the engine of a little Ford 8 motor car belonging to a Miss Wadsworth, who worked in an office in the Brewery. When she left in her car after work, the herring began to fry on the engine as she approached Christchurch Place. Seeing Dickie walking along the street, she stopped and offered him a lift. When he got into the car, he sniffed and said, 'Is there a fish and chip shop here?'

'No,' she said, 'but I can get the smell of fish!'

As they drove towards College Green, the smell worsened and by the time they reached the Bank of Ireland, blue smoke had begun to emerge from the bonnet. They had to stop and Dickie was forced to disconnect the fish, which by now was sizzling. His clothes stank of fish afterwards.

Dickie interfered with yet another car – that of Dr Jackson, who was a scientist in the Brewery. He owned an old-fashioned open 'bull-nosed' Morris car. Dickie gave Cathal a referee's whistle and instructed him to make a wooden plug, one inch in diameter. The whistle was to be set in the plug and several small holes had to be bored around the plug. Cathal was given precise measurements and made the plug very accurately. At an appropriate time, a fitter went outside to Dr Jackson's car, disconnected the silencer and exhaust pipe, and placed the gadget inside the exhaust pipe before reconnecting it.

When Dr Jackson left work at four o'clock, Cathal made it his business to be in the vicinity. He watched Dr Jackson take out the starting handle and crank the engine into life. As soon as it started, the whistle began to shriek; it could be heard all over the place. Dr Jackson tried to make it quieter, but it would not stop, even when the engine was just ticking over. As he realized what had happened and had no tools with him, he simply had to abandon the car, go home by some other means and ask a fitter to remove the whistle the following day.

Twenty-One

*O*n Saturday, 10 February 1945, Carl Hardebeck died; Cathal attended a Radio Éireann-sponsored symphony concert in the Capitol Theatre that began with a graceful tribute to the great man: a sympathetic perform-ance of his orchestral variations upon *Seoithín Seo*.

Cathal attended the state funeral, which was held in St Joseph's Church, Berkeley Road. The church was packed; various government ministers, the Lord Mayor and representatives of the President and Mr de Valera were there. Hardebeck's own *Kyrie* and *Agnus Dei* were performed at the Requiem Mass. He was laid to rest in Glasnevin Cemetery, where the *Benedictus* was chanted by the clergy present. Cathal was sorry to lose his good friend. He would have concurred with the sentiments expressed in a vote of sympathy issued by the Irish National League of the Blind to Hardebeck's widow and relatives, in which the hope was expressed 'that the nation as a whole would not be unmindful of the important contribution which the late Dr Harde-beck had made to Irish culture, music and art'.

When the war ended on 6 August 1945, things slowly began to return to normal; cars reappeared on the roads, gas was restored to full strength and provisions that had been in short supply became available in the shops once again. In Guinness's Brewery, men who had been on service during the war returned to work.

At some point during the year, Bill Lycet retired and Mr Gannon, Cathal's father, was made foreman of the carpenters' 'top shop' in the Brew-ery. The assistant foreman was now a man named Stephen Greene.

Cathal sold his Alexandré harmonium to Pigott's of Grafton Street and in September bought a Schiedmayer upright piano in a private house in Beechwood Avenue. As it was in fair condition, very little restoration work was necessary. It was black, had a marquetry panel at the front and had a good, pleasant tone. The Broadwood square piano that had been in the back sitting room in Herberton Road was moved upstairs to the front spare bedroom and the Schiedmayer put in its place. The Pye radio was probably moved to the breakfast room at this stage, where it could be listened to in less formal surroundings.

From then onwards, Cathal and Margaret began to hold musical evenings in their house on Saturdays. Frequent visitors to the house were the singer Patricia Lalor and her boyfriend Paddy Agnew. The young couple married later and spent their honeymoon in Glengarriff, having heard all about the place from Margaret and Cathal.

Patricia, who lived in Longford Terrace just a few doors away from the Gannons, was one year younger than Cathal's young sister Ethna, who had died when she was nearly twelve; the two girls had been close friends. Patricia was fond of Cathal from an early age and was always anxious to tell him everything that happened in her own household. She loved to sit in the back seat of the Gannons' car in the garage, making clothes for her dolls. When Cathal drove the car down the lane, he encouraged her to steer it; by the age of eleven she was practically able to drive a car.

Patricia developed an interest in music and began to learn the piano, which she often played for Cathal. She remembered the upright piano in the sitting room of the Gannons' house and the two harmoniums, one in Cathal's bedroom and the other in the glass conservatory. Cathal remembered bringing her to some symphony concerts in the Mansion House in the early 1940s in order to encourage her and she remembers sitting beside him in the balcony on the left.

Patricia had fond memories of the musical evenings in Margaret and Cathal's house. Her friend Gertrude Leahy, who was also invited, was a fine pianist and sensitive accompanist. Like Patricia, Gertrude had won several competitions in the Feis Ceoil. Her sister Ada, who came with her to the Gannon household in Rialto, was a good singer. As the two sisters lived in Portrane, quite a distance away, they often stayed overnight in the spare bedroom and caught a train home on Sunday. At the time, Cathal and Margaret were minding a bedroom suite for Kevin Cregan, who was about to get married.

Other guests included Daphne Regan, a pianist and friend of the Leahys, and Molly Concannon, a cellist in the Radio Éireann Symphony Orchestra.

Mai and Billy Gannon came occasionally and invited Cathal and Margaret to their home for a few musical evenings, though as the couple aged the invitations tailed off. Margaret remembered being encouraged to sing by a man who was at one of the parties. He asked her 'Do you sing?' and when she said 'No,' he took her over to the piano, struck a note and asked her to sing it. Margaret was reluctant to do so, but complied as the man was so insistent. He said to her: 'All you've got to do is breathe properly and then you can sing. Your diction is perfect.' He was correct on this point; Margaret always spoke very clearly and precisely, and never lost her English accent.

Apart from enjoying the music, Margaret and Cathal's visitors also relished the suppers that Margaret prepared in advance on Fridays, when she baked various cakes and buns. Sandwiches were made on the Saturday evening before the guests arrived at about eight o'clock. Supper was generally served between ten and eleven o'clock in the front dining room.

As the new piano needed to be tuned now and then, Cathal obtained the services of a piano tuner whom he had used some years previously when living in the Crumlin Road: Cyril Byrne, who lived in Harold's Cross. He worked in Pigott's during the day and in the evenings attended to his own personal customers.

Cyril was a large, burly man with a fat face and a little mouth. He was a great character and had a heart of gold. Cathal loved to listen to his ample stock of funny stories, which were all about the pianos and people that he came in contact with. He frequently complained of the poor quality pianos that he had to tune and usually began grumbling as soon as he entered the hall.

'Where were you, Cyril?' Cathal would ask him.

'Oh, I was across in Ballyfermot tryin' to tune an old mangle of a piano,' he replied on one occasion. He then described the technical details of the instrument. 'While I was tunin' it, the woman put her head round the door and said, "Mr Byrne, are you finished with the piano?" "No, missus – the piano has *me* finished! Where did you buy it?" "I bought it in Pigott's. The man said it was a good piano and it cost £250." "Well, begod, you wouldn't get 250 pence for it now." "But the man said it was a good piano." "What the hell else would he say when he was sellin' it to you?"'

He went into another house in Ballyfermot and was amazed when he discovered a high-class German piano there. Without thinking, he said to the woman: 'I didn't expect to find a piano like that in this neighbourhood.'

'What's wrong with the neighbourhood?' she asked.

'Oh, nothin',' he said hastily, 'the neighbourhood is all right – I'm not saying a word about it, but that fellow Walton down in Camden Street is floggin' awful pianos around this neighbourhood. I've just done them recently and I expected that this was goin' to be another one and I'm agreeably surprised.' This was the way he wriggled out of his faux pas.

He told Cathal on another day when he called, 'I've just come from a house and I found it hard to get into it – the woman wouldn't answer me knocking on the door. Well, I wasn't goin' to go away and so I took it out on the knocker. The next thing this oul' one opened the door. It was easy known she didn't make herself – she was as ugly as sin. I went into the piano and found it was a bloody old spring and looper [a technical term for a certain type of cheap action or mechanism]. I tried to tune this dreadful old thing but you might as well be trying to tune the railings in the park.'

The most unusual party that Margaret and Cathal ever attended had to be the one held by the McNamaras in Christmas 1945, when entertainment by a musical family had been promised. Cathal wondered what lay in store as the McNamaras' piano was old and in very poor condition.

Cathal and Margaret travelled to Rathfarnham by tram. They were surprised to find Grace Plunkett there; she had dropped in unexpectedly. They joined the guests and sat down to a 'knife and fork tea' in the back dining room and afterwards came through the folding doors to the sitting room just as the musical family arrived – they had been delayed. There was a father, a small daughter and two tall sons. The guests now sat around a huge log fire, making polite conversation.

After the musical family had eaten, they joined the guests and set about organizing themselves. Sheaves of music, music cases of songs and piano pieces were pushed over people's heads, followed by a violin and then 'a dreadful-looking banjo, all chromium-plated glitter'. Grace looked horrified. She said, 'Good God, Cathal, did you know that this was going to happen?', got up and left the room, causing a great deal of embarrassment. She went upstairs and joined Mrs McNamara, who was in a delicate state of health and resting in bed. Grace spent the rest of the evening with her.

Cathal said to the girl who was about to play the piano, 'I'm sorry for you because the piano is, as far as I know, a major third down in pitch. Also, the centre is in tune but the extremities are wildly out of tune.'

'Ah,' she said, 'any piano is better than no piano!'

The 'music' started with a rendition of Schubert's Overture to *Rosamund*, performed on the piano, violin and banjo. As the McNamaras' little upright Victorian piano was so low in pitch, and the violin and banjo had to be tuned down to it, the banjo strings were 'loose and flopping around'. The music was dreadful. Despite this, Eva McNamara was ecstatic and repeatedly said: 'Isn't it lovely! Isn't it wonderful!' Cathal's cautious response was: 'I never heard the like of it before – it's most unusual!'

The overture finished, songs were sung and everyone present was encouraged to join in. One of the songs was 'The Teddy Bears' Picnic'. One of the sons, who sang in the Palestrina Choir, handed Margaret a pile of music and asked her to select the songs that she liked best. She unwittingly chose about twenty and the lad proceeded to sing every single one of them.

Afterwards there was a lull and Cathal began to talk about music and concerts. He discovered that the daughter had been to several of the symphony concerts that he had attended in the Round Room of the Mansion House. They also discovered that they had been at the same students' concerts in the Royal Academy of Music in Westland Row.

After a while the father became a little uneasy and said, 'Not so much talk about music – let's get on with the playing!', and it started again.

Matt McNamara, who was sitting back, smoking a big cigar and enjoying the entertainment, was treated to a selection of Negro spirituals, which he was fond of. At this point 'the banjo came into its own', as Cathal said.

As the trams stopped running at about half past nine or ten o'clock, Cathal saw Grace off. 'Cathal,' she said to him, 'how can you stand it?'

'Well, it's so dreadful that it's funny, Grace,' replied Cathal. 'I'm enjoying it!'

'What an awful tribe of people!' she said. 'They look like a family of plumbers!'

He and Margaret eventually left at about one or two o'clock in the morning. They collapsed on to the footpath outside the house, helpless with laughter and could proceed no farther for some minutes. They then walked all the way back to their house in Rialto.

At around this time, Cathal and Margaret travelled by tram to Ranelagh, where they visited Kevin Cregan and his wife Eithne at their home in Moyne Road. They had hesitated about going as they both had slight colds. Eithne convinced them that the best remedy was a shot of poteen, which she happened to have in stock; a bottle of the brew had been sent to her from her relatives in Tubbercurry, County Sligo. After supper she heated some milk and added a generous dash of poteen to it. Cathal and Margaret drank it; it was so strong that Cathal felt that it had 'burned a hole' in his stomach. They then walked all the way home to Rialto, a distance of nearly three miles, went to bed and woke up the following morning feeling completely recovered. However, neither of them could remember walking home!

Apart from live music at home, Cathal was able to enjoy a good selection of music when the new BBC Third Programme (now Radio 3) began broad-casting from London in 1946. At first, programmes were only to be heard in the evenings. Thanks to this station, Cathal became familiar with a wide selection of music from medieval to modern. He stayed with this station for the rest of his life, listening to everything it had to offer and making his own decisions as to what he liked and disliked. Gradually he began to conclude that anything too early or too late did not suit his taste; whilst he showed a great interest in eighteenth-century music, he favoured the classical and romantic composers such as Haydn, Mozart, Beethoven, Schubert, Schumann, Mendelssohn, Brahms, Berlioz and, of course, Chopin and Field.

In 1946, following a strike by laundry girls for longer holidays, the working classes were finally allowed to take two weeks' annual leave. Because the war had ended and restrictions had been lifted, Cathal and Margaret were able to visit Mr and Mrs Clench in Harrow during the summer. Cathal remembered cycling to St Stephen's Green in order to have himself photographed for a passport and leaving his bicycle outside the shop, unlocked. It simply was unnecessary to padlock a bicycle in those days.

As rationing and a scarcity of dairy produce still existed in England, Cathal obtained a special export licence for several dozen eggs, which he brought over in a specially constructed wooden box. However, the customs officials failed to notice small wedges of cheese packed in between the eggs and five pounds of butter hidden underneath the false bottom that Cathal had made. Although the box was quite heavy, Cathal had to give the impression that it was light. Whilst in England, Margaret and Cathal borrowed bicycles and repaid the people for their kindness by giving them a pound of butter.

Whilst travelling over on the mail boat, Margaret and Cathal met an Irish lady who told them that she baked cakes very successfully using liquid paraffin instead of cooking oil or margarine, which were not available then. Margaret and Cathal decided to try it out. Just to make sure that it was safe, Cathal checked with the chemist in Dolphin's Barn, who told them it would be harmless. The results were wonderful and Margaret's cakes and buns rose as they had never risen before. Their friends expressed their horror when Cathal hinted that some people were actually using liquid paraffin for baking.

Mai Gannon was one of the people who sampled Margaret's cakes and enjoyed them. She asked Margaret how she managed to do so much baking. Cathal explained that the lady next door used to give them butter from the country. This she did, but as it was always rancid, they never used it. 'As a matter of fact,' said Cathal to Mai, 'only the other day I heard of somebody who used liquid paraffin for baking.'

'Ooh! The thoughts of it!' said Mai, shuddering.

Margaret and Cathal never told any of their friends about their secret ingredient.

Twenty-Two

C athal met Sir Charles Harvey, assistant managing director and director in charge of personnel, sometime around 1946 in Guinness's Brewery. Having studied at Marlborough and the Royal Military College, Sandhurst, he had become a major general in the British Army and had spent some time in India. Cathal found him a very pleasant and interesting man. Sir Charles made it his business to meet everybody as far as it was possible and put aside days for simply ambling around the Brewery, mixing with the people.

Like Sir Haldane Porter, Sir Charles lived in 98 St James's Street during the time he worked in Guinness's Brewery. With him were his wife, Lady Harvey, his daughter and two sons. One of his sons took some two-hour lessons in carpentry from Cathal and managed to make a couple of picture frames, complete with glass and a backing. He sold them to his brother for 1s. 6d. and wanted to give Cathal half the money. Cathal was very touched by this simple gesture.

When Sir Charles retired in 1962 and became chief steward of Hampton Court Palace in London, he gave Cathal a present of a fountain pen. He made Cathal promise to visit him at Wilderness House, adjacent to Hampton Court but unfortunately Cathal never went. This was typical of him; he often missed opportunities like this, for he always felt uncomfortable about open invitations and having to telephone people out of the blue – he preferred an invitation with a definite time and date agreed by the host with no prompting from him.

Cathal met Bryan Guinness, second Lord Moyne and vice-chairman of the company, sometime in the mid-1940s. Walter Edward Guinness, Lord Moyne's father, had been assassinated in Cairo by the Zionist Stern gang in

1944. In 1929 Bryan married Diana Mitford, sister of the writer Nancy, and had two children: Jonathan (the present Lord Moyne) and Desmond (founder of the Irish Georgian Society). Five years later the couple divorced. Bryan then married Elisabeth Nelson, by whom he had seven children.

When Cathal was introduced to the new Lord Moyne he found himself speaking to a man in his thirties; Cathal was just five years his senior. For some reason, he had expected to see a young boy. Lord Moyne chatted to him for a few minutes and then, in his usual manner, excused himself and hurried off. Cathal met him now and then over the coming years.

Some time afterwards, Cathal remembered Lord Moyne coming to Guinness's from his home in Knockmaroon, Castleknock, on horseback; a small stable was built for his horse in the Brewery. His next mode of transport was a little Fiat car, which he used for many years. Cathal soon realized that people of this calibre rarely indulged in any form of ostentation.

Cathal was always kept busy in the Brewery by men, especially those who worked on early shifts, asking him to fix broken alarm clocks. In most cases the clocks simply needed a drop of oil, though occasionally Cathal discovered that the main spring had broken. He dealt with the latter by shortening and re-hooking it. In most cases he was able to repair the clocks and get the men out of a fix. There was always a clock in his drawer; hardly a day went by when he did not do a little job on one.

Cathal heard a story concerning an ex-army man who went out on pension one Friday evening. He lived in a 'digs' with two younger fellows who shared one bed; he slept in the other. On the Sunday night, much to the two lads' amusement, the man went through his usual ritual of preparing for work on Monday, hanging his trousers over the chair, laying out his clothes in order, winding up his alarm clock and setting the time for seven o'clock. The two young men thought that he had forgotten that he was now on pension and were curious to see what would happen the following morning. They said nothing to him and they all went to bed.

At seven o'clock in the morning the alarm went off. The old fellow jumped up and, taking hold of the alarm clock, ran over to the window and hurled it out into the street.

'I've been waiting to do that for the last forty-five years!' he shouted, jumped back into bed and promptly fell asleep.

Tom Donoghue was a pleasant though pious man, with a great sense of humour. He worked as a labourer in the Brewery. He used to go to St James's Church every evening at five o'clock to do the Stations of the Cross, accompanied by a mentally retarded young fellow named Kevin, whom he looked after.

One day Cathal fixed Tom's broken alarm clock and, setting it for ten past five, put it back into its cardboard box, wrapped it up and tied it with string. Needless to say, it went off in the church, in Tom's pocket. He was most embarrassed by the noise of the bell and the resulting howlings and twistings of young Kevin.

A labourer by the name of Frank Doyle, who lived in a small cottage in Blackhorse Lane, told Cathal that he was due to start work one Monday morning at six o'clock, which meant that he needed to be up by half past four. Unfortunately his alarm clock gave out at the last minute. He brought it to a man who might be able to fix it, but was told that nothing could be done – whatever was broken could not be repaired. The poor man was worried that he might be heavily fined for not waking up in time on the Monday morning.

As it was obviously too late to buy another clock, the man asked Frank what sort of clock he had in the house. Frank told him that it was an old 'wall wagger' with hanging weights that struck the hours, and that they did not have it striking as it kept them awake during the night. The man suggested that he wind the clock on Sunday morning at the time he went to bed in the evening, ten o'clock. He told him to observe the position of the weight at half past four in the afternoon and make a pencil mark on the wall under it. The man then told him to wind the clock once again at ten o'clock that night and place a tin basin on the edge of a table or some object at the level of the pencil line so that the weight would cause it to overbalance and fall to the floor.

Frank thanked the man for his advice and did what he had been instructed to do. In the evening he went out for a few drinks and was given a present of a dog. He brought the dog home and, as it would not settle down in the yard outside, he brought it into the kitchen and tied it to the leg of the table.

At ten o'clock he repaired to bed, having wound the clock and placed a tin basin full of knives, forks and spoons under the weight, at the level of the mark on the wall.

At half past four the following morning there was an unmerciful crash as the basin and its contents hit the floor. Jolted out of his sleep, Frank accidentally thumped his wife, hurting her in the ribs. The new dog was so frightened that it broke its lead and jumped out of the window. Frank certainly woke up!

Cathal and his workmates in the Brewery succeeded in tormenting an individual who was rather fond of drinking. The man, who worked in a small storeroom opposite the carpenters' workshop, frequently had cause to answer the minor call of nature. Because the WC was some distance away from his place of work, he used a little alleyway beside his storeroom. Cathal and his pals watched him from the window of the workshop and, as soon as he went out, they rang his telephone but hung up as soon as he ran back to answer it. Having waited a few moments, he left, and when halfway up the alleyway, the lads telephoned him again. As before, they hung up as soon as he reached the telephone. They were merciless and had the poor man running backwards and forwards.

One may wonder if any work was done in the carpenters' workshop, for Cathal and his colleagues seemed to be forever up to some sort of mischief. Somehow Cathal found the time to construct a primitive hurdy-gurdy in order to demonstrate how this medieval instrument worked and to entertain himself and the lads. He made a simple box, which acted as a soundboard, stretched a metal string over it, constructed a keyboard with keys of different widths, which stopped the string at the correct point for each key, and over the string fixed a circular wooden disc, with rosin on its edge, and a handle to turn the disc. When the handle was turned with the right hand, the disc bowed the string and Cathal was able to play the melody of a tune on the keyboard with his left hand. As Cathal said, 'It worked all right but it had a dreadful sound!'

Cathal also attached an old foot-operated bellows, which had come from a Brewery laboratory, to a tin whistle by means of a rubber tube and played tunes on it. It was handy in that he did not waste any breath playing it – indeed he could talk at the same time – but the disadvantage was that it could not be stopped immediately in an emergency. Cathal was caught one day when the supervisor came running up the stairs and somebody shouted 'nicks!' Cathal tried to hide the contraption in a hurry, but of course the whistle kept sounding until all the air had finally escaped from the bellows. The supervisor, unsurprisingly, wondered where the sound was coming from.

Various characters in the Brewery were given an assortment of nicknames. The 'Ram' Carroll had fought in World War I and was named thus after a phrase probably used in India, *ram-ram* – 'whatever that meant', as Cathal said. He brought his military decorations into work every 11 November,

Armistice Day. In honour of his achievements, he was given plenty of free drink, and was usually well 'plastered' early in the morning.

The 'Moochey' Boyle's nickname apparently derived from a word in some Indian language meaning 'tailor', though why it was applied to him Cathal never knew. The Moochey was no oil painting and spoke through a crooked mouth. He used to help Cathal's brother Jack when he worked on the vats. One of the jobs he was given was filling the vats with water. For this he used a large hose, which he was always careful to drain and put away carefully. He was very annoyed to discover that somebody had left some water in his hose when he was out sick and reported the matter to his supervisor.

Cathal and a friend decided to play a trick on him. When he was absent, they borrowed the keys to his storeroom from Stephen Greene, the assistant foreman, and proceeded to fill his hose with water. When they had filled it, it was so heavy that they had great difficulty replacing it on its hook. Moochey went to fetch it in a hurry on the following day, only to discover that he could hardly lift it. As usual, he ran to Stephen and complained. Stephen winked at Cathal and told the Moochey that he would make an exhibition of the man who had put the water in his hose.

Another individual was nicknamed 'Louse' Brown. The name stuck so well that when he was addressed 'Mouse' Brown by one of the office cleaners, he corrected her by saying, 'I'm not "Mouse" Brown — *"Louse"* Brown is my name!'

The 'Calf' Welsh, who cleaned windows, was so-named because his tongue protruded from his mouth and he often seemed to be 'chewing the cud'. Because his workmates annoyed him by calling him by this name, he went to the head brewer to complain. 'I can do nothing for you,' said the man, who was known for his rather jumpy manner. 'They call me "Hop the Twig"!'

Paddy Carroll, a fitter who had a most dreadful tongue and who could have won first prize for cursing and blaspheming, was known as 'the Bishop'. Cathal, who had once met him near Finglas, had listened to him enthusing about the countryside and wild flowers in the area. He seemed quite a different man and used no bad language. Cathal felt that he was 'playing to the gallery' and simply doing what was expected of him in the Brewery. Cathal was always very obsequious to him, calling him Mr Carroll and opening doors for him. This was enough to 'get him going'.

On Fridays he was given a certain amount of free drink in the morning. Having received his wages, he then spent his money on more drink during the lunch break, and was thus quite inebriated during the afternoon. That was when the 'fun' started. On a certain occasion he was at a hatch under a staircase ordering some nails, screws or hinges for himself. While he was talking to the man in the storeroom, with his head well into the hatch, a colleague took a large piece of plywood and piled it high with sawdust. He then went a little way up the staircase and threw it over the edge on to Paddy's neck. The resulting language was so foul that a man ran out of the door saying, 'Oh God, I wouldn't stand in this place with such blasphemy going on!'

When Paddy retired in about 1945, the head engineer asked him, 'Well, Carroll, what are you going to do with your spare time now that you're going on pension?'

'I'm goin' off on the f—in' foreign missions, sir,' was Paddy's curt reply. Shortly afterwards there was an official unveiling of his portrait in the 'Gluepot' pub in a little street at the back of the Brewery, so named because if one went in, one got stuck in it and could not come out.

Twenty-Three

*C*athal often came home from work, sat down to his tea and began to laugh at the recollection of some funny incident that had happened during the day in the Brewery. Margaret, curious to know what was making him laugh, used to ask him for an explanation.

Some of the best entertainment in the Brewery was unwittingly provided by the many odd characters who worked there, one of them being Paddy Lyons.

Although Paddy was ostensibly employed as a carpenter, his chief job seemed to consist of affixing handles to brush heads and assembling rubber squeegees; occasionally he made very crude temporary ladders and steps. However, he spent an inordinate amount of time pontificating on various subjects and starting rows amongst his workmates. Having raised tempers and set the men arguing, he often sidled over to Cathal and said to him, under his breath, 'I riz [rose] that row!'

As soon as the foreman in charge had left the workshop, he used to shout, 'Now boys, draw your breath! Have a rest!' He opened the door, which was adjacent to his workbench, so that he could observe the staircase and the comings and goings of the workmen. He often hailed a man and invited him into the workshop, saying, 'Come in round the house! Take the weight off your feet!' He then involved the individual in a discussion and before long an argument was set in motion.

As he found plenty of spare time in which to talk and read the newspapers, he formulated many pet theories, which he talked about ad nauseam. He regularly gave out about shopkeepers, accusing them of being 'daylight robbers, robbing unfortunate men, women and children. Then they're stuck up in the front of the church the first thing on a Sunday morning, having robbed unfortunate housewives and overcharged them!' If he did not argue about that all day long, he complained about the law. 'The judges get paid £12,000 a year for trying a man for his life, and yet they have twelve ignorant workmen in the jury box telling them whether the man is guilty or innocent.'

He directed more words of bitterness towards the well-educated and well-spoken members of the Brewery staff. 'The poor workin' man', proclaimed Paddy, 'has no polish: he's just a plain-spoken man but these people have la-de-da accents. You'll hear them talking on the phone to the working man and they'll say: "Kindly repeat that sentence, if you please". The working man says: "What the f—in' hell did you say?" They both mean the same thing!'

Most of Paddy's workmates soon tired of these philosophical ramblings but Cathal put on a pretence of being interested, saying, 'Begod, Paddy, you have a point there, there's no doubt about it – you're right. Every word you say is true!'

Another odd character was a gate porter named Billy Richards. He was extremely gullible and believed any story that he was told. At one time, when they were short of guides to bring visitors around the Brewery, he was given the job. However, his approach was somewhat unorthodox. Apparently he rounded up his first group by saying, 'One, two, three, four, five, six, seven … ah, twenty of you! All together now, keep together! Follow me!'

He brought the bemused visitors around and explained the workings of the Brewery in his own inimitable and repetitive style.

'This is a hopper – this is a hopper here. Now the malt is thrown in here out of the wagons – the malt is thrown in; and it goes up, it goes up, and it goes up through the house and I don't know where the hell it goes after that!'

At one point a man asked him, 'What is this for?'

'For makin' beer – what the bloody hell else do you think it's for? Come on, don't be actin' the fool! One, two, three, four, five, six, seven, eight, nine – come on, gather round me!'

Fortunately, the authorities discovered their mistake after he had brought visitors on just a few tours and he was replaced with somebody more suitable for the job.

It seemed that Billy spoke his mind to everybody, no matter who they might be. On one occasion he saw the managing director, Mr T. B. Case, cycling into the Brewery, which he did every day. On this particular morning Mr Case cycled in through the gate and down the yard, which he was not supposed to do. Billy made a megaphone of his hands and shouted, 'Law makers, law breakers – law makers, law breakers!'

Mr Case immediately jumped off his bicycle and said 'You're quite right, Richards – I shouldn't be cycling in the yard!'

Cathal met Billy shortly afterwards and said to him, 'I heard you ticked off Mr T. B. Case!'

'Oh,' said Billy, 'I did! I didn't really care if he cycled all round the place – I just wanted him to know that I was on my job!'

Billy was also a bird fancier. A friend of his named Johnny, who worked in the medical department, had a cousin who had birds. Billy met Johnny in the pharmacy one day and said to him, 'I have a young bird mopin' on the perch – mopin' on the perch; no song – no song. I don't know what's wrong with it – would you be able to help me?'

'I don't know anything about birds,' said Johnny. 'You're in the medical department!'

'Good heavens almighty,' said Billy, 'you'- supposed to understand medicine and all like that – you *should* be able to help me!'

'Well,' said Johnny, 'it might have the pox!'

'How the hell would it?' said Billy. 'A young bird – never out of the cage – are you gone mad? What do you mean by that?'

A man in the Brewery who could imitate any bird was Ned Pallas. He was extremely good and had once demonstrated his skills on the radio. He was also something of a ventriloquist and once threw his voice into a corner, giving the impression that a cock was buried under a huge pile of heavy timber. Billy heard the cock crowing, felt sorry for it and organized a group of men to release it. Of course when the timber was removed, there was nothing underneath.

Ned teased Billy by whistling like a bird behind him, though Billy never suspected him and blamed an innocent man who was passing by. Billy approached Cathal's father and complained about him, saying, 'That's a proper blackguard you have – I can't go anywhere but he's cat-calling and whistling after me!' The unfortunate man who was blamed could not whistle to save his life.

Some of the teasing that went on in the Brewery could be rather cruel. A hunchbacked labourer in the Brewery was nicknamed the 'Hump' Spillane.

One day he was out walking and had his little son sitting on his shoulders, or to be more precise, on his back. A neighbour came walking down the other side of the road. On account of a recent football match, the 'Hump' encouraged the little boy to humour the man by shouting 'Up Kerry!'

'Up Kerry!' cried the little boy in his high-pitched voice.

'That's right – up Kerry!' replied the man. 'There's a good boy now. You do what your daddy tells you. And when you go home, you'll be able to tell your mammy that you had a ride on a camel!'

A workman whom Cathal met when he returned full-time to the Brewery in 1937 was Charlie O'Connell. Charlie had been there long before Cathal's time and went on pension in the mid-1950s. He was a simple, decent man; he was short, stout and had a round, fresh face.

He played a mouth organ and, like Sir James J. Lawlor of Finglas, was tricked into thinking that he was broadcasting from the Brewery. An electrician had converted an old storeroom, where obsolete DC electrical equipment had been kept, into what looked like a studio, complete with what Charlie called a 'mitrophone' [microphone]. There was even a red light that was switched on when they went 'on air'. Charlie used to introduce himself by saying, 'Ladies and gentlemen, I am broadcasting from an unknown destination and I'm not supposed to tell where I'm broadcasting from. I'm going to play two hornpipes: "The Skillet of Crabs" and "Jenny Pickin' Cockles from the Shore".' The light was switched off in order to give him a short break and later he performed such delights as 'The Kettle on the Hob' and 'The Chapel House Reel'.

Of course, everybody he met congratulated him on his radio broadcasts and reminded him that he was being heard worldwide. All the men in the Brewery knew what he was doing and had been told what to say to him. Even people outside the Brewery knew what he was up to.

One Sunday morning, when Cathal and Margaret were in Harold's Cross Green, having attended Mass at Mount Argus, Cathal espied Charlie sitting on a seat, neatly dressed in a light grey suit. He decided to introduce him to Margaret, but said to her beforehand, 'This is the man I was telling you about. Pretend you heard him playing an accordion.'

Margaret was a little reluctant to do this, but after Cathal had made the introduction she said, 'You play the accordion beautifully.'

'Ah no, ma'am,' he said, 'it was only a sixpenny mouth organ. I hope I won't get into trouble for playing it in Guinness's. I believe I was on from Amsterdam last night – there were a lot of atmospherics but that wasn't my fault! I was on from Birmingham during the week, and I'll be on from London tomorrow night and Paris next week.'

Charlie suffered from high blood pressure and was receiving treatment from the Brewery doctor. At one stage the doctor prescribed a special diet and presented him with a list of food that he was to eat. Charlie looked at it, somewhat perplexed, and asked the doctor, 'Am I supposed to take this before or after meals?'

Cathal remembered a day when Charlie came to him and said, 'Paul,' – he could never remember Cathal's name and always called him Paul – 'there are very decent people in the Brewery.'

'There are, Charlie,' agreed Cathal, 'very nice people, when you get to know them. A lot of decent people.'

'Yes,' he said, 'there's a man gone away on his holidays to London – he went away by aeroplane.' At that time, just after the war, it was a great novelty to fly to England. 'He said to me beforehand, "I won't forget you men when I'm passing over the Brewery on Monday morning. And furthermore, when I'm in London, I'm going to call on Park Royal and find out if we're going to get a double week before Christmas." We were in the cooperage on Monday morning and we were watchin' the sky and wonderin' would his plane pass over the Brewery. Suddenly a plane came over very low – *vvvrrrm* – and we heard a bang behind us. We looked around and there was a big brown paper bag of boiled sweets! He threw them down from the plane – he didn't forget his friends! I've a sore mouth now from sucking them all day long!'

Some of his workmates had gone to a shop in Capel Street where broken chocolate and cheap sweets were sold. They had bought three and a half pounds of sweets for a few shillings. While Charlie and the lads were looking up into the sky, one of the men had lobbed the sweets over a fence behind him. However, Charlie was quite convinced that they had been thrown down from the aeroplane.

Charlie told Cathal that the man was due back on Friday week. He hoped that there would be news of the double week from the Guinness headquarters at Park Royal. Cathal was told that Charlie and his colleagues had watched all the planes on the Friday and, when a particular one passed over, a piece of paper bearing the message 'Dear Charlie, we're getting a double week' floated down from the sky. Delighted, he went around the Brewery, spreading the good news.

In the mornings, Charlie often went to a part of the Brewery where he knew he would find a group of men cooking their own breakfast. The men had a hut and were allowed this privilege as long as they did not take any more than twenty minutes to cook and eat. They used to fry rashers, sausages, eggs and tomatoes on a pan. Charlie usually came along when they had finished eating and were drinking tea. They used to say to him, 'Charlie, will you have a cup of tea?'

'Ah, I'll have a cup of tea all right,' was Charlie's standard response. He would sit down with them, drink some tea and, taking two big slices of dry bread out of his pocket, he would dip them into the remaining fat and fragments of egg and tomato in the pan, and eat them.

However, the men became a little weary of this procedure and decided to try to put a stop to it. On one such morning, they finished eating a little earlier and before Charlie arrived at the usual time, spilled the fat from the pan into a dustbin. They then took about half a pound of yellow axle grease that was used for the railway engines and put it into the pan. By the time Charlie came, it was nicely melted and mixed with the little bits of leftover food.

As usual Charlie was invited to have a cup of tea, which he accepted. Out came the slices of bread; he dipped them in the pan, coating them with grease on both sides, shook off the surplus, ate them both, sang 'Skibbereen' – a song of about forty verses – and went off about his business without making any comment.

Twenty-Four

*T*he man who provided the best amusement for Cathal in Guinness's Brewery was a labourer by the name of Charlie Malone. Cathal had known him since he had first started working in the Brewery. Charlie was a well-built man with a face that resembled an intelligent monkey; his two beady eyes stared sharply at everyone. He claimed the doctor had told him that he had a 'very strong heart'. He worked as a general helper and did all sorts of odd jobs.

He was attached to the carpenters' top shop, but as he was not much use – he always held people up – he was constantly moved from one job to another. It was his boast that he had worked in every part of the Brewery. Little did he know why!

The most remarkable thing about Charlie was his propensity to mispronounce words. Many of Cathal's workmates never noticed his mistakes and Cathal took care never to correct them. He was fascinated by the fact that somebody could mangle the English language in such a comical manner.

He often spoke about the Papal *Nunnico* [Nuncio] in the Park. His sister had a house in Greystones 'surrounded by *eucalilly* [eucalyptus] trees'. The stress in the word 'hereditary' was always shifted to the third syllable: '*he-re-DIT-ary*'. He once referred to a child who had been 'constipated [consecrated] to the Sacred Heart'. Charlie's grammar was not much better; he frequently used constructions such as 'he should have came in' or 'he might have went out'.

Cathal often encouraged him to read passages from the newspaper. Because full stops and commas meant nothing to him, and as he mispronounced most of the words, Cathal never knew what the reports were about.

If the price of meat was going up, he could have been forgiven for believing that it was going down.

'You're a terrible ignorant man, Cathal — you don't know what's going on,' said Charlie one day. 'There's a story here about an accident up in the mountains and the people had to be rescued by *helipeter* [helicopter].' Another newspaper story concerned a burglary and the evidence given in court. 'Evidence was given that the *accursed* [the accused] was seen loitering in the neighbourhood of the *Haemorrhage* [Hermitage] Golf Club with the intent to commit a *larency* [larceny].'

Charlie told Cathal about some shopkeeper — 'a bloody impostor' — who had gone on what he called a *pildrimidge* [pilgrimage] to the *Vacuum* [Vatican] State during the Holy Year, in 1950. He said: 'It's a wonder the Pope didn't kick him out of the *basilium* [basilica], with his over-charging people for stuff in his shop!' Charlie complained that he had 'a *pie-ah* [pious] face on him and he goin' around into St John *Lanteren's* [Lateran] Church.'

On another occasion, Charlie approached Cathal, rattling some loose teeth at him. 'What's wrong with you?' asked Cathal.

'Gonorrhoea of the gums,' said Charlie. What he meant, of course, was pyorrhoea of the gums.

'Well now,' said Cathal, managing not to laugh, 'you go down to the doctor at the medical department and don't wait for him to tell you what's wrong with you — you tell *him*.'

Charlie took Cathal's advice and hurried off to the medical department.

'What's wrong with you?' asked the doctor.

'Gonorrhoea of the gums,' replied Charlie.

'Oh, I see,' said the doctor, 'your teeth are loose. Well, I think we'd better get a second opinion,' and he brought in another doctor.

'What did you say was wrong, Charlie?' asked the second doctor.

'Gonorrhoea of the gums, sir.'

'Yes, it looks like that,' commented the doctor, 'but to be sure, I'd prefer to get another one of my colleagues to look at you.' A third doctor appeared and asked Charlie the same question. Eventually the first doctor said 'Well now gentlemen, what we really need now is the opinion of the dentist,' and he was brought off to see him. Having heard what Charlie had to say for himself, the dentist examined his teeth and treatment was started right away.

Charlie owned a small open car known as a Baby Austin, possibly made in 1923, which Cathal described as looking like 'a little pram'. According to Charlie, the car had *disket* [disc] wheels. The car was also fitted with what Charlie called *shock observers* [shock absorbers] and on the dashboard were various *try-OM-eters* [speedometers and so forth].

He kept the car in very good condition. He painted it 'tay brown' [tea brown] on one occasion with the help of what he called *plummy* [pumice] powder, which somebody had given to him. He told Cathal, 'I painted it and the following night I *plummied* it down, then I gave it another coat of paint.'

He occasionally went out for a drive in it. If it started to rain, he drove it home and went out on his bicycle instead. According to him, getting wet on a bicycle was acceptable, but to get wet in the car was not so pleasant, even though it had a hood.

Charlie only drove along the Naas Road – nowhere else – and invariably ended up in Mrs Lalor's tea house in Naas. This was his standard Saturday afternoon drive. When Cathal told him that he had been up in the Wicklow Mountains in his car, Charlie would say, 'What do you want goin' up there for, breakin' every spring in your car? Why don't you go down for a nice drive to Naas, go into Mrs Lalor's and have a cup of tea?'

Charlie told a fellow worker, Tommy Doherty, that he was going to sell his car and buy a more modern one. Tommy passed on the news to a colleague with a dark complexion known as 'the Nigger' Bean (usually pronounced *Bayne*), who said, 'We'll have a bit of a lark. Tell him I'd be interested in it and ask him to bring it out on Saturday so that we can have a trial run in it.'

The arrangement was made and Charlie met them at Kingsbridge railway station. Predictably, he said, 'I'll bring you up the Naas Road and let you see how it runs.'

'Why don't we go to Kilcullen?' suggested 'the Nigger'.

'Oh God,' said Charlie, 'that's too far – the wife will be waitin' for me.'

'Well,' said 'the Nigger', 'if you want to sell the car to me, I'll need to have a proper trial run.'

Tommy and 'the Nigger' brought him into a pub, gave him a few drinks and succeeded in making him agree to drive them to Kilcullen. When they arrived there, 'the Nigger' called to see his sister-in-law, who gave them bacon, eggs, sausages and tea. She also presented them with cabbages and potatoes from the garden.

Afterwards they drove to somewhere near the Curragh, where 'the

Nigger's' brother-in-law lived, and there they had their supper, despite the fact that Charlie was anxious to get home all the time.

They finally arrived back at Kingsbridge railway station by midnight.

'Well gentlemen,' said Charlie, 'what do you think of the car?'

'It's a lovely car,' said 'the Nigger', 'but I'd like another little run in it before I make up my mind.'

With that, Charlie slammed the door and told them to 'so-and-so off' – he realized that he had been tricked. When he arrived home, his wife nearly threw him out, along with the potatoes and cabbages!

Sadly, Charlie's wife died of cancer. As Cathal had worked with Charlie for a number of years, he felt obliged to attend the funeral in Portlaoise, which took place on a beautiful October day. In the morning he attended the Mass in Meath Street Church. As he had room in the car, he brought Paddy Lyons (the man who put the handles on the brushes), Johnny Byrne (a carpenter) and Stephen Greene (the supervisor) to the graveyard in Portlaoise. Stephen was a deeply religious man but had a good sense of humour.

After they crossed Inchicore Bridge, the cars in the funeral cortège put on a spurt and they travelled at the more civilized speed of forty miles per hour. Stephen, who was sitting in the back of the car, took out his pipe, filled it and began to sing 'The Boys of Wexford'. Charlie joined in and instead of it being like a funeral, it was more like a holiday outing. They duly arrived and attended the ceremony; afterwards there were refreshments in a nearby hotel. It was what Cathal described as 'a jolly funeral'.

It appears that when they returned in the evening, Charlie announced that he was not going to live on his own and that he was going to get a young woman to look after him. This he actually did, marrying a girl of twenty-nine when he was sixty-four.

During the time when he was looking out for a new wife, Cathal introduced him to Margaret. When another man asked him what he thought of Margaret, he said, 'She's not bad for an Englishwoman – it's a pity she's not a widow!'

Soon after the funeral, Charlie put his eye on a girl named Josie in the Brewery canteen. Occasionally, when he could afford it, he gave her a tip of 2s. 6d. on a Friday; this was quite a lot of money in the late 1940s and early 1950s. Some of Charlie's colleagues noticed what was happening and started to give him encouragement, saying that they knew the girl's mother and would talk to her in an effort to make things easier for him.

Cathal followed the events with interest and when the whole business began to fizzle out, he decided to do something about it. As Charlie had given him a good deal of information about the girl, who lived in Rialto, he realized that he had plenty of material to concoct a series of letters. He put pen to paper and, using a dreadful backhand and the worst possible grammar, such as 'I *seen* you yesterday', he started to write love letters supposedly from Josie to Charlie. Just as Cathal expected, Charlie swallowed the whole thing hook, line and sinker. Charlie wrote to Josie, who received his letters and, although somewhat mystified, said nothing because she was still receiving his generous tips.

On one particular day, Charlie placed a rose on the table in front of Josie in the canteen. She was very embarrassed, but took it and said nothing. Naturally everyone saw what had happened and the news spread throughout the Brewery. Charlie received even more encouragement and was told that the girl was crazy about him. The reality, of course, was that the girl did not know what was going on.

Shortly before Christmas, Cathal asked to see the cards that he and Margaret had received the previous year; Margaret was in the habit of keeping them in order to remember who had sent them. Cathal found a large card depicting a stagecoach and a snow scene. As it was too big for any of the envelopes that they possessed, Cathal cut it down in size, and in doing so removed the sender's name. However, there was enough room for a greeting from Josie, which Cathal wrote, along with 'barbed wire' and 'kisses all over the place'. He addressed the envelope to Charlie, care of Guinness's Brewery.

Charlie showed it to Cathal a few days later and asked him what he thought of it. Cathal remarked that it was a nice card. Charlie asked him, 'Do you see anything in the picture?'

'Well,' Cathal said, 'it's a snow scene, there's a stagecoach … typical of the Christmas postcards they produce nowadays …'

'Ah, you're a terrible fool – you can't see through it at all.'

'No, I don't. I don't get the message.'

'It's travel.'

'What do you mean, travel?'

'Well, you see,' Charlie explained, 'I've got a motor car and she's hinting that I bring her out in the car: transport – travel.'

'Oh,' said Cathal, 'it never dawned upon me – that's quite right!'

Charlie was thus emboldened to send her a present of a '*pilastic* handbag' and twelve embroidered handkerchiefs, along with a letter stating that he would call to her over the Christmas and bring her out for a drive. He called to her house but had the misfortune to meet Josie's mother at the door, who gave him a cold reception. She told him that Josie had never written to him and was doing a strong line with a young lad.

'And by the way, I have something for you,' she said, giving him a parcel.

'Oh,' said Charlie, 'she needn't have bothered!'

'It was no bother at all,' said the woman, 'it's your present! My daughter can't accept that present from you – she's going with another man!'

Charlie threw the presents into his car and drove off in high dudgeon. Cathal asked him, 'What did you do with the presents, Charlie?'

'Ah,' he said, 'I sent them down to my niece in Edenderry. They didn't go to waste!'

At the next opportunity, Cathal wrote Charlie a letter from Josie, which began, 'Dear Charlie, where war [were] you over the Christmas? I never seen you ...', deliberately giving the impression that she knew nothing of her mother's intervention and that she was still interested in corresponding with Charlie.

During the following February, when St Valentine's Day was approaching, Cathal went to the newsagent's in Rialto and asked for the biggest and most vulgar valentine card that was available. The girl in the shop found something so large that she had difficulty in finding an envelope for it. The price, 1s. 6d., was pencilled on the back of the card; Cathal carefully rubbed it out and wrote 3s. 6d. instead. Inside, he wrote a message in the usual handwriting, signed it 'Guess Who?' and, when he sealed the envelope, wrote 'SAG' (Saint Anthony Guide) on the back.

When the bold Charlie received it, he was overjoyed and showed it to everyone in the Brewery. A day or two afterwards, Cathal took him aside and said, 'Listen, are you sure that girl sent you the card?'

'If I was as certain as getting into heaven as I am of that valentine, I'd be a happy man,' said Charlie.

'But', said Cathal, 'any fellow could have written that and sent it to you.'

'Now,' he said, 'what man is going to put his hand in his pocket and pay three and sixpence for a card, *plus the postage,* not to mention the trouble? Are you mad?'

'Oh,' said Cathal, 'you have a point there all right.'

'I'm bloody sure I have,' he said.

Eventually the affair with Josie fizzled out and Cathal stopped the correspondence. By this time Charlie had found the new young lady in his life and had decided to marry her. The venue and time of the wedding was supposed to be a secret, but Cathal and his colleagues deduced from what he had said about the priest and the parish in which his beloved lived that it would take place in the elegant church of St Paul's, Arran Quay. Cathal obtained the use of a typewriter and typed six notices that read, 'The wedding of Mr Charles Malone and Miss Byrne will take place tomorrow morning in St Paul's, Arran Quay with nuptial Mass at seven o'clock. All well-wishers are cordially invited to attend.'

As Cathal possessed a key to the official Brewery noticeboards, it was no trouble for him to place his typed notices in some of them. He did this quietly and said nothing.

When Cathal left work that evening at five o'clock, he found a group of men gathered around one of the noticeboards. He asked them if they were about to get a bonus or double week. 'Oh no,' said an elderly man putting his spectacles back into his pocket, 'that old bastard Malone is going to get married and everybody is invited to go to the wedding. What do *we* want to go to the wedding for?'

'Oh, I see,' said Cathal innocently. After a moment's reflection he added, 'It's rather strange, putting that in a Brewery noticeboard!'

Several fellows turned up at the wedding the following morning with large wooden rattles (or corncrakes as they were called) that they used at football matches. When, after the ceremony, Charlie appeared at the door of the church with his new bride on his arm, the lads cranked the rattles, making enough noise to wake the dead. A passing bus skidded on the road as the driver thought that he was being fired upon by a machine gun.

Charlie told Cathal that he and Jim Bocombe, the man who lived in the flat under him, once went to the men's retreat in Meath Street Church on a Friday evening. They had both hoped to get confession afterwards, but it was out of the question as there were so many people there. However, the missioner issued tickets to those who had missed confession and told them to come back the following day, when they would be heard first.

On the Saturday afternoon, Charlie followed the custom of the time and sent two young *gerils* [girls] to the church to reserve places for him and Jim; they arrived later and sat down to wait. There were just a few men in the pew before them. The missioner came in and said, 'Very good. I shall hear confession first from those to whom I gave tickets last night,' and went into the confession box.

The first few men went in and soon it was Charlie's turn. Just as he was about to go in, a man came along and knelt down in the aisle beside him, by the door of the confession box.

'Excuse me, mister,' said Charlie, 'you're at the wrong end of the queue – you want to go behind.'

'Mind your own business,' was the man's curt response.

Charlie looked around and the other men said, 'Hey Charlie, don't let him go in before you. You were here all the afternoon.'

Charlie tapped the fellow on the shoulder and said, 'Look here me good man, I don't mind so much, but the rest of the men are complaining; we've been here all th'afternoon.'

At this point the door of the confession box opened and the man slipped in.

'You're a terrible fool to let him go in before you,' whispered one of the fellows beside Charlie, 'I wouldn't let him get away with it! If I were you I'd pitch him out of the box!' The men kept prodding at Charlie and encouraging him.

'Well,' reported Charlie to Cathal, 'I got up and opened the door of the confession box, grabbed your man by the hasp of the arse and the nape of the neck, and I threw him out and over the seat behind me. I shook the church! The fellow got up and ran out and wasn't seen again.'

Because of the commotion, during which a man's hard hat had been crushed, the missioner pulled back the curtains, looked out and asked for an explanation. Charlie told him what had happened and how he had been offended. The missioner ticked him off, saying that what he had done was rather drastic, that the fellow might have been in a predicament and that he might never come back again.

'Oh,' said Charlie to Cathal, 'I wasn't going to let him get away with it,' and added, 'I left by the back way because I was afraid to go out the front in case your man was waiting for me, maybe with a gang of others.'

Cathal often laughed at the recollection of this crazy incident and wondered what somebody from another denomination might have made of the scene. It certainly could only have happened in Ireland.

Twenty-Five

*A*t the beginning of 1948, the carpenters' old top shop and the building housing it was declared to be derelict, and all the carpenters were shifted to another workshop beside the Mill.

During this year Cathal attempted to make a clavichord – a small and relatively simple keyboard instrument in which thin wire strings are struck from underneath by means of metal 'tangents' affixed directly to the keys. Johann Sebastian Bach's son Carl Philip Emmanuel considered the clavichord to be the instrument par excellence when it came to delicacy and expression, for, due to its simplicity, the fingers had an almost direct connection with the striking of the strings. Having a tiny sound, the instrument was often used for practising.

Cathal constructed the clavichord at home. He based his plans on 'bad photographs and descriptions' found in various woodworking magazines, which, it must be presumed, were the source of his motivation for making the instrument. As he was dissatisfied with the result, he never quite finished the instrument and for many years it lay at home, untouched.

Although he regarded this experiment as a failure, he at least learned some valuable lessons from it and gained a certain amount of knowledge; for example, how to make a keyboard, how to string an instrument and how and where to order the various parts, including the strings, which were unprocurable in Ireland. Most of the components had to be ordered from England. After the restoration of two antique pianos and a harmonium, it was Cathal's next step on the road to constructing a large-scale instrument.

Cathal had met the young musician John O'Sullivan in Mai and Billy Gannon's house in Rathmines soon after he and Margaret were married; he came to Rialto to see the new clavichord, in which he undoubtedly took great interest. He would later become a well-established organist and harpsichordist.

The clavichord did not go to waste; it was finally completed many years later and given to John Beckett for practising on whilst in hospital.

Since 1947, cars had begun to appear once again on the roads. Margaret, who had carefully put aside some money, now purchased a second-hand car of Cathal's choosing: a four-door, eight-horsepower Austin Saloon with a sunroof. After the engine had been rebored, the six-year-old car ran smoothly and lasted for a further eleven years, giving Margaret and Cathal great pleasure. All in all, it proved to be comfortable and reliable. The main expenses were petrol and batteries, which at that period did not last very long. Cathal constructed a garage of wood and corrugated iron in the back garden of the house; it was accessible from a laneway behind the terrace of houses.

Margaret was pleased with the new acquisition – she had always wanted a car. Cathal tried to teach her to drive, but she was a nervous student and never felt safe. When, on one particular day, she managed to hit a sheep on a mountain road and narrowly miss a puppy dog, she decided to give up her attempts on the grounds that she could easily have hit a child.

As they had seen nearly everything within cycling distance of Rialto, they now had the luxury of travelling farther afield. The new car also attracted the attention of some of the local children. On Saturday afternoons, when Cathal and Margaret usually went out for a drive, children such as Joan and Willie Devine, the Bracken girls – Olive, Dorothy and Rona – and the Clarks congregated around the garage, all hoping to be invited to join them. The inevitable question was, 'Mr Gannon, are you going for a picnic?' Margaret helped in deciding who would come; three or four were selected and off they all went for a 'spin'.

The Devines and Brackens remained close friends of Margaret and Cathal and remembered these outings with great pleasure. It would seem that Margaret and Cathal influenced them in many ways as they grew up, especially as regards music, art and taste in furniture. In particular, young Joan Devine took careful note of their views and ideas. All remembered their kindness, pleasant nature and generosity. It would seem that they were a model couple and ideal neighbours. Margaret, because of her English accent and somewhat regal bearing, was always described as a 'lady'.

On 22 November 1948 Cathal's father retired from the Brewery and was succeeded by the man who had been the assistant foreman, Stephen Greene, a 'decent, harmless man'. Cathal was offered promotion by Mr Richardson, one of the engineers, to the now vacant position of assistant foreman, but he declined it in favour of his brother Jack, who was by now married and had a family of four children. Mr Gannon was pleased that Cathal had made this decision. Apparently Jack had been offered the position of foreman but, like Cathal, had allowed Stephen to take the job because of domestic considerations.

When shortly afterwards a position of carpenter with special responsibility for locks became vacant, Cathal applied for and got the job. In fact, the main emphasis of the new job turned out to be maintenance of all the locks in the Brewery with just a little time devoted to carpentry. Cathal remained at this job for the next fifteen years and enjoyed it. He now became a familiar figure around the Brewery and was often to be seen going from one place to another with a small wooden case containing his equipment. Because of this, he was soon nicknamed 'Doctor Lock'. Once this happened, he dared not tell his colleagues that his wife's maiden name had been Key – they would have found a good opportunity for cracking indelicate jokes.

It was reckoned that there were some 20,000 to 30,000 locks in the Brewery. On account of customs and excise, most vessels had to be locked and the keys held by those in charge of the relevant departments. Of course, all safes had to be carefully locked; when a lock gave trouble and the door could not be opened Cathal was immediately called. In most cases he was able to solve the problem but sometimes a safe-expert had to be summoned; while the man was attending to the lock, Cathal was obliged to safeguard the key as a security precaution.

Although there was a rule that locks must be 'sent out' for repair, Cathal was allowed to work on them in cases of emergency. He had a complete set of replacements for various types of small locks. He was also able to make a key, providing he had a blank. He was allowed to distribute keys; he kept a special book containing a list of them and the signatures of those responsible for them. However, when locks broke, he normally sent them to Devine & Sons, South King Street, to be fixed. This company also supplied new keys when the originals were lost.

Often, at nine o'clock on a Monday morning, there was a telephone message to say that some member of the staff had left a key at home and could not open the drawers of his or her desk. Cathal was always ready with his box of tools. Having opened the drawers, he frequently returned at four o'clock in the afternoon to close them again. The most interesting part of the job was meeting the various people and talking to them.

Locks of gates often gave trouble, especially during the winter when they became affected with rust, and Cathal was at hand to fix them. This was a pleasant enough job in good weather but difficult when it was wet or windy. When keys of the boundary gates were lost, a new set of locks had to be made and fitted for security reasons.

When goods were being brought from one part of the Brewery to another, passes had to be presented at the gateways: outwards passes and an inwards passes were required. This was another security measure to ensure that goods did not go missing. In each gatekeeper's hut were special locked boxes with slots, one marked 'in' and another 'out', into which the passes were 'posted'. Unfortunately, much to the continual annoyance of one lady clerk who took her job very seriously, passes were frequently placed in the wrong sections. Occasionally the gatekeepers realized that they had made a mistake and opened the bottom of the boxes with a screwdriver to sort out the passes, but more often than not the boxes arrived in the lady clerk's office every day with several passes in the wrong section.

Cathal received an emergency call one day to sort out a problem with one of the locks of these boxes. He introduced himself to the lady clerk, examined the lock, said, 'I'm afraid the lock will have to be repaired,' and asked her for the key. She was very reluctant to part with both the box and the key – especially the latter – but Cathal patiently explained what he would have to do and managed to convince her that he had been given special responsibility for locks and keys by the authorities. He gave her a solemn promise that he would return both box and key within an hour.

Back at his workshop, he repaired the lock in a few minutes, made a couple of duplicate keys (which he later gave to the gatemen at the bottom and top gates) and returned the box and key to the lady clerk. Consequently the gatekeepers no longer had to resort to opening the boxes with screwdrivers in order to sort out the passes and the lady had no further trouble with misplaced passes.

Years afterwards, when she was about to retire, she sent for Cathal and said to him, 'You may remember that you repaired a lock on a box for me at one time.' Cathal pretended that he had forgotten and she reminded him of what had happened. 'And furthermore,' she added, 'ever since then I never had any more trouble with the passes! You were very helpful to me!'

Towards the end of 1948, a small group of workers including Cathal were transferred back to the top shop, which had still not been demolished, and the rest remained at the Mill.

In the summer of 1949 Margaret, Cathal and the Clenches drove in the new car to Spiddal in Connemara, where they stayed for a week in a guest house run by a Mrs Mary O'Leary, whom they befriended. During the second week they brought the Clenches to Glengarriff and the surrounding area. By all accounts, the holiday was greatly enjoyed by everyone.

1950 was proclaimed a Holy Year or Jubilee by Pope Pius XII. This practice had commenced in 1300 and was generally repeated every fifty years, though there were several 'extraordinary' Holy Years. Following the long-established custom, Catholic pilgrims went to Rome for the celebrations, returning home with certificates of Papal blessings, seraphic offerings (Masses that had been said on request) and holy pictures. Many of the employees in Guinness's Brewery asked Cathal to frame these and so he was kept busy; he made a written record and discovered that he had framed 164 Papal blessings during the year.

The usual procedure when doing these 'nixers' was to glue-up a frame at about half past four in the afternoon, before going home, and leave it overnight. As Cathal knew the sizes of all the certificates off by heart, he rarely bothered to measure them. The next morning, Cathal nailed the frame together and asked a glazier to cut the glass.

Dr Stan Corran, who had come from Park Royal in London, began working in the laboratory of Guinness's Brewery in Dublin during this year. Cathal had heard that he had been one of the three cleverest boys in England for three years. Stan became involved with the St James's Gate Musical Society (later the Guinness choir) and, as he had no piano at his home in Rathmichael, south Dublin, he bought a treble recorder so that he could play his bass parts (two octaves higher!) in order to learn them. He knew that the foreman in the carpentry department was Stephen Greene, that his assistant was Jack Gannon and that his older brother was Cathal, who maintained the 'multitudinous locks in the Brewery'.

Apparently Dr Corran needed keys for something in the laboratory and asked to see Cathal. Cathal went to his office and introduced himself. He noticed that on his desk was the book *Autobiography of William Farrell: Carlow in 1798*, edited by Roger J. McHugh, which he thought was an unusual choice of literature for an Englishman to read.

Once they had finished talking business, they fell to discussing musical matters. Stan had heard that Cathal was interested in music and mentioned that he had bought a recorder. Cathal knew what a recorder was but probably had never heard one being played at that time. He mentioned that he had recently made a clavichord. The two men then discovered that they both shared a love of history. Cathal found Stan a very interesting person. Stan, for his part, found Cathal 'a cheery, hail-fellow-well-met sort of chap with a rather soft voice'. A more accurate description of Cathal's voice, however, would be 'high-pitched', for it was regularly mistaken for that of a woman's on the telephone.

The musician John Beckett, cousin of the famous playwright Samuel Beckett, had been a student at the College of Music in London and had gone to Paris for a year in 1949. He returned to Dublin in 1950, lost his father in September, and stayed in Ireland until about September 1953. He believes that he met Cathal sometime around this period. Although he has long forgotten their first meeting, he obviously obtained a favourable impression of him. 'I took to him like a duck to water,' he said. 'I liked him, I respected him and I respected his knowledge, his interests, his enthusiasm, his simplicity, his directness, and became very, very, very affectionately fond of him.'

In the year 1950, the bicentenary of Bach's death, a performance of his Mass in B minor was given in the Metropolitan Hall in Dublin. The conductor was Otto Matzerath, who was German. The Weber harpsichord of circa 1768 was borrowed from the National Museum for the occasion, but as it could not be tuned up to the correct pitch, John was obliged to transpose and play the continuo part (the 'thorough' or 'figured' bass) in C minor – a semitone higher – while the rest of the orchestra played in the original key. John remembered that the harpsichord was not in good condition.

At around this time, Cathal went to hear the famous Spanish guitarist Andrés Segovia play at the Theatre Royal in Hawkins Street, but because he would not allow any amplification Cathal could hear nothing except people moving about and lavatories being flushed at the back of the hall. He left during the interval, went home, turned on the radio and happened to find a programme of him playing, which he listened to in comfort whilst having his supper.

From the mid-1940s, Cathal had begun to take an interest in the famous eighteenth-century lexicographer, critic and conversationalist Dr Samuel Johnson and his biographer, James Boswell. His general interest in the eighteenth century probably led him to these two notable men. The latter's *London Journal 1762–1763* gave Cathal much amusement.

During the fifties, Margaret and Cathal regularly visited the Clenches in Harrow. Cathal often left Margaret with her parents and, setting off early in the morning with a satchel containing a map and a picnic lunch, travelled by underground train to London and spent many rewarding hours visiting the Science Museum, the National Gallery, the Victoria and Albert Museum, the British Museum, St Paul's Cathedral and many of the other fine churches designed by Sir Christopher Wren. He also went to the various markets. He enjoyed London immensely – it was an education – and he could readily appreciate Dr Johnson's famous maxim: 'When a man is tired of London, he is tired of life.'

It was on one of these treks around London in September 1951, the year of the Festival of Britain and the centenary of the Crystal Palace Exhibition, when Cathal visited Dr Johnson's house in Gough Square, off Fleet Street. In his inimitable manner, Cathal chatted to the curator, who remarked, 'It's a pity you weren't here last week – we had a lovely concert of music.'

'Oh,' said Cathal, 'that's most interesting, but I don't think Dr Johnson liked music!'

'He didn't,' she said, 'but it was an excuse for us to put on a very interesting programme of music of his period and we had a most beautiful harpsichord which was played.'

'Where did you get the harpsichord?' asked Cathal, suddenly interested.

'Oh, we got it from one of our National Trust houses – the Benton Fletcher Collection at 3 Cheyne Walk, Chelsea. If you want to see the collection of harpsichords, go there – it's open to the public. You can see the instruments, play them and examine them.'

Cathal mentioned that he had never heard of the place before.

'You go there,' repeated the lady, 'and make yourself known to Mrs Eileen Jackson, the curator. You have several harpsichords to look at in this wonderful house.'

Cathal arrived at the elegant Queen Anne house two days later, on Wednesday, 19 September, at ten o'clock in the morning and met a lady who was sweeping the front driveway.

'I would like to see the musical instruments,' said Cathal.

'Certainly,' she said, then added, 'do you come from Dublin?'

'I do.'

'So do I – my name is Mrs Jackson. What part of Dublin do you come from?'

Cathal told her that he lived in Herberton Road. She told him that she came from a musical family.

'Are you interested in harpsichords?' she asked.

'I am. I often times think that I'd love to attempt a simple one.'

'Well, why don't you? We have architects, dentists, dentists' mechanics … all sorts and conditions come here and make these instruments. Are you a woodworker?'

'Yes, I'm a carpenter, though I'm more of a cabinetmaker than a carpenter, because I never leave the bench and I do fine work.'

'Well now, you go in and look at the instruments. Pick out whatever you think you'd like and make up your mind to copy it. Take the moving parts out – you won't do any harm – I know you won't!'

Cathal went inside an found an Aladdin's cave of eight lovely harpsichords as well as a collection of spinets, virginals and early pianos. Leaving aside one harpsichord by Ruckers of Antwerp from 1612, which had been loaned by Her Majesty the Queen Mother, he examined all the instruments and finally picked out an impressive harpsichord made in London by Jacob and Abraham Kirckman in 1777. The case was veneered with cross-banded mahogany and was inlaid with herringbone strips of boxwood and ebony. The area of the case over the keys was made from burr walnut. The lid and music stand were made from mahogany. The elegant instrument had two keyboards with ivory naturals (the 'white' notes) and ebony accidentals (the sharps and flats or 'black' notes), like a piano. It also had two pedals; the right one, when depressed, opened a flap in the lid, known as a 'nag's head' swell, to make the sound louder.

Cathal, no doubt excited by his new discovery, approached Mrs Jackson again and told her which harpsichord he had chosen. She told him that he had picked the best one in the house. He said that he would come again on the following morning with his wife, armed with a measuring tape, a drawing pad and a pencil.

When Cathal returned to Harrow that evening, he told Margaret what had happened and asked her to accompany him to the Benton Fletcher Collection the next morning so that she could help him measure the instrument. Not surprisingly, Margaret had never heard of the collection before and hardly knew what a harpsichord was.

On the following morning they arrived at Cheyne Walk before ten o'clock, when it was quiet, and spent almost the whole day there measuring the Kirckman instrument. These original drawings still survive. To the casual observer they look rather careless and disorganized, but they are quite detailed. Amazingly, the correct technical terms are used for all the various parts of the instrument, even though Cathal had had hardly any contact with harpsichords. Cathal was as careful as he could be, measuring everything that he could see, but inevitably he missed several details. A further visit to the Benton Fletcher Collection was necessary to take more measurements and clarify certain points.

Back in Dublin, Cathal set about constructing his copy of the Kirckman harpsichord in the ridiculously small glasshouse between the kitchen-cum-scullery and the garden wall. Cathal procured an 8 by 4 ft sheet of hard-board, covered it with white paper and on it drew a full size plan and section of the instrument. The glasshouse was about $15\frac{1}{2}$ ft long and only a foot wider than the sheet of hardboard; the finished instrument, with its lid, would measure 7 ft 4 by 3 ft $1\frac{1}{2}$ in. As Cathal said, he 'had to get under and over it'.

The next objective was to obtain the materials. Wood – 'old deal' for the case, sycamore for the inside braces and the wrest plank or pin block (to which the strings would be attached by tuning pins), and Sitka spruce for the soundboard – was procured. Cathal wrote for advice to Arnold Dolmetsch Ltd, the musical instrument makers and suppliers in Haslemere, Surrey, ordered the brass and steel strings from J. & J. Goddard, Tottenham Court Road in London and received the celluloid key coverings from H.J. Fletcher & Co. Ltd, Shaftsbury Avenue, London.

Work on the instrument started in November. Construction of the case would have been the first part of the operation. Cathal had to figure out a way of bending the curved side of the case; he used the age-old method of steaming thin layers of wood, forcing them into the shape required and gluing them together. Cathal had to use his imagination for the strengthening braces within the instrument, since he had been unable to see them on the original Kirckman, which had a wooden bottom. Making the lid and legs, and drilling holes into the wrest plank for the tuning pins would not have presented him with too much trouble. He worked slowly and methodically, always obeying his oft-quoted expression, 'measure twice, cut once'. All this work was done after tea in the evenings, after a full day's work in the Brewery. Margaret, who just had enough space to squeeze past and go out to the back garden, observed what he was doing from time to time, but did not take too much notice.

The next phase required a little more precision: making the upper and lower keyboards or 'manuals'. The idea was that each keyboard would have its own set of 'jacks', which plucked the strings at different points, thus producing two different qualities of sound. Since there would be a set of strings tuned to the same pitch for both keyboards, both manuals could be played together or coupled, producing a louder sound.

Having made the key frames, Cathal joined together panels of timber with the grain running in the same direction as the keys and drew the shapes of the keys on them along with the position of their pivots. Having nailed the panels to the key frame, he then drilled the holes for the pivots. This done, he finally cut the keys, using a thin saw. The construction of the case and the keyboards was finished during the summer of 1952.

Cathal would probably have made the soundboard, which was less than a quarter of an inch thick, at the early stage of the construction process, but would not have glued it into the case until the summer when the wood was at its driest. In the autumn, he strung the instrument with brass strings in the bass and steel strings for the rest of the notes up to the treble.

Now came the trickiest and undoubtedly the most tedious part: making the jacks, which plucked the strings. Some 244 of these had to be made. Each keyboard had sixty-one notes; a row of jacks was connected to the top keyboard and two rows connected to the bottom. A fourth row of jacks was dedicated to a 'lute' stop.

In order to give the reader an idea of the complexity of making these fiddly plucking devices, it can be stated that eleven different operations were needed for each one. The body of the jack itself was made of maplewood. The jacks were of different lengths, depending on which keyboard was operating them; some were 'dog-legged', enabling both keyboards to engage with them. A pivoted tongue fitted precisely into a rectangular hole in the jack and projecting from it was the all-important plectrum or plucker, made of leather for the main stops and goose quill for the lute. A spring, made from a hog's bristle, had to be inserted into the body of each jack and fitted into a groove at the back of each pivoted tongue. The function of this natural spring was to return the tongue to its correct position after its passage downward, having plucked the string. (At some later date, Cathal remembered taking apart a 180-year-old jack and seeing the hog's bristle straightening before his eyes.) The cobbler who sold Cathal the hog's bristles was astounded at the number that he ordered and wondered how many years he intended to live – two or three hog's bristles were enough to last the average cobbler a lifetime.

The final operation in the making of the jacks was to cut two slots at the top of each one; these were used to insert small squares of felt, which dampened the strings when the jacks fell downwards, having plucked the strings.

Making these individual components must have taken a fair amount of time and taxed Cathal's patience, especially as he was doing all this for the first time. He had to rely on his own ingenuity to devise methods of making this complicated instrument, for he had no help; little or no literature was available at the time and there was nobody in Ireland who could assist him. It must have required an extraordinary amount of determination to persist. Cathal often wished that he lived in England.

Finally Cathal would have fitted the keyboards and the action into the case and made careful adjustments to the jacks so that they operated smoothly. 'Voicing', or adjusting the length and thickness of the hard leather plectra in order to produce the best sound and evenness of touch, proved to be tricky. Cathal used a very sharp chisel and, at a later stage when his eyesight deteriorated, two pairs of spectacles, one worn in front of the other, to give increased magnification. In time he would substitute the leather and quill with a special type of durable plastic named Delrin.

Unfortunately, at around this stage of the construction, Cathal unwittingly fell into a trap. By pure coincidence, Radio Éireann purchased a Dolmetsch harpsichord in 1952, which Cathal examined when it arrived. This was a typical product of the English company. Traditional methods of construction had not been followed – it was a modern, 'improved' harpsichord. The first thing that Cathal noticed was the lack of a bottom and the presence of heavy bracing, almost like a piano, under the soundboard. Other details were quite different from those of the historical Kirckman; for example, the stringing was heavier. Influenced by what he saw, Cathal now undid some of his good work, removing the bottom, adding extra bracing and putting too many 'cut-off' bars under the soundboard. He revised the stringing and ran the bass strings parallel to the spine. Without realizing it, he was interfering with the sound of the instrument.

Carol and Charles Acton, who were married in 1951 and who came into contact with Cathal at around this period, possibly through Michael Morrow, a friend of Dr Stan Corran and John Beckett, saw the new instrument being constructed. Charles became music critic for *The Irish Times*. Carol taught both violin and piano in the Royal Irish Academy of Music, and was the leader and only professional player in the Dublin Orchestral Players. Charles loved the visits to Herberton Road and both greatly appreciated the friendship that Cathal offered them. Charles felt that he and Cathal had many things in common.

When the harpsichord was finally completed in December 1952 it still needed to be painted. Although English harpsichords were generally veneered with choice wood, Cathal painted his in the Flemish style, in black lacquer for the outer case and Dutch orange for the inner. Having painted the lid, he passed it over the back garden wall to Mr Hicks, a painter who lived in the house next door. Cathal watched, fascinated, as he quickly sketched and painted the Latin motto: *Musica magnorum est solamen dulce laborum* ('Music is the sweet solace of work').

What Cathal had achieved was nothing short of a miracle. Despite the faults of the instrument, he had managed to recreate an elegant and fully functional harpsichord, having had virtually no past experience or training – and in so doing, had revived the art of harpsichord building in Dublin, which had died out some 154 years previously. His childhood dream had finally come true: he was now the possessor – and the creator – of a harpsichord. Cathal was thrilled with his achievement; now he could understand why one of these instruments cost the prohibitive sum of £1000. He wrote, 'by Christmas I had the pleasure of hearing it play for the first time. It would be hard to describe the pleasure I derived from hearing the sonatas of Scarlatti being played on an instrument of my own making; my efforts were well rewarded'. When his mother saw and heard the new instrument she was delighted and justifiably proud of her son.

This not-too-faithful reproduction of a Kirckman harpsichord, housed in the sitting room of a small Dublin suburban house, was still not finished, however; Cathal, following the example of the Dolmetsch harpsichord, intended to fit it with seven pedals, so that the player could comfortably change the various stops whilst playing. Fortunately he never added them.

Shortly afterwards the novelty wore off and Cathal began to find fault with the new instrument, as he had done with the clavichord; whilst it had a fine treble, it lacked resonance and the bass was weak owing to the unnecessarily heavy construction and shortened length (the original Kirckman was several inches longer). Regrettably (or perhaps fortunately) it was left unfinished and Cathal relegated it to the spare bedroom, where it remained for some time, virtually untouched. Dublin would have to wait for a few more years before it was revived and played in public.

Twenty-Six

*I*n early October 1951 Cathal was asked to hang some Japanese prints, owned by Lord Moyne, on the walls of the staff dining room in Guinness's Brewery. The prints had been purchased by Lord Moyne's father in Japan. Cathal met Lord Moyne and together they carried the framed prints to the dining room. Lord Moyne seemed a little surprised that Cathal knew that the pictures were Japanese; Cathal of course had framed a couple of similar prints for Grace Plunkett, he owned at least one and he had seen many in London. While he hung them, he and Lord Moyne discussed the pictures. When Cathal expressed his interest on hearing that Lord Moyne owned several masterpieces by the renowned artists Hiroshige and Hokusai, Lord Moyne asked him if he would like to see them. Cathal said yes and Lord Moyne promised to invite him to his home at Knockmaroon in Castleknock when his next play-reading session was held. Involving members of the Guinness Players, these evening gatherings were held every autumn.

Accordingly, on 31 October Cathal received an invitation from Lord Moyne's secretary, Miss Anderson, in which he was informed that some members of the play-reading group would be going to Knockmaroon on 6 November and that the Brewery bus would leave St James's Gate at 6.45 pm. He received a second letter on the following day, in which Miss Anderson apologized for not having included Margaret in the invitation; Lord Moyne did not know whether Cathal was married or not. Margaret and Cathal both accepted the invitation.

They duly arrived at Knockmaroon House on the appointed day, approaching it along an impressive tree-lined avenue. A large, plain structure of no great architectural merit, it was nonetheless, as Cathal recollected, 'a most glorious house'. Originally dark and drab, it had been recently painted and decorated; Lord and Lady Moyne had given their home a 'lovely light atmosphere'. A new grey carpet had been placed in the drawing room and display cases had been fitted in the corners. 'When I went into this most elegant house,' Cathal said, 'I thought it was absolutely wonderful. It was everything that I could have desired.' Cathal admired the pictures on the walls and enjoyed mixing with the guests. Among them were Brewery people, such as Dr A. H. Hughes and D. O. Williams; other guests included Mr Figgis of the Hodges Figgis bookshop, the writer Monk Gibbon, Lady Honor Svejdar, and Garech Browne and his mother. Cathal recognized several of his colleagues amongst the Guinness Players, including Dessie Brennan and Jack Bolger. Al Byrne, brother of the radio broadcaster and television presenter Gay Byrne, and author of the book *Guinness Times*, also took part in the play-readings and may have been there that evening.

Lady Moyne approached Cathal and Margaret and welcomed them. She said to Cathal, 'I haven't met you before.'

'No,' said Cathal, not realizing who he was speaking to, 'my name is Gannon.'

'Oh,' she said, 'we've been expecting you – you're interested in Japanese prints.'

'I'm interested in many things,' said Cathal and proceeded to tell her about visiting the Benton Fletcher Collection in Cheyne Walk.

'That's most interesting,' she said, 'and what brought you there?'

Cathal told her about how he and Margaret had measured one of the harpsichords with a view to making one. Once again Lady Moyne expressed her interest and mentioned that they had a clavichord in England.

Margaret had felt rather nervous about going to Knockmaroon House, not having met any titled people before, but was put quite at ease by Lady Moyne's pleasant manner.

When everyone had assembled they all sat down in the drawing room and the play-reading commenced. Unfortunately, Cathal could not remember which play was read on that particular evening.

Afterwards, Lord Moyne pressed the bell to summon the servants for supper and everyone adjourned to the dining room. There Cathal was able to admire the extensive collection of Japanese prints that literally covered the entire walls. He was very impressed by them. He and Margaret then applied themselves to the buffet supper, assisted by the butler and the elegantly dressed female staff, who wore mob caps, striped blouses, linen dresses and white aprons with a large bow at the back. Some of the younger children, who had been allowed to stay up, offered nuts and titbits to accompany the drinks; Cathal remembered that Tamsy was aged about three or four and that Erskine wore a little kilt. Wine and porter were available, but not spirits, for Lord Moyne did not approve of them. Apparently the Guinness served in Knockmaroon was always in poor condition.

All in all, it was a most enjoyable evening for Margaret and Cathal. They were soon invited to the next play-reading and once again fell into easy conversation with Lady Moyne, who showed Cathal several illustrated magazines with pictures of clavichords in them. When Lord Moyne met Cathal soon after the first invitation he had said, 'My wife was telling me in bed last night that you're interested in harpsichords and clavichords.'

From then on, Margaret and Cathal were invited to Knockmaroon on a regular basis to attend the play-readings, until they finally died out in the 1960s. For Cathal it was an education, for he was being exposed to plays that normally he would not have gone to see; he found them very rewarding. Normally he sat and listened, though occasionally he was persuaded to read a minor part. He was a little reluctant to participate, thinking that his 'tinny' voice was unsuitable; doubtless he felt a little out of his depth.

Kathleen Kelly, the granddaughter of Alderman Tom Kelly (who had been the first president of the Old Dublin Society) was a member of the Guinness Players for a while and came several times to Knockmaroon House to read plays. Cathal, who had met her whilst attending to locks in the various offices in the Brewery, gave her lifts home. Cathal found her an interesting person and enjoyed talking to her. Like him, she was interested in art and music.

When Cathal and Margaret arrived at Knockmaroon House during the following year for one of the play-readings, they thought that they had come on the wrong night as the place was in darkness. Lord Moyne opened the door and said, 'I'm afraid we have no electricity and we're putting candles all over the house.' The female servants were flitting about with candlesticks and to Cathal the interior looked 'absolutely lovely'. Just as they were about to commence the play-reading, the lights came on.

During the war years and the 1950s Cathal remembered a hideous-looking crude wooden dummy, made to the same size and weight of a man, which was used in the Brewery for training ambulancemen and firemen to rescue wounded people from burning buildings and the like. The Brewery had its own ambulance and fire engine. He often saw the dummy strapped to a stretcher and being lowered from a roof by means of ropes. When not in use, it was kept in a storeroom along with various pieces of equipment. Cathal remembered talking to somebody and having the uneasy feeling that he was being watched. When he looked up he saw the dummy sitting on a platform near the roof, its heavy boots dangling over the edge.

Every year, soccer teams from the upper and lower levels of the Brewery used to compete for what was known as the La Touche Cup, which had been presented by Managing Director Christopher Digges La Touche in 1906. There was an unwritten law entitling the winning team to spend about one hour parading – and drinking – around the Brewery.

On one such occasion there was great razzmatazz when the parade included a small truck towing a trailer, on which had been placed a large wooden box like a coffin with the wooden dummy lying on top, dressed in the opposing team's colours. Surrounding this macabre spectacle were ribbons and bunting; the soccer team members, who walked beside it, waved flags, rang bells, rattled 'corncrakes' and cheered.

Cathal witnessed the parade emerging from the main gate of the Brewery on its way down towards Watling Street, Cook's Lane and the traffic department. One of three elderly women standing nearby pointed to the dummy and asked him, 'What's wrong with the man, mister?'

'Ah,' said Cathal, 'he's been involved in an accident and they're bringing him down to Steeven's Hospital!'

'Jaysus, Mary and Joseph,' said the woman, 'he'll be dead by the time he gets down there! That's no way to treat a poor injured man! Sure they'll kill him that way! Look at the face of him – God help him!'

Cathal was still up to his tricks at this period. As Cathal was friendly with the pharmacist in the Brewery dispensary, he often asked him for a small quantity of sulphuretted hydrogen (hydrogen sulphide) and acid, with which he was able to make stink bombs. The resulting smell was like rotten eggs.

On one particular day, Cathal was passing a closed-up doorway at the back of a temporary wash room at about ten minutes to five, when the men were preparing to go home. He could hear the animated voices inside. As there was a north wind blowing through the bottom of this ill-fitting door – there was a gap of several inches – he decided to use his ingredients for a stink bomb, which he had been unable to use elsewhere. He placed a small tin under the door, poured the acid over quite a large amount of sulphuretted hydrogen and quickly walked around to the front entrance of the wash room, rolling up his sleeves as if he were about to wash his hands. As he went in, the men came out in droves. Innocently, Cathal asked, 'What's wrong?'

'Oh, mother of Christ!' said one of the men. 'There's an awful smell in there! A man has already got sick!'

'What is it?' asked Cathal. 'Surely it's nothing to worry about – it's only Keefe's the knackers that you're smelling!' O'Keefe's were the manufacturers of glue, grease, fertilisers and feeding stuffs, and had their premises in nearby Mill Street – everyone referred to them as 'Keefe's'.

'Oh my God,' said the man, 'it's worse than Keefe's the knackers!'

Cathal remembered how the men came out in waves and how appalling their language was. The smell cleared the whole place in minutes.

At around this period, Cathal made a second clavichord, which was a little better than the first, and completed it some time in 1952. Veneered in mahogany, it was based on plans published in a *Woodworker* magazine from 1950. Cathal was still not fully satisfied with the resulting instrument and made no more clavichords; he decided that he did not care for them. He gave this second instrument to D.O. Williams in 1968. Mr Williams kept it for a number of years and offered to return it to Cathal, who refused it.

As we have seen, Cathal made several instruments that did not come up to his high expectations. Although he had a strong spirit of determination and always strove to make his next instrument better than his previous one, Professor Kevin B. Nowlan may have put his finger on it when he said that the actual making of the instruments was possibly more important to him than the end result.

At around this time, Cathal met the colourful antique dealer Rosie Black in John Burke's house. Cathal gave her a lift to her home in Appian Way; she brought him inside and showed him some pictures and antiques that she had for sale.

One of Dublin's great characters, Rosie worked as a nurse in the Mass Radiography Centre in Lord Edward Street. This was the place that Cathal telephoned if he wanted to get in touch with her. A storeroom at the back of the premises housed the various antiques that she purchased in the auction rooms along the quays until they were moved to her house. Apparently the man in charge of the Centre was interested in antiques and allowed Rosie to do this.

Rosie never received any formal training in antique dealing – she simply developed the knack of buying something good without knowing why it was good.

Although she was the cause of many a laugh, she was not a funny person and often did not appreciate a joke. She was quite eccentric. She shared the house in Appian Way with a Miss Crawford, who knew little of Rosie's dealings – everything was done in strict secrecy. Rosie eventually had to move to a house in Moyne Road, where her dealings were done in the same degree of secrecy, as she seemed to be afraid of the people living opposite. On answering one's knock on the door, she ushered the person in, saying, 'Come in quick, come in quick!' and shut the door immediately. Cathal regularly teased her by telling her that somebody was peeping at her from behind curtains across the road.

Once inside, the visitor was brought to a back room and invited to sit by a tiny stove that made very little difference to the temperature of the room. Wielding a poker, she would say, 'That's a great fire!' She spoke rapidly and very dramatically, and always dressed in old, worn clothes. Her clients were always strictly segregated and never allowed to meet; names were never mentioned. She had no qualms about asking people to leave if someone else arrived. She constantly pestered people to run messages for her or drive her from one place to another; Cathal was always at her beck and call. She often telephoned him and said, 'I can't talk to you now. Come down to me.' When Cathal arrived at her house, he was usually asked to run some small errand. On one occasion he had to loan her his car for a week.

Despite her eccentricities, she was a person who was well worth knowing. Cathal bought many good paintings and antiques from her at affordable prices. She was an interesting person and a constant source of amusement.

Sadly, at the beginning of 1953 Cathal began to lose his old friend Grace Plunkett, who by this stage was ill. She had become somewhat demanding and, at times, unreasonable with her friends. Early in January, Cathal received a bitter letter from her, in which she reminded him of his 'aunt's indictment' that his forty-two years 'had produced only a "purveyor of dirty stories"'. She then accused him of a 'regular refusal to do anything not pleasing' to himself.

She reminded him of how he had said to her, in the previous May, that he would not be seeing her 'for a long time' and put this down to the fact that she, in his estimation, was 'too much trouble in asking help in very small matters which I could not do myself'. She told him that she had been seriously ill for the past month and that he had only called once. Her doctor, Dr O'Hogain, had told her that she had not long to live; however a relic of the Jesuit priest Fr John Sullivan was brought to her and a 'miracle occurred'. More bitter words flowed, accusing Cathal of neglecting her and reminding him of how she had selflessly helped others. A postscript asked him to 'remember how you used to call on me every week before marriage and how you dropped all visits for nine months'.

Unaware that Grace was treating many of her friends in a similar manner, Cathal immediately sprang to his own defence. A pencilled draft of his reply begins, 'Your letter which arrived Tuesday evening surprised and worried me as it contained many exaggerated and sweeping accusations.' He stated that he was not aware that he had deliberately refused to do any turns she had asked of him, though he admitted to having been slow on occasions to answer some of her requests. He told her about his long hours at work and the fact that he only had three hours for recreation in the evenings. He mentioned that he was obliged to make 'duty visits' to his parents and relatives, and that he insisted on having Sunday evening free so that Margaret and he could enjoy each other's company. His explanation for not being able to visit Grace 'for a long time' was his having to attend to Margaret's parents, who had come to stay with them at their home in Rialto. However, he reminded her that he had visited her several times after they had returned home and that he had taken her out for two picnics. 'The extra work entailed in getting a home together' accounted for his absence for some nine months after he and Margaret were married. 'Margaret takes first place in my affections and I hope she will never have cause to say I neglected her or denied her my company', Cathal wrote.

Grace's last letter to Cathal, in answer to this defence, was posted on 21 January. In it, she stated, 'Your letter amazed me. Every statement was untrue.' She defended the accusation of Cathal's that she had subjected many of her friends 'to various tests and trials' and cited examples of long friendships, such as with the McNamara sisters. She was unconvinced by Cathal's explanation for 'dropping' her for nine months, saying that his home was 'an already perfect house'. She concluded her letter by stating, 'I would not trouble to answer your letter only that I think you have a fine character under it all. With best regards, G.'

In January 1953, Cathal's mother began to go 'a little odd' and was sent to St Patrick's Hospital in Dublin. After five or six weeks she was sent to St Edmundsbury's in Lucan for a while. She stayed in Margaret and Cathal's home in Rialto for a weekend at the end of February and in early March was discharged from St Edmundsbury's and sent home, to all intents and purposes cured. She attended the Brewery medical department for the last time on 19 March, was sent to Dr Steeven's Hospital on the 23rd and died of a brain haemorrhage on 8 April. She was seventy-one years of age. She was buried at Mount Jerome Cemetery. Mr Gannon was heartbroken and from that time onwards he never let anyone sit in her seat in his Austin 10 saloon car. He finally sold the car for scrap and had it destroyed in front of his eyes.

That autumn, a German acquaintance of Michael Morrow, Werner Schürmann from Munich, returned to Dublin from Galway. He had stayed in Dublin briefly in 1952. Werner was a sculptor, singer and amateur musician and had met Michael Morrow in Germany, where he had been studying for one year on a scholarship. Werner had come to Dublin with him out of curiosity and with a vague notion of obtaining a job at the National College of Art. Michael, who was a friend of John Beckett, Dr Stan Corran and the Actons, was a competent painter, lutenist and recorder player. During the sixties, he and John Beckett founded Musica Reservata, a group dedicated to the performance of early music.

Whilst in Dublin, Michael introduced Werner to John Beckett and John O'Sullivan. Werner, Michael, his sister Brigid and John Beckett played recorders, and Werner's small octavino (a portable spinet tuned an octave higher than normal pitch) came in handy as a continuo instrument. John Beckett persuaded Werner to sing some German songs for a Radio Éireann broadcast. Somehow Werner was invited to Cathal's home in Rialto. He was shown the new harpsichord, which at this stage was probably kept upstairs in the spare bedroom. He remembers the black case and the Dutch orange lid. However, as Werner was too occupied trying to set up a place in which he could do bronze casting, he saw little of Cathal at this period.

By now, Cathal's sister Maureen was married and had two sets of twins: Peter and Stephen and Kathleen and Anne. Sadly, her husband Stephen

Moran died on 26 December 1953 – St Stephen's Day, as it happened. As Maureen had to return to work in order to make ends meet, the two baby boys were sent to her brother Jack's home and Margaret and Cathal agreed to take young Kathleen and Anne, who were aged four and a half at the time. Margaret had decided to mind the girls as she knew nothing about babies – the boys were barely one year old.

Naturally, having two small girls in the house gave Margaret extra work, but she managed as they were well behaved. She took them to the national school at Loreto Convent on the Crumlin Road every day and collected them. Although she did not realize it at the time, looking after the children proved to be good preparation for what was about to come.

In May 1954, Margaret and Cathal went on another holiday to Spiddal, taking Mr and Mrs Clench, Mr Gannon and the two young girls, Kathleen and Anne. Because there were too many people for one car, they took two; Mr Gannon drove his. By all accounts the holiday was very pleasant; according to Cathal, it was the only time that he saw Spiddal under ideal conditions. Mrs O'Leary from the guest house claimed that my life began there.

She was absolutely right for, amazingly, Margaret discovered that she was pregnant only in November of that year; the doctor told her that her baby was due to be born in February 1955. Possibly because of her age (she was now forty-two), she hardly expanded; as the weather was cold and she wore a thick fur coat when out and about, nobody noticed her condition.

The doctor also advised Margaret to have young Kathleen and Anne looked after elsewhere, for he did not want to put any undue strain on her and wanted her to carry the baby for as long as possible. The two girls were sent to St Mary's Dominican Convent in Cabra, where they stayed as boarders and were brought home to their mother and grandfather at weekends by Cathal. There were tears every time he drove them back on Sunday evenings.

By all accounts the pregnancy developed without any hitches and Margaret remained in surprisingly good spirits. Only the news from England that her stepfather was ill upset her a little. Indeed, her mother was not in the best of health either.

Despite the onset of labour pains on the morning of Saturday, 5 February, some ten days before they were expected, Margaret innocently went out shopping. When Cathal arrived home from work and she told him what had happened, he said, 'For God's sake – the nursing home is the place for you!' Margaret packed up some things and Cathal drove her to the Eveleen

Nursing Home in Eccles Street, where she was ensconced in an elegant Georgian room with comfortable furniture – it was more like a sitting room than a hospital ward. As the weather was quite cold, a fire was lit.

Margaret's labour dragged on and on, lasting from Saturday morning until Tuesday afternoon. By this time she was exhausted. Doctor John F. Boyle, who was looking after her, said, 'I think we can't go on like this,' and decided to call the anaesthetist.

Margaret was happy to fall in with this plan and end the torture, knowing that she would wake up and find the baby already born. It did not matter to her much whether it would be a girl or a boy. However, she and Cathal had agreed that, should she give birth to a boy, it would be named Charles after Cathal's father, since none of his grandchildren had been given that name.

PART TWO

My Father 1955–99

Twenty-Seven

*B*y a curious twist of fate, my birth – at mid-afternoon on 8 February 1955 – occurred mid-way in my father's life. He was forty-four years of age at the time and was to live for another forty-four years. Also, we both managed to inflict on our mothers difficult births that required the use of anaesthetic. Unlike my father, I was not born to the sound of music, but was destined to develop a love–hate relationship with it some years later.

I was presented to my mother when she came out of the anaesthetic and she heaved a sigh of relief – the ordeal was over. Cathal sent a telegram to her parents and shortly afterwards they wrote, conveying their congratulations, love and pride. It was clear that they were overjoyed. Soon, letters and presents began arriving from all of Cathal and Margaret's friends and relatives.

Margaret stayed in the nursing home, recuperating, and after a couple of days I was taken to Berkeley Road Church to be baptised. Kevin Cregan's wife, Eithne, was my godmother. I was returned to my mother, and both she and I came home to Herberton Road after a fortnight.

My father was delighted that he now had a son, and was both congratulated and teased by his colleagues at work. He 'wound up' one fellow by telling him that on account of his wife's nationality, he had named me Charles after Prince Charles of England.

I weighed six and a quarter pounds and photographs prove that I had a shock of dark brown hair. One snapshot shows my mother looking well and smiling at the camera, and my father looking down at me. His hair is also dark but is receding; as yet he is not bespectacled. He looks pleased at the new arrival. Another photo is of the christening cake and cards.

As I had to be fed during the night, my father took to sleeping in the front spare bedroom (where the harpsichord was kept) so that he could have a good night's rest. He rejoined Margaret at a later stage.

Apparently I was a reasonably well-behaved baby. In June, my grandparents came from Harrow to see me. A photograph shows me in my grandmother's arms, wearing a potty on my head — my father had placed it there for a joke.

On 13 December 1955, Grace Plunkett died alone, in bed, in her apartment in South Richmond Street. My mother cannot remember my father's reaction; as he had known her so well and for so long, he must have been saddened. Yet her two final letters had embittered him and it appears that he did not attend the state funeral that was accorded to her.

My father had met Jack Brady, owner of the granite quarries in Ballyknockan, County Wicklow, in 1950, through John Burke and his family. Jack Brady was married to Máire Burke's sister, Eileen.

In 1955 Jack offered Cathal a little cottage near his house in Ballyknockan for £25, on condition that he renovate it. It was situated beside a bog road, facing an unfinished statue of the Madonna, which had been carved in local granite, and overlooked the spectacular reservoir. Thinking that it would make an ideal weekend house, Cathal bought it. He worked hard on the cottage at weekends during 1955 and 1956, enlarging the windows, making sashes and fitting a new hall door. He replastered the inside walls and put compo on the outside. He put down two new timber floors and a concrete floor in the kitchen. The cottage had been built on rock and as one floor was higher than the other he had a difficult job lowering it.

Cathal furnished the cottage with various bits and pieces given to him by his aunt Cissie. I can well remember being at Ballyknockan. One approached the timeless old-world village of grey stone cottages and houses, which looked as though they had grown there naturally, and ascended a steep hill to the Brady's house, which I loved. My memory of the cottage itself is rather hazy. There was a wooden shed to one side and a short walk through a field behind the house brought one to a little spring and then a quarry.

An elderly man who lived in the village often came to the cottage to talk to my father. Apparently he often asked my father to buy him various things in Dublin; Cathal once supplied him with a chimney pot. The man was also very interested in royalty and nobility. Cathal teased him by telling him that his wife was a daughter of the Earl of Harrow (of course there was no such person) and he introduced our young neighbour, Joan Devine, as the daughter of Sir Charles Harvey. Joan had done a secretarial course with Sir Charles Harvey's daughter.

Sadly, Jack Brady died in November 1957. After this my father gradually lost interest in the cottage, the village and villagers, and in 1963 he sold the cottage for £350.

I can clearly remember our house in Rialto, its neatness and cleanliness, and the amount of time my mother spent every day keeping everything in order. The decor was simple yet refined and everything was in good taste. Right from the beginning I grew up surrounded by elegant furniture, good pictures and musical instruments, which I always respected and loved. Even the simple furniture made by my father was restrained and tasteful. I can remember the colour scheme and layout of most of the rooms in that little house and often wonder what it is like now.

Most of my childhood memories are connected with my mother, who was with me all day, every day. My father was a more shadowy figure. During weekdays I saw him only at mealtimes and for a little while in the evening before I was dispatched to bed. I often shrank from him in terror and ran to my mother for comfort, for, when I grew a little older and was naughty during the day, my mother always threatened me by saying, 'Wait until I tell your father.' As soon as he arrived home from work (always through the back door into the scullery), he was told what I had done – usually something minor, I am sure, for I was not a deliberately naughty child – and punishment was administered in the form of a 'box in the ears' and a lecture. Although I was good most of the time, I soon began to dread his arrival in the evenings. I cannot remember being slapped by my mother; although strict like my father as regards discipline, she was more gentle.

By September 1956, Werner Schürmann, his wife Gerda and their son Wenzel had settled in Ireland, living at Woodtown Park near Rathfarnham. During the previous spring, Werner had bought an early Broadwood square piano, which Cathal helped to put into some sort of playing order. He went to the Schürmanns' house, where he restrung the instrument and tuned it.

After this Werner came frequently to Herberton Road, where he played piano duets with Cathal and introduced him to some of the wonderful

German *Lieder* or songs. Although Cathal did not understand a word of German (Werner remembers how he always mispronounced his name), he adored the songs, especially those by Schubert and Brahms. Cathal became a sensitive accompanist for singers, mastering the difficult art of following a singer's whims and idiosyncrasies.

Werner's music-making was listened to with interest by Margaret, who later in the evenings prepared her usual 'sumptuous' suppers, which Werner relished. I can remember Werner's visits with pleasure; the fact that he was German fascinated me and I loved his rich, resonant voice, both when he spoke and sang.

Werner purchased more pianos in the following years: another square piano, a fine Erard grand and a Bechstein boudoir grand, all of which Cathal found for him and bought for around £20. Cathal often went to his house to tune, maintain and play these instruments. When Cathal worked at the pianos, Werner watched carefully and made a mental note of everything that he did, which later was of great help to him when he restored these instruments in Germany.

Werner noted how careful and precise Cathal was about the smallest details; he felt that his accuracy was astounding and that nobody could equal him. According to Werner, Cathal was quite unlike anybody he had ever met before. Although Cathal was older than he was, they became good friends. This was typical of Cathal; he preferred the company of younger people and had the sense to keep them as friends for his latter years.

Werner greatly admired Cathal's collections of pianos, watches, clocks and pictures, and his knowledge about every item in the house. He can still remember my father's face keen with interest and concentration as he tuned an instrument, yet still able to talk and impart detailed information about what he was doing.

In 1957, probably in the autumn, Cathal heard a talk by the instrument collector and harpsichord expert Raymond Russell on the BBC Third Programme. Mr Russell advocated the accurate copying of old harpsichords and condemned the modern 'improved' instruments with their heavy construction, foot pedals and sixteen-foot stops, tuned an octave below normal pitch. To illustrate his point, he made reference to the history of the violin, which had reached its zenith in the 1730s and thereafter had been left unchanged. He reasoned that, just like the great violin makers such as Stradivarius and

Amati, the old masters of the harpsichord knew what they were doing.

Having listened attentively to Mr Russell's talk, Cathal went upstairs to the bedroom in which the harpsichord had been put and began to undo some of his mistakes. He removed the unnecessary bars from under the sound-board, unstrung it and put in lighter strings. The effect was immediate; suddenly the instrument 'was absolutely lovely'. Cathal abandoned his plan to fit seven pedals and moved the harpsichord downstairs to the sitting room, where it was used for the Saturday musical evenings.

Two regular guests at Lord Moyne's play-readings in Knockmaroon were the Honourable Desmond Guinness, Bryan's second son, and his wife Mariga, born Hermione Marie-Gabrielle, Princess of Urach and a descendant of the royal house of Württemberg in Germany. The couple had married in 1954 at Oxford, had come to Ireland the following year, and had rented the beautiful Carton House near Maynooth, County Kildare, where the Duke of Leinster had once lived. Desmond believes that he met Cathal at the meetings of the Old Dublin Society some time previously. Margaret and Cathal now renewed the friendship and they were invited to visit the Guinnesses at Carton.

Desmond and Mariga were a striking couple: Desmond a handsome young man with intense blue eyes and Mariga an imperious, dramatic young lady with long dark hair and a slight cast in one eye. Although highly unconventional and quite eccentric, she was both amusing and likeable. Cathal and Margaret took to her immediately. As befitted her rank, she was inclined to order 'lesser mortals' around like servants, but nobody seemed to mind this. She always spoke her mind and never minded what others thought about her. To Cathal, who always enjoyed eccentric people, she must have been a breath of fresh air. At times she could be hilarious; she had a wicked sense of humour and could silence a person she disliked with a word or two. Like Cathal, her mind was razor-sharp and she could always retort when provoked – she gave as good as she got. She spoke in a very emphatic manner in a characteristic breathy voice and constantly used imperatives such as 'you *must* come for dinner' or '*do* come and visit us'. She loved to organize parties and picnics, and was famous for arriving at functions 'fashionably late' – often with an entourage of uninvited friends. Her introductions were short but stimulating – 'this is Mr *Gawnnon* who makes harpsichords' – and always left both parties with something to talk about. Margaret felt at ease with her. Apparently Mariga was very fond of me as a child.

Cathal, Desmond and Mariga had a common interest: a passionate love of old Dublin and its Georgian buildings, and a horror at the neglect and wanton destruction of so many fine eighteenth-century houses both in Dublin and around the country. Inspired by Maurice Craig's scholarly book, *Dublin 1660–1860*, which had been published in 1952, and shocked by the recent demolition of Georgian houses in Dominick Street and Kildare Place, Desmond and Mariga founded the Irish Georgian Society in 1958 in an effort to arouse public awareness and save the crumbling mansions. Cathal and Margaret joined (no doubt they were *persuaded* to join, as so many others were) and attended the meetings, which were held in various different locations, such as Ely House, where Mariga once gave a talk about a proposed journey to Russia. Unfortunately Cathal could not remember the details of these early meetings.

In 1958 Desmond and Mariga bought Leixlip Castle in County Kildare and restored it with the help of many people, including Cathal and his brother Jack, who journeyed there at weekends to lend a hand. Apparently Jack worked on the staircase. Anybody and everybody was invited to do some work on the castle. When it was completed, the three of us were invited and we became regular guests over the years.

In 1958, Cathal bought an 1815 Clementi square piano for 30s. from the elderly Bullard sisters, who owned a tiny shop in Chancery Place. The piano was in bad shape, although nothing was missing. Cathal restored it to playing condition and was quite happy with the sound. He loaned it to the Royal Irish Academy of Music for a dramatization of *Jane Eyre*, which was staged in the Dagg Hall in November. It ran for three nights and only Margaret attended one of the performances.

In the spring of 1958, Dr Stan Corran was walking across the Brewery yard one morning when Cathal stopped him.

'Dr Corran,' said Cathal, 'I've got a nice little Clementi square piano that I've restored and I'd like to show it to you.'

Stan protested that he had no skill on the keyboard, but as Cathal was so keen for him to see it he agreed to go to the house in Rialto. Cathal ushered him into the front dining room, where he showed him the 'rather beautiful square piano'. Stan played a few bars of a piece by Clementi and agreed that the sound was quite marvellous.

As he had heard of the harpsichord, which D.O. Williams had ridiculed by saying that it made no noise whatsoever (he was an excellent pianist), Stan asked Cathal, 'What of the harpsichord?'

'Ah,' said Cathal, 'I never finished it.' However, he brought Stan into the sitting room and showed him the instrument. Stan admired it, sat down and played a few chords on it.

'But it's perfect,' he said. 'What isn't finished?'

'I never completed the lute stop,' replied Cathal.

'Be blowed to that!' said Stan. 'It's marvellous without that!'

Stan then told him that he had played music at one of Lord Moyne's social evenings and that he would like to use the harpsichord at the next performance. Cathal agreed to this and, when the time came, made all the necessary arrangements.

Cathal kept the Clementi square piano for a while in the dining room, where I have a vague memory of seeing it. At a later date he stored it on its side and finally gave it as a wedding present to Kathleen Kelly when she married Desmond Duncan in 1968.

Cathal by now had become quite methodical in his approach to restoring old pianos, taking note of the original string thicknesses and other details before restoration and writing them down. When finished, he took care to write an inscription somewhere inside the instrument, detailing his name, the date of restoration and what exactly he had done, so that a future restorer would know what was original and what had been replaced.

Cathal was always fascinated by the inscriptions that he found inside instruments, especially on the keyboards. For him it was evidence that labour was subdivided. It was obvious that various individuals made the parts, which they often signed, and that an assembler bought them and put them together. Consequently, the name painted on an early piano or even harpsichord was more likely to be that of the assembler; keyboard instruments were, in effect, mass produced. The same system was also applied to the manufacture of clocks.

Shortly before Margaret and Cathal's sixteenth wedding anniversary in November 1958, they were invited to Knockmaroon for one of the regular play-reading evenings. On that occasion Cathal met the poet and dramatist Pádraig Colum, 'a nice, quiet old man' aged seventy-seven, who spent most of his time in New York. When Cathal introduced himself, Pádraig mentioned that the name Gannon rang a bell. It turned out that as a young man he had been involved in amateur theatricals with Cathal's father in the Father O'Donovan Hall in Lower Clanbrassil Street, which was later turned into a weaving mill.

Cathal's first harpsichord was finally inaugurated and introduced to the public in Knockmaroon House by Lord Moyne either on or near the date of the wedding anniversary, 28 November. Lord Moyne had fallen in with Dr Stan Corran's plan to borrow Cathal's harpsichord for his next musical evening.

A Brewery colleague of Cathal's helped him transport the harpsichord to Knockmaroon during the afternoon of the appointed day. As they were lifting the instrument into position, Lord Moyne came into the room. Obviously the instrument and the Latin motto took his fancy, for Cathal remembered him saying, 'What elegance!' He then invited Cathal's colleague to come to the evening performance. The man was delighted.

The musical evening, which was a great success, was held in the fine ballroom. Cathal and Dr Stan Corran performed Georg Philipp Telemann's *Wedding Divertissement* on harpsichord and recorder, and Tom Tierney performed a piece by Mozart on the new instrument. Mrs Elizabeth Hannon (née Colclogh) sang and played her accompaniment on the guitar.

While Cathal was demonstrating his harpsichord to some interested people during the interval, Lord Moyne approached him and said, 'You are badly needed in the dining room.' When Cathal arrived, he found it in darkness. On the table was an iced fruit cake, with sixteen lighted candles and the inscription 'Happy 16th Wedding Anniversary', which had been added by the children's nanny, Miss Nevett. As far as Cathal could remember, a piper marched up and down the hall, playing. He was extremely surprised, not having expected it at all.

Margaret had gone to the dining room before him, had seen the cake and had assumed that it was for somebody's birthday. When Lady Moyne congratulated her, she thought that she was referring to the new harpsichord. When she discovered that Lady Moyne knew about their wedding anniversary and that the cake was in fact for them, she was flabbergasted. When Margaret asked her how she knew about the anniversary, she merely laughed. It turned out that Lord Moyne's secretary, Miss Anderson, had told him. Margaret and Cathal cut the cake to a round of applause.

Cathal's workmate, who enjoyed the evening, was able to witness everything and report it to his colleagues on the following morning – Cathal did not need to say anything. The man purposely embellished his account, which annoyed several of the workers.

Thereafter, Cathal often met Lord Moyne at concerts, especially at those given by the St James's Gate Musical Society, conducted by Victor Leeson. Lord Moyne often chose to sit beside Cathal.

This was an exciting and stimulating time for Cathal; his horizons were being broadened by mixing with the likes of the Guinnesses and their acquaintances. They appreciated him because of his knowledge and his unusual skill of being able to make a harpsichord and restore old keyboard instruments. He led a busy life, working every day in the Brewery, attending concerts on various days of the week and entertaining guests almost every Saturday evening. Stan Corran, his wife Olive and a group of recorder players were now regular guests, as well as a friend of the Corrans, Mrs Andreas, who lived in Blackrock. Over the weekends, Cathal often drove to Ballyknockan or off to the countryside for picnics, and of course there were visits to friends, films to be seen and Irish Georgian Society lectures to attend. Cathal, it could be said, was living life to the full.

Twenty-Eight

*I*n 1959 Victor Leeson, the conductor of the St James's Gate Musical Society, planned a performance of Bach's *Saint Matthew Passion* in the relatively new St Francis Xavier Hall in Upper Sherrard Street. Having heard about Cathal's harpsichord, he asked John Beckett to go to our house to try it out; if John liked it, he would ask Cathal's permission to use it. As John thought it was a good instrument, he reported his approval to Victor and the instrument was borrowed for the performance.

The *Passion* was held on 15 March and performed, in its entirety, in two parts, the first in the afternoon and the second in the evening. On the back of a promotional leaflet was printed the following note:

> Last year the St James's Gate Musical Society gave the first complete performance in Dublin of Bach's *St Matthew Passion*. In response to many requests, we have decided to give another performance this year, on Passion Sunday, 15 March.
>
> Last year, we had to improvise a harpsichord, using a piano with drawing-pins stuck into the hammers. This year through the kindness of Mr. Cathal Gannon, we have been most fortunate in obtaining the use of a genuine instrument. Mr. Gannon, who works in St James's Gate Brewery, has for many years been interested in old musical instruments. He has restored many old square pianos, and some years ago built himself a clavichord. This harpsichord, which has taken him almost two years in building, is based on a classical design, taken from an instrument at Fenton House near London [to which the Benton Fletcher Collection had been moved in 1952]. It will be played by Mr. John Beckett.

Although poorly attended because of a gala concert at the Gaiety Theatre on the same evening, the performance was a tremendous success and critiques in praise of it appeared in four national newspapers on the following day. One reviewer wrote:

> Betty Sullivan and John Beckett were a lovely continuo. Mr. Beckett was a little insistent at times in the orchestral passages, but his realisation of the harpsichord part was at all times beautifully apt and exciting. It was especially interesting to hear him play on what seemed a lovely harpsichord made in Dublin by Cathal Gannon — I hope we may hear this instrument in solo or chamber music performances.

John O'Donovan of the *Evening Press* wrote:

> The playing of the double orchestra was excellent, and all due praise must go to David Lee, the organist, and John Beckett, the harpsichordist.
>
> The harpsichord, by the way, deserves special mention. It was entirely built by a Dublin craftsman, Mr. Cathal Gannon, and is a credit alike to his patience and to his skill ... I hope to renew its public acquaintance again and again.

Although Cathal probably found the performance too long — over four hours — and the music not entirely to his taste, he must have been tremendously proud that his harpsichord had been used at such a great occasion and heard by members of the public. It also must have been immensely satisfying to read such good reports in the newspapers. This was not the first time his name had been in print; in February he had been featured in 'Tatler's Parade' in the *Irish Independent*. The article, entitled 'The Musical Carpenter', described his interest in early keyboard instruments, how he went about building a clavichord and then a harpsichord.

> It took nearly four years of winter spare-time work and a second visit to London, although Mr Gannon, with the quiet air of the perfectionist, admitted: 'I built and re-built it several times before I was satisfied.'

The article concluded:

> Modestly brushing aside his accomplishments as a mere 'hobby', this soft-speaking craftsman has the quiet, confident air of a man with no limit in the 'do it yourself' sphere.

The reporter had touched on a side of Cathal's character that I have not yet described: his extreme modesty. Although he obviously had a driving ambition to achieve perfection (despite the lack of impetus he had suffered when his first harpsichord was almost completed), he was always self-effacing when his work was praised. When admirers expressed amazement, he always tried to convince them that there was no mystery attached to what he had done or achieved, explaining that anybody could do it given enough commitment and training. Knowing that others had managed to produce these fine instruments in the past, he saw nothing unusual about what he had done; he merely thought of himself as someone who was continuing a tradition that had been interrupted for a number of years.

Eamonn Delaney, writing in the March–April edition of the Guinness *Harp* magazine, also noticed Cathal's modesty. His short article was entitled 'The Quiet Carpenter'.

> *Musica magnorum est solamen dulce laborum* ... Few of our Irish readers are by this time unaware of Cathal Gannon's distinction of giving Dublin its first harpsichord in one hundred and sixty years. Hardly a columnist in our daily papers missed the opportunity of writing of this fascinating and inspiring achievement. The motto quoted above, telling us that music is a delightful consolation after toil or trouble, is inscribed inside the lid of this beautiful musical instrument and sums up the fruit of [two] years of patient, talented labour. Our Musical Society's recent performance of J. S. Bach's *St Matthew Passion*, in which the same harpsichord played no small part, has been so favourably received by the critics that we must be forgiven if all this makes us a little proud. All concerned, however, are fully conscious of John Beckett's contribution to this notable success, for his playing of the harpsichord had all the gentle quality of the Master.
>
> And what can we now add to the story of this quiet carpenter who only last year restored by his own hands an 1808 Clementi table piano, out of a deteriorated model he had purchased almost as scrap? We are privileged to report that this wonder man is busy again. This time, and to complete the group, he has set himself the task of building a Virginal. This is an instrument that can best be described as a simplified version of the harpsichord, which was to be found in most of the well-to-do homes of the 17th century. In this particular work, Cathal will follow the design of an instrument by Robert Hatley (1664), London.
>
> What then, you might well ask, is the driving force behind such

enthusiasm and effort? An absorbing love of music certainly, coupled with the craftsman's instinctive and natural enjoyment of a job well done. But greater still than these important ingredients is the never failing devotion and encouragement of his wife.

For while Cathal Gannon has accepted, somewhat shyly, the plaudits and the praise, always in the background is this lady of talents, the inspiration of all his toil and his faithful helper.

To them both, on behalf of the entire personnel of St James's Gate, we send our sincerest congratulations.

Unfortunately, Cathal was rather dismissive about the virginal referred to in the article and said very little about it. He did make it and finished it during the following year, but because he 'never liked it', he gave it away to a friend. Whilst on one of our regular holidays in Harrow, journeyed into London and headed for the Benton Fletcher Collection once again, now in the elegant Fenton House, Hampstead. Cathal must have been struck by the beauty of the original virginal; a rectangular box-like instrument with jacks like a harpsichord, it measured five and a half feet long and had a keyboard of black ebony naturals and white ivory accidentals on its long side, offset to the left. The inside of the case and the keyboard surround were covered with gilt embossed paper; the insides of the lid and the drop-front cover were decorated with paintings depicting rustic scenes.

Cathal was disappointed in the sound of his much plainer copy. A photograph of Cathal playing this virginal, watched by Dr Stan Corran holding a recorder, Andrew Healy (a Brewery clerk) holding an oboe and a very youthful Liam Fitzgerald (then a Guinness apprentice electrician) holding his violin, appeared in the March–April edition of the *Harp* magazine for 1960. The four had played a quartet by Telemann at one of Lord Moyne's parties at Knockmaroon. 'I don't recall any performance ever giving me such satisfaction,' wrote Dr Corran to me many years later.

However, we have jumped ahead a little. In June 1959 Cathal's harpsichord was used again, this time in a recital of Vivaldi concertos given in the Gaiety Theatre by I Virtuosi di Roma, a small but highly-regarded orchestra of thirteen players, dedicated to the performance of pre-classical music, conducted by Renato Fasano. The harpsichordist on this occasion was Riccardo Castagnone. Once again, the newspaper critics were ecstatic, especially Charles Acton, who reported that although the theatre was only half full, the audience 'produced a louder volume of applause than I have ever heard there

– and achieved an encore'. He continued: 'How fortunate we are now to have Mr. Gannon's new harpsichord for these events. In Riccardo Castagnone's sensitive hands, it shewed [*sic*] its beautiful tone, and the balance was always perfect.' Cathal was lucky, for Charles Acton always had a good word for his harpsichords.

Towards the end of June, Cathal and Margaret received a formal invitation for a reception at the American Ambassador's residence in the Phoenix Park, which they accepted and attended. The Ambassador, Mr Scott McLeod, had invited members of the Irish Georgian Society to attend between six and eight o'clock on the 26th. However, only some of the guests arrived on time at the residence; as the ambiguously worded invitation read 'RSVP US Embassy Phoenix Park', a busload of Americans were driven from their hotel to the US Embassy in Ballsbridge. When they eventually arrived, they sidled past the Ambassador and avoided shaking hands with him. The Americans were well aware that Mr McLeod had been an embarrassment to the administration and had been sent to Ireland by President Eisenhower as a means of getting him out of the country. In the residence, the guests nibbled sandwiches, sipped drinks and chatted, and a group of musicians, dressed in eighteenth-century costume, played. However, as some of them were obliged to wear spectacles in order to see their music, the ensemble looked very strange indeed.

At one stage during the reception, Margaret and Cathal found themselves smiling at a familiar-looking man, who stood at the foot of the staircase holding a little dog and conversing with Mrs McLeod. The man returned their smiles. It was some time afterwards when they realized who he was: Walt Disney.

Around this time, Dr Stan Corran bought Cathal's Schiedmayer upright piano and brought Cathal to a recital featuring the English Consort of Viols, held in the St John Ambulance Hall, Upper Leeson Street. Cathal was familiar with viols (the six-stringed and fretted precursors of the violin family), having heard them on the Third Programme and seen examples in the Victoria and Albert Museum. Unfortunately, the hall was illuminated by gas lights, which gave out moisture and continually caused the delicate gut-stringed instruments to go out of tune. One of the bass viols was played by Mrs Elizabeth Goble, wife of the English harpsichord maker Robert Goble, whose workshop was situated in Headington, Oxford. Cathal met and spoke with Mrs Goble at a lunch held in Guinness's Brewery after the concert.

Nineteen fifty-nine was the year of the bicentenary celebrations in Guinness's Brewery and everyone who worked there was given a complimentary china ashtray bearing a portrait of Arthur Guinness. As Cathal had been out sick, he went to the registry office to collect his sick pay and the pensions for four other elderly men, including his father. He was given five ashtrays, packaged in small cardboard boxes.

Cathal caught a bus home and sat opposite a woman who obviously had collected her husband's pension. She eyed the five boxes and said, 'You're only entitled to one of those.'

'The ashtrays?' asked Cathal.

'Yes,' she said.

'Oh well,' said Cathal, 'I got four extra ones.'

'You're not supposed to get them,' snapped the woman. 'I was in there and the man would only give me one.'

'Ah well,' said Cathal, 'I spun a tale to him and I got four extra! That's the best of influence!'

'Well, be Jaysus,' said the woman resolutely, 'I'm goin' to go back and talk to him!' and jumped off the bus. Cathal often wondered what happened when she tackled the man in the office!

The Howth tram also ran for the last time that year and I can remember travelling in it with my mother, looking at the surroundings from the open top. My father followed in his new Morris Minor car, which he had bought in March. It was dark green in colour. The letters and numbers of the registration plate are etched in my memory: EYI 767. It was a good car and we kept it for a number of years.

In November I can remember going with my parents to an Irish Georgian Society event at 8–10 Henrietta Street in Dublin to raise funds for repairing these three houses, which were occupied by the Sisters of Charity of St Vincent de Paul. The roofs were in danger of collapse. I have a vague recollection of mingling with guests during a reception in the front room of one of these large Georgian houses.

I can then clearly remember walking along a path in the back garden, magically illuminated by lighted candles in jars, to a hall, where we watched a preview of unedited footage taken during a recent architectural visit to America.

My father remembered being in one of the tenement houses in Henrietta Street with Mariga Guinness at around this period, admiring the fine plasterwork. They found the people in the house all very pleasant, especially the woman who had shown them in.

After Mariga had left, the woman said to Cathal, 'Your friend is a terrible well-spoken lady!'

'Oh,' said Cathal, 'you mean Mrs Guinness?'

'Yes, I think she's called Mrs Guinness. She often comes in to see us here.'

'Did you know she's a princess?'

'Oh, for God's sake – a princess?'

'Yes, she's a real German princess, married to Desmond Guinness.'

The woman was delighted. 'Well,' she said, 'I never thought I'd have a princess in the house!'

In early 1960, Cathal was introduced by Desmond Guinness to Sir George and Lady Mahon, who lived in Castleknock Lodge. Sir George owned a virginal that needed some attention and Cathal fixed it for him. Afterwards Cathal saw Sir George and his wife at various musical events.

In May, Desmond asked Cathal to repair a Broadwood grand piano of 1802, which he had at Leixlip Castle and which, he had been told, could never be played again. As he and Mariga were going to Italy for a two-month holiday, he invited us all to stay in the castle until their return, giving Cathal ample time to work on the instrument. As Cathal had to go to work and as I had to attend school, we had to decline this enticing offer and settle on staying there over eight consecutive weekends. The castle was staffed with a butler and a few maids and so we had our meals in style – something that Cathal relished.

I remember those magical weekends with great pleasure. I had been brought to Leixlip Castle before by my parents, but now I had the golden opportunity of actually staying there. I was ensconced in a large mahogany bed hung with blue and white toile curtains in an elegant bedroom decorated with Chinese yellow wallpaper; blue and white Chinese plates hung on the walls. My parents used an adjoining bedroom.

While my mother and I regularly adjourned to the nursery to join the nanny, Mary Fitzgerald, and the two adorable children, Patrick and Marina (who were younger than I was by one and two years respectively), my father worked on the piano. He did a job on the action and put new coverings on the hammers. As the keyboard was in a bad way and many of the ivories were missing, he fitted new ones. Having finished the action, he then restrung the instrument and got it playing. By the time he finished, it was in good condition. However, as the Guinnesses kept it beside a radiator, the heat soon played havoc with it.

In between times, my father brought us all out for drives in the Morris Minor. On one memorable occasion we went to the generating station at Poulaphouca near Blessington, where we children rolled down the grassy slopes, surrounded by buttercups and bluebells. There are photographs to remind me of this occasion; in one of them, my father smiles at the camera, clutching a small flower. By now he looks exactly as I always remember him: his hair has receded and is almost grey, his face is fuller and he wears the type of horn-rimmed glasses that he would use for many years to come.

He remembered this outing too; whilst walking with Margaret, myself, Miss Fitzgerald and the two Guinness children, he passed a workmate, who afterwards asked him about the children and the nanny. My father spun some yarn about Miss Fitzgerald being *my* nanny.

Over the years, when I was a little older, I was invited to many children's parties at Leixlip. Although I adored the unique atmosphere of the castle, I felt a little ill at ease amongst the children. We often chased about the house, in and out of rooms and up and down staircases. Cakes and other delights were served at a number of tables in the octagonal dining room. Desmond often produced his cine projector and showed us Charlie Chaplin films, which we enjoyed hugely.

On Saturday, 30 July, Cathal and a photographer friend, Hugh Doran, joined a two-day Irish Georgian Society expedition to Limerick and Clare. Desmond Guinness had written a short letter to Cathal a little earlier telling him that they were keeping a bed for him at Glin Castle, home of Desmond Fitzgerald, Knight of Glin. Cathal drove to Limerick with Hugh, arriving at the Customs House by two o'clock, when everyone met. Having toured the County Courthouse, the Town Hall and St John's Square, they then went to nearby Shannongrove, the earliest eighteenth-century house in counties Limerick and Clare, built in 1710 and owned by Mr and Mrs Armitage.

Having spent a couple of hours at the Hell Fire Club at Askeaton, they then went to the elegant Glin Castle, built between 1790 and 1812. Here they were entertained and Cathal and Hugh stayed the night.

The following day they all met at Bunratty Castle, then a ruin, and proceeded to Mount Ievers at Sixmilebridge, County Clare, where they picnicked. Having toured this fine house with its two facades, one of red brick and the other of cut stone, they then moved to Carnelly House, built by the Stamer family in 1740. Later they drove to New Hall, dating from 1764, in which they admired the imitation organ in the octagonal hall. The excursion finished at Kilnasoola Church, where they admired the monument to Sir Donatus O'Brien Bart.

In September, Cathal bought a Broadwood square piano, made in about 1814, at Battersby's auction rooms, Westmoreland Street for £25 plus fees. Although it was in reasonable condition when he bought it, the piano needed restringing. It turned out to be a good instrument and so Cathal retained it for many years. A handsome piano, I can remember it in Herberton Road.

In February 1961, Bach's *Saint Matthew Passion* was performed in the City Hall, Cork using almost the same forces that had been used in Dublin in 1959, and Cathal's harpsichord was once again employed. It was sent to Cork by train; Cathal and Margaret travelled with it, staying overnight in Cork.

Although the performance was not particularly well attended, it was enthusiastically applauded and received a favourable review in the press.

By this time, Trinity College had purchased Townley Hall, a fine house by the River Boyne near Drogheda in County Louth, with the intention of turning it into an agricultural college. During 1961 a badly broken-up Kirckman harpsichord of 1772 was discovered in this house and brought to Dublin, where it was housed temporarily in Trinity College. As soon as Cathal heard about it, he went to look at it and examined it in detail. As he felt inclined to restore it but had nowhere to put it, he encouraged the authorities to write to Lord Moyne, in the hope that he would ask Cathal to work on it in Guinness's Brewery. Following Cathal's directions, they wrote the letter, but there was no response. Lord Moyne later claimed that he had never received any letter. In all probability, a secretary had consigned it to the waste-paper basket.

In the end, money was collected and the instrument was sent to Robert Morley & Co. Ltd in Lewisham, London, where it was restored in a not completely sympathetic manner. When it returned to Dublin, Cathal was employed to maintain and tune it over the years.

When discovered at Townley Hall, this interesting instrument was unstrung, one of the keyboards had been removed and two-thirds of the

mechanism was missing. Because of this, Cathal was able to measure everything very accurately. He was given permission to remove the bottom and
was therefore able to see under the soundboard in a way that had not been
possible when examining the Kirckman in the Benton Fletcher Collection.
He thus had all the information he needed to make an accurate copy of it;
this he proceeded to do, working once again in the narrow glasshouse at
home. Having learned several lessons from making his first harpsichord,
work on the second was that little bit easier and took less time; he completed it in about one year. The new instrument, which was made to the
same length as the original, was a good deal more satisfactory than the first.
Cathal used this instrument as a pattern for five more harpsichords that he
would construct over the coming years. These instruments were not painted
like Cathal's first harpsichord; instead they were veneered in a style similar
to the original. The second harpsichord was veneered in choice mahogany.

As, unsurprisingly, I had been showing an interest in music – I can remember picking out a melody on one of my father's square pianos in the front
dining room – it was decided that I should learn the piano and I was sent to
the School of Music in Chatham Street. My first lessons were held in a classroom with other children. I enjoyed the experience of learning music at
first, though, as we shall see, the enjoyment was to be short-lived.

During this year a violinist by the name of Michael Clifton, who had formed
a small musical ensemble, formulated a plan to enter the Feis Ceoil Chamber Music competition. What the ensemble lacked was a harpsichord. Somehow or other Michael heard about Cathal's instrument – probably by reading the newspapers or by attending the recent concerts in which it had been
used – and came to the house. The ensemble, which included people such as
Emer O'Reilly (a cellist who later married Michael), Kieran Egar, a violinist, and Liam and Margaret Fitzgerald, managed to fit themselves into the
back room and practise their repertory of baroque music with Cathal playing the continuo part on the harpsichord as best he could. My father was
regularly cajoled into playing a movement or two of Bach's difficult solo
harpsichord piece, the *Italian Concerto*, which he played indifferently, apolo-
gizing all the time for his mistakes.

 During the summer months, our next-door neighbours opened their
windows or sat in their back garden, enjoying the free concert. A rehearsal

of this group took place nearly every Saturday evening and on each occasion my mother provided her usual supper of tea, sandwiches and cakes, which apparently was enjoyed by everyone. More people were encouraged to join the ensemble and eventually it blossomed into a small orchestra – the Dublin Baroque Players – with Liam Fitzgerald as its energetic conductor.

Twenty-Nine

*O*n 12 January 1962 Cathal's aunt Cissie passed away in the Hospice for the Dying in Harold's Cross and was buried in Dean's Grange Cemetery in the south of Dublin. Circumstances had separated Cissie and her sister Peggy and they had not seen each other for the past couple of years. Cathal had brought Cissie to visit Peggy in St Kevin's Hospital, James's Street, and they had spent a few hours together. This was to be their last meeting.

On the evening of Cissie's death, Cathal and Margaret went to a packed public meeting held in the Round Room of the Mansion House. Organized by the Irish Georgian Society and the ESB Fitzwilliam Street Protest Committee, it was a lively debate on the demolition of sixteen Georgian houses in Lower Fitzwilliam Street in order to make way for a modern office block for the Electricity Supply Board. Cathal had promised Mariga Guinness that he would go.

One of the principal speakers in favour of retaining the houses and using the land behind them for the building of an office tower was the British architect Sir Alfred Richardson. Cathal was very impressed by his argument in favour of preserving the houses. Sir Alfred Richardson declared that it was a most wonderful thing to see half a mile of Georgian architecture from Holles Street Hospital to Leeson Street Bridge, with mountains in the background. He told his audience that no place in the world could boast half a mile of Georgian architecture.

He had two blackboards behind him on the stage and on one of them he quickly drew the skyline of the Georgian houses as they stood. His depiction was quite accurate. He spoke about the good qualities of the houses and mentioned the beautiful colour of the bricks, which was particular to Dublin.

He then turned to the other blackboard and drew the modern office block proposed by the ESB. He deplored the bland replacement, which he said would ruin the character of the street, though he said he did not despise modern architecture, for he himself had designed buildings for New York and other cities in America.

Sir Alfred Richardson was given a great ovation, but a group of students from UCD with placards, who were in favour of destroying the old houses, heckled him. Cathal remembered Mariga Guinness pleading with them to be quiet, but they jeered her.

Unfortunately Sir Alfred, the Committee and the Irish Georgian Society were overruled by Dublin Corporation's decision to approve the ESB's plan and furious correspondence raged in the newspapers. Ultimately, as everyone knows, the Georgian houses were pulled down, and a dreary office block was erected.

A couple of days after this meeting, something uncanny happened. Cathal went to visit his aunt Peggy, who told him that she had dreamed that he was with a group of people. She said that it was not a concert because there was no music. Cathal told her about the Fitzwilliam Street meeting.

'That sounds like it,' she concluded, then added, 'I also had another dream about Cissie. How is she going on?'

Rather than tell her that she had died, Cathal said, 'Ah, she'll never get out of bed any more – she's confined now to bed.'

'I had a dream that she was dying and that there were nuns surrounding her,' Peggy said. 'She had a candle in her hand and they were all deploring the fact that they would miss her very much. But it was just a stupid dream.' Cathal found this quite extraordinary.

Peggy died in St Mary's Hospital in the Phoenix Park (I can remember seeing her there) in October 1962 and, like Cissie, was laid to rest in Dean's Grange Cemetery.

Although the little house in Rialto was perfect in every way, the area was beginning to become a little rough and noisy. Cathal often wished to live in a quieter house – especially at night-time when a neighbour's dog barked continuously and kept him awake. Towards the end of January, Cathal chanced on a newspaper advertisement for a house for sale in Lucan. It was one of eight elegant Georgian houses that formed a crescent behind the Spa Hotel. Margaret and Cathal drove to the house, number 3, and spoke to the owner, an elderly lady by the name of Miss Helen McGovern. She asked them how they knew the house was for sale and Cathal told her that he had read about it in the newspaper.

'I didn't give any authority to Adam's to put it up for sale,' said Miss McGovern. 'We were *discussing* putting it up for sale.'

However, she brought them inside and showed them around. Overlooking an extensive golf course at the back, the house, with a basement and three storeys, was idyllic. Cathal learned that it had been built in the 1790s for people who wanted to take the waters at Lucan Spa. The windows still retained their original glazing bars and glass. He and Margaret were greatly taken with the fine house, which had recently been redecorated. They also got on very well with Miss McGovern – no doubt Cathal used his charm to good effect.

Cathal decided to buy the house and put his own up for sale. He then began to look for a school for me. A friend who had some influence with the Presentation Nuns tried his best to get me into the local national school, but it transpired that the school was overcrowded and that the nuns were not inclined to take a non-local. As I was only seven years of age at the time and not old enough to travel on my own to Dublin every day by bus, Cathal began to lose heart.

He finally 'got the jitters' on a Sunday evening and decided to cancel everything before signing on the following Tuesday. He got in touch with the solicitor and succeeded in getting a buyer for Miss McGovern. Cathal decided to continue living in Herberton Road for the time being and made a decision to build an attic in the roof in preparation for the arrival of Margaret's parents, who had decided to leave England and live with us in Ireland. By this time they had lost most of their friends and neighbours and were becoming too old to look after themselves.

Although it was a great pity to miss this wonderful house – I can remember being enchanted by it – Cathal later realized that he had made the right decision and everything worked out for the best. There were too many stairs in the house and it would have been difficult to maintain. We remained friendly with Miss McGovern for many years afterwards. She went to live in England and when she returned we often visited her on a farm in Trim. Although a little eccentric, we remembered her for her warmth and kindness.

At some stage during the proceedings Cathal had shown the house in Lucan to Desmond Guinness, who was charmed by it. Lord Moyne heard from Desmond that Cathal was to buy the house and congratulated him, but Cathal had to explain that he had backed out of the agreement. He was sorry to hear this. Cathal mentioned to him his cherished dream of living somewhere near Knockmaroon and asked him to tell him if a house or some land were to be sold. Lord Moyne would never agree to sell any of his land, but promised to bear him in mind if any house in the area became available.

In February we attended a concert in the newly restored Pillar Room, under the Gate Theatre, which had been closed for the previous three years. It had narrowly escaped modernization. The elegant ballroom and oval room had been redecorated on the advice of the Irish Georgian Society; Mariga and Desmond Guinness had suggested a sympathetic colour scheme.

Organized by Dr Stan Corran, the concert was entitled 'Dublin musical life in the late eighteenth century' and featured Cathal's first harpsichord, played by a relatively new acquaintance, Florence Ryan, a fine pianist who came regularly to Herberton Road. On the evening of the concert, it was bitterly cold and hot-water bottles had to be brought for the musicians. Cathal was very glad when the recital finished and he was able to return to a warm home. Whilst I can remember little of the concert, I can remember the wonderful hall, the pillars and the hot-water bottles.

It may have been here or at another concert at around this period when I was introduced to the famous portraitist Seán O'Sullivan who, as we have noted in an earlier chapter, was a friend of John Burke's. I seem to recollect him sketching something. Seán was forever promising John to do a drawing of me, but it was not to be; unfortunately by this stage he had become addicted to the bottle.

Also at around this period I made my First Holy Communion at Loreto College. After the ceremony, Mum and Dad brought me to the zoo in the Phoenix Park where I looked at the animals and was taken around, with other children, in a pony and cart. Dad took some very good photographs of a neighbour's daughter and me using his sister Maureen's camera. He was well able to compose a shot. A photo, presumably taken by Mum, shows him seated on a bench with me balanced on the top. Here my father looks exactly as he did for the rest of his life: his hair is grey and sparse and his face is full. His slightly forced and idiosyncratic smile reveals his upper teeth.

I can remember such moments with my father with pleasure – weekend outings to Ballyknockan or to the countryside and so forth – but I was beginning to fear him more and more. His temper was very short and any small mistake or misdemeanour on my part was enough to make him slap me with increasing vigour. I quickly realized how strong he was. He often threatened me with the words 'I'll give you a box on the ears,' or 'I'll give you a kick in the teeth.' Cocooned in our little haven of peace with my mother during the day, I often trembled when he returned home from work in the evenings, no doubt tired after a hard day's work. I do not resent being slapped or beaten by him; it was what was done in those days – few children escaped physical chastisement – and it was undoubtedly due to his strict discipline that I was such a well-behaved child in general. I was not allowed to get away with anything; meals had to be eaten and wasting food was never permitted.

My mother and I did not escape my father's teasing. Dad often tried to 'take a rise' out of my mother, who frequently fell into his traps. Whenever she hesitated over the number of items to be bought in a shop, my father always said 'Buy six of them!' My mother invariably snapped at him, saying, 'Cathal, I don't want six!'

I can remember one occasion when my father frightened the life out of me. My mother had read me a Noddy story in which the little hero had become so conceited that he had got a swelled head and his cap no longer fitted him. When my father accused me of having a swelled head, he fetched my school cap and placed it on my head. I was horrified to discover that indeed it did *not* fit and I began to cry. What I had not realized was that Dad had made it smaller by means of a safety pin at the back.

For some obscure reason, my father nicknamed me 'Nucker' and often sang a song about 'Mr Nucker' to the tune of 'Frosty the Snowman'. Another, sung to a different melody, began as follows:

> Oh, there was a little man called Nucker
> Who lived in a great big house ...

He knew perfectly well that I hated the name, but deliberately used it to provoke me. When I wailed, 'My name's not Nucker!' he always responded by saying, 'Oh – I forgot,' then addressed me in the same manner a few moments later. I often screamed in frustration. Of course, if I had had any sense, I would have ignored his taunts. Another nickname that he used, though less frequently, was 'Codge-Box' – whatever that meant.

At other times my father used to amuse me by making funny faces, twisting one of his eyes, pretending to take out one eye in order to polish it, bestowing mock blessings on me and various objects in the manner of a priest ('Dominick Street, Patrick Street, Francis Street and The Coombe, Amen' he used to intone instead of the usual Latin words), endeavouring to make me (and other children) laugh at inappropriate moments, such as when drinking, and uttering snippets of nonsense verse such as:

> *The day before yesterday, the year before last,*
> *A man with a hammer was breaking his fast ...*

or

> *I come behind you to announce before you,*
> *Next Tuesday being Ash Wednesday ...*

I can remember being tickled by various expressions that he used, such as 'It's the same – only different.' An object that defied description was usually called 'a thing off a door for a gate'. I often heard him say, 'Instead of improving, it's getting better!' Another favourite of his was, 'What's the hurry? Sure, your mother had to wait nine months for you!' (I undoubtedly heard this when I was older.) When things were neither going too well nor too quickly, he often suggested saying a prayer 'to Saint Expedite'. He was not very fond of American parlance and hated the word 'guy', but he did use the expression 'That shook you!' for effect. In order to encourage someone to put more energy into the task at hand, he often cried, 'Give it lackery!' or, when circumstances allowed, 'Give it bollocky!' In situations when someone had to admit defeat or suffer an injustice, his usual advice was, 'Offer it up!' A phrase that he had once heard and was fond of repeating was 'Marry in haste and repent in the Coombe,' referring to the famous maternity hospital of that name. 'You'd need a letter from the Pope,' indicated that special permission was required. When speaking of a person who 'enjoyed bad health', as he put it, he often commented that 'it was either an arse or an elbow' when referring to a particular complaint.

Whenever he came across the name of a house such as Sea View, overlooking the sea or Mountain View, facing a nearby mountain, he loved to feign astonishment and say, 'Isn't that very clever? How did they think of that?'

When the need arose, Cathal could be very tactful – and yet funny at the same time. If he were asked for his opinion about something that he found not to his liking, he would say with great caution, 'Well, I've never seen anything like that before!'

In general, my father loved children and liked to amuse them in various ways. Whenever he saw a child falling and starting to cry, he used to say in a tone of great amazement, 'Oh, look at the big hole in the ground!' Invariably, his trick worked; the child, curious to discover where the non-existent hole might be, was immediately distracted and forgot to cry.

If a child showed a reluctance to take a second helping of food, he often said, 'I know a man who ate two of them and he's still alive!' At suppertime, he often recounted a story of how a young boy was encouraged to 'tuck in' by his parents, who said, in the presence of their guests, 'Eat up – see how the visitors eat!'

I often noticed that when my father spoke to someone, he rarely looked the person in the eye, preferring to look past his or her head and direct his remarks into one of the acquaintance's ears. I discovered that other Brewery workers were inclined to do the same thing; no doubt it was a practice developed to counteract the noisy environment in which they worked.

From my earliest years I can remember my father tackling his heavy stubble with an electric razor. When younger, he had used ordinary razor blades, which had hurt his face and cut him. Because his beard was so heavy, he often had to shave twice a day, especially if he was going out in the evening.

As in most houses, we were plagued with flies during the summer when the windows were opened. Whenever a fly made its way into our house, my father always became very agitated and did his best either to kill or catch the intruder. He had an uncanny knack of being able to outwit a fly by a deft inward move of his hand – more often than not he managed to catch it.

We would regularly sit around the radio listening to Roy Plomley's *Desert Island Discs*, to which my father attended with interest. He was always curious about people's taste in music and would often *tut-tut* when a piece that did not meet with his approval was played. Another favourite was Anthony Hopkins's *Talking About Music* on the Third Programme, in which various works were analysed. He was always anxious to listen to the news and frequently silenced my mother with an impatient '*Sssh!*' if she attempted to say something during a bulletin.

It could have been at around this time that I started to stammer. Initially I picked it up from a young girl who lived in the neighbourhood. I can remember my parents trying to stop me in the early stages, but my increasing nervousness and tension aggravated the stammer until it became an embarrassment. Already isolated by my rather sheltered upbringing – I had no brothers or sisters and almost completely missed out on the rough and tumble of knocking around with other lads of my age – I began to retreat into myself and became wary of speaking to others. However, left to my own devices and amongst the people I knew and liked, I was reasonably at ease.

Every Sunday we all went to Mass. Although there was a simple church within walking distance of the house, my father usually preferred to drive to one of the more classical and elegant churches in town. I can remember going to St Audoen's, High Street, the University Church in St Stephen's Green and the lovely chapel in Dublin Castle. I can also recollect, with some amusement, playing at being a priest at home; I used the kitchen table as an altar and managed to secure my mother as a 'congregation'. She had to cut slices of banana for me and these I used as communion hosts. Thinking about it now, I wonder how she managed to keep a straight face.

The meals she cooked at home were simple and nourishing. She bought most of her fresh vegetables from a tiny shop at the end of the terrace of houses in Herberton Road. Like my father, she had a fondness for sweet things and always produced some type of pudding as a dessert. I can remember my father eating biscuits and drinking coffee after a full dinner in the middle of the day. To me, he always had an unusual way of eating. A corner of bread was always tasted before butter or anything else was applied. Instead of eating all the food on his dinner plate together, he tended to eat everything separately, one after another, in a prescribed order. When he grew older, this habit regularly irritated my mother. Like his father, he relished ice cream and, when in season, blackberries.

Cathal had a liking for strong tastes, for he always applied mustard to his meat; he piled butter on bread, salt on his savoury dishes and sugar into his tea, coffee, cocoa and even on his desserts when they were not sweet enough for him. Apart from destroying his teeth, this excess of sugar, salt and butter never seemed to upset his general health, for he burned it all up when sawing, hammering, walking and cycling. Although he liked to take at least ten minutes' rest after his midday meal, he generally returned to his physical exertions far too soon after eating, which undoubtedly caused the indigestion from which he so frequently suffered.

In May of this year, a lump was discovered on Margaret's right breast and Cathal urged her to see her doctor, which she was somewhat reluctant to do. Just as Cathal had feared, it was cancer; fortunately it had been discovered in time, before it worked its way down her right arm. Margaret was rushed to Baggot Street Hospital on the day that we had been due to move to the house in Lucan and was operated on immediately. The surgeon told Cathal that if the condition had been left any longer without treatment, there would have been little hope for her.

Margaret was given a private room in the hospital and stayed there only two weeks after the operation, instead of the customary four weeks, as she was a fast healer. Flowers and many letters expressing the hope for a speedy recovery were posted to her; the senders included Mariga Guinness and the Schürmann family. It appears that the Clenches in Wealdstone were not informed; undoubtedly Margaret did not wish to give them cause for concern. She was soon back to normal, though not necessarily feeling the best, when she returned home. Very soon afterwards, Michael Clifton and the group came for one of the usual Saturday musical evenings, and she and Cathal attended their friend Olive Bracken's wedding.

By the summer of 1962, Cathal's second harpsichord was almost complete, though for some reason he left it unfinished for a considerable time – until 1968 to be exact. Cathal was nonetheless very pleased with the result. Like the original, it had two eight-foot stops, one four-foot stop, a lute and buff stops, but no coupler. The casework consisted of Cuban mahogany panels banded with Honduras mahogany; the wood came from a large Victorian office desk purchased from the Brewery. Strips of boxwood and ebony inlay also adorned the case; this 'stringing' had been bought by Cathal's father in London, probably in 1907. The keyboard surrounds were of burr walnut, tulip wood and more inlay. It was a very handsome instrument and was beautifully constructed.

In the meantime, Lord Moyne told Cathal that the original instrument from Townley Hall, which by this stage was restored and in Trinity College, was giving a little bit of trouble; Cathal was asked to fix it. Lord Moyne said, 'If I had known about that harpsichord, I would have had you repair it in the Brewery.' Cathal told him that a letter had been written to him about the matter and that he had not replied to it.

The winter of 1962–3 was harsh and the tank in our attic burst. My father climbed up into the roof to fix it. It was probably soon after this incident that he began to build a room in the attic, in preparation for the arrival of my mother's parents in September 1963. I watched with interest as he increased the size of the opening in the ceiling and built a staircase from the landing to it. In the attic, the tank and joists were covered by sheets of timber, a lino-covered floor was laid and a window installed. When electrical sockets were fitted, I wondered what would happen if I placed a short piece of discarded cable in the holes. Amazingly, my father encouraged me to find out for myself. The effect, as one can imagine, was quite dramatic: as soon as I pushed the wire in, there was a flash and I was thrown back by the force of the electric shock. I am certain that my father had to replace a fuse. Needless to say, I did not repeat the experiment again.

Thirty

*T*hroughout 1963 the Saturday musical evenings continued in Herberton Road. At some point during the year the small ensemble was augmented by another member, Arthur Agnew. Originally from Belfast, the Agnews had moved to Dublin when Arthur was a boy of eleven. He had studied the violin and then had turned his attention to singing, studying under Jean Bertin at the School of Music, Chatham Street. Possessed of a fine tenor voice, he won prizes at the Feis Ceoil and went on to perform as a musician in the Din Joe programme, jokingly described as 'Irish dancing on radio'. Later he would sing on the *Town Hall Tonight* radio programmes and play in the Dublin Symphony Orchestra. A man of many talents, he also played the double bass, the piano and the guitar. Arthur had been playing with Michael Clifton elsewhere and had been told about Cathal. He arrived at the tiny house in Rialto with his double-bass and a new reel-to-reel tape recorder, which he was anxious to try. When the others had fitted themselves into the small sitting room, Arthur came in last with his 'bull fiddle' and the door was shut. Once Arthur was in place, there was no coming in or going out. Arthur can remember the people who played on a regular basis in our house: Kieran Egar, Liam Fitzgerald and Neil Downes on violins, Michael Clifton on viola, Emer O'Reilly and Margaret Fitzgerald on cellos, and either Cathal or Florence Ryan on the harpsichord. They played all sorts of music; Arthur can remember tackling the Bach double violin concerto with Dinah Molloy.

On Arthur's first evening in our house, he recorded Florence Ryan playing on my father's Broadwood square piano; I remember him playing the recording many years later.

At some later date, Arthur recorded John Beckett playing my father's first harpsichord in the sitting room and the recording, which I believe was mostly of music by Bach, was made into a record. We were given a complimentary copy and my father tried it out on a record player given to us by Werner Schürmann. For some reason, Cathal had placed the record player on the floor of the sitting room. Having started it, he stood up and accidentally kicked it, which sent the arm skidding across the new record. Needless to say, it was badly scratched.

Arthur had married in 1956; although his wife Bernadette did not come to our house in Rialto we were to meet her some years later. She and Arthur remained good friends of the family for many years. Arthur was always interested in my father's pursuits and my father always enjoyed encouraging him in his.

At around this time the Caltex harp, which had been made by John Quinn of Dublin and donated to Guinness's Brewery in 1959, had begun to give a bit of trouble; the frame had become somewhat distorted. Cathal was asked to fix it. In order to increase the size of his workbench, Cathal nailed a large table top to it, so that it overhung the bench on two sides. Unfortunately, somebody removed the table top in his absence, used it and threw it back without bothering to nail it down again. Consequently, when Cathal placed the harp on it the next time, the instrument overbalanced, fell to the floor and broke into three pieces.

Undaunted, Cathal removed the strings and, with the help of one of his colleagues, glued it together again. According to Cathal, he made 'a better job of it than ever'. Like Mozart, Cathal had little time for harps.

Unbeknownst to my father, important decisions about his future career were now being made behind the scenes. At the end of April, John Beckett (who had come to Dublin to give a recital) made an appointment to talk to his friend Owen Williams, the assistant managing director of Guinness's Brewery. Mr Williams's mother-in-law had been a neighbour of the Becketts; John's father had befriended Owen and had played piano duets with him. John now reminded Mr Williams of Cathal's talents and suggested that they be put to better use; instead of looking after locks, he should be allowed to make harpsichords in the Brewery. The instruments could then be donated or sold to interested institutions or individuals and, as a result, Guinness's could be seen to be a patron of the arts. John stated that, in his opinion, 'the two harpsichords that Cathal Gannon has made are as good as, or even better than, any harpsichords now being made in England'.

According to John, Mr Williams was 'very sympathetic' to the idea. A Board Meeting was held on 1 May and Owen submitted a report on his interview with John. It was decided that Mr Williams should write to Mr W.E. Phillips of Park Royal in London, 'to find out whether Park Royal would consider making a gift of such a harpsichord to some suitable body; failing this it would be considered whether to present a harpsichord to one of the Dublin musical colleges'. Owen wrote two days later to Mr Phillips, who responded by showing a certain amount of interest but suggesting that it was 'primarily a possible operation for the Dublin Company to mount'. He concluded, however, by saying that there was 'spare cash' in the budget that could be put towards such a project.

On 4 May a concert was given in the Examination Hall of Trinity College to inaugurate the recently restored Kirckman harpsichord that had been discovered in Townley Hall and sent to Morley's in England for restoration. Behind the scenes, Cathal had to 'work very hard at it to get the thing into any sort of playing condition'. Professor Brian Boydell of the music department saw to it that Cathal was remunerated for his maintenance of the instrument throughout the following years.

The concert, which Cathal attended, featured the soprano Barbara Elsy, the recorder player John Sothcott, John Beckett on the harpsichord, and Daphne Webb on the cello. Most of the music was by Georg Philipp Telemann. The long list of people who had contributed money towards the restoration of the harpsichord included the Provost, Professor Boydell, Lord Moyne, John O'Sullivan and David Lee.

Judging by the amount of correspondence that flowed back and forth between the various parties over the coming months, the whole matter of Cathal building harpsichords in Guinness's Brewery was being taken very seriously by the authorities in Dublin and Park Royal. John Beckett, now back in London, wrote a couple of times to Owen Williams in order to apply pressure. 'There is no make of harpsichord amongst those I have used, that I would rather play than one of Cahill [sic] Gannon's – I would with delight sign an undertaking to that effect,' he wrote.

Dublin and Park Royal were anxious to get a second opinion about

Cathal's work before committing themselves. In July, Mr Phillips of Park Royal wrote to George Malcolm, the noted English harpsichordist, pianist and one-time director of music at Westminster Cathedral, asking him if he would examine Cathal's instruments in Dublin. However, it turned out that Mr Malcolm was in Germany and would not be able to come to Dublin until February of the following year. 'I think this is too long to wait,' wrote Mr Phillips to Owen Williams. Undecided, the authorities did no more for the time being and Cathal continued with his normal duties at work – maintaining locks and keys and some carpentry.

Although I knew little of what went on in the Brewery, I was acquainted with one individual who caused a certain amount of amusement and annoyance there. This was Danny Power, who fancied himself as a singer. Danny lived in Rialto Buildings and sang operatic arias to anyone who cared – or did not care – to listen. I can remember unsuccessfully trying to go to sleep one evening in my little bedroom in the front of the house while Danny roared his version of Mussorgsky's *Song of the Flea,* in what my father called 'bog Russian', from the back of a stationary number 19 bus.

He often sang on the street near the post office at Rialto. As my father had heard that he had 'hounded' some local to play his accompaniment on the piano, he took care to leave and enter the house by the back door any time Danny was around.

Danny also sang in Italian. Cathal said to him once, 'You've wonderful Italian, Danny – where did you get it?'

'I go down to the Florentine Cafe in Dolphin's Barn,' he said, 'and the Italian man behind the counter teaches me how to pronounce the words.'

Another technique of his was to listen carefully to a gramophone record of the aria he was learning in order to master the pronunciation. If he was still in doubt about some of the words, he brought the sheet music to the Italian waiter in the cafe.

One day Cathal was passing Rialto Buildings on his bicycle and heard the unmistakable sound of Danny singing at the top of his voice. When he reached Danny's flat, he found him leaning out of his window and bellowing through the horn of an old gramophone player to a collection of children in the street, who applauded and cheered him.

On another day, Danny was busy practising his scales while his son was resting in his bedroom at the back. A man in the flat upstairs, who had heard enough, shouted, 'Give up that singing or I'll burst you!'

Danny's son, who realized that his father had not heard the threat, opened the door and shouted, 'You will in your arse!'

With that, the man ran down the stairs, entered the front room and hit the bewildered Danny.

'That'll teach you to sing and keep the children awake!' he said angrily and stormed out. As my father remarked, 'That stopped it for a while!'

Cathal always made Danny feel that he was intensely interested in his singing career and often asked him what he was studying. Danny respected Cathal's judgment as he had the reputation of making and restoring musical instruments. Cathal often chose a cold, miserable winter's morning to ask him what his latest aria was. Whilst discussing the music, he would lead Danny into a narrow passageway in the Brewery, where he was in every-body's way, and there he would start him singing. As none of the workmen was interested in being serenaded at ten to eight on a winter's morning, they cursed him roundly. 'It was priceless to hear the remarks,' Cathal said, 'but he was oblivious to all this – he just sang away. And when I had him at full steam, I'd just drift away myself.'

It appears that Danny once appeared on television. Whilst pushing his bicycle along Thomas Street, he was approached by a reporter from the new station, Telefís Éireann, and his opinion was asked about opera. This, of course, was a golden opportunity for Danny and he lost no time in treating the interviewer to a sample of his singing. Cathal never saw the transmission, which apparently was very funny. Undoubtedly Danny sang in his usual man-ner, 'the whites of his eyes turned out like saucers – you just couldn't see the pupils of his eyes, whichever way he looked up to heaven. It was the funni-est sight in the world to [see] him singing: he was oblivious to everything!'

Another colleague of Cathal's, a stout, swarthy man by the name of Mick Corcoran, was adept at imitating Italians and opera singers like Caruso. He often encouraged Danny to sing duets with him by bursting into song and approaching him with arms outstretched. Danny always fell for the ploy and responded accordingly. On one particular day, he and Danny began to sing under a window at the flats in Bellevue, near Guinness's Brewery. As Cathal commented, 'It was the most dreadful bawling match you ever heard!' While they sang, Mick noticed some activity at the window. He backed away, still singing, and a woman emptied a basin of water over Danny, who simply stopped long enough to say 'F— you!' and continued with the song. When at last he finished he looked up to find the woman, but of course she had disappeared from view.

Cathal had known Danny since the 1930s. At one stage he had been nicknamed 'China' Power; it appeared that he had been in China during World War I. Despite his eccentricities, he was a nice fellow and spoke well. He was always involved in something; at one time he was interested in nature cures and read everything he could find on the subject. He always had some new discovery to tell his workmates about. He was telling everyone about vitamins in the 1930s when few people knew anything about them.

He went through a phase of being interested in Shakespeare's plays and, as he had a terrific memory, he boasted that he could recite the entire text of *Julius Caesar* from the beginning to the end. Cathal believed that he could do it. Woe betide the person who quizzed him about his boast, for once he started reciting the play there was no telling when he would finish.

At one time there were allotments on the South Circular Road where Fatima Church now stands. Danny often worked his plot at night-time, arriving with a torch and an alarm clock. When Danny was planting seed potatoes and used far too many of them, the man who was helping him asked him how many he had put into each hole.

'I put two,' replied Danny.

'You need only have put one,' said the man. 'Why did you put two?'

'Ah,' said Danny, 'I thought they might want to mate!'

At the outbreak of the war, relatives of his who lived in Wexford and who owned a horse asked him if he could buy a trap for them. The idea was that they would be able to use the horse and trap when the cars went off the road. Danny succeeded in buying one at an auction. He then had to devise a way of transporting it all the way down to Wexford. He hit on a plan, which he described to Cathal. Rising at about two o'clock in the morning, when he reckoned that no Gardaí would be on the roads, he made a harness of ropes for himself, placed his motorbike and sidecar between the shafts and set off in the dark, pulling the trap. All went well until he approached Newtownmountkennedy in County Wicklow; the trap gathered momentum as he drove downhill and the brakes on the motorbike proved to be useless. Fortunately for him, he escaped possible injury by making it to the next uphill stretch in time and taking it at a terrific speed. He met no Gardaí and arrived safely in Wexford with the trap.

Poor Danny ended his days at a nursing home in Cork Street, where he slipped, fell on his head and died. He was always in good health and should have lived much longer.

I can remember hearing Danny singing (and being cursed) in the old medical department around the back of the Brewery in Robert Street. My mother often brought me along the gloomy cobble-stoned streets, the stench of hops in our nostrils, to visit the doctor or dentist. Visiting the doctor used to be an intimidating business; I can remember people waiting by the open door, listening to every word that was being said by the doctor and patient. Many men were ticked off for feigning illness and certificates were denied them. Patients were summoned to the doctor's presence by a peremptory 'next!'

Cathal was not the only trickster in the Brewery. A chubby and jovial van driver by the name of Billy Hawkins had a sense of humour that others often did not appreciate. Cathal unwittingly fell into one of his traps when out walking along James's Street. Billy stopped his van and said, 'Where are you going?'

'I'm in a hurry,' replied Cathal. 'I'm going up to what we call the top shop.'

Indicating the passenger's seat, Billy said, 'Jump in there now and I'll bring you up,' but instead brought Cathal for an unexpected drive around the Phoenix Park. Thanks to him, Cathal was unable to make an urgent telephone call.

Billy offered another man a lift from one part of the Brewery to another. As it was inclined to rain, the man gratefully accepted his offer and was whisked off to Howth, where Billy had to do a message. He was left back to the Brewery about an hour later and fortunately was not missed.

At some stage, Billy purchased a big false nose with a pair of spectacles attached. As the nose blended perfectly with his face, he became unrecognizable. He fooled at least one individual with this disguise. Putting on the nose and spectacles, he passed by a man on his way into a building, to which there was only one entrance. He went upstairs, delayed for a couple of minutes, took off the disguise and came down. Meeting the fellow in the hall again, he said, 'Who's that man up there?'

'I don't know who he is,' was the reply, 'but he must know his way around the place.'

Billy left, went around the corner, put the nose and spectacles back on and re-entered the building. The man could not believe his eyes when he saw him coming in, for he had not seen him leaving. Once again he went upstairs and came down a few minutes later without the disguise.

'Who's that fellow up there?' he asked again.

'I don't know who he is,' replied the man, thoroughly perplexed. 'He's an ignorant bastard – he walked by me without passing the time of day!'

'Where is he now?'

'He's upstairs, but he ... he must have got over the roof because he ... he didn't come down and he came in the door a second time!'

Billy left, came in yet again with the disguise and repeated the procedure about four or five more times. The man in the hall, who should have been minding his own business, assumed that the 'stranger' was in charge of some workmen nearby and did not want to be too cheeky. He was completely mystified by the comings and goings.

Cathal used to tell a story about one of his workmates who kept bending down and disappearing under his workbench in order to do something. Cathal sidled over to him and found him trying to file his false teeth.

'What's wrong?' Cathal asked, bemused.

'Ah – it's me false teeth,' said the man. 'For some reason they don't seem to fit me properly today and I'm trying to make them a bit more comfortable. I think I've nearly got them right now.'

Cathal saw him make a few more adjustments to them during the day and at last he seemed satisfied.

On the following morning, Cathal greeted him with 'Well, how are the false teeth this morning?'

'Oh, don't talk about that!' said the man. 'There was feckin' murder when I got home yesterday – it was the wife's teeth that I had in by mistake!'

Thirty-One

*I*t was probably in the autumn of 1963 when I was upgraded to a better piano teacher in the School of Music. Unfortunately, as she was unsuited to teaching children and regularly rapped me over the knuckles when I made mistakes, I began to dislike her. At this early age I realized that I had poor co-ordination between my two hands and was a bad sight-reader. The only way I could master a piece of music was to learn the notes for the right hand first, then the left, and then attempt to play the two together; I could never read and play both lines together. By the time I managed to play the piece using both hands, I had memorized it and felt it unnecessary to refer to the printed music, preferring instead to look at my fingers. This infuriated my teacher, who constantly instructed me to 'look at the music'.

Up to this point I had been practising on the Broadwood square piano in our sitting room. By October, my father decided that I needed a more modern instrument and bought an upright Bentley piano from a private house in Milltown. The square piano was moved into the dining room. I can remember coming home from school at lunchtime, hurriedly eating my meal and excitedly sitting down to play the new piano.

We kept this instrument for only about one year. Unfortunately, I have unhappy memories of playing it. My father insisted on supervising me when I practised my music and became increasingly frustrated by my ineptness. Being a perfectionist, he obviously could not tolerate anything beneath his own standards. He vented his frustration on me by losing his temper and boxing my ears whenever I made a mistake. Owing to my nervousness and fear of him, I made plenty of mistakes. Looking back, it seemed that every practice session ended in tears. Learning music was turning into a nightmare for me and I could feel that my relationship with my father was becoming strained. I can remember feeling so annoyed with him that I once managed to push him off his chair in the kitchen; he narrowly escaped falling into the fire. Obviously I had inherited his hot temper.

Like most children, I enjoyed collecting stamps. On one occasion I can remember soaking stamps off the corners of envelopes and leaving them to dry on a sheet of newspaper before the fire. My father, who was angry with me for some forgotten reason, seized the newspaper and threw the stamps into the flames.

Thinking about it now, there must have been some explanation for his behaviour towards me, which at times was simply unreasonable. I seem to remember my mother taking my side after the incident with the stamps. At fifty-three years of age, was he simply too old to deal with an eight-year-old boy? Would he have been more reasonable if he had been twenty years younger? My mother thought that he may have been. Through no fault of either my mother or father, it was my misfortune to be born rather late in their lives. Attending a school that I did not like (St Mary's in Rathmines) and being bullied by a strict father made this period of my life quite miserable and, not surprisingly, my stammer worsened.

It is possible that at around this time, my father's attitude began to harden towards my mother. Everyone knows that marriage is not a bed of roses and that all couples argue. Although my parents were careful to air their disagreements in private, I do have hazy memories of an occasional sharp word from my father to my mother. My mother's normal response was a bout of silence – what my father described as 'a nark'.

A further cause of tension may have been the fact that my mother's parents came to live with us in September of that year, 1963. They had sold their house in Harrow and had moved to Dublin, which they soon began to dislike. Being elderly, they could not adapt to living in a country where they knew so few people. They missed their friends, neighbours and everything that was familiar to them. My father looked at Mrs Clench in the same light that most married men regard their mothers-in-law and inwardly criticized her for talking too much about trivial matters, as he had once criticized my own mother. I noticed that Mrs Clench tended to be quite argumentative at times. However, she and 'Pa' Clench were kind to me and gave me pocket-money every week – either sixpence or a shilling. By now they had both gone very deaf. They slept in what had been the spare front bedroom, which I had been using for a while previously. I think that the second harpsichord had been removed to the Brewery by this stage.

In October Lord Moyne wrote to a friend of his, the harpsichord and clavichord maker Thomas R.C. Goff, who was indirectly related to the royal family and who lived at 46 Pont Street, London. He invited him to Dublin to attend the Ardilaun lectures at Alexandra College and, more importantly, to give an opinion on the two harpsichords made by Cathal. He hoped that he might give Cathal some help and encouragement. Mr Goff replied on the following day, 24 October, 'John Beckett is a very fine player of the harpsichord and I am sure that he would not praise Mr Gannon's work if it was not very good. I wish I could show Mr Gannon my workshop and instruments. Might the Company wish to send him to London at any time?'

It is obvious from a letter written to Mr Phillips in Park Royal that Lord Moyne was very satisfied with this response. 'As you see, he would put great reliance on Beckett's opinion,' he wrote. Mr Phillips, however, was a little more cautious and, a little later in the month, wrote to George Malcolm, inviting him to examine one of Cathal's instruments when he would be in Dublin the following February.

A handwritten document detailing Cathal's wages at the time and how his work could be shared out amongst other employees was submitted to somebody in authority and on 7 November a board meeting was held, during which it was agreed to adopt Mr D.O. William's proposal that 'Cathal Gannon should be allowed to make a Harpsichord during Brewery time and that his general carpentry work should be looked after by other arrangements.' It was an important and unusual decision. When John Beckett received news of it, he wrote, 'this is a humane and civilized gesture, which I am sure nobody concerned will regret'.

Soon the cat was out of the bag. Lord Moyne approached Cathal privately and said, 'Certain people in the Brewery are hoping you would make a harpsichord for them to donate to the Academy of Music, and to be made in the Brewery.'

'Well,' Cathal said, 'if that is to be, I would have to have a workshop to myself.' Lord Moyne indicated that a special workshop would be set up for him, but asked him to say nothing for the time being.

When Cathal was eventually summoned by the board of directors, he knew what to expect, but put on a pretence of being surprised when Mr

Williams asked him if he would make a harpsichord for the Royal Irish Academy of Music. Cathal said that he would and Mr Williams informed him that he would be given a workshop in the building that had formerly housed the old carpenters' workshops.

In mid-November Cathal sold the cottage in Ballyknockan. Cathal had various reasons for selling it, one of which was its small size – it would have been impossible to house five people in it.

A little later in the month, Lord Moyne forwarded Cathal a copy of a letter he had written to Tom Goff. In it, Lord Moyne thanked Mr Goff for his letter about John Beckett's recommendation of Cathal's harpsichords and for his kind offer to let Cathal see his workshop and instruments. Lord Moyne stated that the Irish Board of Guinness's had decided to let Cathal make a harpsichord for the Brewery, which would probably be presented to the Royal Irish Academy of Music. An important point in the letter was the reference to Mr Goff's endorsement of John Beckett's capability as a judge of Cathal's instruments.

Cathal had been told previously of a proposed visit to Tom Goff, for Lord Moyne wrote, 'Mr Gannon is most anxious to avail himself of your kind offer and we are ready to send him over at any time convenient to you.' Goff's scribbled note to Cathal suggested that he come either at the end of November or early in December.

Cathal flew to London on 29 November and spent a week there at the Brewery's expense. However, he stayed with his brother Willie at Hove in Sussex and took the train into London's Victoria Station – a day ticket then cost the princely sum of 14s.

After Willie and Kathleen had married they had moved to Shinrone in County Offaly. They decided to emigrate to England after Willie had an argument with the parish priest, who refused to allow the local youths to play billiards in the hall on Sundays. He worked for a time in the aircraft industry and in 1953 formed his own engineering consultancy, Gale Design Consultants, with the aim of exploring the field of computers. In 1962, Systemation Limited was formed in Hove to produce low-priced computers. Willie designed two computers called Betsea and Sadie, which I remember him showing to us in my aunt's house in Dundrum at around this time.

In London, Cathal discovered that Mr Goff owned a very elegant house, lived well and kept a butler. He was very kind to Cathal and brought him to his cramped attic workshop, where he was given tea and cake. Cathal spent an afternoon chatting with him and learning the tricks of his trade. In truth, Mr Goff misdirected him, for Cathal would, in time, have to undo some of the things that he had learned from him. Tom showed Cathal a couple of his own clavichords, one decorated by Rex Whistler and another by Ronald Pym, the illustrator of Bryan Guinness's (Lord Moyne's) books. He brought Cathal around the house and showed him his various harpsichords, most of which were available for hire. They were constructed with aluminium frames and featured a sixteen-foot stop, which Cathal did not approve of.

Although Tom was not the right person to send Cathal to, he did give my father some valuable information as to where he could purchase timber and materials. He wrote to D.O. Williams, 'Mr Gannon came and saw my harpsichords yesterday and I explained them very fully to him and gave him all the addresses where he can get all he needs.'

Whilst in London, Cathal bought pear wood for making the jacks and holly for making the pivoted tongues of the jacks. Cathal had used Swiss pine, ordered from Germany through Walton's in Dublin, for the soundboard of the second harpsichord, but now he ordered silver spruce. He ordered pine or spruce for the cases.

Whilst in London, Cathal also visited Michael Thomas, another harpsichord maker (albeit a rather disorganized one, according to W. J. Zuckermann in his book, *The Modern Harpsichord*), who lived in The Manor House, Hurley, in Berkshire. Michael would later visit Cathal in Dublin. Cathal also went to the Victoria and Albert Museum and revisited Fenton House, where he once again examined the collection of keyboard instruments.

When Cathal returned from England, Margaret told him that a salesman by the name of Joe Devine had called and had tried to interest her in buying a complete set of the *Children's Britannica* for me. Margaret had told Joe that he would have to wait until her husband came back. She and Cathal discussed the matter, welcomed Joe when he called again and decided to buy the encyclopaedias.

My parents befriended Joe, who was a teacher, and his wife Helen, a pianist and organist; I remember them visiting us in Herberton Road with their baby son Vivian. We kept in touch for many years and remained very good friends. When my mother was widowed, Helen regularly telephoned her and drove her to her house for a meal or for an evening's entertainment.

Her sister Susan regularly used to send my mother magazines in the post. Now that my mother is gone, we still keep in touch.

Towards the end of 1963, the new workshop was made ready for Cathal. It was in a building on the left as one entered the Brewery's main gate in James's Street. One approached it by means of a wide staircase. It measured about 24 ft by 18 and had three windows that looked out over the yard below. Cathal was supplied with a bench 8 ft long by 4 ft wide, a circular saw and a drilling machine. The workshop was lit by large fluorescent lights and heated by radiators. As Cathal had stipulated, it was in a quiet part of the Brewery. Cathal was delighted with his new work area.

The unfinished second harpsichord was installed, along with the timber, materials and tools that would be needed to build the next instrument. Cathal asked for a helper and was given the man he requested, Billy Sexton. Like Cathal, Billy was a very competent and neat carpenter. Cathal had watched him closely over the years and reckoned that he was the best woodworker in the Brewery. His only fault was to work a little too quickly and take short cuts, which were not always successful.

Billy, a well-built, stocky man with strong features, hailed from Newcastle West in County Limerick and spoke with such a thick accent that when Cathal first met him in about 1950 he thought that he was a Hungarian refugee. Despite the unusual accent, he pronounced his words in a 'studied manner'; even the final -*ing* of a well-known swear word was precisely articulated. I can clearly remember his way of saying 'Do you see, Cathal?' – 'Do 'oo see, Ca-al?' He had a wonderful turn of phrase and was very droll. At their time of meeting, Billy was working for McLaughlin and Harvey's and was temporarily employed by the Brewery for the building of a power station. Cathal found him very interesting. He spoke to him about musical instruments and discovered that he knew quite a lot about violins; his father had repaired them. Billy was also knowledgeable about old furniture.

Billy wore a pair of half spectacles over which he would peer when not engaged in close work. One day Cathal brought in a tiny pair of antique spectacles and wore them whilst working. When two workmates looked in, both Billy and Cathal pretended not to see them and continued with their work.

'Now the other f—er's at it,' muttered one of the fellows as they walked away.

A telephone was installed in the new workshop and Cathal received many calls from members of the Board, especially D.O. Williams, who would say, 'At about half past two I'll bring up Colonel somebody; I'd like him to see what you're doing.' Such visitors often stayed long enough to interrupt Cathal's work and 'put a hole' in the afternoon. Anybody musical was brought to visit the workshop; he remembered the clarinettist Gervaise de Peyer being shown around. At a later period, Cathal himself invited various organists and harpsichord players to the workshop, including John O'Sullivan and David Lee; any time they were about, Cathal telephoned one of the lady clerks, Elizabeth Neuman, whom Jack had introduced to him, and invited her to join the gathering if she was free.

Lord Dunleath, who was an expert on organs, visited the workshop on a few occasions. Cathal remembered him looking slightly mystified at an old print of King Billy crossing the Boyne and a picture of the Pope that Cathal had hung on the wall, side by side. Also on the wall were portraits of Bach and Beethoven, which had been taken from a record sleeve. When workmates asked Cathal who they were, he always told them that they were two famous harpsichord makers.

While Cathal set about making the third harpsichord, based on the second, Billy regaled him with his wonderful store of anecdotes, many of which were unintentionally funny.

One of them, which Cathal often retold, concerned Billy's father, who not only repaired violins but worked as a carpenter on the railway around Limerick. He often was away from home for the best part of a week, doing maintenance work, for example, in a signal cabin or on the gates of a level crossing. When in a certain part of the county, he always endeavoured to stay with an elderly lady who took in gentleman boarders, such as commercial travellers. She had a very comfortable house and 'kept a good table'. Most importantly, however, she put flannel sheets on the beds during the winter months. These made the beds warm and cosy before the days of the electric blanket.

On one particular evening, Billy's father was shown into a large bedroom with two beds in opposite corners. He was on the point of falling asleep when the landlady tapped on the door and said, 'Excuse me, Mr Sexton, there's a travelling tailor who wants to stay the night. Do you mind if he shares the room with you?'

'Not at all,' said Mr Sexton. 'Let him come up!'

A man came in with a parcel under his arm, spoke for a few minutes to Mr Sexton, got into the other bed and fell asleep.

On the following morning, when Mr Sexton was shaving himself in the mirror, he noticed the tailor jumping out of bed. He pulled back the bed-clothes, smoothed the flannel sheets and, taking from his pocket some paper patterns and a pair of scissors, he proceeded to cut himself the makings of two pairs of 'inside drawers'. He pinned them together, rolled them up care-fully with the paper patterns and put them in his inside pocket, leaving just a few triangles of flannel remaining. He pulled the cover back over the bed, went downstairs, had his breakfast and 'off with him along the road'.

When Billy was a boy, he often brought his father's lunch to him – a flask of tea and 'sangwiches', as Billy called them – when he worked in the local railway station. When he arrived at the station one day with the lunch, there was a certain amount of commotion. Some unfortunate man had been involved in a shunting accident and had lost his leg. Amazingly, the man was seated on a trailer, smoking a cigarette and talking to the people who were attending to him. Somebody had tied a towel around the remaining stump of his leg to stop the bleeding.

After a few minutes, an ambulance arrived and the man was transferred to a stretcher. As they were lifting him into the ambulance, the man shouted, 'Throw up that old leg – there's a good boot and sock on it!'

Billy told a 'wonderful' story about a Wren Boys' party, which took place on the evening of St Stephen's Day in a small cottage in the middle of a big field. The men, who were mostly dairy workers, had collected some money and had bought a tierce of porter. (A tierce is an obsolete measure of capac-ity, equal to forty-two wine gallons.) Apart from the drinking, the enter-tainment included singing, an old fellow playing a button melodeon and an expert tap-dancer: a young lad who sported a fine pair of hand-made shoes. Apparently the dancer was held in high regard in County Limerick.

Later in the evening, the young man was asked to dance 'The Blackbird', but by this stage the melodeon player was beginning to get a little tipsy. His playing was becoming careless and he was slowing down too much for the dancer, who was 'battering out the fancy steps'. He danced round in a cir-cle, and when the musician had the melodeon stretched out he kicked it up into the air, leaving the old fellow with only the two straps around his wrists. The melodeon fell over the cross-stick of the house, where it sagged limply and groaned – 'uuuuh'. That finished the night – an unmerciful row began and Billy had to run out of the cottage.

Apparently, during 'the Troubles' in Ireland, a unit of Black and Tans came to Newcastle West. The men, who came principally from the north of England, had brought bagpipes with them. According to Billy, they were decent men and did not want to interfere with anyone. They wanted to be friendly with the locals, but nobody would have anything to do with them because of their reputation. Occasionally they used to play their pipes in the town centre in an effort to entertain the people, but nobody listened to them.

On one such occasion, an elderly man by the name of Maurice, who lived up in the mountains and was mad about bagpipes, decided to come to listen to them. He walked down the mountainside 'with the most miserable set of patched and repaired pipes you ever saw, as Billy said, "hanging across his arm like a sick f—ing goose"'. He approached the Black and Tans, who made a great fuss of him. They called him 'Paddy' and gave him an opportunity to try to play the big war pipes, but he could not manage them. They produced white linen handkerchiefs and stuffed them into the drones in order to make it easier for him, but he made little progress.

Maurice greatly appreciated all the attention he was given, but the locals took no further notice of him because he had fraternized with the hated Black and Tans.

A story of Billy's concerned a country family who regularly attended a yearly fair in a small Limerick town on New Year's Eve. On one particular year, they got the date mixed up. They rose very early in the morning on New Year's Day, made themselves ready, changed into their best clothes, ate their breakfast, piled all their wares into their cart, hitched up the horse and set off for the town. They arrived to find the streets deserted and not a soul to be seen. As they gazed around, mystified, a window was opened, a man stuck his head out and shouted, 'Go back to where you came from! You're a day too late and a year too soon!'

Perhaps Billy's best story – and certainly my favourite – concerned an elderly couple who lived in the middle of nowhere, on a mountainside, about five miles away from the nearest town. The woman had a heart condition and was in delicate health. During one very bad evening, when it was pouring rain and a storm was blowing, she got a 'little turn' and thought that she was going to die. Her husband felt that he could neither leave her nor risk the journey to the local parish priest. The woman was concerned about making her last confession. They were at their wits' end wondering what to do. However, the husband suddenly had a brainwave.

'Mary,' he said, 'isn't there conditional baptism?'

'Faith, there is John,' said his wife, 'there is such a thing.'

'Well,' he mused, 'there could be conditional confession.'

'That could be so, too,' agreed the old woman.

The husband went out into the kitchen, where he put on his navy-blue waistcoat back to front, made an imitation priest's collar from a piece of white linen, and put on his best suit. Carrying a lighted candle, a crucifix and a little saucer of holy water with a piece of blessed palm in it, he walked back into the bedroom with a serious face, sat down beside the bed and began to tell his wife about confession and the importance of it. He explained that if anything happened to her, he would convey whatever she said to the parish priest.

She began by telling him her little sins, such as how she had poured tea on white eggs and had sold them as brown, and how she had robbed a rick of turf when the children were young because they had no money for fuel. She enumerated other minor transgressions and then began to hesitate.

'Come on, out with it Mary – you're going before your maker,' said her husband in an effort to encourage her.

'Do you remember the fair of Knocknagree forty years ago?' she asked. 'You sold a white-faced heifer.'

'I do well.'

'I went to the fair too.'

'Well, you didn't come with me.'

'No,' she said, 'I followed you about half an hour afterwards in a creel car with John Doney.'

'Oh, I remember that. Well?'

The old woman hesitated again.

'Come on – out with it,' said the husband, 'this might be your last chance.'

'Well,' she said, 'I ... I misbehaved myself in the creel car with him.'

'You dirty oul' trollop!' he exploded. 'If it wasn't for the sacred f——ing collar I'm wearing, I'd kick the arse out of you in the bed!'

Thirty-Two

*T*hroughout 1964, Cathal and Billy were busy constructing the harpsichord that was to be donated to the Royal Irish Academy of Music,
modelling it on the copy of the Townley Hall instrument. However, Cathal
made this instrument several inches longer than the original in order to
improve the quality of the bass. The case was veneered with panels of Cuban
mahogany, cross banded with Honduras mahogany and inlaid with ebony and
boxwood 'stringing'. The keyboard surround was veneered with panels of
burr walnut, cross banded with tulip wood. Contrary to Kirckman's usual
practice, the naturals on the keyboard were covered in ebony and the accidentals (the sharps or flats) in ivory.

In January and February of this year, Cathal's first harpsichord was used
in two concerts, the first given by the Ulrich Gebel Chamber Ensemble at
the German Institute for Cultural Relations in Merrion Square. The second
was also presented by the German Institute but performed in the St Francis
Xavier Hall, Dublin. It was given by the Collegium Musicum der Berliner
Philharmoniker. Charles Acton wrote enthusiastically about this recital of
chamber music. The harpsichordist, Irmgard Lechner, 'gave us real harpsichord realisations, instead of the too usual succession of plonks – and, of
course, Cathal Gannon's harpsichord responded beautifully.'

On 18 February the English harpsichordist George Malcolm arrived in
Dublin and, along with Professor Brian Boydell of Trinity College, attended
a lunch given in Guinness's Brewery by D.O. Williams. Afterwards the three
men drove to our house in Rialto, where George was to examine Cathal's
first harpsichord. Writing from Guernsey in 1989, D.O. Williams described
the scene:

> I remember so well the day I came to your house in [Rialto]. As we walked up the path to your front [door] George Malcolm plucked me by the sleeve and said 'you know this is going to be very awkward. There are only a handful of people who can make a harpsichord worth playing on.' And then he sat down and touched yours. A light came into his eyes and he went on playing as if he could never stop.

According to Cathal, George pronounced the harpsichord to be as good as any of the other instruments that he had played. He also ran his hands over the Broadwood square piano. He was most impressed by the little instrument and did not believe that it could be so good. He had played a square piano in London, but it was his impression that Cathal's was superior.

Mr Malcolm then presented Cathal with a visitors' book, something that he thought Cathal should possess. Inscribed on the first page is, 'To Mr and Mrs Gannon with best wishes and congratulations on the harpsichord, from George Malcolm 18.2.1964.' On the following page, a list of the people who have visited us over the years begins. The first two names are Brian Boydell and Owen Williams. (Other familiar names are John O'Sullivan, Anthony Hughes, Kieran Egar, Emer O'Reilly and Michael Clifton, who all came on 29 February. In March I see my grandfather's name, C.W. Gannon and also Guy Jackson's. He was an assistant managing director in Guinness's and was tragically killed in the Trident air crash at Heathrow in 1972.)

Delighted with Mr Malcolm's assessment of my father's harpsichord, D.O. Williams wrote immediately to Lord Moyne. 'I have just returned from a visit to Cathal Gannon's house with George Malcolm. You will be very pleased to hear, I know, that Malcolm thinks Cathal Gannon's harpsichord one of the most beautiful instruments he has ever played, and absolutely miraculous for a first attempt. He seems to be quite clear that Cathal Gannon should go on with the good work and will inform Will [W.E.] Phillips accordingly.' On the same day he sent a telex to Mr Phillips in Park Royal:

MALCOLM THINKS GANNON'S HARPSICHORD IS
ABSOLUTELY FIRST RATE, AND WILL BE INFORMING
YOU ACCORDINGLY IN DUE COURSE.

Mr Phillips wrote to Mr Malcolm on the following day, thanking him for having examined Cathal's harpsichord. 'It will be great encouragement both to Gannon and ourselves to have your good opinion of the instruments he makes,' he added.

Mr Williams also wrote to John Beckett in London, informing him of what had happened. 'I am pleased, but not surprised, to hear that George Malcolm's opinion of Cathal Gannon's harpsichord is synonymous with mine,' he wrote. 'When the time comes for me to buy a harpsichord I shall get one of Cathal's.' He went on to say that the BBC was considering buying a new instrument and that he had already suggested that they buy one of Cathal's.

On the 20th, George Malcolm gave a harpsichord recital, organized by the University of Dublin Central Music Committee. He used the restored Kirckman harpsichord belonging to Trinity College and played music by Bach, Haydn, Rameau, Scarlatti and some pieces by early English composers contained in the Fitzwilliam Virginal Book.

He was quite happy to play this Kirckman harpsichord and paid Cathal a great compliment by telling him that he had removed all the 'ugly gremlins' and that Dublin was lucky to have him. Cathal was invited to lunch with him and Professor Brian Boydell in Commons at the university.

In April, an article entitled 'Carpenter's Unusual Job' was printed in the 'Tatler's Parade' section of the *Irish Independent*. Including a photograph of Cathal seated at his virginal, it described him making harpsichords in Guinness's Brewery. It mentions that one of his instruments would be used in the following month for a recital to be given by John Beckett. It told briefly of how Cathal's imagination had been fired by an article in *The Children's Newspaper* and how he had made his first instrument. It also described how the instrument that he was presently working on was based on the Kirckman found in Townley Hall. It concluded by mentioning that on most weekends a group of 'young people' went to his house to 'play a little bit of good music'.

It was typical of Cathal to make little or no comment on the effect that all this praise and attention had on him; he affected to be quite dismissive about it. However, I am sure that he was rather pleased at the time.

Lord Moyne had not forgotten Cathal's disappointment in losing such a fine house in Lucan and his desire to live somewhere adjacent to Knockmaroon in Castleknock. In April, he came into Cathal's workshop in the Brewery and told him that he had a 'maisonette' in Knockmaroon that he would like us to live in. Cathal explained that he was having his house in Rialto repainted and that he intended living there for a little longer, but Lord Moyne insisted that we come to see the house on the following Sunday, 19 April. He asked in particular that I be brought.

We arrived on a beautifully sunny afternoon. Never having been in Knockmaroon before, I was captivated by the long, tree-lined avenue, the spring flowers, the big house, the fields and trees. The grounds contained a little less than 200 acres of land.

The 'maisonette' turned out to be a sturdy, three-bedroomed corner house in a square of half red-bricked, half pebble-dashed, mock Tudor residences, built in 1904 around a central cinder-covered courtyard. The courtyard was entered by an archway, over which were a clock and a weather vane on the roof. To one side of the archway were stables for the Guinness horses and to the other side was a long room full of hens busily clucking and laying eggs. Small black and red bantam cocks ran freely around the yard, pecking and crowing. There were three houses and one flat in the yard.

Lord Moyne led us through an old laundry, full of antiquated sinks, equipment and a huge wooden washing machine, to the house on the other side, which had once been lived in by the laundry maids. The garden was a wilderness and the house, although it had recently been given a quick dash of paint, was in very bad repair. The walls were pitted and children had carved their initials on the banisters. A huge, ugly range stood in the large kitchen. The scullery simply contained an old sink with just one tap. Off the scullery was the one and only primitive toilet and a filthy coal cellar, in which a dog (and its fleas) had been kept. The bath and wash-hand basin upstairs were Victorian in style, with wrought-iron decorations.

My mother was not impressed by the house but my father realized that the house and grounds would be a lovely place for me in which to grow up. Inwardly, I hoped that my parents would move to this enchanted spot. While they and Lord Moyne surveyed the place and talked about it, I played on a simple swing made from a long, thick rope, which hung from a nearby tree.

We had afternoon tea in the dining room of the big house, where I gazed in admiration at the numerous Japanese prints, and later we were brought around the gardens. A pergola, festooned with flowers, led past Lord Moyne's summer house, in which he often wrote his poetry and books, to a lily pond; beyond were smaller gardens, surrounded by high hedges, in which were statues, a wrought-iron pavilion and trees bright with blossom.

Although my mother was most reluctant to move to a house in such poor condition, my father succeeded in putting her mind at ease, telling her that the sale of our house in Rialto would pay for all the necessary renovations. It was agreed that we would move to Knockmaroon provided that I could be sent to a local school and if the rent were not too high. Fortunately the sum agreed was well within Cathal's means.

Lord Moyne spoke with the nuns in nearby Mount Sackville Convent and I was guaranteed a place for a year; thereafter I would have to be sent elsewhere as boys were only taken up to the age of ten.

The deal settled, Cathal approached the workmen who were busy painting and decorating our home in Rialto to ask them if they would work on another house when they were finished; they said that they would. Cathal then set about putting his own house on the market. Most people, I am sure, would have told my father that he was mad to sell his house in Rialto and move to rented accommodation. Any business-like person would have held on to the house for security and let it to someone else. However, Cathal was happy to escape the worry and hassle that troublesome tenants might bring him. He wanted to live a carefree life; as long as he had enough to live on, he was satisfied. He deliberately turned his back on monetary gambles like stocks and shares, investments and schemes such as life insurance.

As soon as the workmen finished in Rialto they moved to Knockmaroon and tackled the house. The walls were repaired and papered, then painted. The hall, sitting room, landing and bathroom were painted white. The range was removed from the kitchen, a fireplace was installed, the walls painted pale blue, the cold flagstones covered and carpeted and the room made into a large, comfortable living room. The sink was taken out of the scullery and the room was converted into a small but neat kitchen, complete with cupboards to the ceiling. The flagstones were covered in linoleum and the room painted blue and white. The coal cellar was cleaned out, painted white and turned into a pantry, with shelves once again to the ceiling.

In the sitting room, Cathal sanded the wooden floor, carpeted it, fitted skirting boards, blocked up the door to the old laundry, converted the doorway into a china alcove, and made an elegant wooden surround for the fireplace. He bought chandeliers and hung them in the living and sitting rooms.

Upstairs, the ugly Victorian bath and wash-hand basin (now very much in demand!) were removed and, permission having been granted by Lady Moyne, a modern bathroom suite, including a much-needed toilet, was installed. This room was also painted white. The master bedroom, directly over the living room, was painted pale blue and white. It was decided that Mr and Mrs Clench would use this room; they could also use it as a sitting room if they did not care to join us and our friends downstairs. My parents' bedroom faced the front of the house, looking towards a wood. It was painted pale yellow. For some strange reason, I asked for my room, which faced the courtyard, to be painted pale pink.

In all the rooms, Cathal fitted white wooden pelmets over the curtain rails, as he had done in Herberton Road, and painted the ceilings white. I was delighted that we would have so much more space in the new house. Being at school, I saw little of the work that was being done; I only got occasional glimpses at weekends.

I was introduced to the children who lived in the neighbouring houses; I was lucky in that they were all about my age. Next door to us lived the man who milked the cows, Mr Redmond. He and his wife came from Wexford. Two of their five daughters, Phyllis and Patricia, were of my age group. The other corner house, on our side of the square, was lived in by the manager, Mr Daunt Smyth, his wife and their two sons, Peter and Stuart; Peter was the same age as myself. By this stage I had probably met Mirabel Guinness, Lord Moyne's youngest daughter, who was a little younger than I was. Although we didn't play with them very often, there were two boys who lived in one of the gate lodges; their father, Mr Wood, also worked on the farm.

We were not allowed to keep a dog because of the sheep, which were looked after by Mr Daunt Smyth. The cows were milked by Mr Redmond in the red-bricked farmyard, a couple of minutes' walk away from the courtyard towards the road. At that time there was little traffic on the roads in the area; two young girls, Veronica and Olive Smith, whom we were to meet later, could remember a time when they could leave a skipping rope tied across the Carpenterstown Road all day. They had to untie it at five o'clock, when a car came along.

According to our new visitors' book, John Beckett came to the house in Rialto in May, no doubt to practise on the harpsichord for a solo recital that was held three days later in the Royal College of Physicians, Kildare Street. In the 'Irishman's Diary' section of *The Irish Times*, printed on the day of John's visit, notice was given of the forthcoming recital, which would be given under the auspices of the Musical Association of Ireland. In the article, the author styled Cathal the 'Stradivarius in the harpsichord field'.

The recital comprised three of Johann Sebastian Bach's partitas. Charles Acton, in his review, praised John's faultless and seemingly effortless technique, as well as his superb sense of phrasing. He concluded, 'I felt that Bach would have found here a performance and a player after his own heart.'

What Cathal thought at this time about John's interpretation of Bach's work must remain a mystery. No doubt he was very impressed by his technique; both men were perfectionists. I have a feeling however, that he probably found an evening of music devoted entirely to the works of Bach somewhat dry and tedious, though he would not have admitted this publicly. It must be reiterated that Cathal's favourite instrument was the piano, not the harpsichord, despite the fact that he was constantly portrayed as a dedicated harpsichord maker (which he was). Although he did attempt to play Baroque music with his friends at home, his preference was for the Classical and Romantic composers; his youthful love for the lush melodies of Field and Chopin had not diminished.

An article by John Horgan entitled 'He makes harpsichords in a brewery' appeared in *The Irish Times* in June. Accompanied by four photographs of Cathal at work in the Brewery, it described how he had received letters from people who had found old keyboard instruments 'in the attic' and wondered how much they were worth. Having described how he had become interested in harpsichords and how he had made his first one, it went on to mention the discovery of the Townley Hall Kirckman and the making of two copies. 'He is not unaware of the need for improvement,' wrote Mr Horgan, 'and hopes modestly that each successive instrument he makes will be slightly better than its predecessor – even if only by the most minute change, as long as this has been found necessary.'

The article concluded, 'After he made his first harpsichord, thinking that it would also be the last, he threw away the complicated working drawing from which he made the templates and which he used as his guide.' It is obvious that Cathal's pessimism at the time was overcome by his later success.

At around this time, a fair amount of written communication took place between D.O. Williams in Dublin and W.E. Phillips in Park Royal as to whether harpsichords made by Cathal in Guinness's Brewery should be sold to Park Royal. Mr Williams, who was obviously far more enthusiastic about the venture than Mr Phillips, wrote, 'Park Royal are of course under no obligation to buy from us any of the Guinness–Gannon harpsichords, but I think it very likely that in time they will become so sought after that you may well wish to be concerned with their distribution.'

In early June, it was mooted by Tibor Paul, the musician, conductor and director of music at Radio Éireann, that the station should get a new harpsichord as he was dissatisfied with the Dolmetsch instrument that had been purchased. This was reported by D. O. Williams, who had lunched with him at the Brewery, to Lord Moyne. The latter agreed that more publicity could be gained by donating a harpsichord to Telefís Éireann but suggested that, as the first harpsichord to be made in the Brewery had been promised to the Royal Irish Academy of Music, a *second* be given to Telefís Éireann. The Academy having been consulted about the matter, a decision was made at a board meeting shortly afterwards to offer the first instrument to Telefís Éireann, but one year later it was decided, as Lord Moyne suggested, that the first be presented to the Royal Irish Academy of Music as the fledgling television station had not yet made up its mind as to whether it should buy a second instrument or not.

On Friday, 31 July, the first harpsichord was brought to Wexford for the Opera Festival by McCullough's of Dawson Street. It was probably on this occasion that the instrument was bundled into a large pantechnicon, much to the horror of my mother. She feared the worst and told my father what had happened when he came home from work in the evening. He was not too pleased to hear of how the harpsichord had been treated. My mother did have cause for concern, for the instrument returned with the case damaged. My father would be a little more cautious about loaning it in future.

This, in fact, was our last day in Rialto, for that evening we left the locality for good and moved to Knockmaroon. Removal of our furniture and belongings had begun the day before. I can remember nothing of the move – I am told that Mr and Mrs Clench stayed with Mr Gannon and my aunt Maureen in Dundrum while it all happened – but I can clearly remember the thrill of waking to bright sunshine in my new, sparsely furnished pink bedroom and reading a comic album – either *The Dandy* or *The Beano*. I swallowed some breakfast and ran out to play with the children in the yard: Peter Daunt Smyth and the two Redmond girls, Phyllis and Patricia. Undoubtedly, while we amused ourselves, my parents were busy putting the new house in order. Very soon it became an elegant residence, thanks to my father's excellent taste. My mother was now happy that we had made the move.

Her parents were installed in the master bedroom and all was well, though Mr and Mrs Clench felt even more ill at ease in the country, far away from the shops and bustle of the suburbs.

When we first came to Knockmaroon, quite a number of people worked on the farm and fresh fruit and vegetables were grown. I have happy memories of picking fruit, such as strawberries and raspberries, with the local children in summertime. One of the farmhands came regularly to our house with a basket of vegetables for my mother to buy. He was inclined to mix up his words, with humorous results. He spoke of a man who 'walked with a lisp'; described how his newly married son had bought a 'dive-in' [divan] bed, how another couple had not had a church wedding but had been married 'in one of them off-licence places' [a registry office] and how a 'pineapple' [piebald] horse had jumped out of a field.

There were apple trees in the field opposite our house and Mr Daunt Smyth kept bees nearby. The honey was bottled *in situ* and was stored in one of the laundry rooms. Nothing could be more different from the world of concrete into which I had been born.

That summer was a glorious one for me. I was free to run about the grounds, playing with my young friends. One of the first things they said to me was, 'What? You've never heard of the Beatles?' My curiosity was roused and suddenly I was hooked on pop music. Before that, I had hardly known that it had existed. Much to the disgust of my father, I twiddled with the tuning knob of our new plastic transistor radio and succeeded in finding Radio Caroline. He ordered me to turn off the racket. I turned it off when he was around, but switched it on when he was at work.

When the decoration and furnishing of the house were finally finished, Lord and Lady Moyne, Desmond Guinness and maybe a few others called on a tour of inspection. My parents admitted them and showed them around the entire house. They were understandably tense while their work was being scrutinized, but there was no reason to be worried; the reaction was favourable. My father was complimented on the excellent job that he had done on the house. No doubt he heaved a sigh of relief.

In the autumn, he bought another upright piano for himself and for me to practise on. This time it was a Broadwood of 1924, purchased at a house in Rathfarnham. I continued to attend the dreaded piano lessons and started school in Mount Sackville Convent, which I soon began to dislike. The journey there and back, by bicycle across the fields when weather permitted, was pleasant enough, but the nuns were short-tempered and shouted at us.

One of the girls in my class was Veronica Kerr, who in later years became a well-known singer. She remembered me, but I have no recollection of her as a student then. Another girl was Deirdre Byrne, who later introduced me to her brother, Thomas. They, their parents and their younger brother John lived in Porterstown, near the small Catholic church where we often attended Mass. The parish priest was Father Brown, a down-to-earth man who, much to my father's delight, could say Mass in about twenty-five minutes — there were no 'trimmings' (my father's term for extra prayers and additions). A keen farmer, he was known locally as 'Flash' Brown. What my father liked best about the church was the total absence of music; he had very little time for the usual Catholic hymns, especially when badly performed or sung, and had no time at all for folk Masses or the music associated with them.

Once a week, after school, I walked to Castleknock village, caught a bus and travelled into town for my piano lessons. As my teacher became more and more frustrated by my attempts to master the piano and as my father became more impatient, matters came to a head and I decided to put my foot down. At the end of the term during Easter 1965, I suddenly announced that I would not return to my lessons at the School of Music. My parents were so taken aback that my act of rebellion worked. The teacher was informed that regretfully I would not be attending any more lessons. My father was angry but my mother had some sympathy for me; she was not too surprised by my decision. At last I was free from the weekly torture.

Whilst I do regret not having continued, I realize that what had happened was inevitable. Under such circumstances I would never have made any headway with a career in music. The outcome of my rebellion was to distance myself as much as I could from my father; from then on I never attempted to do anything that he could do, for I realized that he would never tolerate my poor standards. For a few years I played no music at all; I merely listened to pop music on Radio Caroline and Radio Luxembourg when the coast was clear. Finally I demanded a guitar for Christmas and was given one; obviously my father thought that any music was better than none at all.

Thirty-Three

*B*etween January and May of 1965 Margaret kept a short diary, which she wrote in a notebook in her small, neat handwriting. The entries refer mostly to visits made and received. Billy Sexton and his wife visited us in January; other events during the month included Jack and Eileen Gannon's silver wedding anniversary, a visit to the McNamara sisters, a visit from Rosie Black, an evening in Kathleen Kelly's house, and a couple of musical evenings at home. On the second of these, the 23rd, Florence Ryan came and with her a new acquaintance of ours, Cormac Flanagan, who worked in the sound department of Telefís Éireann. He was a friend of Arthur Agnew's.

On Saturday, 30 January, we visited some new friends introduced to us by Kathleen Kelly: Harry Siberry and his wife Rita. Harry, who worked as an architect for the Guinness Permanent Building Society (hence the connection with Kathleen), was a competent pianist with a wicked sense of humour and a liking for jazz. The Siberrys lived in a bungalow on Glenamuck Road, near Kiltiernan. The house was full of cats, which were owned by Rita, and a large dog named Buster, who regularly rolled around on the carpet of the living room. Old Mr Siberry, Harry's father, entertained us with various tricks and puzzles. He was quite deaf and watched television using headphones. He ignored most of the music until he suddenly discovered that his favourite piece, Schubert's 'Trout' Quintet, was being played. When this happened, he invariably made a dive for his two hearing aids, crying, 'They're at it — they're at it!' In the absence of a cellist, the cello part was played on Harry's electric organ, which fascinated me.

It was in the Siberrys' delightful home that we met the violinist, Lorna

Thompson, whom Margaret and Cathal held in very high regard. In time we were to be invited to her house in Monkstown.

I was present at all these musical evenings, either at home or in our friends' houses. Undoubtedly this was quite unusual for a child of my age; most nine- and ten-year-old boys prefer to be with children of their own age. Whilst I did have pals of my own at Knockmaroon, I was happy enough to be included amongst the adults, though like my mother I felt completely overshadowed by my father. He was the one who did all the talking; my mother and I merely listened. He had become a great raconteur, entertaining his listeners by telling them funny stories about Guinness's Brewery or astounding them by his knowledge of history, people, architecture, clocks and watches, and the arts. He had an amazing ability to remember dates. However, apart from recounting the various things that he had done throughout his life, he generally avoided talking about himself or his personal feelings. Whenever anyone asked him questions concerning his views or opinions, he normally hesitated, said as little as possible and deftly changed the subject of conversation to something else. I never managed to discover why he was so reluctant to air his personal feelings or emotions.

On 1 April my parents went to Belvedere College in Dublin for an interview. On completion of the school year at Mount Sackville, I would be obliged to leave. The nuns had suggested Belvedere College, run by the Jesuits, as a suitable school for me. My father, always prone to name-dropping, wrote to the Father Rector, 'Lord Moyne is most anxious that [Charles] should attend your school as is Dr Kevin Nowlan of National University who is a past pupil of Belvedere. They are both willing to write to you if necessary.' The priest – probably Father Rector – who interviewed my parents set a date later in the month for me to sit a short examination.

About one week later, Cathal and Margaret attended a cocktail party given by Lord Moyne and on the following day, John Beckett came to practise on Cathal's first harpsichord. This was for a concert that took place in the Aberdeen Hall of the Gresham Hotel on the 8th. Cathal remembered bringing a special chair to the hotel for him; John had discovered that it was just the right height for playing the instrument.

On the following day, Professor Brian Boydell of Trinity College wrote to Lord Moyne. Guinness's Brewery had donated money towards the restoration by Morley's of the Kirckman harpsichord, which now, Professor Boydell claimed, would 'not stand up to the demands it has created'. Would

Cathal, he wondered, make a new instrument for Trinity College? Earlier in the year, John Beckett had suggested that the School of Music in Chatham Street receive one of the Guinness–Gannon harpsichords. As the Guinness authorities were aware that Cathal could not mass produce his instruments, they were careful to give non-committal replies.

A couple of days later a large party was given in our house. The guests included Lord and Lady Moyne and three of their children, Finn, Catriona and Erskine, the cellist Coral Bognuda, Werner and Gerda Schürmann, Michael Clifton and Emer O'Reilly (who married later in the year), the pianist Gillian Smith, her husband the oboist Lindsay Armstrong, Gillian's mother Olive Smith, and David Lillis and his wife. I have a vague memory of this musical evening. My mother's comment in her diary is short and to the point: 'very successful'.

By now the third harpsichord had been completed. John Beckett had tried it earlier in the year and had conveyed his impressions to his friend D.O. Williams, who wrote to Lord Moyne. 'He was extremely pleased with it and says it has an even fuller tone than the two previous ones,' he wrote. Cathal received a letter from Tom Goff in Pont Street, in which he said, 'I am sending you my congratulations on completing your new harpsichord. You must be very pleased and proud and I think of all the musicians and students of the Royal Irish Academy of Music and their audiences who are going to derive such enormous pleasure from your work. I hope that there will be a day when I can see and play it, but I do not think I can come to the 'opening' ceremony (to which Lord Moyne has so kindly asked me). I retain the happiest memories of the day you spent with me and this brings you my warmest good wishes and rejoicing at the completion of your lovely instrument.'

On 12 April the harpsichord was presented by Guinness's Brewery to the Royal Irish Academy of Music at a special luncheon ceremony. As Cathal stated, 'it was quite an occasion'. The specially printed invitations, complete with a gold harp, were grandly worded. 'The Board of Directors of Arthur Guinness Son & Co. (Dublin) Ltd request the pleasure of the company of Mr and Mrs Cathal Gannon at a Luncheon in St James's Gate Brewery on Monday, 12 April 1965, at one o'clock on the occasion of the presentation of the First Guinness Gannon Harpsichord to the Royal Irish Academy of Music.' I was invited too and undoubtedly was let off school for the day.

We donned our best clothes and arrived for the meal, which consisted of smoked eel (I confess to have felt a little nervous eating this), poached salmon with mousseline sauce, then Chicken St James with sprouting broccoli and croquette potatoes, followed by Bombe Moka and finally coffee. Our hosts were Lord and Lady Moyne. I sat between young Mirabel Guinness and Miss Harte Barry; on the other side of the table was the pianist Dina Copeman, who lived on the South Circular Road and to whose playing Cathal had listened with great interest when he was a young man. Various people of note were present; Mr W.E. Phillips of Park Royal had been invited but was unable to come.

The handing-over ceremony was somewhat facetiously described by the author of 'An Irishman's Diary' in *The Irish Times*, dated 13 April:

> Among the guests were eleven members of the Guinness family, a number of very top-drawer Guinness executives, including three Assistant Managing Directors and two Brewers (any one of whom speaks only to God on far more easy terms than the Lowells or Cabots), Dr John Larchet, Mr and Mrs Tibor Paul, Mr Maurice Dockrell, TD, Mr and Mrs Charles Acton, Mrs Olive Lyall (Concert-Hall) Smith, and the Tanaiste-elect and Mrs Aiken.
>
> For once in a way, the Minister for External Affairs was very much Mr Maud Aiken, because Mrs Aiken was there in her capacity as President of the Royal Irish Academy of Music, to receive from Lord Moyne the harpsichord made by Cathal Gannon of Guinness's – on behalf of the Academy. Mr and Mrs Gannon were there; so was their son, Charles, who is a very competent harpsichord player at the age of ten; so was his friend, eight-year-old beautiful blonde Mirabel Guinness, youngest of eleven Moynes, and interested in two things – ponies and harps. 'Concert harps or Lager Harps?' I asked. 'Neither,' said Mirabel (obviously refraining with difficulty from adding 'Stupid!') 'I play an Irish knee-harp, but Charles plays the harpsichord quite beautifully.' She then concentrated on her ice-cream, and having consumed same, told me that her family will be showing a bull and four heifers at the Spring Show.
>
> Mirabel's Papa, who is as consistent a devotee of Donegal tweed suits as Maurice Gorham, made a short little speech in which he likened the occasion to 'a christening party with Bach and Scarlatti as sponsors.' He thanked Dr John Beckett for coming from London for the luncheon, and also for convincing Guinness's of Cathal Gannon's quality as a harpsichord maker. Mr. Gannon, a white-haired, monkish-looking cherub with a most self-deprecating manner, thanked the Board of Guinness's and Lord Moyne for 'allowing me to indulge my hobby and paying me at the same time.' He also thanked his wife,

'who put up with a lot,' and told us that the only difference between this harpsichord and the Trinity one is that 'the white notes are black and the black notes are white.'

Mrs Aiken then went through the motions of taking delivery of the instrument from Lord Moyne, thanked everybody, and then Dr John Beckett played us two little Bach pieces and three Scarlatti sonatinas, leaving nobody in any doubt that the Gannon harpsichord is a beauty and that, in John Beckett, it has a beautiful interpreter.

In the concluding (and more serious) section of the article, the author mentions the woods used in the construction of this instrument: tulip, mahogany, silver spruce and rosewood. Pear and holly wood had been used in the construction of the jacks.

Elsewhere in *The Irish Times* for that day was a photograph of me, looking suitably angelic, playing the new harpsichord and being watched by five of Lord Moyne's children: Mirabel, Catriona, Tamsy, Kieran and Erskine. An article and photograph, showing John Beckett at the keyboard observed by Mr Frank Aiken TD and Mrs Aiken, Cathal, and Lord and Lady Moyne, appeared in the *Irish Press*. A photograph of John once again playing the instrument, watched by Mrs Aiken, Cathal, Lord Moyne, Mirabel and myself, appeared in the *Evening Herald*.

The event marked another important milestone in Cathal's life; inwardly he must have felt quite chuffed at the fuss being made about him, though the recognition that he was Ireland's only harpsichord maker bent on reproducing the elegant and excellent instruments of the past did not go to his head. He still realized that he could probably do better and that life had to go on. Like everyone else, he had to work in order to earn money and live. He was still being paid a carpenter's wage by the Brewery and was still essentially a carpenter.

When the idea was put to him that, in fifty odd years' time, his harpsichords would be compared favourably or put on a par with the instruments of old, Cathal scoffed at it, explaining that he had always been hampered by a lack of knowledge and materials, and that he had taken chances that were often 'wide of the mark'. His view was that any instrument of his could not possibly equal those of the great masters – they could only be pale imitations.

When writing to Mr D.O. Williams to apologize for not being able to come to the presentation of the harpsichord to the Royal Irish Academy of Music, Mr W.E. Phillips of Park Royal had mentioned that the Brewery in

Dublin might be interested in selling an instrument to Harrods of London. On the day after the presentation, Mr Williams wrote to Mr Stanley J. Murdoch, buyer in the piano department of Harrods, to say that 'we can sell you one of the Guinness–Gannon harpsichords at price of £950 in Dublin'. A response from Mr Murdoch, indicating that he was interested, arrived on the following day. Accordingly, it was decided at a Board Meeting in Guinness's Brewery that the next harpsichord would be sold to Harrods and that, instead of donating or selling a new instrument to Trinity College, Cathal would restring and provide the existing Kirckman harpsichord with new jacks in July.

Now that the Guinness–Gannon brand of harpsichord had effectively been created, the Brewery was anxious to show it off to the general public. A few days later, on 17 April, which was Easter Saturday, Cathal appeared briefly on Gay Byrne's long-running television chat programme, *The Late Late Show*, with the instrument. I can remember watching the fuzzy black-and-white images on the Daunt Smyths' television set in Knockmaroon. Cathal was not very enthusiastic about appearing on the show – at first he had stubbornly refused, confessing that he was 'of a nervous disposition' – but reluctantly did it for the sake of the Brewery. The instrument, which was still in the workshop, was collected and transported to Telefís Éireann in Donnybrook, where it was carried into Studio 1. Gay recognized Cathal immediately and mentioned to him that he had seen him somewhere before. Cathal explained that he used to live near his family home in Rialto.

The live interview was short and Cathal played a couple of pieces, including an Irish jig with the harp stop on, to demonstrate the harpsichord. Gay Byrne wrote to D.O. Williams that he was very happy with the performance. After the programme, which was shortened because of it being Easter, Cathal and Margaret left in the van with the driver and the instrument, never having been offered a fee. They returned to the Brewery late at night and, because nobody else was available, Margaret had to help lift the harpsichord into the visitors' waiting room. Needless to say, they were not very impressed by what had happened.

Despite Cathal's reservations about appearing on television, his brief stint brought him more into the eyes of the public. Some years later, when ascending the steps of St Paul's dome in London, he encountered two Irish ladies on their way down. One of them greeted him in a familiar manner. As Cathal continued his ascent, he could hear the ladies' voices wafting up to him from below.

'Do you know that man?'

'Yes, I do – I saw him on *The Late Late Show* some time ago!'

From now on, Cathal was known affectionately as 'the man who makes the harpsichords', though there were several variations on this phrase. Some people thought he made pianos or organs. When a man hollered across the road at him, 'Hey Cathal, are you still makin' the harmoniums?', he merely smiled and said, 'Oh, yes!' and refrained from correcting him.

He also came across some original mispronunciations of the name of the instrument; *harpischord* was frequently encountered but the best of all had to be *whipsichord*, uttered by one of the farmhands at Knockmaroon.

Unfortunately, one person who did not see Cathal on television was his uncle Billy, who sadly died on 11 April of that year. Ironically, he had been watching *The Late Late Show* on the previous Saturday.

As Cathal's brother Willie and his wife Kathleen were over from England on a visit to Maureen, Cathal's sister, they saw the programme. On Easter Sunday they came to Knockmaroon for tea.

Praise for Cathal's harpsichord at home came from another quarter a few days afterwards; we received a visit from the English harpsichordist Colin Tilney, who later wrote, 'I am grateful to you for letting me see (which was a minor revelation) what I can do if I have a wonderful congenial harpsichord under my fingers. I am very much looking forward to when you come to London – I'll try to show you all that's going on in harpsichord-building.'

Colin came again to Knockmaroon on the following day for a musical evening with other guests of ours, including Kathleen Kelly, Michael Clifton, Neil Downes and Werner Schürmann. My mother's diary pronounced it to be a 'wonderful evening'.

Margaret recorded various other social occasions for the end of April and beginning of May, including a series of recitals given by the Aeolian String Quartet in the Rupert Guinness Hall and musical evenings at the homes of Lorna Thompson, the Siberrys, Florence Ryan and Kathleen Kelly. It was around this time that I gave up studying the piano.

On 21 May, she wrote in her usual terse manner, 'Cathal wrecked the car.' This was not the first time that Cathal had damaged a car. Just a year or so previously he had fallen asleep at the wheel of his Morris Minor whilst driving to Dundrum to visit his father and sister Maureen. My mother's parents and I were in the car. Just as we approached the viaduct between Rathgar and Milltown, the car suddenly left the road and gracefully went up on the footpath. A little puzzled at first, I suspected nothing unusual until the car approached a lamp post. I screamed, 'Daddy, Daddy!' just as the car squeezed itself between the lamp post and a high concrete wall to our left. This woke my father and the car came to a stop. He got out and surveyed the damage; according to him, the car looked 'like an accordion'.

The car behind us stopped to see what had happened. The driver remarked that he had been thinking that my father was a very careful driver until we left the road for the footpath. My father explained that he had fallen asleep because of the heater, which he had switched on for my grandparents as they had felt cold. He took a philosophical view of the affair, saying that he had been thinking of buying a new car and now he would have to.

His next car was a tiny Austin Mini. This turned out to be a 'Friday car': various bits and pieces came adrift and fell off, and my father was disappointed with his purchase. How he managed to 'wreck' the car on the occasion recorded by my mother has long since been forgotten.

It was just as well that Cathal never had to do a driving test, for doubtless he would have failed. After he started to teach me to drive many years later, I had to unlearn many bad habits when I attended proper lessons with a driving instructor. Two things irritated him constantly when driving: undipped headlights shining into his eyes from an oncoming car and 'oul' fellas with soft hats driving in the middle of the road' (invariably in a Morris Minor) holding up the traffic. According to him, slow drivers like these 'navigated' around corners. Moving off slowly from traffic lights also annoyed him. He always approached and drove away from traffic lights at a 'good lick'.

With the mention of a retreat beginning on 23 May and another musical evening at Knockmaroon on 29th, Margaret's diary comes to a close. Where the retreat took place and whether it was a men's or women's retreat is not recorded. Although my father went to Mass every Sunday morning and was satisfied if it was short and to the point, he was not what could be called a very religious man. Whether he attended the retreat out of genuine piety or a sense of duty is difficult to say – I rather suspect that it might have been the latter. It must be remembered that his view of the Catholic faith would have been tarnished by bitter recollections of the treatment meted out to him by the dreaded Christian Brothers when he was at school. However, as everyone knows, the Church authorities were stricter in the 1960s and the absolute necessity of attending such a retreat would have been drilled into the minds of the congregation from the pulpit.

Throughout this period, several letters passed between the authorities in Guinness's Brewery and Harrods about the price and mark-up of the harpsichord that Cathal was now working on; after much deliberation, the price was lowered to £850. It was proposed that the new instrument be displayed at an exhibition of Irish-made goods, due to open in August.

In June of 1965, the Guinness–Gannon harpsichord now belonging to the Royal Irish Academy of Music was used in the first of a series of three concerts dedicated to the music of J. S. Bach. The instrument was played by John Beckett, with Betty Sullivan providing the basso continuo. Other artistes included Edward Beckett on flute, John Ronayne and Mary Gallagher on violins, and the singers Violet Twomey (soprano) and Frank Patterson (tenor). John Beckett remembered rehearsing with Frank in Cathal's workshop at the Brewery.

Cathal undoubtedly attended all three concerts, the third being a production of Bach's Cantata No. 11 (the Ascension Oratorio) and the B minor Mass at St Andrew's Church in Dublin. It was performed by the Radio Éireann Symphony Orchestra and the St James's Gate Musical Society. As Cathal found the music too wearisome, he left about halfway through and walked around St Stephen's Green, watching 'the ladies of pleasure and things like that'.

In the 1960s a museum was opened in Guinness's Brewery; Dr Stan Corran was in charge. Believing Cathal to be suitable for the job, Stan wanted him to become its curator. However, the authorities would not allow this as they wanted Cathal to continue making harpsichords. Cathal was pleased that he was not given the job, for he was not very enthusiastic and knew that he would always have to show people around. He preferred the comfort of his own workshop, where he could lock himself away and take a short nap after lunch.

Sometime in 1965 Cathal bought a Longman and Broderip square piano, made in London between 1796 and 1798, at a house in Donnybrook. Although it was in poor condition, he stored it for two years without touching it. A handsome instrument, it was a typical late eighteenth-century square piano in the Sheraton style. It stood on four legs and the mahogany case and legs were inlaid with tulip wood and boxwood stringing. The nameboard over the keys was made of satinwood and bore an enamel plaque bearing the inscription, 'New Patent, Longman and Broderip, London'. This was actually a firm of music dealers and publishers that had published all of Joseph Haydn's music in London during the 1790s. The firm was taken over by Muzzio Clementi in 1800, with Frederick Collard as the foreman. The Irish composer John Field, who was buried in Moscow, demonstrated the instruments. Clementi was a pianist and composer but now embarked on a career of music publishing and piano making.

The keyboard of Cathal's piano had five and a half octaves; there was one sustaining pedal and a shelf underneath for volumes of music. Most of the strings were missing, as well as many of the hammers and ivory key coverings.

On 22 July Cathal began restoring an unplayable Broadwood square piano that had once belonged to the poet Thomas Moore, composer of the famous Irish melodies. The instrument belonged to Lord and Lady Elveden (later Lord and Lady Iveagh), who lived in Farmleigh House, adjacent to Knockmaroon. Lord Elveden's father had bought the instrument in 1900. The piano had been used by Moore when he had lived in Kent, where he wrote many of his poems. After Moore's death, it passed through several hands before Lord Iveagh purchased it. An inscription, written in the poet's handwriting, was found at the back of the keyboard. It read, 'Bought this instrument and played it for dear little Isobel. July 15, 1813. T. Moore'. Isobel was one of Moore's daughters; all of them died of tuberculosis.

Before and during the restoration, Cathal became acquainted with Miranda and Benjamin Guinness (the Elvedens) and visited them at Farmleigh – the house is now owned by the government. Miranda and he got on particularly well together; despite Benjamin's shyness, Cathal had several interesting conversations with him. Cathal also met his elderly father, Lord Iveagh, who was then in a wheelchair.

My mother and I were brought to Farmleigh on a few occasions and I played with the two young daughters, Emma and Louise. When Emma, at some later stage, borrowed a book that I had written (modelled closely on Richmal Crompton's *William* books and, needless to say, never published), I received a gushing letter in childish handwriting, full of praise and thanks.

Both Miranda and Benjamin were suitably amazed when Cathal, working at the piano in his Brewery workshop, restored it to playing condition. The strings all had to be replaced, the covers of the hammers had to be renewed and the hammers themselves had to be fitted with new vellum hinges. One of the six legs had broken and had been replaced with a more modern one, which did not match the style of the piano. As luck would have it, Cathal had some legs from an old Broadwood square piano that suited it perfectly and so he was able to supply a leg of the correct style.

In September 1965 an article, complete with a photograph of Cathal bending over the instrument, appeared in the *Sunday Press*. It reported that he expected to complete the work in a month or six weeks. Another article, entitled 'Stradivarius of the harpsichord', appeared in the *Evening Herald* during the same month. It reported the restoration of Moore's piano, which, it stated, would be 'a labour of love', and mentioned that Cathal's latest harpsichord was on sale at Harrods in London.

This fourth harpsichord was based once again on the Kirckman of 1772 found in Townley Hall and was effectively a copy of the previous instrument as regards layout and materials. By 11 August it had been completed and was on display in Harrods until 18 September. According to the *Daily Express*, it was one of the highlights in this 'Charm of Ireland' promotion and was priced at 1400 guineas. Other items on display were a Spanish guitar made by Laurence Egar from Cork, an 18-inch high miniature Brian Boru knee harp, examples of Waterford crystal and even a gaily painted horse-drawn travellers' caravan, used for holiday tours.

Billy Sexton, Cathal's helper in the workshop, visited London during the promotion and wrote to him, describing what he had seen at Harrods:

> The harpsichord was displayed against a harmonised mellow background of Donegal carpeting in a corner of the main exhibition hall. The main cover was down and a book of Irish jig music was on the stand. We stood a while listening to the comments which were very praising all round, to quote: 'a damn fine job', or 'Oh! how beautiful' or even the one ample word 'splendid'.
>
> The price listed was a stunner to a lot of people. It is to retail at 1400 gns or can be bought by a down payment of £124 + 24 monthly payments of £60.

Cathal received an invitation from the Irish Ambassador in London to attend a cocktail party at the Irish Embassy in Grosvenor Place on Tuesday, 14 September. The Brewery sent him to London so that he could attend the party, see the exhibition for himself and buy more materials for his next batch of three harpsichords. Cathal flew to London on the 14th, travelled by train to Victoria Station and took afternoon tea in the Grosvenor Hotel, possibly with his brother Willie who met him in London. The two men travelled to the embassy by taxi in order 'to do things properly'.

During the course of the evening, Cathal and Willie had a long conversation with the Irish ambassador. By all accounts, it was a very pleasant occasion. Afterwards, Cathal and Willie took the train to Brighton.

On Wednesday, Cathal travelled into London and arrived at Harrods by 12.45 pm. There he met Mr Stanley J. Murdoch, buyer in the piano department, and lunched with him. Afterwards he examined the instruments on sale and then went to Goddard's, the piano suppliers in Tottenham Court Road, where he ordered parts, such as tuning pins, felt for the dampers and key coverings for the next three harpsichords.

On the following day he lunched again in Harrods with Mr Murdoch and two other executives, then went to Mallinson's, where he ordered timber and veneers; in the evening he had supper with Willie and Kathleen.

On Friday Cathal went to Greenwich and later to Morley's, the keyboard instrument makers (more correctly, 'pianoforte and harpsichord galleries') in Lewisham, where he undoubtedly examined the instruments on view and possibly spoke to John Morley, designer and head of the firm.

The London piano-key makers J.F. Pyne & Co. in Duncombe Road were visited on Saturday and Cathal ordered more components for his instruments. He also found his way to Holloway Road, where Margaret had been born, and later went to St Paul's Cathedral. Cathal finally returned home on the following Tuesday.

The harpsichord at Harrods was finally sold, presumably at the asking price. Some time afterwards, Mr Murdoch asked Cathal if he would be willing to restore Victorian and early pianos for Harrods. It was proposed that they would be sent to Ireland for Cathal to work on. Unfortunately, as Cathal was doing a full day's work at Guinness's Brewery and could not entertain the idea, he had to turn down the job, despite the fact that he was told that the money would be good and that he could charge whatever he liked. He admitted to not being a businessman and preferred the safety of working for a large company that could supply him with a steady, albeit rather low, income and pension; he considered the idea of working freelance to be too precarious.

A proposal like this indicates the high regard in which Cathal must have been held by the authorities at Harrods. Doubtless there were many others in England who could have done this type of work to perfection; however, Harrods must have been duly impressed by Cathal's high standard of work. Much more recently I was told of how impressed a noted English harpsichord restorer, Christopher Nobbs, had been by Cathal's standard when he had occasion to work on the harpsichord that Cathal had made for the Royal

Irish Academy of Music in Dublin. In a report on the instrument, written at the beginning of 2003, he wrote, 'Gannon's building after historical models was pioneering in 1965 and ... he twice worked on the instrument later to bring it closer to the originals as taste changed and knowledge increased'. According to him, instrument makers were only beginning to get into their stride in England in the 1960s and many were still floundering. Cathal had been ahead of his time; instead of trying to improve or modernize the harpsichord, as many of the British makers were doing, he simply made faithful copies of an historical model, believing that this was the only way to make good instruments. In his estimation, the makers of old knew what they were doing. His idea was very simple, yet radical.

We have noted Cathal's reservations upon meeting Tom Goff in London and yet we have also discovered him complaining about the lack of knowledge and materials in Ireland. Somehow, he had managed to overcome these shortcomings as he pushed ahead, continually striving for perfection. 'I'm not satisfied with anything I did,' Cathal once said in a radio interview many years later, 'I can find fault with everything.' It was John Beckett who had dubbed him 'the equivalent of a Stradivarius in the harpsichord field'; it seems that there was not too much exaggeration in this description after all. An article in *The Financial Times* dated September 1965 describes Cathal as 'shy and erudite' and concludes, 'he is still far from happy with his own work.' The accompanying photograph shows him in a characteristic pose: instead of looking directly into the lens of the camera, he humbly looks downwards.

Back in 1963, Dr Stan Corran of Guinness's Brewery had written to Cathal, suggesting that he might become a member of the Galpin Society, which specialized in the history of musical instruments and regularly published a journal. He thought that back numbers of the journal might be of interest to him. Although Cathal did not become a member, in October 1965 he received a letter and some printed papers from Charles Mould, Lieutenant Colonel, Royal Tank Regiment, who lived in Berkshire, which informed him that a list of makers of historical keyboard instruments was about to be published in the next edition of the Galpin Society Journal. He had learned of Cathal's existence from the aforementioned article in *The Financial Times* only after he had returned the galley proofs to the editor and hoped that somehow his name might be included in the journal or at least in the next section of the list. Cathal was asked to fill out a form and return it as quickly as possible. In his letter, Lt Col Mould wrote, 'I must say that your instruments look most handsome, and I feel that any survey of this nature would be incomplete without mention of your work.'

Cathal complied with the instructions and his name, address and the technical details of just his first two harpsichords (representing the two 'models' that he had produced) were included in the forthcoming index, which was published early in 1966. They appear on page 117 of the reprint of the Galpin Society Journal XIX: An Index of British Makers of Historical Keyboard Instruments, by Charles Mould.

In thanking Cathal for his letter and completed form, Lt Col Mould wrote:

> You sound very modest about your building, but I am sure by the way you speak that you have no cause for modesty. I feel sure that we still have a tremendous amount to learn by the full and careful study of these old instruments. So many makers today (including myself) have started out with the idea that we know much better than those who have followed a rigorous apprenticeship in a craft which had enjoyed a period of development over several hundred years. The fact that (as in the case of the Dublin instrument you mention) the work of some modern builders cannot even survive a few years use cuts us all down to size.

Lt Col Mould had also informed Cathal that the second edition of Donald Boalch's important book, *Makers of the Harpsichord and Clavichord, 1440–1840*, was about to be printed and that Mr Boalch, who lived in Oxford and was a friend of Mould's, would be grateful for any additional information or corrections that Cathal could supply. The book had originally been printed in 1956. Cathal sent Lt Col Mould some information about the Weber harpsichord in the National Museum in Dublin, which he passed on to Boalch. Once again, here is proof of the high regard in which Cathal was held abroad, even by people who only knew him by repute.

Also in October 1965, Cathal travelled with his own harpsichord in a Brewery estate car to Wexford, where the instrument was used in the Opera Festival. It had been used there previously. In Wexford, Cathal handed the instrument over to Dr Walsh, set it up, tuned it and returned home the same evening. He had been invited to a 'Guinness Night' at the Talbot Hotel prior to a production of Verdi's *La Traviata* but it is unlikely that he attended it, for as we have noted, Cathal simply did not care for opera.

Later in the month, Lord Elveden wrote a note to Owen Williams asking if Cathal could repair a piano made by the Dublin maker William Southwell, which he owned. It was Southwell who, in 1798, turned the square piano on its side to produce a small upright. Lord Elveden wondered if the work could be completed before starting on the Radio Éireann harpsichord. However, having spoken to Mr Williams, he learned that the Radio Éireann harpsichord had to be finished by April of the following year and realized that having his piano ready before then might not be feasible.

On 30 October, Stanley Murdoch of the piano department in Harrods wrote to D.O. Williams, informing him that the department store had decided to loan the Guinness–Gannon harpsichord for a series of three concerts at the Commonwealth Institute, Kensington High Street, in aid of the Arnold Goldsbrough Memorial Fund, and asking that Cathal be informed about this.

At around this time, Lord Moyne wrote to James Callery, secretary at the Royal Irish Academy of Music, asking if Cathal's harpsichord could be available for George Malcolm to play upon; the Philomusica of London was due to give two concerts at the Royal Dublin Society. The request was granted and George Malcolm played the instrument at the beginning of November. During the rehearsal, he turned to Cathal and in front of everyone said, 'Are you going to go on making these instruments?'

'Mr Malcolm,' said Cathal, 'it's the only sort of harpsichord I know anything about.'

'You're only working for antiquarians,' he said. 'You want to make a larger instrument with a sixteen-foot register and foot pedals.'

'Well,' said Cathal, 'I'm afraid that would be beyond me.'

The famous double-bass player Francis Baines, who was performing in the orchestra, later approached Cathal and said, 'That man doesn't know what a harpsichord is – we've never played with such a satisfying instrument.' According to him, the balance was perfect. However, Cathal was convinced that Mr Malcolm was not very happy playing his harpsichord because he had heard it said that 'he played more with his feet than his hands'. It is strange that Mr Malcolm, who had given Cathal such high praise just over one year previously, was now so critical of his instrument.

A little earlier, John Beckett had written to D.O. Williams requesting that Cathal make him a harpsichord as he did not possess an instrument of his own. He was prepared to pay £500 if a plain, unadorned instrument could be made for him at that price. In August of the previous year, Tibor Paul of Radio

Éireann had written to Mr Williams to thank him for the offer to present a harpsichord to the station. However, because of 'restrictions imposed on Radio Éireann by the terms of its legal constitution', it was not possible for them to accept gifts. However, he did agree to buy an instrument.

On 1 November, official confirmation came from D.O. Williams and Lord Moyne that Cathal would make three harpsichords concurrently. One of these would be sold to Radio Éireann for £750 and another to John Beckett for £500. Writing to Cathal a couple of days later, John admitted to being thrilled on receiving this news ('a word I don't remember often using'). However, he then went on to write:

> BUT, having thought the project over, as you must have done, are YOU agreeable also? It seems to me terribly cheap for such an instrument. I fear that I may be exploiting your great skill, and your friendship. If you have any such feeling please tell me. If you think the price too little, which it is − too inadequately little for your work and time, say so now. I mean that seriously.
>
> Francis Baines (double bass player in the Philomusica) said to me this morning, apropos of you: 'He has got nearer the truth in his instruments than anyone else.'

Cathal, who realized that John could only just afford the price of the instrument, did not ask for a penny more and the deal was settled. Several letters passed between the two men concerning the look and specifications of the proposed instrument. John stated that he would prefer ebony naturals and ivory sharps on the keyboards (no celluloid coverings), a moving coupling device with two separate eight-foot stops, no buff stop and a plain waxed walnut case. John, having waited so long for an instrument of his own, was prepared to wait a little longer to get the exact specifications that he requested.

Meanwhile the fate of the third harpsichord in the batch of three had yet to be decided. Letters passed between Guinness's Brewery in Dublin and Park Royal in London about the possibility of selling the instrument for £700 to a gentleman named Philip Ledger of the University of East Anglia, who had probably seen Cathal's instrument at Harrods. In the end, the correspondence came to nothing and the instrument was eventually sold to the Irish harpsichordist David Lee.

Thirty-Four

*I*n the meantime, I had started school at Belvedere College in September, having passed the entrance examination during the summer. Deirdre Byrne, whom I had met in Mount Sackville Convent, had by now introduced me to her brother Thomas, who also attended Belvedere. Although he was some two years older than I was, we became fast friends and his father kindly gave us both a lift into town every weekday morning. On Saturdays my father collected us from Belvedere at midday and often brought us to the Hugh Lane Municipal Gallery in Parnell Square or to the Orkens' antique store, which was like an Aladdin's cave for us. I can remember the visits to the gallery with pleasure. Years later, Thomas admitted that my father had left a lasting impression on him and encouraged him to take an interest in the arts. My father influenced many young people in this manner.

At weekends, Thomas and I used to visit each other – I believe I spent more time in his house than he in ours – and play pop music. For me, the great attraction in the Byrnes' house was their television set. My father was always vehemently against having a television at home and many years would elapse before we finally acquired one. We did not even have a telephone.

Whilst my father helped me occasionally with homework, in general I tended to avoid him and ignored what he was doing. Influenced by the boys around me, I continued to listen to and compose pop music and started to wear my hair long, which was the fashion then. Although I did some things that pleased my father, such as playing the recorder, painting and drawing, writing books (which I 'printed' in longhand, illustrated and bound myself) and even devising and writing a school magazine, which was printed and circulated, he was disappointed in me and often told me so. The fact that I had given up learning to play the piano and seemed to have no inclination to follow in his footsteps was a bitter disappointment to him. Despite his public modesty and charm, he still had a very hot temper and had no qualms about laying down the law at home. He was impulsive and often stubborn; he rarely took 'no' for an answer and always considered himself to be in the right. Like his own father, he was a strict disciplinarian.

At some time around this period, the City Basin in Basin Lane near James's Street was being demolished to make way for flats. The city water course had terminated at this point. Cathal had often visited this pleasant spot and admired a simple yet handsome early eighteenth-century gateway and stone surround with a fine architrave and wrought iron gate, which had been illustrated in drawings. He approached the foreman and asked him what was about to happen to the gate.

'It's going to be pulled down,' was the answer.

'Has anyone shown an interest in it?' asked Cathal.

'No, but if they have, they'd better hurry up because it's going to be pulled down in a week or two.'

Cathal alerted Desmond Guinness, who managed to salvage it and incorporate it into his garden at Leixlip Castle.

During the last couple of months in 1965 Cathal did some restoration work on the original Kirckman harpsichord in Trinity College and in January of the following year he was sent to London to do an emergency job on the instrument owned by Harrods, which John Beckett was about to use for a BBC Third Programme recording. The instrument had been sadly neglected and then over-voiced by some zealous piano tuner, who had tried to make it sound as loud as possible. Cathal flew over on the evening of the 4th, worked on it during the following day in Broadcasting House and flew home that evening. He had the pleasure of meeting Patricia Hughes, an announcer whom he had often heard on the Third Programme, and had 'a great chat with her'.

In May, Cathal received a letter from Lt Col Charles Mould, enclosing the Galpin Society Journal mentioned in the previous chapter and the news that his harpsichord in Harrods was so badly out of tune and regulation that it was impossible to play. Lt Col Mould was horrified to see how Harrods were treating the instrument and begged Cathal to make some arrangement with a professional in London to keep it tuned and maintained. A few days later, Harrods wrote to D.O. Williams in Guinness's Brewery to ask where they might buy replacement Delrin plastic plectra for the instrument. Cathal wrote back to say that Delrin was unobtainable in Dublin and that leather should be used; he enclosed some strips with his letter.

In March 1966 Cathal's harpsichord was used for a production of J. S. Bach's *Saint Matthew Passion*, performed in the Concert Hall of the Royal Dublin Society by two orchestras conducted by Victor Leeson, The Guinness Choir, The O'Connell School Boys' Choir and the soloists Peter Bamber (Evangelist), William Young (Christus), Honor Sheppard (soprano), Bernadette Greevy (contralto), Richard Cooper (tenor) and Christopher Keyte (bass). John O'Sullivan played the organ, John Beckett the harpsichord and Betty Sullivan the cello.

Sadly, Margaret's elderly parents died during this month. Old Mr Clench had a heart condition and so we were not too surprised when he passed away peacefully on 15 March. What did take us by surprise, however, was the fact that Mrs Clench, who had been fit enough to walk to church on Sunday, caught a cold that quickly turned into pneumonia; she died two days later. She had been hoping to return to England. At the same time, I lay in bed, suffering from influenza. Mr Clench's funeral was delayed and both he and Mrs Clench were buried together. My mother was in a state of shock, a condition that soon developed into high blood pressure.

Everyone we knew showed great sympathy towards my mother and wrote letters of condolence to her. Even the Rector of St Brigid's Church, Castleknock kindly wrote to her, stating, 'your mother's erect figure at the front of our Church is sadly missed'. Letters from people living in Spencer Road, Wealdstone told of what good neighbours the Clenches had been; they had always been ready to help others.

As soon as everything was straightened out, my father suggested that we take a two-week holiday in Switzerland. This was our first time to travel on the continent; I remember feeling very excited at the prospect of going abroad. The arrangements were made with Thomas Cook & Son and the holiday started on 20 June. Never having been in an airport before, never mind an aeroplane, I was delighted with everything. We checked in and all went well until an announcement informed us that our flight would be delayed. My father grew increasingly restless and annoyed until he declared that he had had enough and was going home. My mother and I implored him to be patient and wait for the flight.

Once we had arrived and my father had settled down, he began to enjoy the holiday. He was delighted with the pretty little town of Interlaken, where we admired the fine scenery and marvelled at how so many souvenirs were displayed on tables outside the shops without any danger of being stolen. We travelled to the snow-covered top of the Jungfraujoch mountain by funicular railway and visited Lake Thun, where Brahms had stayed and composed some of his best music. My father was enchanted by the area.

We then journeyed to Lucerne, where we crossed the lake by walking on the wonderful old wooden bridge, which sadly was destroyed by fire many years later. I can remember being brought to an aquarium; I was fascinated by the electric eels. We visited my parents' old friend Maria Schönenberger in nearby Zug and she showed us her brother-in-law's carvings in a local church. The treasury was opened specially for us and we were shown the silver and gold artefacts that were kept in it.

Our last place to stay in was Lugano, which my father did not like; I think it was too modern and lacking in character for him. I can remember travelling by boat along the lake. All in all it was a wonderful holiday – it gave my mother (and later me) an appetite for foreign travel – and helped to dispel the gloom caused by the sudden death of my grandparents, though my mother remained upset for some time afterwards.

On returning home that summer, the Clenches' beds and furniture were removed from the master bedroom and I used it as a playroom for some time until my father moved in and it became his bedroom. I can remember playing with my electric train set, which I had received one Christmas whilst living in Rialto, on the floor. On the whole, my toys continued to be basic and I made my own using cardboard boxes. Inspired, no doubt, by our neighbours, I even made my own television set. My father fitted it with an electric light bulb and I made cardboard shadow puppets for my programmes and shows.

In June 1966 Cathal sold our Broadwood square piano to Helen and Joe Devine and bought a Chappell baby grand from Andrew Tynan's piano shop in Rathmines. Cathal had got to know Mr Tynan at around this time.

The Chappell was kept in the sitting room at Knockmaroon until it was sold four years later to my parents' friends, John and Mary Byrne, who had come to our musical evenings for the first time in May 1966. John had worked in Guinness's Brewery; his wife Mary sang beautifully, her speciality

being German *Lieder*. A fluent German speaker, John taught her to pronounce the words correctly. He positively worshipped Mary; when she sang,
he watched her, enchanted, and listened to every word intently. Mary won
several prizes for her singing, including some awarded at the Feis Ceoil.
Cathal loved to play her accompaniment. Sadly her husband died whilst
swimming on holidays and she died at a relatively young age of cancer.

By mid-September 1966 the Radio Telefís Éireann harpsichord was completed (the first of the batch of three mentioned earlier) and on the 20th it
was formally handed over by Lord Elveden to Kevin McCourt, director general of the station, at an evening reception. Another grandly-worded invitation was sent to us and a buffet supper was served. After the ceremony,
music by Henry Purcell was performed by John Beckett, Betty Sullivan and
Frank Patterson. The list of people who attended is impressive; it included
the Minister of Posts and Telegraphs, Mr Brennan and his wife, Mr and Mrs
Michael Noonan, Mr and Mrs Tibor Paul, Mr and Mrs Roibeard Ó
Faracháin, the Minister for External Affairs Mr Aiken and his wife, Professor
and Mrs Brian Boydell, Dr J.F. Larchet, Mrs Olive and Miss Gillian Smith,
Charles and Carol Acton, and various high-ranking Brewery figures includ-
ing Lord and Lady Elveden, Lord and Lady Moyne, Lady Honor and Mr
Frank Svejdar, Dr and Mrs A.H. Hughes, Mr and Mrs D.O. Williams, Mr and
Mrs G.P. Jackson, Dr and Mrs Stan Corran and Mr and Mrs Hely-Hutchin-
son. At the very bottom of the list are my parents and the Sextons: Billy
(Cathal's helper) and his wife. My name is missing and I am fairly sure that I
did not attend.

As before, the event was reported in the national press. A photograph of
John Beckett at the new harpsichord, watched by Cathal and Billy Sexton,
appeared in the *Evening Press*. In *The Irish Times*, Charles Acton reported how
Kevin McCourt had said, when receiving the key, that 'it was a matter of
pride that an Irish broadcasting authority could receive such a beautiful
instrument made by a superb Irish craftsman employed by an Irish company'.

The instrument was used mostly in concerts given by the RTÉ Symphony
Orchestra and also by Seán Ó Riada, the eminent composer and traditional
Irish musician, who regularly played it when performing with his group
Ceoltóirí Cualann. He believed that the sound of it was close to that of the
old Celtic wire-strung harp, examples of which were not available then.

Despite Cathal's fame as regards harpsichord building, he sometimes felt rather thoughtlessly neglected. On one occasion, Lord Moyne complained to Cathal that he had not been invited to a function at which one of Cathal's instruments had been used. Cathal reminded him that he too had not been invited, despite the fact that he had both made and supplied the harpsichord. 'The trouble is,' Cathal concluded, 'that you and I are not high-up civil servants!' He often had to tune his harpsichords in adverse conditions; people did not realize that peace and quiet are needed to tune such delicate instruments.

The entry in the Galpin Society Journal had not gone unnoticed, for in September Mr Meredith M. Moon of the Music Department of the Bodleian Library, Oxford, wrote to Cathal asking how much he would charge for a two-manual Kirckman harpsichord. An official answer was sent from the Brewery, stating that an instrument similar to the one supplied to the Royal Irish Academy of Music, with a veneered case, would cost £1355. To the best of my knowledge, that was the end of the correspondence.

At around this time, Cathal's skill was employed for something a little more unusual, for he received a letter from one of Lord Moyne's daughters, Fiona, thanking him for the work that he had done on her Indian sitar. I have a faint recollection of my father fixing it for her. I was more fascinated by this exotic instrument than he was.

Towards the end of November, Elizabeth Neuman, whom Cathal knew from Guinness's Brewery, came to visit us at Knockmaroon. She was to remain a good friend for many years to come. I have fond memories of her. She took a keen interest in me and, when I was a few years older, sent some of the children's books that I had written to various publishers. Naturally none of them was ever published, but I received favourable comments from the publishers. It was not surprising that Elizabeth left Guinness's Brewery and became a child psychologist.

Some time in 1967, RTÉ contacted Cathal in the Brewery and asked him if he had a harpsichord in playing order. He did; in fact, he had three instruments in his workshop. One was completed, one half finished and one just started. An RTÉ representative told Cathal that it would be to the Brewery's advantage to televise the workshop and interview Cathal about his instruments; he agreed to it. Plans were made to lay cables at nine o'clock in the morning, either on the following Wednesday or Thursday. When the day was finally decided, Cathal was casually informed that the programme was to be in Irish. 'Well then,' he said, 'the programme is off.'

Surprised, the RTÉ people tried to reason with him and talk him back into co-operating with them. 'No,' said Cathal. 'If I had known it was to be in Irish, I wouldn't have been interested in it.' Naturally they wanted to know why Cathal would not agree to the programme being made. 'Because,' he said, 'I had such a nasty time with the Christian Brothers over the Irish language that I just have no interest in it, and I am not going to be used.' Apparently Cathal told them that they would be better off making a programme about bagpipes or some other traditional instruments. He stated that he was available for a programme to be done in English, but refused to be 'in the hands of the Irish contingent'.

Needless to say, the incident caused a certain amount of embarrassment in the Brewery. Mr D.O. Williams heard about what had happened and Cathal went to speak with him. 'I feel very strong about the Irish language and the way they're using it and I was a victim of the same language,' Cathal explained.

'I'm a Welshman and I know how extreme some people can be,' said Mr Williams sympathetically. 'You don't have to worry in the least about it.'

'Well,' said Cathal, 'I am very sorry that it happened, I assure you, because I *do* want to help the Brewery in any way possible.'

Apparently Billy Sexton took a different view of the matter. 'If you can't beat them, join them,' he said.

'Look, Billy,' said Cathal, 'people know me for my attitude towards the language and the way it's being abused and ill-used. I'm not going to talk in that language – I switched it off in 1925 when I left school. I left school disillusioned and badly beaten by one of the Brothers over the same language, and I just don't want to remember that; it's a phase of my life which is finished. Good luck to the people who want to carry on and speak Irish – that's their business and they're entitled to it, but I'm just *not* interested.'

This is not exactly the meek harpsichord maker portrayed by the press; this is the Cathal whom I remember: decisive and at times stubborn. Here is an instance of him putting his foot down firmly and sticking to his ideas. Although he had nothing against the Irish language per se, he did have a grudge against those who insisted on 'ramming it down people's throats', as he liked to say. I can remember him using these words in connection with the compulsory study of the Irish language to the headmaster in Belvedere, who looked understandably displeased. I knew from experience that it was useless to turn to my father for help if I got into difficulties with Irish grammar or vocabulary when doing my homework.

Throughout 1967 Cathal continued work on the remaining two harpsi-chords in the Brewery workshop – by April it was confirmed that David Lee would buy one of them for £900 – and also restored the Southwell piano for Lord Elveden.

In May we went on a holiday to the Netherlands, spending most of it in Amsterdam, which Cathal was interested to see. He particularly enjoyed vis-iting the famous Rijksmuseum, where he examined the Rembrandt master-pieces, including 'The Night Watch'. He often recollected how an American tourist had sat down beside him and asked him what the value of the painting was, a question to which Cathal had no answer. He named some figure and the man left, satisfied. At the souvenir shop, my parents overheard another American tourist saying, 'Gimme a copy of the painting that sells best.'

Cathal was very much impressed by the way that the old merchants' houses along the canals were being restored with great attention to detail. He enjoyed visiting the various museums and churches in the city, pointing out all the wonderful details to Margaret and me. We stayed in the Museum Hotel in PC Hooftstraat, a fairly comfortable hotel, though my father com-plained of the tepid food served on cold plates. If food was meant to be hot, Cathal wanted it *hot*, not warm. At this stage Cathal, in a fit of piety, had us kneeling every evening and reciting the Rosary. I can remember us praying together in my parents' bedroom in the hotel. Every time we started, a record player in an apartment across the street began to play the Beatles' song 'All You Need Is Love' at top volume, much to my father's annoyance.

We went on several day trips from Amsterdam: to Maarken and Volen-dam, the tulip auction houses at Alkmaar, the cheese factory at Gouda, the Frans Hals Museum and the St Bavo organ in Haarlem, and the Mauritshuis in the Hague, where we saw Vermeer's 'View of Delft', one of Cathal's favourite paintings.

Douglas Gunn, the recorder player and founder of the Douglas Gunn Ensemble, paid a visit to Knockmaroon in June and wrote to my parents from Cork a few days later to thank them for their hospitality. He wondered if Cathal could make him a 'small instrument of the spinet or virginals type' by November, when the quatercentenary of Monteverdi's birth would be celebrated. In the event, such an instrument was never made for him.

By the end of June, work on David Lee's harpsichord was completed in the Brewery workshop and the instrument was delivered to him. Soon afterwards it was inaugurated at a recital given by David in St Bartholomew's Church, Clyde Road. He was joined by his friend David Ledbetter, who read a short lecture on the history of the harpsichord and the programme to be played. Mr Ledbetter also played the recorder with Robert Frost in a trio sonata by Telemann. Our friend Werner Schürmann sang a couple of songs.

Charles Acton wrote in *The Irish Times*, 'I came away from St Bartholomew's with the impression that this latest [harpsichord of Cathal's] had a remarkably strong and even tone, and that the duration of sound is unusually great, even when heard at the back of the church.

'David Lee played the first two items, the Couperin and the Handel suite with obvious love for his new instrument, and it was in the Couperin that the richness was particularly noticeable while the Handel showed its carrying clarity.'

The fact that David was delighted with his new instrument is borne out by a letter written early in the following year. In it he wrote, 'in short it is the most splendid (and the word is carefully chosen) harpsichord I have ever played, seen or heard.' Indeed, it was Cathal's opinion that the three harpsichords he made at this period were the best to date; the availability of the original Kirckman instrument in Trinity College was of immense help to him, as he was able to recheck his measurements at any given stage.

In August, D.O. Williams in the Brewery received a request from James King, General Manager of Kilkenny Design Workshops Ltd, Kilkenny, for a Guinness–Gannon harpsichord for a German friend of his. He had second thoughts when he was informed that the price would be £2150. Clearly the authorities were beginning to think that it was time to wind up the harpsichord-making business. Early in the following month a board meeting was held at which it was decided that production of more harpsichords should cease 'because of lack of demand'.

Cathal now heard from a colleague in Guinness's Brewery that the owner of two popular shops in Liffey Street that sold low-priced goods, Hector Grey, had a piano for sale: a Blüthner boudoir grand. As Hector wanted to get rid of it, he said that he would accept £100 from the first person to take it away.

Cathal drove to his house in Grange Road, Raheny, looked at it and bought it. It was in a bad state of repair; it had been knocked about and the lid was covered in beer stains. Cathal removed the polish and stripped it down to the wood with Nitromors, which 'nearly choked' him. He then waxed the wood. He cleaned the action and soundboard, polished the strings and re-surfaced the ivories. It was a hard job, but it was worth it. We now had two grand pianos in our sitting room at Knockmaroon. They were often used for the performance of two-piano duets at our regular Saturday musical evenings. Harry Siberry or Helen Devine usually played with Cathal.

Hector Grey, whose real name was Scott, was a familiar figure on the quays on Sunday mornings, when he used to stand out in the cold selling all manner of goods to an interested crowd of onlookers. By all accounts, he was a good salesman. Apparently he once produced a brace and bit, which he brandished in the air in front of the people. 'This brace and bit is made in China and it's a heap of rubbish,' he announced. 'However, if you have one of these at home, your neighbour is sure to ask you for a loan of it. It'll break when he uses it and then he'll have to go out and buy you a good one.' Needless to say, every one of them was sold.

In October, Cathal and Margaret attended four wonderful concerts at the RDS of all Brahms's solo piano music performed by the great American pianist Julius Katchen. Cathal had the pleasure of speaking to him after one of the recitals. One of the works performed was the *Variations and Fugue on a Theme by Handel*, which Cathal had heard played by Paderewski in 1928. Julius Katchen told him that he had also heard Paderewski play when he was a boy, and that even at that time there was still a little bit of magic in his fingers. Also at the concerts was Cathal and Margaret's good friend, Helen Devine.

By mid-November, John Beckett's new harpsichord was completed and shipped to his home in London. Like David, he was delighted with it. The batch of three instruments was now finished.

In between times, Cathal had been busy restoring his Longman and Broderip square piano during the year. This he had been doing in his spare time at home. All in all, Cathal reckoned that he spent approximately 300 hours working on the instrument. The restoration, when complete, was a great success. Cathal was delighted with the sound, which was bright and crisp owing to the light stringing, thin soundboard and small hammers covered in buckskin. This was the type of sound with which Haydn would have been familiar. The little piano turned out to be Cathal's favourite. John Beckett was enchanted with it also and, as we shall see, used it for several radio broadcasts. It was also featured in a couple of television programmes made about Cathal.

In January 1968 an article about harpsichords and Cathal, written by

John O'Sullivan, appeared in *Hibernia*. A photograph of David Lee playing his new harpsichord in St Ann's Church, Dawson Street appeared in the *Evening Press* a month later and Charles Acton reviewed this short lunchtime recital, given in an icy-cold church. Once again, Mr Acton was enthralled by the sound of the instrument.

As Cathal was continually being pestered for loans of his own harpsichord (his first instrument), he allowed Dr Stan Corran to take it off his hands sometime around this period. He now, therefore, was able to tell people that he no longer possessed a harpsichord. It would seem that he was beginning to tire of being in the eye of the public and at the beck and call of everyone who needed an instrument.

Soon after Cathal completed John Beckett's harpsichord in the previous year, he had begun to restore a handsome Broadwood grand piano of 1809, also discovered in Townley Hall near Drogheda when Trinity College took over the house and grounds. The piano was in an unplayable condition, but nothing was missing. The restoration involved restringing the instrument, working on the action and replacing the doe skin coverings on the hammers.

The piano had no metal braces to support the wooden frame (although such braces were introduced at this period) and had three pedals. The left-hand one slid the keyboard and action to one side, producing an una corda effect, whereby only one or two strings were struck and the others sounded in sympathy. The other two were separate sustaining pedals for the two halves of the keyboard. Despite these interesting features, Cathal was disappointed in the quality of the sound when he finished the restoration; for him, the treble lacked clarity.

Nonetheless, a big fuss was made of the instrument when it was inaugurated in the magnificent saloon of the Provost's House in Trinity College in June 1968. Professor Brian Boydell gave an introductory speech about the instrument in its context, 'an account packed with fact and interest' as Charles Acton wrote in *The Irish Times*. Professor Anthony Hughes of University College Dublin then played the instrument for the assembled guests. They first heard a Fantasy in C minor by Mozart, then a Beethoven piano sonata, a piece probably better suited to the instrument. Like Cathal, Charles Acton expressed reservations about the sound; he found it lacking the necessary brilliance and clarity needed for the Mozart. In his report he stated that 'such an instrument poses problems of usage. The solution surely is that its existence in a learned institution enables us to study the relationship between technique and art in that period, the better to play music in modern terms on modern pianos.'

With the completion of work on this historic instrument, Cathal ceased to work on keyboard instruments for Guinness's Brewery. As the building in which Cathal had been working was due for demolition, he was approached by the board of directors and asked if he wished to continue making harpsichords. No doubt he had been told about the decision at the board meeting in November of the previous year. As he claimed to have lost interest in making harpsichords and as he had been interrupted too often during his work, he said what the directors expected him to say: 'no'. Accordingly, the workshop was closed. He was offered the contents of the workshop for a ridiculously small nominal sum – £1 or 30s. was suggested – so that it could be said that he bought them. Cathal, who knew the true value of everything, offered £50 and it was reluctantly accepted. He had a small wooden workshop built in the field opposite his house in Knockmaroon, in which he installed all the timber, tools, electrical equipment, workbench and even the lights that he had had in the Brewery. The second harpsichord, the initial instrument modelled on the Townley Hall Kirckman, was put in the living room of our house.

Thus, in a rather abrupt manner, a chapter in Cathal's life ended. The few short years in which his skills were proudly brought to the public's eye were the culmination of years of perseverance, observation and hard work. He had progressed from what he regarded as an indifferent first attempt at harpsichord building to the finesse of his last Kirckman copy and had discovered the joy of bringing old pianos back to life.

Although Cathal was not to make a harpsichord for another four years, his name was not yet to be forgotten and he would, in time, produce and restore many more fine instruments.

Thirty-Five

C athal was now given the job of maintenance inspector in Guinness's Brewery. This involved examining the windows, doors and roofs of the various buildings in the large complex and reporting on the need of repairs. He was given a desk in the corner of a general office, which could be reached by means of one of two lifts. According to Cathal, each floor of the building had a plant growing in a pot and everything was 'very slick'. However, working in this environment did not appeal to him; he realized that he was more suited to standing at a bench and using his hands. As carpenters of such a high calibre were of no particular use in the Brewery at this stage, the job was merely an excuse for keeping him occupied.

Cathal worked from a large map in his office, which was divided into squares. His method was to concentrate on one area at a time, visiting all the buildings and writing reports, which were submitted to an engineer. When the area had been examined, Cathal crossed off the square and proceeded to the next. In this way, he managed to visit all the buildings in the Brewery in a period of a few months. Once he had examined them all, he started all over again, reporting on repairs that had been carried out and others that had not.

The job was hardly very pleasant; Cathal found himself in basements or else climbing up to dangerous walks on the roofs of buildings that had lain derelict over a number of years. He once found a dead snake on the top of a roof; he surmised that a seagull might possibly have left it there. Gradually he began to think that it was not safe for a man of his age to be on rooftops. However, he continued at this rather unsuitable work until he retired two years later.

At around this time, Cathal gave D.O. Williams one of the clavichords that he had made some years previously. Mr Williams had been looking for such an instrument and was delighted to receive it. He wrote a short note of thanks to Cathal in September and gave him a book entitled *The Keyboard Music of C.P.E. Bach* by Philip Barford. Occasionally Cathal went to Mr Williams's fine house in Herbert Park to tune and regulate the instrument and sometimes I went with him.

Very little seems to have happened in 1968. Whilst Cathal liked to reminisce about his childhood, growing up in Dublin, working in the Brewery, making harpsichords and restoring old pianos, he rarely had much to say about himself or the events that happened after 1965 or 1966. It was as if the good times and treasured memories stopped at around this period.

Nonetheless, his life continued to be interesting and his circle of friends became wider. In December 1968 a name appears in our visitors' book that was to be a familiar one for many years to come: Anthony Harrison, who had come with his sister Carmel to one of our musical evenings. Anthony, who was studying in the National College of Art in Kildare Street, had learned of Cathal's existence through his interest in historical musical instruments and the revival of the harpsichord; he visited Cathal in his workshop in Guinness's Brewery a few times before it was demolished. Despite the age gap, they became fast friends and remained so until Cathal's death.

A couple of years later, Anthony left college and began working at art conservation, restoring paintings firstly with Richard Kingston and then for Patrick Dunfoy of the Dublin Antique Brass Shop in Lad Lane. Cathal always enjoyed Anthony's company and often went to visit him at his house in Pembroke Place, Baggot Street. His sister Carmel studied harpsichord with John Beckett at the Royal Irish Academy of Music and Anthony, thanks to Cathal's help, later began to make her a magnificent copy of a French harpsichord, which unfortunately he never finished. He decorated the soundboard with beautiful painted floral arrangements. I clearly remember our visits to his basement workshop. Later he made tapes for me of Renaissance and Baroque music, which helped me to appreciate other types of music rather than just pop.

In March 1969 the Royal Irish Academy of Music's Guinness–Gannon harpsichord was used in a performance of Bach's 'Peasant Cantata' given in the RDS by the Ulster Orchestra under Janos Fürst. Other items included a

Mozart symphony and a divertimento by Bartók. Charles Acton once again praised Cathal's instrument, calling it 'a magnificent continuo instrument with a large and fine tone supporting the orchestra'.

During the following month, Cathal received a letter from an earnest 23-year-old Mr James Bump of Pennsylvania, USA, who wrote to ask if he might become his apprentice. He had studied a variety of subjects at university: music, the piano, the harpsichord, literature, art history and ceramics. He had taught himself woodworking, had built four clavichords and had made some other early musical instruments. He included a list of worthies who would furnish Cathal with references.

Cathal replied to this request by saying that he had lost interest in his hobby and that his workshop would be dismantled in the near future. He advised Mr Bump to concentrate on England, where more people were engaged in the revival of the harpsichord. It is clear that Cathal had no intention whatsoever of taking a chance and engaging Mr Bump as a student; at this stage in his career he only wanted to be left alone.

It is regrettable that Cathal never took on anyone as an apprentice, either in Guinness's Brewery or later at his workshop at home. It seems that there was nobody in Ireland who had the necessary interest in music and skill in carpentry. There were many fine musicians and good carpenters but the musicians could not have made instruments and none of the carpenters had enough interest in making copies of old musical instruments.

This was not the only correspondence from America. The day after Mr Bump typed his letter, Wolfgang J. Zuckermann of Zuckermann Harpsichords, Inc., New York, wrote to Cathal to say that he was writing a book about present-day harpsichord makers and to ask him if he would like to be included. A form, to be filled in, was enclosed. Cathal replied, in a very similar manner to that used when writing to Mr Bump:

> Dear Mr Zuckermann,
> I am not a professional harpsichord maker in the accepted sense. Between the years 1952–1967 I made 7 copies of a 2 manual Kirckman of 1772 with no concession to modern trends. This represents the sum total of my efforts in this realm. I don't intend to construct any more harpsichords as I have other interests and would prefer not to be mentioned in any publication.
> > Sincerely,
> > Charles Gannon.

Although Cathal strove for anonymity, the book, entitled *The Modern Harpsichord*, which was published later in the year, had the following entry:

CHARLES GANNON
Ireland
Charles Gannon has made seven double harpsichords, exact copies of a Kirckman of 1772, in the course of 15 years. In 1967 he ceased his building activities and is not now planning to resume them.

Earlier in the year old Mr Gannon had begun to behave rather oddly and had tried to slit his throat with a kitchen knife. He had read of an attack in a newspaper and had a hallucination that he was being attacked. He was put into St Patrick's nursing home for a while, then moved to Dr Steevens's hospital, Dublin. In December, Mr Gannon was moved to Our Lady's Manor nursing home in Dalkey.

'We had to put him into a home for the elderly, which he hated though he had every comfort,' wrote Cathal to a friend many years later. 'He was aware that he was somewhat confused and, apart from the family, did not welcome visitors. He was never certain whether I was his son or his brother! This arose from the fact that I looked older than he did and the nuns who ran the home often said "here come the two brothers".'

We visited Mr Gannon regularly and often brought him out for drives in the car. On one occasion, he managed to walk out of the building, catch a bus and travel into town, where fortunately a friend recognized and rescued him.

Cathal continued to buy some pictures from Rosie Black at around this period, along with a couple of Regency chairs and a large Chinese blue and white plate or 'charger'.

Rosie, who was a rather colourful character, was given to wearing tweed hats – even in her own house, which was generally very cold. On one particular day, she decided to go into town. She met a friend in Grafton Street who asked her where she was going. 'I'm going down to have my lunch in Switzer's,' was the reply.

'Well, if you are,' said the other lady, 'you have two hats on you!'

Obviously, Rosie had absent-mindedly placed another hat on top of the one she wore at home.

Cathal often saw her outside the various auction rooms, ordering people about and organizing the collection of furniture by men in vans.

Rosie was notorious for walking into people's houses, eyeing a painting, asking, 'Did I sell you that picture?' and groaning when she heard how much she had sold it for.

All sorts of people now came to our home, including the harpsichordist Colin Tilney (who performed at the Royal College of Physicians in Dublin) and Geeta Alvarés Meneses from the Indian Embassy, who was brought by our friend Elizabeth Neuman on a couple of occasions. From now on, Lord Moyne brought various acquaintances of his, including Jo Grimond, the well-known Liberal MP, to see 'Mr Gannon's harpsichord'. Unfortunately, no record was kept of these visits and often we did not know who we had the honour of meeting, for Lord Moyne's voice, which was always soft, had the unfortunate habit of trailing off when he announced the person's name.

Visitors were either brought by our friends or else found their own way to our house. One day in March 1970 there was a knock on the door and I answered it. A tall young man with black hair, a moustache, spectacles and a long German military coat stood before me. Speaking in a gentle Northern accent, he introduced himself as William Stuart and asked to see Cathal. I believe I brought him into our sitting room and summoned my father. He had heard of the name before; William, who was interested in old pianos, had tried to contact him in the Brewery and had left a telephone number, but my father had not bothered to ring him.

It transpired that William had given a lift to an elderly lady who had told him where we lived. When Cathal met him on that day, he immediately found him to be a very interesting young man. Twenty-five years of age, he hailed from Ballymoney in County Antrim, had studied biology at Trinity College and was now a teacher. The two men discovered that they had much in common and fell into easy conversation. Cathal showed William the pianos and the harpsichord that we owned and William showed an interest in the clocks that Cathal had acquired over the years and placed in different rooms. Cathal also showed him a display case containing his antique watches, but William merely glanced at them and said that he was not particularly interested in them.

Cathal invited our new friend and his fiancée, June Orr, to come the following week and they duly arrived in William's red MG sports car. Both were given a tour around the house and, interestingly, William asked to look at the watches again. Soon he became hooked on them; in the end, Cathal claimed he had built up one of the biggest collections of antique watches in Ireland.

Despite the difference in age, William and Cathal became close friends and spent a considerable amount of time together, discussing, planning and doing things, as we shall see. The friendship lasted until William's untimely death from cancer in 1995 at the age of fifty. Whenever William felt that he had to escape from stress or domestic strife, he invariably beat a path to Cathal's door, spending hours with him in his little wooden workshop amongst the trees or with us in our house. Although William had rejected religion (a consequence of the bitterness and animosity that he had encountered between the different religious communities in Northern Ireland), he lived his life true to Christian principles. He was a model of goodness and kindness; he was generous, helpful, pleasant to everyone, always interesting and always willing to show interest. He rarely came to our house empty-handed; he regularly offered a gift of food to my mother in thanks for the meals that she had provided for him. I liked him too; he was good enough to talk to me and show an interest in whatever I was doing.

However, like most people, he was not without faults; he could be stubborn and outspoken at times, and was inclined to use strong language at inappropriate moments. He and Cathal exchanged many coarse jokes and laughed a good deal; in this regard, they were well matched. Cathal admired young William's vitality, which no doubt spurred him on, and William obviously admired Cathal for his knowledge. Nonetheless, it was William who had a wider range of interests; unlike him, Cathal could not converse on science, sport and a range of more up-to-date topics. Cathal, despite the fact that he listened to the news every day, virtually lived in the past, for most of what he loved dated from the seventeenth or eighteenth centuries; William, who appreciated things from this period but was in contact with young people, lived in the present.

My father, as we have noted, was not particularly religious; whilst he avoided discussing religion with William, he no doubt was influenced by William's iconoclastic views on the subject and may have become somewhat more sceptical in his beliefs at this stage in his life. Although Cathal was not greatly interested in politics, he made it clear that he didn't support Fianna Fáil and preferred to vote for Fine Gael, the members of which he regarded as being a little more civilized. When 'the Troubles' began in Northern Ireland at around this time, he took a keen interest in the events, turning on the radio for news bulletins and requesting silence in order to listen carefully. BBC Radio 3 was his constant companion in the workshop when he worked alone; he listened to everything, including modern music and sometimes opera. He liked to listen to every type of music at least once before forming an opinion about it.

He disliked sport of any description – he cursed Radio 3 when they interrupted their music programmes for coverage of cricket – and had lost interest in films and film stars. He loathed television and considered it to be a killer of conversation. Although he could do simple electrical repairs, he was unimpressed by most modern electrical gadgets. He would not have a telephone in the house at this period for fear of people ringing him and asking for help with some musical instrument; he wanted to be left alone. He had obviously developed a love–hate relationship with the harpsichords he had made and the pianos that he had restored.

Approaching his sixtieth birthday and bored with his job as a maintenance inspector, Cathal now began to think that it was time for him to retire from Guinness's Brewery. Although he was due to retire at sixty-five, he managed to persuade the board of directors to let him go. It had been hinted that it would be in his best interests to stay on for another five years and be awarded with a better pension, but Cathal was anxious to leave.

Cathal drove into Guinness's Brewery for the last time on Friday, 12 June 1970. During the morning, members of the staff presented him with a book token and Victor Leeson gave him a copy of *The Harvard Dictionary of Music* by Willi Apel. The men he worked with clubbed together and gave him a leather wallet containing £40.

As Cathal wanted no ceremony, he simply said goodbye to his colleagues and walked out of the gate at about two o'clock. A porter approached him and asked him if he could look at a broken lock, which he would bring in on Monday morning.

'There's no use in bringing it in – I'm going on pension this very moment,' said Cathal.

'Is there no farewell party?' the man asked.

'They wanted to give me one but I didn't want one,' said Cathal. 'I just want to slip out.'

Slip out he did; he got into his car, which he had parked on Victoria Quay, and within half an hour he was in Carton House tuning a harpsichord for a concert.

The board of directors respected Cathal's wish to leave Guinness's Brewery quietly but on 31 August gave him a tea party and a 'golden handshake'. Dr A.H. Hughes presented him with what he called 'a scrap of paper': a cheque for £2000, which was considered to be quite a lot of money then. Classifying Cathal as a 'unique person', Mr G.N. Cairns, one of the directors, had proposed that he receive this *ex gratia* payment. With this gesture, Arthur Guinness, Son & Co., Ltd formally said farewell to one of its most talented workmen; a man who had been with the firm for forty-five years, who had been engaged in a most unusual job and who had brought a certain amount of extra respectability to the company, which could now be regarded as a patron of music and the arts.

Thirty-Six

*F*or most people, retirement means putting one's feet up and taking it easy; life becomes less hectic and often less interesting. With Cathal it was the complete opposite; if anything, he became busier than ever. If he had lived his life up to this point in third gear, he now shifted into fourth. Over the next twenty years he would work extremely hard, not for gain, but for the benefit of many people who wanted instruments made or restored by him. It could be argued that he worked far harder than he did in the past, for now he no longer had the entertainment provided by what he called the 'funny characters' in Guinness's Brewery; those days were gone forever.

Regularly ensconced in his little workshop facing the house, Cathal made seven small single-manual harpsichords in the Italian style for various friends, three large double-manual French harpsichords after the famous maker Pascal Taskin, three simplified versions of the same with just one keyboard, helped two people (Tom Wilson and Hughie Doherty) construct harpsichords, assembled a harpsichord kit for Loretta Keating, and assembled a fortepiano from a kit shipped to him from America. The final four harpsichords that he had begun were eventually shipped to England, where they were completed by a friend of his, Patrick Horsley. In between times, he restored eleven antique pianos, two barrel organs, two barrel pianos, and did endless maintenance work on the instruments that he had made. Instruments were constantly coming and going and being shifted from one room to another in the house. One of the pianos he restored was another Broadwood belonging to Trinity College. He was constantly in demand as a piano and harpsichord tuner.

Any visitor who had managed to leg it over the wire fence, cross the small field and enter Cathal's black wooden workshop during this period would have encountered a stocky, grey-haired, balding middle-aged man, wearing horn-rimmed spectacles and a shabby, faded brown shop coat, busy at work. In cold weather, the workshop was heated only by a small electric fire. In the centre was the workbench and around the walls were antique pianos and sheets of timber. Along the wall facing our house was the door and two windows, under which ran a counter and shelves. Against the opposite wall, which had one window overlooking the woods, was a grey electric drilling machine. As the surrounding trees tended to shade the building, the workshop was always well lit with the neon lights taken from the Brewery. The ceiling and interior walls of the workshop – or at least those that could still be discerned – were painted white.

Cathal, usually stooped and peering through strong spectacles (he had several pairs), worked slowly and methodically, usually to the accompaniment of music supplied by his transistor radio. To my inexperienced eyes he seemed to spend an inordinate amount of time checking and double checking things before actually doing anything. Because of the limited size of the workshop, he was obliged to clear unwanted timber and tools away as he worked; therefore, he knew where everything was and could find what he wanted instantly. Nails and screws were kept in glass jars, ranged neatly on shelves. Files were kept in one drawer, chisels in another and so forth. Only occasionally did he mislay something and then all work stopped until the missing item was found. Details of all the work that he did were meticulously recorded in a notebook and either written in pencil (his preferred writing implement) or ballpoint pen. He noted dates of commencement and completion of work, names and dates of instruments, the number of hours worked, measurements and, most importantly, string thicknesses for the various instruments. Occasionally diagrams were drawn in the notebook. Interestingly, the entries in the notebook are often not in sequence; they may have been copied from records written on scraps of paper and the backs of envelopes – nothing was wasted. He often drew diagrams or wrote memoranda on pieces of wood, which he later used for some other purpose. In the drawers of his workbench he kept letters and documents, particularly itemized receipts from suppliers. Most of these still survive.

In this environment, Cathal was cool, calm and calculating; it was as if he had switched off the impetuous side of his nature. His concentration was intense once he started working. I was impressed by both his tremendous strength when sawing or hammering and the delicacy of his touch when he applied himself to something small and neat: his work was never sloppy. I can still picture his large, strong hands and the expression on his face as he peered intently through his spectacles.

The floor of the workshop was strewn with wood shavings or sawdust, which I hated, but it was regularly swept clean. Whilst Cathal was completely at home in this atmosphere of wood and shavings, I was not. I was always happy to help him spin strings for an instrument or hold something when he needed an extra pair of hands, but I was usually glad to leave the cold, dusty workshop. Many a time I managed to get a splinter in my finger when handling timber.

Many of Cathal's friends and acquaintances called to this cramped workshop, especially those who knew that a harpsichord was being made for them. Although Cathal put in long hours devoted to making the various harpsichords, he by no means shut himself off from the world, and he continued with his social engagements.

During the summer of 1972, Cathal's second harpsichord was purchased by the Park Royal branch of Guinness's Brewery and sent to the Gardner Centre, University of Sussex, where it still is to this day. One of the small Italian harpsichords was bought by the Dublin Baroque Players; a double-manual French harpsichord was made for the up-and-coming harpsichordist Emer Buckley, and one of the single-manual models was donated to Trinity College, Dublin by the Russian cellist Mstislav Rostropovich. Two of the pianos restored – an upright cabinet piano by Robert Wornum and a 'pianino' by Lichtenthal of Brussels – were kept at home, along with a fine double-manual French harpsichord, the soundboard of which I painted. [Details of all these instruments can be found in Appendices A and B.]

An entry in my diary in August 1972 records an excursion up the Wicklow Mountains, via Glenmacnass (where we stopped for a picnic lunch) to Glendalough. This may have been the first of many such outings, which my parents always relished. Cathal was always ready, on good sunny days, to drop everything and drive to County Wicklow for a picnic, after which he would always take a short siesta in the car. Although there was a certain amount of repetition in these little journeys – we tended to revisit the same places time and time again – I also enjoyed them.

Later in the year, Margaret and Cathal went to Charles Healy's house for a meeting about the formation of an Irish branch of the Antiquarian

Horological Society, which William Stuart was interested in establishing. He successfully founded the new society, which Cathal eagerly joined, and meetings were held at first in the horological school in Blanchardstown, not far from our home at Knockmaroon. Cathal now found himself amongst a host of new friends, who all enjoyed his company – the likes of Charlie Healy, John White, Maurice Blake, Daniel Gilman and David and John Boles. Cathal was able to share his experiences of working with clocks and watches with his new friends, who listened with interest. On at least one occasion he prepared and gave a talk; one was about buying clocks and watches during the 1930s and 1940s. Cathal described the group as 'a very lively bunch'. Many of the meetings turned into late-night parties; either the members sat around talking shop in the college or adjourned to William's house, where they were supplied with tea, drinks and supper.

Excursions were often organized in order to view a watch collection or admire an important clock. On one occasion my mother and I were invited to join the group at Farmleigh, where we climbed the clock tower and admired both the movement and the view. On another occasion we went by train to Cork, where we were shown the bells of Shandon and an important collection of clocks and watches. Cathal and Margaret also went on a trip to Italy with the group.

During this period, I used to spend Christmas Day with my school friend Thomas Byrne and his family. I had been going to the Byrnes for the simple reason that Christmas at home was a rather fraught occasion. My father dreaded the festivities and the food that he was expected to eat (he was not keen on turkey and he loathed Brussels sprouts), and he was generally cranky. He hated the idea of sitting around, doing nothing. On the other hand my mother wanted to cook a traditional Christmas dinner. As everyone knows, dinner on Christmas Day rarely appears on time; when his meal was not served at one o'clock, my father generally became impatient and annoyed. Tension mounted and an argument often ensued. I was always glad to escape and join my young friends.

At the beginning of 1973 we listened to a BBC radio programme about Samuel Pepys' London and the Great Fire of 1666. Cathal was interested in anything connected with London and was fascinated by Samuel Pepys. He had read Arthur Bryant's books on the famous diarist and was aware of their shortcomings. He was delighted to discover that a complete and unexpurgated edition of the diaries had been published, and that the volumes were now available in one of the Dublin libraries – probably in Rathmines. He now began to borrow them one by one and read them in any spare time that he had – often at mealtimes and always before bed. He loved the original spelling, the phraseology, the descriptions of events and, above all, the spicy bits. Whilst reading, he often laughed aloud and read out some lewd passage that Pepys had written. Over a period of time he worked his way through all nine volumes, the last of which was published in London in 1976.

Early in the following year, Cathal bought the two volumes of *Carolan: The Life Times and Music of an Irish Harper* by Donal O'Sullivan. For a man who disliked harps and was rather dismissive of traditional Irish culture, this would seem to have been an odd purchase. However, he had developed a great respect for Carl Hardebeck's revival of Irish melodies. Indeed, Cathal relished these two books and immediately applied himself to the music. My interest was also aroused and, thanks to my ability to harmonize a melody, we devised two-piano arrangements of the lovely Carolan airs. Cathal, following the printed music, played the melody and I improvised a chordal accompaniment.

Although Cathal generally took music quite seriously, he also could make fun of it. At around this time he often amused me (and himself) by playing some erudite piece of music – generally by Brahms – in waltz time and furnishing a very basic 'oom-pah-pah' accompaniment in the bass. When requested to play some of his 'party pieces' on someone else's piano, he often played a rapid scale in C major with one hand and C sharp major with the other, resulting in an unpleasant cacophony. Grimacing, he would then say, 'Oh my God, this piano's terribly out of tune,' in an effort to get out of performing in front of others.

By now my father and I were on easy terms and often went out walking together along the quiet roads near Knockmaroon. Our interests were similar and we used these occasions to discuss all manner of topics. A large part of my father's conversations was devoted to his past and his work in Guinness's Brewery. Aged sixty-four, Cathal was now beginning to mellow. He was still as strong and energetic as ever but was becoming a good deal more tolerant towards me. Hard work and late nights were offset by extended afternoon siestas. He normally took the phone off the hook when sleeping. He confided to a friend that he kept these siestas secret, feeling that Irish people were unable to appreciate the benefits of an afternoon nap. Now enjoying an idyllic lifestyle (he seldom worried and had little to worry about), he was developing a healthy attitude towards life. He was fond of quoting a maxim, which he attributed to George Bernard Shaw, that the two greatest comforts in life were 'old shoes and loose bowels'. He was generous as regards money – he regularly gave donations to charity and got rid of unwanted possessions by giving them away to friends and acquaintances – and was generous with his time. He liked to stop to talk to people, and had the ability to speak to all types of people at their own level. He often returned home late for meals, having been delayed in conversation. He was always courteous and regularly checked young people in shops for not saying 'please' or 'thank you'. He always held a door open for others and offered his seat to a lady, and expected to be thanked. He firmly believed in good manners; as a child I was never allowed to be rude or arrogant.

Not only was he able to converse easily with everyone, but he was able to extract information by subtle means. I well remember when, during one of our walks along the Carpenterstown Road, he spied a neighbour in his garden and said to me quietly, 'I bet I can find out from him what rent he's paying for his house.'

Having greeted the man, my father casually said, 'That's a fine house and garden you've got.'

'Yes,' replied the man, 'and would you believe it, I'm only paying £10 rent for it every month!'

Along the Carpenterstown Road were houses where dogs were kept. Cathal often entertained me with his skill at barking and 'setting them off'. One of the dogs regularly walked with us and returned to its house afterwards. Cathal could also imitate the crowing of the bantam cocks in our yard and puzzle them into responding. He still retained his impish sense of humour and enjoyed a good prank.

Cathal's dress was never flamboyant. On formal occasions he donned a suit and looked very presentable, though at home he felt more relaxed in what he called his 'old duds': an open-necked shirt (often the worse for wear), an old jumper, the faded shop coat used in his workshop and, when the weather demanded it, an anorak when he went out walking. His head was invariably adorned with a peaked cap when he was outdoors.

One of his oddities was that he often talked to himself when alone – a habit that I, either consciously or unconsciously, picked up from him. On several occasions I entered the kitchen or his workshop to discover him whispering something to himself. I often wondered if he was rehearsing a conversation or simply thinking aloud.

Although he listened to music and news bulletins on the radio most of the time, he also applied himself to *Talking about Antiques* with Bernard Price and Arthur Negus on BBC Radio 4. I seem to remember him and my mother listening to *Gardeners' Question Time*, also on the same station. During Sunday lunch, we laughed at the various BBC comedy programmes such as *Around the Horn* and *The Clitheroe Kid*. We also listened to RTÉ's comedy programmes featuring Maureen Potter and others. For something completely different, my father switched to RTÉ Radio One for Ciarán Mac Mahúna's *Mo Cheol Thú* and *Sunday Miscellany* on Sunday mornings; on Saturday at lunchtime there was *The Walton's Programme* with Leo Maguire, during which he hummed the signature tune and made faces suggesting mock approval of the music. He also pretended to cheer for teams during sports results after the news, often mischievously adding in a knowing way, 'You can't beat a bit of kickin'!'

He often attempted to sing along with the music that he heard on the radio. As his voice was rather high-pitched by nature, he could almost sing falsetto, though the result was far from musical. When 'accompanying' or imitating music that did not please him, he usually screeched the melody with a pronounced nasal or Dublin twang. He often termed the vocal efforts of female popular singers as 'a hoor wailing for a policeman'. He could be merciless when criticizing and sometimes made acerbic remarks about people behind their backs. However, such remarks were generally reserved for strangers; his friends were carefully picked and remained dear to his heart.

Cathal loved mixing with people, listening to what they had to say and learning from them. He made it his business to get on well with everybody; as he often said to me, he could 'pull with the devil'. Whenever he had to deal with an unpleasant individual he made the best of the situation. Using a little basic psychology, he would put on a show of agreeing with everything the disgruntled person had to say and, having gone out of his way to please the individual, he would eventually gain the person's respect and admiration. In no time at all they would be friends. With the use of a little tact and diplomacy, he could 'patch up' broken friendships between those who had argued and fallen out with each other.

The number of people that Cathal met and befriended during his lifetime was quite extraordinary; I think it would be safe to say that very few people disliked him. What was it that drew so many people to him? It seems that most of his many acquaintances found him refreshing, great fun and full of life; they also respected him for his vast store of knowledge – he always had an interesting story to relate. A quality that endeared him to many was his modesty. He was never dogmatic and was willing to listen to other people's views. However, a failing of his was his love of name-dropping; his sister and family in Dundrum must have grown weary listening to him constantly telling them about the comings and goings of the Guinness family.

Cathal had a sensible and relaxed attitude to life; he avoided anything that might make life more complicated for himself and never envied others. He delighted in living in a rented house – his theory being that, if anything should go wrong with it, it was not his responsibility. He always believed that if something was made in too complicated a manner, there were more things to go wrong. It could be said that his motto was 'keep it simple'.

Most people remember my father for his wit. His was a typical Dublin wit, full of colourful colloquialisms and quick retorts. Cathal loved to entertain his friends and guests with the many funny stories and jokes that he had remembered over the years. For some reason, he had a penchant for morbid jokes, such as the one in which a man called to a house and asked the woman who opened the door, 'Is this the house where the dead man lives?'

'No,' she said. 'He's gone and I'm the remains.'

Another story concerned a lady who was sympathizing with a woman who had just lost her husband. 'I believe he died rather suddenly,' she remarked.

'Suddenly is not the word for it,' declared the widow. 'Sure, the water boilin' for his tea shaved him and he a corpse!'

With his good buddies (William Stuart being the closest), my father often recounted coarse jokes and employed the Dubliner's habit of using an insult as a compliment and vice versa. An insulting remark was also used by way of a friendly greeting; those in the know responded in like manner and laughed heartily. Although he often threw caution to the wind and told an inappropriate joke in mixed or female company, often shocking his listeners, he was wise enough to be more circumspect when mixing with those 'above his station in life'.

Cathal was honoured in March 1974 by a special concert of music by Bach, performed in the Examination Hall of Trinity College on three of his harpsichords. In a short article in the Dublin Arts Festival programme, of which the concert was the first event, John Beckett explained that the concert would be a tribute to Cathal's work.

The three Guinness–Gannon harpsichords (belonging to John Beckett, the Royal Irish Academy of Music and RTÉ) were played by John O'Sullivan, David Lee and David Ledbetter, and the New Irish Chamber Orchestra was conducted by André Prieur. The concert was highly successful and the subsequent newspaper reviews were ecstatic. Fanny Feehan, writing in the *Evening Herald,* hailed the recital as 'a unique event' and mentioned that the 'packed, enthusiastic audience who were predominantly young, gave Mr. Gannon an ovation at the end'. Charles Acton in *The Irish Times* called it 'a most happy occasion' and, despite a few small reservations, was quite satisfied with 'the interlacing sounds of two (and then three) splendidly played harpsichords with the beautifully and precisely delicate playing from NICO'. Judith Segal, writing in the *Evening Press*, said of Cathal, 'Without his craftsmanship, it is extremely unlikely that the opportunity to hear a Bach concerto for three harpsichords would have been possible.' She concluded, 'On behalf of all those who gathered together to pay tribute to Cathal Gannon, may I extend to him our warmest greetings – and to the festival committee which gave the opportunity of lauding him, our grateful thanks.'

The author of a short review in *Hibernia* described the Examination Hall as being 'hearteningly packed to the ceiling' and continued:

> Cathal Gannon quite rightly received an ovation. (Someone near me asked was that the composer.) It is rarely that a craftsman lives to tell the tale, never mind enjoy hearing what posterity thinks of his work. Mr Gannon has been one of the lucky ones. He is the centre of a whole pride of harpsichords, and since he made his first instrument in 1951 has now made some superlatively beautiful ones. I can do no better than quote from John Beckett's programme note for this concert. 'In all Mr. Gannon's instruments the craftsmanship is masterly and they are made with a musical and historical sensibility that is, I think, exceptionally perceptive.'
>
> All that is left for one to add to that is hear! hear! It is a nightmare to tune a harpsichord; tuning two would land a normal person into an asylum; but *tuning three* of them, especially 'up' to the idiotic RTÉ pitch was nothing short of a miracle.

What did Cathal make of all this? I seem to remember him being somewhat bemused; when applauded at the end of the evening's music, he may have looked behind him as if to find the maker of the instruments before acknowledging the applause and standing up. I know that he did this on at least one occasion. Whilst he undoubtedly must have felt a thrill on receiving such an ovation from a packed hall, I do know that he was glad when it was all over. That he found some of the music rather tedious was evident; he dismissively described the final work to me as 'three harpsichords clattering away'. Tuning the three instruments *had* been something of a nightmare.

I was sensible enough to bring along my recording equipment and make a rather indifferent tape of the concert, due to my lack of skill and inadequate microphones. Listening to the recording now, it sounds, by today's superior standards, rather scrappy; a more modern-day and enlightened orchestra using instruments of the correct period could play the music far more sympathetically. However, it was a very good effort for the time. In all, the evening was a wonderful occasion and it finished up with us repairing to Mr and Mrs William Dillon's fine Georgian house in North Great George's Street, where there was a lavish reception for all those involved.

In this way Cathal's work was fittingly acknowledged and music lovers in Dublin were, I believe, proud of him.

Thirty-Seven

*I*n March 1974 Cathal bought himself a lightweight bicycle with ten gears, exactly fifty years to the day after he had learned to ride a bicycle on the Crumlin Road. He was very pleased with himself and his new acquisition. Over the coming years he would regularly go off in good weather for a cycle around the neighbourhood; I often accompanied him when I had time to spare.

Towards the end of the year, Cathal received a letter from Edward Hamilton of the Dublin Baroque Players, informing him that at the recent annual general meeting he had been elected an honorary member. 'I must tell you that this is a mark of special esteem for you by the Players,' wrote Edward. He continued, 'I hope you will accept the Membership as a token of our great appreciation for you personally, and for your work in the harpsichord field.'

Cathal gratefully accepted this honour and from then onwards we were entitled to free tickets to any of the Dublin Baroque Players' concerts that we chose to attend.

During the summer of the following year, my father and I flew to Rome. Cathal had been invited to tune the harpsichords used for concerts to be given by the New Irish Chamber Orchestra and Our Lady's Choral Society. John Beckett was to conduct. The concerts, given in Rome and Perugia, were very successful and featured some of the 'Brandenburg' Concertos by Johann Sebastian Bach.

Our holiday in Rome was one to remember. My father and I got on very well together. Cathal brought me to all the major sights of the city, including the Forum and the Colosseum, where, by sheer coincidence, we bumped into my mother and her friend Maisie Cronly, who had gone to Italy on a tour at the same time. As Cathal said later, if he had been doing anything improper, he would have been found out!

We (and, amazingly, John Beckett) attended a televised production of Handel's *Messiah* in the large church of St Ignatius and afterwards the choir and orchestra travelled home. Cathal and I stayed for another week, during which we did more energetic sightseeing, visited Emer Buckley in her flat (she was now living in Rome) and climbed to the top of the dome of St Peter's. We saw the famous Sistine Chapel and visited the Vatican museums, where we were overwhelmed by the opulence.

Home again, Cathal and I went to hear the new Austrian Rieger organ that had been built and installed in St Michael's Church, Dun Laoghaire the previous year; we were suitably impressed by it. David Lee played it that evening and showed off the fine instrument to its best advantage. We were back again the following week to hear Nicholas Danby perform. After the recital we were introduced to him by Professor Gerard Gillen, who had had the new organ built and who had organized the series of recitals. My father and I would go to many more organ recitals in St Michael's Church, especially when the Dublin International Organ Festival was founded in 1980 and when Cathal, who became a patron, received complimentary tickets.

Soon afterwards, the musician John O'Sullivan came to interview Cathal and play musical examples on the various instruments for two RTÉ radio programmes, entitled 'Music Magazine', which were broadcast in July and August. A further session was held in RTÉ, where Cathal's harpsichord was recorded. Listening to the programmes now, they sound stiff and lacking in spontaneity. Cathal sounds as though he is reading from notes and is doing his best to put on a 'posh' accent.

Towards the end of 1975 we were introduced to the young Malcolm Proud, who was destined to become, in my firm opinion, Ireland's finest harpsichordist. I noted in my diary his hearty appetite and fondness for cups of tea. We found him to be very knowledgeable about the interpretation of music; he was concerned that early music be performed in an authentic manner. We were to see more of the easy-going Malcolm in the years to come. Around this time he often cycled across the city to visit my father in his workshop to see what he was working at.

A typical 'working' day for Cathal at this period of harpsichord building generally began at a quarter to eight in the morning, when he awoke to the sound of his old alarm clock (which he kept under the bed) and birdsong. Opening the curtains of his bedroom, he looked out over the fields to the gardens behind the big house and to a distant view of the Dublin Mountains. He then put his head around the door of my bedroom to wake me up. (By now I was working at commercial art.)

Downstairs, still dressed in his pyjamas, he ate a simple breakfast in our tiny kitchen. He always paid full attention to the local news on the radio, then switched to his favourite Radio 3 for music. He often perused a book over breakfast but never a newspaper; by this stage he had given up reading them. By the time I left for work, he began to wash, dress and shave, always in the confines of the warm kitchen. He was generally out of the way by the time my mother came down from her bedroom.

By nine or half past nine he was usually in his workshop, hard at work. If no one called or interrupted him, he generally pressed on until he felt the need to stop. Relief was often in the form of a long, vigorous walk down one of the neighbouring roads, generally taken before his midday meal. If some- one did call or if he met one of the locals whilst out walking, he always stopped for a chat. Everyone in the locality knew him and recognized his jaunty gait from a distance.

Dinner, his main meal of the day, was announced by a momentary switching off of the electricity in the workshop by my mother at about one o'clock. Sometimes the signal had to be repeated if he did not notice the light or radio going off, or if he had something important to finish.

Needless to say, by this time he had worked up a hearty appetite. In cold weather he welcomed a bowl of hot soup, often taken with a slice of bread. Never fussy about the quality of food, tinned or packaged soup was accept- able; as long as it was piping hot, he was satisfied. The meal – a main course and a dessert – was washed down with diluted orangeade, coffee or both. Cathal disliked the tap water; he complained that it tasted nasty.

My father, who hated the sight of unwashed dishes, generally washed them up immediately after eating. He then either sat down in the living room to read and have a nap or else, if he was particularly tired, repaired to bed for a siesta.

Refreshed, he then returned to the workshop, where, if there were no interruptions, he would work until six o'clock. He then came over for his 'tea'. This was also the time for news on the radio, to which he liked to lis- ten. Thirsty by this time, Cathal quickly swallowed two or three cups of tea while he ate a few slices of bread with butter and jam, then some home-made cake. The news over, he often relaxed over a book.

If no plans had been made for the evening, he continued to work until about half past ten or eleven o'clock, when he generally went out for another stiff walk. If I was around, I often joined him. Before bed we always had a supper of hot cocoa, bread and jam, and biscuits. Usually wide awake by this time, despite the long hours of work, Cathal once again applied himself to the radio and a good book and did not retire to bed until half past twelve or one o'clock in the morning.

Cathal was content with life as it was; he wanted nothing more than his peaceful surroundings, his workshop, his radio and his simple, wholesome meals. As he became older, he was satisfied to stay at home and had no desire to travel abroad; he was content to look at the view from the kitchen window and read about other countries in books – 'armchair travel' as he called it. Although he quarrelled with my mother from time to time, he could not have wished for a better wife, a fact that he sometimes confided to his friends.

His daily routine was never rigid, for there were always unexpected callers and arrangements made to tune or maintain various people's instruments. However, he did like to be home for his meals on time whenever possible. The lack of his afternoon nap or his cup of tea at six o'clock could and often did annoy him. Often, when the weather was fine, he put everything to one side and took off on his bicycle for a couple of hours, or else drove up into the Wicklow Mountains with my mother for a picnic.

Evenings were often spent in the company of friends, either at Knock-maroon or in their homes. Concerts were regularly attended at this period; Cathal frequently met acquaintances afterwards and invited them home.

In short, Cathal was enjoying his retirement; aged sixty-five, he was still in rude health and showed no signs of flagging.

On a Saturday afternoon at the end of March 1976 we visited Justin and Loretta Keating at their home in Ballymore Eustace, County Wicklow. My father had met Loretta a few times before but I had not. She was a pleasantly chatty lady, small in stature and with jet-black hair tied up at the back of her head. Her mother was one of the antique-dealing Wines of Grafton Street. Over dinner, Cathal spoke to Justin about the respect that he had had for his father, Seán Keating, whose lectures he had attended at the Academy of Christian Art in the 1930s. Cathal frequently employed this technique of establishing some type of link when beginning a conversation with somebody he had never met before. Justin responded, opened up and chatted volubly.

Just three days later, Loretta's Hubbard harpsichord kit was delivered to Cathal at Knockmaroon for assembly.

In early April, Emer Buckley, wearing an elegant and flowing green dress that matched the colour of the new harpsichord that Cathal had recently completed for her, gave a wonderful recital of Italian music in the National Gallery to a large and appreciative audience. The recital was a tremendous success. Charles Acton warmly praised both the new harpsichord and the playing, concluding, 'Emer Buckley is clearly a real master of her instrument.'

Soon afterwards, a gentleman from BBC Northern Ireland called on Cathal to ask if a crew could film him in his workshop for a television programme named 'Gallery'. He said that he would ask Emer Buckley to play one of the harpsichords that Cathal was making.

The film crew arrived a few days later. Cathal was exhausted and fed up when I returned from work that evening; he had been denied his afternoon nap. The BBC people returned after two days and filmed Emer playing the harpsichord in the ballroom of the big house.

The programme was shown later in the month; we watched it on television in my mother's friends' house. At the time we were suitably impressed, though when watching it recently on videotape I realized how stiff and formal it was by modern standards. Cathal, who was interviewed by Andy O'Mahony, looked quite ill at ease. The item on harpsichord building was quite short and the rest of the programme was devoted to a northern craftsman who made guitars, Jan Mullyaert with an Irish harp and Charles Guard playing it. Both Jan and Charles had come to Knockmaroon to meet my father.

In July, Tamsy Guinness invited my father to meet the British Ambassador to Ireland, Christopher Ewart-Biggs, who was visiting Lord Moyne one Sunday morning. I had noticed the blue Jaguar parked outside the house. Cathal, who was tuning his harpsichord, which was still in the big house, excused himself and turned down the invitation, probably because he was not suitably dressed. By Wednesday, 21 July, we were shocked to hear the news that the ambassador and his 26-year-old secretary, Judith Cooke, had been blown up in his car in Sandyford, County Dublin. Naturally, the Guinnesses were very upset to hear of the tragedy. Cathal, who considered such acts of savagery to be pointless, simply said that he was 'ashamed of the Irish people'.

There were many IRA bombings and atrocities during the 1970s, which

Cathal privately condemned, though he rarely spoke about his political convictions to anyone. Essentially he was a man of peace. He was familiar with Ireland's troubled history and understood why the Irish should be bitter towards the British and the British government, yet he was convinced that there was little point in bombing, shooting and blowing up innocent British citizens. Cathal always had the greatest respect for British culture; however, he had very little interest in the royal family. Margaret, on the other hand, still worshipped the Queen and the Queen Mother.

Cathal was always reluctant to travel to Northern Ireland because he felt that it was not safe and that he could not feel comfortable there. However, William Stuart managed to persuade him once to join him on a journey to the North. (In his latter years he came on holidays to Counties Fermanagh and Antrim with my mother, Anthony Harrison and me.) He could not fathom why people of different religions and traditions could not get on together in the North as they did in the South. He, of course, had married an English Protestant and many of his best friends were Protestants. His 'neutral' interests in music, musical instruments, clocks and watches, art and architecture crossed all divides and attracted all sorts of people.

Because of the number of clocks and watches that Cathal had accumulated by now, he was constantly winding up, cleaning and oiling them when they needed attention. Whilst the watches tended to remain in a display case, the clocks were all in working order and in use. In almost every room of the house could be heard the gentle ticking of at least one clock; on the hour a host of them would chime together. The sound gave the house, which was normally very quiet, a wonderfully magical atmosphere. Visitors found it easy to forget their troubles in Knockmaroon and, like the clocks, were able to unwind.

As Cathal was so involved in his clocks and watches and liked to have them all displaying the correct time, he was a stickler for punctuality. Although he often was a little late, he always strove to arrive at a friend's house at an appointed hour and was often irritated by my mother not being ready to leave on time. When Cathal tired of calling to her to hurry up, he would sit down at the piano and play something until she was ready, probably in an effort to calm himself down.

I concluded my diary for 1976 by noting that my parents were beginning to age and become more settled; my father, who was becoming reluctant to be 'out and about', just wanted to be left alone. He had told me that his ambition was to work himself to death – he wanted to simply drop dead and not have to suffer any lingering illness. My mother's high blood pressure was beginning to get the better of her; hectic social activities were becoming a strain on her nerves. However, my parents continued to entertain and be entertained for several more years and a casual observer would have been easily fooled into believing that both of them had an extraordinary amount of energy. Their long afternoon siestas were instrumental in keeping them in good fettle, for many of the parties they attended did not end until the small hours of the morning.

Now equipped with a new desk in my bedroom (made by my father), I could escape from the living room where my parents slept in the afternoons. However, this, I soon discovered, was only possible in warmer weather. As we had no central heating in the house, the rooms upstairs had to be heated by means of electric fires; my bedroom was the coldest of them all. Even the living room could be extremely cold in winter, despite a roaring fire. My father kept the fire going all through the winters, placing a peat briquette over the glowing embers at night and smothering the whole with ash. The fire was coaxed back into life the following morning by means of paper, sticks and a great deal of blowing. We often placed an old copper kettle on the fire to boil water, especially for tea. Cleaning out the fire was a messy business; Cathal always looked after it.

Knockmaroon was covered in a carpet of snow at the beginning of January 1977. Despite the coldness and discomfort, the trees and fields always looked wonderful when clothed in their winter garments; I always enjoyed tramping across virgin snow in my wellington boots. Cathal was not so enchanted by wintry scenes; he preferred to work and keep himself warm by physical exertion.

On the second Saturday of the new year, my father brought Emer Buckley to the Keatings' house in Wicklow, left her to her house, tuned her harpsichord so that it would be ready for a forthcoming recital in the National Gallery and returned home late. On Sunday morning he was greeted by my mother with a stony silence that lasted most of the day and finally erupted into a row during the evening. My mother, who felt that my father was not paying enough attention to her, effectively accused him of having an affair with Emer as she considered that he was spending so much of his time tuning her harpsichord and running around on her behalf. Having got on her high horse, she then accused him of relationships with other women and of wanting nothing to do with her friends. It was the most vicious row I had ever heard between my parents and I went to bed feeling quite upset. My father was shaken by the accusations and slept badly that night.

Of course there are cases of men in their mid-sixties falling for women in their mid-twenties, resulting in happy relationships. The truth of the matter was that my father loved the stimulating company of younger people and to seek them out was an escape from the relative loneliness of working on his own. Emer, who at that time could not have been without male admirers of her own age, was young, vibrant and hardly interested in an old fogey like my father. Emer has confirmed that there was nothing in my father's behaviour that could have given my mother cause for concern. Cathal did indeed volunteer to tune her harpsichord perhaps a little too often, but spent most of his time in the Buckleys' home laughing and joking with Mrs Buckley, who enjoyed his company.

The drudgery of life at home was the cause of my mother's unhappiness. It was many years later when she admitted to me that she hated cooking dinners – a chore that she did day after day. Coupled with this was her growing inability to cope with the numerous parties that she was expected to attend and host at home. Unable to drive and lacking the great number of friends that my father had, she had less freedom to leave the house, go out and enjoy herself. With little else to do but cook and keep the house in order, it was understandable that she became jealous when Cathal seemed to show too much interest in another woman, especially one who was so much younger than she.

As my mother put her foot down in such a determined manner, my father was obliged to give in to her and stop seeing Emer. With a heavy heart I went on my own to a recital given by her in the National Gallery and made vague excuses for my parents' absence. She played a programme of luscious French music to a small but appreciative audience; because the weather was very cold and the roads were icy, few people had come to hear her play.

Although my father and I were to meet Emer a few more times soon afterwards, she began to spend more time on the continent and eventually settled in Paris.

At around this time, Cathal received a letter from Victor Leeson, director of the St James's Gate Musical Society, inviting him and Margaret to join a proposed trip to Italy at the end of March. He hoped that they would be able to bring one of Cathal's small Italian harpsichords. William offered the use of his instrument and Cathal made a special wooden case for it to travel in.

My parents left in March 1977 and travelled to Italy with the New Irish Chamber Orchestra and the Guinness Choir. Soloists included Bernadette Greevy, Irene Sandford and Frank Patterson, 'magnificent in a white mafia coat and hat', as Bernard Share wrote in his hilarious account of the somewhat chaotic tour in *The Irish Times*. Throughout the trip they performed Bach's *Saint John Passion*; once in Turin and four times in Sicily. William's little instrument was used in four of the performances 'as the orchestra and public couldn't hear the huge Neupert concert ("Bach") instruments offered to us'. The weather proved to be as contrary as in Ireland and performances, which were often poorly attended, had to start early in the evening in Sicily for safety.

In May, armed with as much knowledge of the country and the language as I could muster, I set off on a three-week tour of China. It was my first time to go abroad completely on my own. However, as I was a member of a tightly controlled organized tour, there was no need for my parents to worry, though I am sure that they did at times.

My parents heaved a sigh of relief when I arrived home in one piece. They were interested to hear all about my holiday and when the cine films that I had shot were developed and carefully edited they were fascinated by what they saw.

During the following month, Cathal and his friend William left in the car for London, for William had bought a Southwell square piano of c.1805 at Christie's. They stayed with my cousin Anne at her house in Ealing and spent ten days visiting various art galleries, museums and places of interest, including Greenwich. They went to Fenton House, Hampstead and examined the musical instruments; however, William came to the conclusion that none of the harpsichords was as good as the one that Cathal had made for Emer Buckley. The Southwell piano that William collected from Christie's turned out to be disappointing, as it was in very poor condition. Both of them bought armfuls of books, which were packed into William's car. Whilst in London, they met Cathal's friend Patrick Horsley and had dinner with him at a restaurant in Fulham Road.

By now we were having regular musical evenings with the man who had taught me some Chinese in UCD, Professor Jiang Tao (or Tao Kiang as he was known). Tao played the recorder and lived in Castleknock. In his house we met Nuala Staines, who sang well, and her son David, who played the flute. From then onwards we were often invited to the Staines's house for musical evenings. A little later we met Nuala's piano teacher, Valerie Walker, who lived in Howth. Greta Lynch, wife of pianist Seán Lynch, joined us and played the violin.

Now that my cine film of China was edited, my parents and I were invited to various friends' homes to show it. One of the couples who asked to see the film was Gillian and Lindsay Armstrong. The reason for their interest was that they wondered if the New Irish Chamber Orchestra could be invited to China on a cultural exchange visit. I told them that I would speak with some new acquaintances of mine in the Irish Chinese Cultural Society, who might know how to organize such a visit.

In mid-May 1978 Cathal was invited to attend a special dinner for the Guinness Choir, which was held in Molesworth Street church. His friend Mary Byrne sang and he accompanied her on the piano. He had been taken by surprise by the amount of fuss made about him; it transpired that he was the guest of honour. He was given the best seat at the table and afterwards presented with two small pictures. After the meal, Victor Leeson conducted the choir and following the celebrations, Cathal and his friends adjourned to Frank Dunne's house for more music and song.

There was good reason for the attention showered on Cathal that evening. In January, Cathal had received a letter from G.H.H. Giltrap, Secretary to Trinity College, which began, 'The Board of Trinity College is anxious to submit to the Senate of the University of Dublin a Grace proposing that the degree of Master in Arts (MA) *honoris causa* should be conferred upon you.'

Cathal was astounded that he should be considered for an honorary degree – obviously Professor Brian Boydell had suggested that he receive one – and shortly afterwards he replied: 'Many thanks for your letter conveying the unexpected honour proposed to be conferred upon me by the Board of Trinity College. After some hesitation I have decided that my name may be submitted to the Senate.'

Soon all his friends and immediate family were informed; they were delighted for him. Many sent him presents and cards conveying their congratulations. Towards the end of February, he was informed that at a meeting of the Senate, it was resolved that he should be offered the honorary degree at the Commencements in July. In June he was sent a map of the college, various instructions and a request for his height and cap size, so that he could be assured of a good fit for the ceremonial robes and cap.

Cathal, who undoubtedly was delighted, knew that such a gesture was the greatest tribute that could be offered to him for his pioneering work in the sphere of keyboard musical instruments over the years.

Thirty-Eight

*T*he conferring of Cathal's degree took place on 6 July 1978. We were admitted to the Examination Hall at three o'clock and entered to the strains of music played on the organ. Shortly afterwards a solemn procession of robed dignitaries and students made its way up the aisle, accompanied by the music. As well as Cathal, Sir Frederick Charles Frank, Professor of Physics at the University of Bristol, the Scots poet Christopher Murray Grieve (Hugh MacDiarmid), Michael Joseph Dargan, former chief executive of Aer Lingus, Winifred Gahan, vice-president of the Royal Dublin Society, Seán MacBride, outstanding European jurist and former Minister for External Affairs, and Mabel Smith, chairman of the Musical Association of Ireland were to receive honorary degrees, though only Cathal would be given an MA. It was somewhat ironic that he was now sharing the limelight with the vice-president of the Royal Dublin Society, an organization that had resolutely refused him admission to its ranks so many years previously.

After a lengthy ceremony, during which degrees were conferred on a host of university students, Cathal's name was called by the Senior Proctor and he stepped forward, resplendent in his black gown and blue hood. He turned towards the Public Orator, who began a fine eulogy of Cathal in Latin. The oration was greeted by an enthusiastic ovation, which lasted some considerable time. Cathal smiled and meekly bowed to the audience and dignitaries. The Chancellor rose, read a short text and conferred the honorary degree on Cathal. While the Chancellor congratulated him and shook hands with him, there was more applause. Cathal signed his name in the large Proctor's Book that was placed on a table and resumed his seat to a final ovation. Officially he was now Charles William Gannon, MA *honoris causa*.

I was intensely proud of my father that day and felt that he certainly deserved the honour bestowed upon him, despite the fact that he had such a poor education and had never been to university. My mother was very pleased for him. The scene in the Examination Hall that day was a stark contrast to the humble surroundings into which he had been born. The ceremony, which had been a novelty to my mother and me, had been a very moving occasion and the use of Latin in the oration had bestowed a tremendous amount of gravity on the proceedings.

In the evening, my parents returned to the college. There they joined guests in the Common Room and proceeded to the magnificent Dining Hall, where they were placed near the end of the principal table, close to the Chancellor. After the excellent meal, toasts to Ireland, the University of Dublin and its new graduates were made by the Chancellor.

I waited up until my parents returned home and, before retiring to bed, I offered Cathal my heartiest congratulations. The humble carpenter that was my father had, after sixty-eight eventful years of his life, received the highest form of recognition that could be accorded to him and I was extremely happy for him.

Towards the end of November, my father finally gave in to my mother's pleading and bought our first television set, which my cousin Cathal supplied from his television shop. My fears of possible arguments over this intrusion into the household were well founded; soon the set was banished to my bedroom, where my mother watched her programmes in peace, though not in comfort. At least she was away from my father, who did not approve of them. Cathal was content to watch an erudite documentary programme on some subject that interested him, but the likes of *Coronation Street* annoyed him intensely.

In December, my father left with William in his car for England in order to collect another early Irish-made square piano. Once again they stayed with my cousin Anne in Ealing but for three nights only. This time they visited John Beckett at his home in Greenwich. Like the Southwell that William had bought in London, the square piano turned out to be very disappointing. Both men bought a quantity of books and Cathal purchased a handsome bracket clock that was believed to be by the famous seventeenth-century English maker Edward East. Despite the fact that William's car battery was nearly flat, they made it to Holmbury-St-Mary, where they collected and paid for a bass viol for me, then safely made it to the ferry, having nearly run out of petrol in Wales. My father must have found such carelessness very frustrating, for he was meticulous about checking his own car before setting off on a long journey. William's mind, however, was always elsewhere – on more important matters, in his opinion. Nevertheless, my father rarely became hot under the collar when such incidents took place, for he knew that William had a knack of wriggling out of most awkward situations.

Towards the end of November in the following year, another film crew descended on our home in Knockmaroon. Justin Keating and the producer Deirdre McCartin had arrived at the end of the previous month and had talked Cathal into being filmed for part of a new series to be called *A Sense of Excellence*, which would be presented by Justin and shown on RTÉ. Initially Cathal had not wanted to be featured; he feared that any more publicity would land him in trouble with the income tax people. However, Justin and Deirdre managed to put his mind at ease and agreed to film only what suited him.

Apparently things were a little chaotic on the first day of shooting; Cathal was filmed at work in his workshop and then playing his harpsichord in the living room. The instrument had been moved there as it was becoming damp in the sitting room. I was present on the second day of filming. Cathal was filmed walking across to the house from the workshop, then more footage was shot in the living room. This time they concentrated on the square piano. When Cathal and Justin had to get up and walk out of the room so many times because of re-takes, Cathal became exasperated. At one stage he shut the door and muttered, 'F— the lot of them!' As he was wearing a radio microphone, the sound engineer heard the remark and repeated it to his colleagues, who burst out laughing.

Whilst in our house, the film crew drank many cups of tea and ate a considerable number of my mother's home-made buns, which they obviously relished. The third and last session took place on 11 December. When Cathal was offered the paltry sum of £50 for his trouble, he asked the producer to donate it to a charity of her choice.

One morning in May 1980 I received a telephone call from Lindsay Armstrong. The New Irish Chamber Orchestra had finally received an invitation to tour China. He now wanted to ask me several questions about conditions and facilities available there. The plan was to bring a harpsichord (preferably one of Cathal's) and possibly donate it to some Chinese institution as a gift from Ireland. Lindsay proceeded to telephone anybody he knew who had one of Cathal's instruments to see if one could be sold. As it turned out, this generous gesture had to be abandoned. He later telephoned Cathal and invited him to come on the tour. He was thrilled to be asked but wondered how he would cope with the hot weather.

Shortly afterwards, Cathal received news of the proposed itinerary in China: the orchestra would go firstly to Beijing, then Chengdu in Sichuan province and finally Xi'an in Shaanxi province. William Stuart gave permission for his little harpsichord to be brought on the trip; Cathal repainted the case for the occasion. Irene Sandford, having been coached by Professor Tao Kiang, had learned to sing a couple of songs in Chinese and her pronunciation was declared to be almost faultless.

The much-anticipated journey to China finally began on 26 July with a two-day stop in Bruges, where the New Irish Chamber Orchestra was due to perform at the beginning of the annual Flanders Festival. The orchestra, John Beckett and Cathal then set off for China. The journey was the longest that Cathal was ever to make. Although the temperature in Beijing was hot, Cathal found it 'bearable'. John greatly enjoyed sharing a room (or 'sweating together in the same room', as he picturesquely described it) and being with Cathal; it seems that both men got on extremely well together.

The trip to China was made up of concerts performed in each of the three cities and various sightseeing tours. Cathal saw many interesting places such as the Forbidden City in Beijing, the Great Wall of China, one of the Ming tombs and the famous Teracotta Warriors in Xi'an. Cathal was quite overawed by the latter and wrote that it was 'a most impressive sight which I shall never forget'. For him, however, the highlight of the tour was celebrating his birthday on the lake of the Summer Palace in Beijing, in one of two covered barges pulled by a motor boat, and being serenaded by Chinese student musicians who played on traditional instruments. Some members of the Irish orchestra played Irish music for the students.

In each city the orchestra enjoyed banquets hosted in their honour and met interested musicians and students, most of whom had never seen a harpsichord before. John Beckett demonstrated the instrument and Cathal tuned it before the concerts, all of which were well received, though John, who conducted, found the audiences somewhat noisy. Irene Sandford's rendition of Irish songs and her performance of the two Chinese songs brought the house down on several occasions.

In Chengdu, Cathal and John slipped out of their hotel early in the morning and, avoiding the guides, went walking 'in the old part of this most interesting town. We met all the people young and old, took snaps and had our breakfast in a little native restaurant.' John even bought the chopsticks with which he had eaten his breakfast. From then on, the two men managed to escape the crippling officialdom and regularly went out on their own in the mornings to wander amongst the people.

In Xi'an they were taken to see a wonderful collection of Tang Dynasty glazed pottery figures of horses, horsemen and camels, which Cathal had often seen illustrated in books. 'This museum thrilled me,' he wrote in his diary. In the evening they were taken to a three-hour-long classical Xi'an opera, which 'at times was hard going. The costumes were exquisite, the acting fine. We had an interpreter who helped us with the plot.' Lindsay Armstrong noted that there was a lull in the translation of the story for quite some time. He turned around to discover the interpreter lying slumped in his seat fast asleep, 'presumably from linguistic exhaustion'.

When, at the end of the trip, my mother and I drove to the airport to meet my father, Elizabeth Neuman was there to welcome him home and wish him a happy birthday. Cathal appeared pushing the harpsichord on a trolley, struggling to get it through a narrow doorway. True to form, he bustled about, calling to people, securing his luggage and running after the harpsichord in order to see that all was in order. Various members of the orchestra marvelled at his tremendous energy and ability to keep going despite the heat. He was glad to be home again as he had begun to feel homesick over the final few days. He told us that he would be glad to return to plain fare; although the food had been delicious, he had eaten far too much of it.

Cathal's holiday in China, which he enjoyed tremendously and about which he often spoke with great enthusiasm, was one of the great highlights of his life. It was fortuitous that it had taken place at a significant milestone; one of his greatest boasts was that he had been serenaded by Chinese musicians on the lake of the Summer Palace in Beijing on his seventieth birthday.

It transpired that Cathal had not yet finished with things Chinese for 1980; in November he contributed to the entertainment of a Chinese delegation of six people who had been given a special lunch in Guinness's Brewery, and in mid-December he and Margaret went to Carroll's Theatre to see a film about the Summer Palace in Beijing.

Although Cathal was still busy restoring pianos, tuning harpsichords and helping his friend William Stuart refurbish a period house in Celbridge that he had bought recently, he now settled down to enjoying life. He spent his time taking long walks, often with me, visiting his various friends, attending some more organ recitals in St Michael's Church, Dun Laoghaire, playing a little music with Professor Kiang, Nuala Staines and myself, going to some Antiquarian Horological Society meetings, fixing a couple of clocks for his sister Maureen, reading books borrowed from the local library and perusing the Saturday edition of *The Irish Times*, which he now liked to read. He was interested particularly in the 'Weekend' section and the reviews of auctions contained in the main part of the paper.

The weather over Christmas 1981 was quite severe. As Cathal wrote to Patrick Horsley in England, 'The older one gets the more one feels the cold. For nearly a week we had no running water and I spent a considerable time filling the cisterns of both toilets with buckets of water and attending to the fires, however things have improved over the past two days.'

Christmas Eve was bitterly cold and icy; it was a little unfortunate that Mariga Guinness had invited us to a party in Leixlip Castle on that very evening. Prepared for the worst, we donned the warmest clothes that we possessed – Cathal and I wore long johns. Just as we expected, the castle was freezing, but fortunately there were blazing fires in some of the rooms. Mariga met us in the dimly lit hall and, in her usual manner, gushingly introduced us to some of her guests, describing me as 'a great expert on China'. One of the guests was Peter Pearson, the artist and conservationist. His eccentric brother Charles, a fine organist, was elsewhere in the castle, repairing a telephone for Mariga. Whilst chatting to Gerard White, an old friend of Cathal's, mulled wine was served – it was very welcome.

When we eventually left, very early on Christmas morning, we offered Mariga some peat briquettes that Cathal had brought in the car in case of emergencies. She readily accepted them and we handed them to her through the library window as it was the most convenient way of getting them into the castle. The scene was both bizarre and sad: a working-class family handing turf through a window to a former German princess.

It was hardly surprising that we all came down with colds over Christmas; and early in the new year we had such heavy snow and severe blizzards that we were unable to leave the house. The snow fell so thickly that cars in the yard and on the avenue were buried almost up to their roofs. Fortunately we had a good stock of food at home; we baked our own bread and obtained deliciously fresh, creamy milk from the farm. Cathal spent much of the time falling asleep in an armchair by the fire. Outside, everything ground to a halt for a few days.

A couple of days before the blizzard, my father and I had listened with interest to the Russian Orthodox Christmas service, broadcast on Radio 3 on the night of 6 January. Cathal, who had enjoyed seeing the slides that I had taken during a recent holiday in Russia, had always been interested in Russian architecture and history. The last Tsar, Nicholas II and Rasputin fascinated him in particular. He had read several books about them and was always saddened by the way the unfortunate royal family had been butchered by the Bolsheviks. In much the same manner in which he had respected the Jews and their customs, his heart went out to the oppressed Russian peasants with their strong, undying faith. On that cold January night, he listened, enchanted, to the powerful singing of the choir during the long Orthodox service.

We attended another Christmas party at Leixlip Castle in the following year; it was much the same as before, though this time we were spared the icy weather. Cathal found himself in conversation with the lively Dr David Norris about the possibilities of establishing a piano museum; David was all on for it. Over supper and mulled wine, Mariga's son Patrick approached us and thanked us for all the attention that we had given him and Marina when they were children; he had fond memories of the outings that we had brought them on.

Summer began badly for Cathal. Thanks to a botched job that had been carried out on pipes in nearby Farmleigh, we were receiving water directly from the River Liffey in our taps, and because of this we were all afflicted with bad doses of diarrhoea. On the morning of 1 June, Cathal awoke with an urge to rush to the bathroom. Unfortunately, he discovered that, at the same time, he had developed cramps in both legs. In his effort to get out of bed, he collapsed on to the floor and broke his left leg. We got him into the car with the help of a walking stick and I drove him to the Guinness medical department. After he had been examined thoroughly, I brought him to St James's Hospital, where his foot was X-rayed. A fracture was discovered just above his ankle. His leg was plastered, crutches were supplied by the Guinness medical department and I drove him home. To save him climbing up and down stairs, I made up my small camp bed for him in the living room and slept in his bedroom upstairs.

On the following morning the plaster was checked and he was told that it would have to remain on his leg for the next two weeks. It caused him a considerable amount of discomfort. Having been in good health for most of his life, Cathal made a poor patient. However, he cheered up whenever visitors and well-wishers came to see him. He came with us to a special reception for a visiting Chinese delegation, which was held – rather unusually – in Dublin Zoo. There he met Brian Farrell, the noted broadcaster, Eileen O'Casey, widow of the famous playwright Seán O'Casey and Paddy Maloney of the Chieftains, who supplied music on his tin whistle. When it was time to leave, Cathal was deep in conversation with the well-oiled Paddy, laughing and joking.

Towards the end of June, we met Mariga Guinness again, this time in William and June Stuart's house in Leixlip. Due to matrimonial difficulties, she was now obliged to leave Leixlip Castle in a week's time and take all her belongings with her. She had no idea as to where she would go. She invited us to her last party in Leixlip Castle on the following Wednesday evening and we went. At the door, we were met by a butler and asked our names. Mariga had asked us to bring cushions as there was nothing to sit on; indeed, the castle was very bare. Cathal was lucky enough to find a chair and sit down. He spent a considerable time chatting to Mr Cholmeley Harrison, owner of Emo Court, who invited us to visit his wonderful house and grounds in County Laois. Cathal thanked him for the invitation, but never followed it up.

The main topic of conversation that evening was Mariga, the castle and where she would go. It was said that she might move to Birr. We managed to speak to her for a while; she was in good form and did not seem to be bitter in the least. She now was sleeping on bubbly plastic wrapping paper with an old coat thrown over her by way of a blanket. When at last we made a move to leave, she kissed us goodbye. We felt sad that we would never see Mariga again in the castle.

After John O'Sullivan had come to Knockmaroon several times to practise music on our various instruments, he, his wife Venetia, Ray Lynott and a couple of radio technicians from RTÉ arrived in the afternoon of 9 August 1983 to record three programmes about Cathal and his musical instruments. My mother and I escaped to the garden, where we read books in the sunshine.

The three programmes, which were broadcast later in August and early in September of the same year, were the best interviews with Cathal to date; Cathal was at ease with Ray and the people around him, and spoke well. Venetia produced the programmes in a very professional manner and Ray proved to be a very sensitive interviewer.

The interviews ended on a poignant note. 'What do you look forward to in the long years we hope that are left to you?' Ray asked.

'Well, I would hope to have the same interest in all these things and also the gift of enjoying books which I have all my life. I'm a great reader, particularly biography and autobiography and books on collecting. And these coffee table books, plenty of pictures; photography ... I'm interested in everything.'

Cathal did indeed continue to enjoy reading many more books and taking an interest in everything. He was mellowing with age, slowing down – he admitted to have lost interest in making harpsichords in one of the interviews – and, despite his recent accident, enjoying life to the full. I can still picture my father wearing a light cream-coloured linen jacket, with a straw hat upon his head and a cane walking stick in his hand during that wonderfully sunny summer.

It was thus attired that I remember him in Luttrellstown Castle shortly afterwards, putting Mrs Aileen Plunket's mind at ease as regards the valuations that Christie's had put on her antique pianos. It was the first time that I had been in the castle; I came as Cathal's chauffeur, as his leg was still supposed to be stiff. It was a unique opportunity for me to see the impressive castle before its contents were auctioned. What amazed me most of all was the silence and peacefulness of the extensive grounds and the expansive vista of fields, trees and mountains in the distance, with no sign of any other building of any description; it was as if we were in another world.

Just as Cathal had mellowed with age, my relationship with him had improved too; not only were we father and son, but we were good friends, sharing interests and opinions. However, as is so often the case in the evening of a man's life, the more time he spent in the house, in my mother's territory, the more irritable she tended to become. Understandably, she had her own way of doing things and resented my father's intrusion; more often than not he was in her way. He, for his part, did his best to help her prepare meals and wash up afterwards; he also went off in the car every few days to do the shopping in the local supermarket, where he had made friends with the checkout girls. They had presented him with a Christmas card towards the end of the previous year.

Cathal began to see more of Peter Pearson at this stage. He was invited to Peter's new ramshackle period house in Montpelier Parade, Monkstown, and found it chock-a-block with bits and pieces salvaged from skips and old houses. Peter, now bent on saving buildings that were being wantonly destroyed in Dublin and around the country, turned up at all sorts of functions. He was present at a lecture on Irish houses given by Mark Bence-Jones in Carroll's Theatre at the end of November, a talk that Cathal attended and found very interesting.

At the end of the year, Cathal attended a party in Maurice Blake's house to celebrate the tenth anniversary of the Antiquarian Horological Society and went to see the Walter Osborne exhibition in the National Gallery with me. He pointed out a study of people and horses by a canal lock in England, which John Burke had offered to him some thirty years previously for £150, and which he could not afford at the time.

From May to July 1984, Cathal repainted the house at Knockmaroon; now aged seventy-four, he was still strong and energetic. In mid-July, Cathal went with David Bolcs, Joe Ennis, Maurice Blake, John White and other members of the Antiquarian Horological Society to Liverpool on the boat for a three-day 'clock and watch hunting expedition'. In September, Cathal set off with William Stuart for a week's holiday in London, where they had a hectic but enjoyable time. William wanted to visit the Victoria and Albert Museum, do some research in the British Museum, attend an auction at Sotheby's, visit a 'celebrated pair of horologists at Tonbridge' and visit the Fitzwilliam Museum in Cambridge. They visited John Beckett and Patrick Horsley, and attended a dinner given by a graduate friend of William's in Cambridge. Writing later to Patrick Horsley, Cathal described the journey home on 4 November:

> After leaving you we enjoyed the descent to the beautiful dale and river and thanks to your clear instructions we found our way to Holyhead without trouble. Traffic was slow but we got to the boat with about 20 minutes to spare only to discover that William had mislaid his tickets. After some filling in of forms we were allowed aboard and we reached Knockmaroon at 9 pm. William afterwards discovered the tickets in a folder with some money he had over-

looked so all was well. The following morning Williams battery let him down so he was half an hour late for school. What a man, he takes chances. He had an idea that the battery was coming to the end of it's life.

We both felt tired on arrival home and Margaret and Charles thought I looked ghastly! I popped into bed and did not surface for three days except for meals. I was exhausted and listless and only about now do I feel my old self. Last Monday I saw my doctor to obtain a certificate of fitness to drive so I asked him to give me a complete check over which he did. Everything was normal but he reminded me that I was not as young as I imagined I was! I am a creature of habit and missed my afternoon nap every day for a whole week. William, out of his great kindness, likes to include me in some of his activities and providing these occasions are widely spaced out I am always 'game' but in future when a high pressure week is proposed I shall have to plead the 'old man'. We have enjoyed a great friendship for fifteen years despite the difference in age, we seem to think alike on most topics.

By now, Cathal was spending relatively little time in his workshop and began to make plans to send his four unfinished harpsichords to Patrick Horsley. By December, Patrick had decided to accept Cathal's offer of the unfinished harpsichords but on condition that he accept some payment for them. 'You are kind to offer me money for them,' Cathal wrote, 'but let us not discuss this matter at present.' He was delighted that they would end up in Patrick's 'competent hands'. From now on, a great deal was written about how the instruments would be transported to Patrick. In the letter written to him in December, Cathal described the various 'small jobs' that he had been doing in his workshop. 'Last week I altered a hideous carved oak Victorian lectern for the Chapel of the local college, ecclesiastical work! The locals bring all their problems to me and I have said on many occasions that "if the local cat was going to have kittens I would be consulted".' This expression may have reminded him of a fellow in Guinness's Brewery who, when told how clever Cathal was, sarcastically declared that he could 'put a new arse on a cat'.

Thirty-Nine

A t this stage in his life, Cathal had lost none of his sense of humour – he had watched a series of Marx Brothers and Jacques Tati films on television with pleasure – and still had an inclination to play pranks. One evening he and I took the *RTÉ Guide* and made some subtle alterations, ageing people and giving them twisted eyes. We wanted to see if my mother would notice. When she perused the magazine during the following morning, she remarked that the actor Frank Kelly looked rather old. Having looked through the rest of the magazine in silence, she finally said, 'Well, you've made a fine old mess of this week's edition of the *Guide!*'

Cathal was still driving the car; however, because of his age, he was now obliged to undergo a medical test every year to qualify for his driving licence. He had no trouble passing it. He had an idea that he would like to live to be one hundred years of age, as did his friend Professor Tao Kiang. The two men jokingly put a bet on their chances of reaching one hundred. If Cathal did not reach that age, he certainly wanted to see the new millennium.

During this period, Cathal helped William Stuart with the restoration of his new house. An ugly Victorian porch was pulled down. Cathal's main work was to reconstruct the wooden panelling. He and William visited three houses in counties Limerick and Clare that had been designed by the architect who had built William's home, Thomas Burgh (1670–1730); Cathal made drawings of the panelling, sections of mouldings, and door and window architraves. He then made scaled drawings of the panelling required in William's hall, one wall of which retained the original panelling and mouldings, and also of the panelling needed in the drawing and dining room, and the sitting room on the ground floor. He also designed and made an architrave for the hall door.

Towards the end of September 1985 Cathal and William visited two important houses in Dublin city centre that were due to be pulled down. 'They contain wonderful staircases and panelled rooms complete with timber cornices,' Cathal wrote to Patrick Horsley, who by now had received the four unfinished harpsichords. 'William will endeavour to purchase what we need if available. I find this very exciting but time consuming. My bench is like an architect's office with plans, elevations etc. strewn about the place but it is all great fun.'

Before Christmas, my father and I went to Dunsink Observatory to see Halley's Comet – as Cathal had been born during the year of the last visitation, he wanted to see it again – but could not get near the telescope because of the crowds of people there. Instead, we managed to see it at home using Cathal's powerful binoculars. It was rather disappointing.

Cathal's brother Jack, who had suffered a heart attack and had been ailing, now died peacefully on 29 December, aged seventy-three. He was laid to rest in Balgriffin Cemetery on a cold, frosty morning. The entire family gathered for the sad occasion. Cathal's niece Eithne, who had journeyed from Switzerland, was most affected by the loss of her father. Cathal joined her, expressed his sorrow and lifted her spirits by employing the simplest – and perhaps best – remedy that he knew: humour. By the time he had finished with her, she was helplessly doubled up with laughter. Unsurprisingly, Eithne formed a deep liking for my father.

Over the Easter weekend of 1986, Cathal set off with his pals William Stuart and Peter Pearson to the beautiful small Georgian town of Birr in County Offaly. Whilst there, they met Mariga Guinness, now living in nearby Tullynisk, and Cathal tuned her old Erard piano. They also met the Earl and Countess of Rosse at Birr Castle, who invited them to visit their home, 'a hard place to gain entrance to'. They stayed overnight in Mariga's quarters, which were in a poor state of repair. When Cathal was shown to his bedroom, Mariga pointed to an umbrella, which, she said, he could use if the roof leaked. He played music for her on the piano and joined a tour of historical houses in the area. 'Altogether we had great fun but I required an afternoon sleep to recover,' Cathal reported to Patrick Horsley.

Cathal had by now developed a love of excursions such as these, especially if they involved William or Peter, both of whom he found to be refreshingly unorthodox and stimulating. They in turn relished his company; he was never stuck for something to say and was full of interesting information and funny stories. Despite his increasing age, Cathal still had a terrific memory, though I had begun to notice that he was more inclined to embroider his oft-repeated stories about Guinness's Brewery. He was beginning to slow down – as one would expect – and get flustered easily. Decision making was now slower than before. A favourite phrase of his was 'Wait now …!', which he frequently uttered when trying to collect his thoughts. Getting him out of the house on time for an appointment was becoming more and more difficult; more often than not he was late. He often became agitated in situations in which he did not feel comfortable; it might be because he was in a certain place, with certain people or because I was driving the car a little too fast for his liking. As his reactions were noticeably slower than mine, he was inclined to think that I was taking too many risks and not paying enough attention when driving. Despite these little shortcomings, he was still strong, healthy, good-humoured and forthright; people loved him because of his ebullience and willingness to help and comfort others. He was happy with life and wanted nothing more than what he had.

In April, Cathal suddenly took us by surprise by shaking off some of his lethargy of late and resuming work on a harpsichord that had lain in his workshop, unfinished, since the end of 1979. He also began restoration work on an antique grand piano that William had bought. He had now got back into his stride. This was characteristic of him; it was always difficult to get him to do things that he did not want to do, but he willingly threw himself at work that interested him – usually for other people. Many jobs that needed to be done around the house were put on the long finger; my mother often nagged him, but to no avail.

By the beginning of July, William's grand piano was strung and Cathal was able to play it for him; by the end of the month, Cathal had finished stringing the harpsichord. Miraculously, the instruments in Cathal's workshop survived Hurricane Charlie, the effects of which we felt towards the end of August, for half a tree came crashing down, damaging the roof. It had to be removed by a small crane.

Shortly afterwards, Cathal's first harpsichord, which had been in the possession of his friend Dr Stan Corran, was returned to us; plans were made for its restoration but it was soon forgotten about and was left, untouched, in a harness room at Knockmaroon for many years.

In mid-September, one of the harpsichords that Cathal's friend Patrick

Horsley had successfully completed in England and which had been ear-marked for St Patrick's College, Maynooth, arrived at customs in Dun Laoghaire; Cathal and William went out to meet Patrick and complete the formalities. It was returned to Knockmaroon for the time being.

Soon afterwards, Cathal bought a new car. He wrote to Patrick, 'I finally got my Citroën back repaired but with the warning that the back shock absorbers were giving out so I went out shopping the following Monday morning while Margaret was doing the washing and bought a Nissan Micra with which I am very pleased.'

Cathal reported to Patrick that he had been having quite a number of interruptions 'which makes it difficult to get on with the numerous jobs I should be completing'. He had had two medical checks given by two differ-ent doctors, one for his driving licence and the other for his car insurance; he passed both successfully. He was assured that he was in good shape and that his blood pressure had not altered over the years. 'I suffer from slight colour blindness which debars me from being an air pilot!!' This indeed was true; we had noticed that he always had difficulty in distinguishing between grey and pastel shades of green and blue, and that he was unable to discern a red light from a distance, especially at night. There then follow the prophetic words: a 'slight heart murmur the result of a touch of rheumatic fever in 1933'. Little did he know, as his doctor subsequently said to him, that his chickens were about to come home to roost.

On the morning of Christmas Eve, Cathal found himself to be rather befuddled; he did not know what was wrong with him and could not find the words that he wished to say. He suspected that he had suffered a mild stroke and was right; a visit to his doctor after Christmas confirmed that he had suf-fered a transitory ischemic attack (TIA). Although he recovered from it very quickly, a slow and inevitable decline to dementia had begun. This was to be the first of several such attacks that he would suffer over the next few years.

Shortly afterwards he became short of breath following any type of phys-ical exertion; his doctor diagnosed fibrillation in the heart and prescribed tablets. However, when Cathal visited the doctor later in the new year, it was discovered that he now had fluid in the lungs and so diuretic tablets were given to him. These proved to be effective and soon Cathal was more or less back to normal. Whilst he continued to busy himself with small jobs – he tuned harpsichords for friends and made a cabinet for some new hi-fi equip-ment that I had bought – he took care to take plenty of rest.

In February of 1987 the last harpsichord that Cathal was ever to make, belonging to his friend Rhoda Draper, was finally delivered to her; Rhoda had been waiting patiently for it for about seven years!

In May, the harpsichord that Patrick Horsley had completed and a Clementi grand piano that Cathal had restored were formally presented to St Patrick's College, Maynooth in an inauguration ceremony held in the Education Hall. The head of the music department, Professor Gerard Gillen, began the proceedings by welcoming everyone and introduced Cathal, who read a short paper that he had written about Muzio Clementi, the composer and maker of the piano. As Cathal had caught a slight cold, his voice was hoarse and he stumbled over his words several times. 'I sounded like a crow,' he wrote to Patrick Horsley, who was unable to come to the ceremony. He enlivened his rather stiff delivery by throwing in a few light-hearted ad-lib remarks, which people enjoyed better than his prepared speech. 'The College seemed to be very pleased to accept the piano (as I was to give it to them!),' Cathal wrote to Patrick. 'It looked very well, better than it sounded.'

Following this, our friend Malcolm Proud performed works by Scarlatti, Couperin, Sweelinck and Bach on the harpsichord. The harpsichord 'behaved beautifully and Malcolm was very happy with it', Cathal reported. 'I left him last Friday morning and Saturday afternoon to practice with a sheet of paper and pencil to note any faults which I could rectify, if necessary, but all I found was a blank sheet. The tone was excellent and many commented on it.'

Malcolm ended his recital by playing two nocturnes by John Field on the Clementi piano, which by this stage had unfortunately gone out of tune. The very note that was repeated twelve times in Field's 'Midi' Nocturne was badly out. The music was recorded by BBC Northern Ireland and broadcast subsequently.

Towards the end of the month, Cathal's old friend and helper in Guinness's Brewery, Billy Sexton, died; he and Margaret went to his funeral in Wicklow. Cathal had been visiting Billy on a regular basis until fairly recently, when he had become unable to look after himself. Undoubtedly Cathal was sorry to lose him; he had enjoyed many years of friendship with him and had comforted him in his loneliness after he had lost his wife. They had had many interesting conversations (or 'chin-wags', as Cathal would have called them) together.

As Cathal was now beginning to spend more of his time at home, he had more leisure time to fraternize with the locals. Three people who always attended my holiday slide shows were Catherine Bracken (sister of the local bard Tommy Bracken and better known as Katie), a young man named Oliver Burns and Jack Lovely, all of whom lived nearby. Jack, who was involved in the Boy Scouts, cycled everywhere and often called at odd moments to chat to Cathal. Oliver was showing an interest in music and Cathal succeeded in finding an upright piano for him to buy.

Two young ladies who greatly appreciated Cathal's company were Olive and Veronica (known to all as Ronnie or Ron) Smith, whose family home was on the Carpenterstown Road. Veronica had married a builder named Terry Murphy earlier in the year and we had been invited to the wedding. She now lived in Fortunestown Lane, near Saggart. Both the Smith girls were struck by Cathal's generosity of time and willingness to speak to anyone and everyone. With them he was open and frank, telling them his true feelings about others; they remembered how he often stressed his conviction that money could not buy happiness. He always succeeded in cheering up Olive, who was prone to illness and depression, by cracking jokes or asking her for the latest scandal, and captivating Veronica by his conversation, which, as she told me, could wander over many topics in a most unpredictable but interesting way. As she never knew what he might talk about, every conversation was like an exciting mystery tour. Like her sister Olive, she found that Cathal's company could offer her relief from stress; having spoken with him, she always felt refreshed.

Beside the Smiths lived Mr Harford, a man who worked in the Ordnance Survey and who often stopped to chat to Cathal. Farther up the Carpenterstown Road lived Paddy Madden, who had worked in Guinness's Brewery – Cathal frequently chatted with him – the Inglis family next door, Paddy Malone and his family, and Joe Malone, his brother, who owned a small shop near the level crossing. At the level crossing (now Coolmine railway station) lived Mrs Byrne, who opened and closed the gates. Our walks up the Carpenterstown Road either went as far as the level crossing, where we often stopped to chat to Mrs Byrne, or to a tree just before the bend in the road, where there is now a housing estate and a roundabout.

Another couple with whom Cathal became friendly at this period was Charles and Máire Lawler, who lived a little farther on, in Coolmine. Their son, Adrian, had fallen off a railway station platform and had part of his leg so badly damaged by a train that it had to be amputated. Cathal felt intensely sorry for the boy and went to see him in hospital with Mr Lawler. We remained friendly with this family for several years.

Frequent visitors to our house at this time, now that the musical evenings were finally petering out, were Ned Cronly, an old Brewery colleague and his wife Maisie, who had accompanied my mother on several holidays, and another workmate from Guinness's Brewery, Peter Nevin, who had lost his wife some time previously. Peter sometimes went with Cathal to the Antiquarian Horological Society meetings. He also enjoyed foreign travel and sometimes came to see my holiday slides. Occasionally we visited Helen and Joe Devine at their house in Clondalkin and their neighbours the Mullarkeys. There were also visits to Joan and Jerry Doyle in Rathfarnham; Joan, whose maiden name was Devine, was one of the little girls whom my parents had brought out for drives in their first car. We also visited Olive Lavelle, who had once lived in Rialto, and her husband Dermot, and two sisters whom my mother had met whilst on a holiday in Russia: Dolie and Stella Lalor. My parents still did some entertaining, but not as much as before.

The year 1988 was not a particularly eventful one for Cathal and yet it was busy enough. He spent most of his spare time working on the panelling and restoration of William's house. Cathal and I helped with the final move from William and June's temporary home in Jarretstown to Celbridge in early October, loading boxes of books into our cars and driving there. Despite engaging in various activities, Cathal wrote to Patrick Horsley, 'I am developing into a lazy, carefree old man. I get tired very easily and need rest after any activity such as gardening. Reading presents a problem, I am inclined to drop off asleep and lose the trend of the narrative and must retrace what I have already read. Still, what can I expect at 77, I shall be 78 in August.'

In June, the Irish Conservation Directory was launched in the National Gallery; as Cathal had written a short article about himself and his work for the publication, he was invited to the reception. There he had the pleasure of speaking to various people, including Professor Kevin B. Nowlan, whom he had not met for a long time, and Nick and Senator Mary Robinson. On the following day, he and William Stuart joined a horological tour to Belfast.

During the following month, three of Cathal's antique pianos – a Longman and Broderip square, a Lichtenthal pianino and a copy of a Stein fortepiano – were transported to RTÉ, where they were used by John O'Conor for one of his *Piano Plus* television programmes, directed by Anne Makower. John and Anne had come to Knockmaroon a little while previously to look at the instruments. Cathal tuned the instruments in the studio and was quite astounded to discover that he too was to be featured and interviewed in the programme. As he was dressed casually in an open-necked shirt and in a brown jumper knitted by my mother, he tried to excuse himself, but John and Anne would hear none of it. During the programme, which I had the pleasure to vision mix (there were two Gannons on the final credits!), Cathal appeared somewhat ill at ease, and when interviewed looked at the floor for most of the time. Nonetheless, he spoke well enough and it turned out to be an interesting programme. It was transmitted on 30 October.

In January 1989, Cathal wrote to Patrick Horsley. 'I wish I had your facility to write an intelligent and readable letter!' he began. 'One time I could – or thought I could, but the moment I take a pen in my hand my brain ceases to function. Old age I suppose.' An interesting passage appears later in the letter: 'I am pleased to hear that Emma [Patrick's daughter] is doing well at the music but she must not be forced. I made the mistake of forcing Charles until he rebelled, then I had to survive a few years of "pop" until he returned to the good music. Now it is nothing but Bach, Beethoven and Brahms – we have great times together especially listening to the CDs into the small hours of the morning.'

Cathal continued to work now and then at William's new house in Celbridge, though William's falling ill with shingles later in the year set things back considerably. 'I don't seem to be much help to him nowadays as I tire easily,' Cathal wrote to Patrick.

While I was away on a holiday in China (an event that coincided with the Beijing massacre of that year, causing my parents to fear for my safety), Mariga Guinness died whilst travelling on the ferry from Holyhead to Dun Laoghaire. My parents were greatly saddened to hear the news and shortly afterwards attended the simple burial ceremony at the Connolly folly near Castletown House, an architectural structure that had become the symbol of the Irish Georgian Society.

The highlight of the year was the conferring of a second honorary MA degree upon Cathal, this time by St Patrick's College, Maynooth. The main movers behind this were the head of music, Professor Gerard Gillen and the president, Monsignor Ledwith, who had received the Gannon–Horsley harpsichord and Clementi grand piano two years previously. At the end of that ceremony, Professor Gillen had whispered to me that there was a possibility that Cathal might receive another honorary degree, but begged me to keep this information to myself. Cathal heard about it for the first time in early November 1989, when Professor Gillen telephoned him with the news. A formal request for acceptance arrived by post at the end of the month. Cathal was allowed to invite his own friends and relatives. 'God help me,' he wrote to Patrick Horsley, 'I don't look forward to the ordeal, I have already one from Trinity College given in 1978 surely that's enough. The one redeeming feature is that it will be informal, a monkey suit is not favoured.'

The conferring took place in the Renehan Hall of the college on 20 December. Although it lacked the elaborate pomp and ceremony of the conferring in Trinity College, it nonetheless was an impressive occasion. Cathal, wearing a robe, was conducted into the hall by Professor Gillen and the proceedings began with two songs by Handel sung by Emmanuel Lawler and accompanied on the Gannon–Horsley harpsichord by Professor Gillen. Following this, the Registrar of the National University of Ireland, Dr John Nolan, declared the Meeting of the University to be open, and an introductory address was delivered by Monsignor Mícheál Ledwith. In it, mention was made of Cathal restoring the grand piano for Desmond Guinness and the Guinness Brewery's decision to set up a special workshop for Cathal. The speech concluded by asking the assembled listeners to 'lift a master's glass to Cathal Gannon for the many fragments of the world of old melodies saved by his soul and hands.'

Cathal was then presented by Monsignor Ledwith. The Chancellor, Dr T.K. Whitaker, admitted him and conferred him with his honorary degree. Finally, the Registrar announced the closing of the ceremony and the Maynooth Chamber Choir sang 'Tomorrow Shall be my Dancing Day'. The conferring concluded with a long burst of heartfelt applause.

Towards the end of July 1990 William's grand piano, which Cathal had restored, was finally transported to his house in Celbridge. Although Cathal did not realize it, this was in readiness for his eightieth birthday, which was celebrated in style on Wednesday, 1 August. It was a bright sunny day and, in order to satisfy a whim of his (something that he had hoped to do ten years previously), I took him on a tour of his former homes. First of all I drove him to 82 Crumlin Road (formerly 20 Longford Terrace), where I knocked on the door and spoke to the lady who opened it. She knew that my father had once lived in the house and readily invited us inside. Cathal recognized various parts of his former home and was fascinated to discover that the garage and part of the glasshouse that his father had constructed still existed at the back of the house. We spoke at length with the lady and after I had taken some photographs we drove to 31 Darley Street in Harold's Cross, the house in which Cathal had been born. He was rather disappointed to discover that the original windows had been replaced with modern ones made of PVC. As there was nobody at home, we were unable to see inside.

Before returning home, we stopped at 169 Herberton Road, Rialto, where I had been born, and I photographed my father standing in front of the familiar house. He was delighted with the little tour.

When we prepared to leave for William and June's house in the evening, Cathal wondered why my mother and I were dressing up – he thought that we had been invited over for a quiet evening – and decided to dress casually. We left, bearing a magnificent cake that featured a miniature piano, which had been made by our neighbour Ron.

When we reached Celbridge, some of Cathal's friends from the Antiquarian Horological Society met him outside William's house and, telling him quietly that some young ladies were swimming naked in the River Liffey, succeeded in coaxing him out of the car. They walked with him to the gates of Castletown House and turned down a lane that led to the river. By then the nude women had mysteriously disappeared and in their stead was William seated in a little wooden boat. He encouraged Cathal to get in and they drifted down the river together towards the house. Cathal sat at the fore of the boat, facing William at the aft. It was a fine, balmy evening. William chatted to him and, when they had reached the bottom of his garden, he told Cathal to look around. Much to his amazement, he found about fifty people gathered to greet him. We sang 'Happy Birthday' and gave him three cheers. Needless to say, everything had been arranged in secret; he genuinely had no idea that so many people had been invited. As he clambered ashore, he shook hands, hugged and kissed the guests, delighted to see so many of his old friends. Most of the people had arrived earlier, left their presents in the house and, bearing glasses of wine, had wandered out into the garden.

Shortly afterwards, when it began to grow cool, we went into the house and applied ourselves to a delicious buffet supper supplied by June and various helpers from her school. The large sitting room upstairs had been cleared of builders' rubble and was lit solely by candles. When darkness descended, the garden was lit up with flares, which added to the wonderfully magical atmosphere. Another birthday cake was presented by Olive Lavelle and Cathal was obliged to blow out the candles. After tea and coffee were served, our friend Mary Byrne sang some songs, accompanied by Helen Devine on the antique grand piano. Afterwards, Cathal played and encouraged Arthur Agnew to sing.

Following this, people began to leave, but Cathal, now completely at his ease, played more music and was applauded. Finally we loaded all the presents into our car and reluctantly left the wonderful house. By the time we fell into bed, dawn was breaking. It had been a wonderful day and a fitting way to celebrate such a great occasion. Cathal wrote to Patrick Horsley, 'the opinion held by all is that it was one of the best parties ever given'.

Forty

Now that Cathal had reached the grand old age of eighty, he was content to rest on his laurels and take life easy. He saw no reason to exert himself any more, save for some minor domestic jobs. He used to chuckle and say to his friends, 'I'm being paid two pensions for doing nothing, so why the hell should I do anything?' He was strong, healthy and maintained his good humour; indeed, he was at his very best during this period. He spent much of his spare time during the end of 1990 and the following year visiting his friends, going off for picnics in the car with my mother and making countless trips to Kilcoole in order to visit the McNamara sisters, who had moved there recently and who always looked forward to his arrival and my mother's cooking.

Just when everything seemed to be going swimmingly, Cathal suffered another TIA towards the end of March 1992; the effects were to be far more serious than the last. I sought medical advice and he was ordered to rest. Although he had the presence of mind to put all the clocks back one hour, his appetite was poor and he had little energy. More confusion followed and I brought him to Dr O'Shea in the Guinness medical department. She concluded that he had pneumonia and prescribed antibiotics. Shortly afterwards he returned to the clinic and was given blood tests. Many of our friends were very concerned and telephoned us for the latest news; my mother was worried and consequently her blood pressure rose.

Slowly, however, Cathal recovered and by Easter Sunday I was able to bring him and my mother to William and June's house, where we sat outside in the sunshine and examined the newly made cottage for June's parents. In the evening, Cathal was seated at the television, watching snooker. He soon regained his energy and we took long walks together in the neighbourhood. From this time onwards I brought him regularly to Dr O'Shea in the Guinness medical department; he loved to talk and joke with her and she always enjoyed his good spirits, even though he was often confused.

While Cathal lived and flourished, his contemporaries continued to pass away. Peter Nevin, his old friend from Guinness's Brewery, died at around this time.

Soon after his eighty-second birthday, Cathal was helping Margaret to paint some of the rooms in Knockmaroon. A new fireplace surround, which Cathal had made some time previously, and a marble centrepiece were installed at this stage. This spurt of decoration was in preparation for the arrival of a friend of my mother's, Margaret Clarke, from England. She stayed for a week and we brought her out for excursions in the car. I made sure to do all the driving, for Dr O'Shea had warned me against allowing my father to drive for long periods. Cathal proved to be a little troublesome at times.

Earlier in the year, in July, Lord Moyne had died. Cathal was sorry to learn of his passing away; he had liked him very much and had regarded him as being a very accommodating landlord and neighbour. A memorial service in Trinity College, to which we were invited, was held in mid-October.

At around this time I left home to share a house in Cornelscourt with some good friends of mine. At thirty-seven years of age and still unmarried, it was time for me to leave the family home and finally learn to fend for myself – I had relied on my parents for far too long. Although I had not really been spoiled as a child, I was always happy to take advantage of being an only child and allow my mother to cook meals for me, wash my clothes and clean up after me. After so many years of dithering over whether I should find a place of my own or not, I now had a golden opportunity to be with people of my own age and to gain some independence. I had always been little more than 'Cathal Gannon's son' and could do little more than talk about my father – an ex-girlfriend had once complained that I had virtually nothing to say about myself. At least working, first of all at commercial art in a small establishment in town (where I made friends with my boss Maurice O'Connor and his wife Claire) and then in RTÉ at television sound, followed by vision mixing, had broadened my horizons. Thanks to my sheltered upbringing, I was not outgoing by nature and always had to put a certain amount of effort into mixing and integrating with people. Fortunately my stammer had finally disappeared when I left school and moved around in the outside world.

I now tackled the restoration and decoration of the house in Cornelscourt with gusto, learning as we progressed, and subsequently became reasonably adept at cooking, cleaning, ironing and looking after the new home, which was conveniently close to RTÉ. Although my parents had been somewhat shocked by my decision to leave Knockmaroon, in the end they were pleased for me and my mother pronounced me to be 'quite domesticated'. However, as we shall see shortly, the timing of my move to Cornelscourt proved to be rather unfortunate.

On 25 October another big party was held in William and June's house for my parents – this time for their fiftieth wedding anniversary. (A party had been given the previous year for my mother's birthday.) Many friends of old attended; presents were showered on Margaret and Cathal, a wonderful meal was served, a special cake (once again made by our next-door neighbour Ron) was cut, and songs were sung. Cathal even managed to play some music on William's piano. During the evening, Cathal stumbled through a short speech that my mother and I had written. Although he undoubtedly enjoyed the evening, he looked a little unhappy in the photographs that were taken of him.

The following year, 1993, began with a meal in the Old Dublin Restaurant in Francis Street; we used vouchers given to us by some friends of my parents. Neither Margaret nor Cathal were comfortable about eating in such a high-class restaurant; as usual, Cathal managed to embarrass my mother by extracting from his mouth a plate containing a couple of false teeth that he found uncomfortable when eating. He was very much inclined to do this at unexpected moments; he usually left the offending object sitting on the table somewhere beside him.

Later in the year, Cathal probably suffered from another TIA, or at least a small clot of blood found its way to his brain, for at the beginning of June we discovered that he was suffering from double vision. Examinations at the Eye and Ear Hospital revealed that a muscle in his right eye no longer functioned properly. In time, the problem rectified itself, though from then on Cathal's eyes never moved correctly together. When sitting at the kitchen table, I often noticed him observing the scenery through the window with one eye shut. Cathal was now put on a course of warfarin and aspirin to prevent his blood clotting and he was obliged to have a blood test every so often; this necessitated many visits to the Guinness medical centre.

Towards the end of August, he was well enough to come on the first of several annual fortnightly holidays with Margaret, Anthony Harrison and me, staying in a rented house or cottage. This year we chose a remote corner of County Cavan, beside Lough Oughter. Apart from one day, when we travelled a little too far and he became cranky and tired, he enjoyed the experience. He meekly allowed us to take him over the border into County Fermanagh, where we were able to see Upper Lough Erne and other beauty spots.

Just before Christmas, Cathal passed his medical test for the car insurance. We kept a careful eye on his driving, allowing him to tackle only short distances or at least routes that he knew very well.

On speaking to my father early in the new year, I concluded that he was feeling down and lonely; Ron had come to this same conclusion. Although he did see some of his friends from time to time, very little was happening in his life by now and he probably felt that he was being ignored. The death of another good friend, Mary Byrne, who had sung so beautifully in the past, probably upset him further. Whilst walking with him in Luggala in April, he told me that I was better off not living in Knockmaroon for, he told me, it was 'a depressing place'. My mother, who had fallen and injured her foot, was in bad humour. She was finding it hard to cope with my father's forgetfulness and uselessness and did not know how to handle the situation. She was inclined to treat him like a naughty child, and so when he did something wrong she lost patience with him and scolded him. Initially he was able to offer some resistance, but he soon realized that giving in was all he could do in the interests of 'anything for a quiet life'. At the time, I was glad not to be at home on a permanent basis, yet torn between wanting to be with my friends and my parents. I felt sorry for my father, but felt that there was little that I could do to help. Cathal anxiously awaited my visits to Knockmaroon, for he felt completely at ease with me and knew that I could bring a little peace to the household. Now I regret that I did not spend more time with my parents, helping my mother, but I could not have been there all the time because of work. Also, I would have been affected by the constant bickering over trivial matters and would have ended up arguing with them both.

A two-week holiday in a rented bungalow near Schull, West Cork in August cheered us up a little, though Cathal was not too pleased with some of the excursions. He did not care for windswept areas and wide, uninterrupted vistas of the sea; what he preferred was gentle scenery with signs of habitation. The highlight of the holiday was a trip, via Bantry, to Glengarriff, where my parents had met some fifty-eight years previously. They hardly recognized the place. We took the boat out to Garinish Island, where we visited the Italian garden. We wandered into what had once been the Poulgorm Hotel – now the Blue Pool Hotel – and found it to be quite different from what my parents had remembered.

By this stage my father's long-term memory was becoming defective; he either forgot incidents that had happened in the past or was inclined to mix them up. His short-term memory was very poor and he was unable to remember what he had said five minutes previously. We became more anxious about Cathal's ability to drive when he accidentally knocked a woman off a bicycle when leaving the local shopping centre, yet amazingly he managed to pass his medical test for the car insurance shortly afterwards.

In mid-December, William Stuart called on my parents out of the blue. He told us that he had been out sick from school for six weeks with sinusitis – or at least that was what he thought was wrong. He told us that he was inclined to suffer from headaches. A couple of days later, Cathal suffered another TIA.

In March of the following year, 1995, William Stuart died suddenly from cancer of the liver; an autopsy revealed that his whole body had been affected and that the cancer of the liver was secondary. Anthony Harrison and my parents went to see William for the last time in the Meath Hospital; he died two days later. We were very upset by this turn of events and now realized why we had seen so little of him recently. William's coffin was brought directly from the house to the graveyard, where various friends made speeches. He was laid to rest in the shade of a large oak tree, surrounded by bouquets of flowers.

We had one of our best holidays together during this summer. Taking advantage of the IRA ceasefire, we drove to County Antrim in Northern Ireland. We stayed in a very comfortable and brand-new modern bungalow near Bushmills and, as the weather was excellent almost all the time, set off for daily excursions from there. Cathal managed to cross the famous rope bridge at Carrick-a-Rede, which my mother was afraid to tackle. He seemed to enjoy the holiday and gave no trouble whatsoever. On the way home we visited friends of my mother in Belfast and my father played a few short pieces on the piano for them.

By this stage Cathal had stopped driving as he had begun to make too many mistakes; once or twice he had set out to go somewhere and had returned, having forgotten his destination. At first he was disappointed at not being allowed to drive but soon accepted the situation. He and I continued to walk together; although a little unsteady on his feet from time to time, he was still able to manage a couple of miles.

The following year began with all the symptoms of another TIA, but it turned out to be a cold that had developed into a chest infection. Once again Cathal was very confused. Ron and Terry's spare bed was fetched and placed in the living room. Much to my mother's dismay, Cathal now showed signs of becoming incontinent; from now on there would be wettings and the constant chore of cleaning up after him. Fortunately he recovered from his infection by the end of January and was able to go out walking again. Every time I went to Knockmaroon to visit my parents, I had to shave him, for he could no longer see the sides of his face and could only tackle the area around his mouth.

On Cathal's birthday, June Stuart brought us out in her car and we visited the elegant Casino at Marino, the interior of which we had not seen since its restoration. Cathal enjoyed seeing this fine example of eighteenth-century architecture. June took photographs of us at the Casino — shots that my mother treasured for many years afterwards. Some time later I brought my parents to see Emo Court, now open to the public. My mother and I were suitably impressed; Cathal, on the other hand, seemed not very taken with the house.

During a summer holiday in the Dingle peninsula, my father was confused and sleepy, but was determined to find the house belonging to the Fox family when we visited Dingle town. This was where he had stayed during his holiday with his aunt Cissie in 1926. We found the house and spoke to the man who lived in it, a son of the couple whom my father had known.

Because of increasing age and inactivity, Cathal now became unsteady on his feet. When out walking, he had to hold on to me in order to avoid toppling over. I encouraged him to use a walking stick, but he never managed to use it correctly. Instead, he used it to threaten the dogs at Knockmaroon House, who invariably gave us a noisy greeting whenever we passed them. He still derived fun from barking back at them or imitating the cocks crowing. By now he had developed the mildly irritating habit of pretending to cry (as he had done to amuse me when I was young) when he was unhappy or something had gone wrong; in time this would develop into real crying or whimpering.

The beginning of 1997 brought more bad health, once again in the form of a chest infection, to which he had become prone. His doctor in the Guinness medical department prescribed medication and soon he was well again. He showed a certain amount of interest in a family tree that I had begun to research at this time, but was confused by the information. It was unfortunate that I had not tackled this some years previously, when he was more alert, for he had often wished to learn more about his family's history.

By now, my father was receiving regular attention from district nurses, who came to wash and dress him in the mornings; my mother was no longer able to cope with his slowness and inability to look after himself. I did as much as I could do whenever I had time.

On the day after Cathal's birthday, we received a visit from his second cousin, Patrick Gannon, his wife Betty and their daughter Judith. In the process of making the family tree, I had rediscovered this 'lost' branch of the family. Judith, a talented musician then aged fourteen, sat down at the Blüthner piano and played John Field's Nocturne No. 5 — one of my father's favourite party pieces. It was uncanny.

Shortly afterwards, Cathal was assessed by a geriatrician in Blanchardstown Hospital and given a CT brain scan at the Bon Secours Hospital. He was then interviewed by a psychiatrist, whose conclusion was that he should be left as he was for the time being. From then on I brought him, and my mother, to a chiropodist for regular treatment. Walking now became painful for Cathal, whose hips were beginning to trouble him, but he still liked to go out for some exercise.

I had finished the family tree by the beginning of the following year. I presented my father with a copy of it; he perused it for a while and then fell asleep in his armchair.

Despite my father's worsening condition, we decided to go on another holiday and set off in May for Ramelton in County Donegal. Cathal, although he slept for much of the time, was in reasonably good form, though there were accidents due to his incontinence. We visited his old friend Pat Agnew, who lived in Fanad; as a young girl, she had lived on the Crumlin Road a few doors away from the Gannons.

As if things were not difficult enough for my mother, another misfortune occurred: whilst walking in Thomas Street with me, having visited her doctor, she tripped on a loose piece of paving stone, fell and fractured a bone in her upper arm. I now had to cook and clean for both parents as well as work. One of the district nurses who washed and dressed my father suggested meals on wheels and so my parents were lucky enough to avail of the service almost immediately. Other friends stepped in and helped now and then. Anthony Harrison and I went off on a month-long holiday to America and by the time we returned my mother's arm had totally recovered, much to the amazement of the hospital doctors. Fortunately for her, the meals on wheels service was not discontinued.

In the meantime, Cathal continued to decline. As he was no longer walking, his feet began to swell due to the lack of circulation, and fluid began to accumulate in his lungs. His behaviour now became very erratic and Christmas in Cornelscourt was a disaster owing to his increasing incontinence. We realized that something had to be done. Thanks to the good offices of my parents' friend Helen Devine, our public health nurse called to us in January of the following year, 1999 and proposed that Cathal be moved to a nursing home as he would from now on need professional care. As this was the one thing that he had vehemently opposed throughout his life, I felt that it would be cruel to subject him to this but it seemed to be the only sensible solution. On 9 February he was admitted into the elegant surroundings of the Riversdale Nursing Home in Palmerstown, a fine eighteenth-century building that could be seen from our house in Knockmaroon. Little did he know that when I brought him out for 'a drive' that sunny afternoon, he would never set foot in his own house again.

For my mother it was a huge relief but it must have hurt her terribly when Cathal hardly acknowledged her presence on some occasions when we went to visit him at Riversdale. His mind had gone back to his childhood and I overheard him telling the inmates that he lived on the Crumlin Road.

His stay in the nursing home lasted just three months, during which his decline hastened alarmingly. Nonetheless, he retained his love of music – which was his salvation at all times – and his impish sense of humour. Whenever I visited him, he contorted his face into a crooked grin, twisting one eye as he used to do in order to amuse me when I was a child, and bestowed me with a mock blessing, in imitation of a priest. His face would then relax and he would quietly chuckle to himself, laughing at his own impudence. When not sleeping or dozing, he often listened to music on cassette tapes and then to RTÉ Lyric FM when it came on air in May.

I moved back to Knockmaroon in order to keep my mother company.

Now that my parents' money was rapidly being used up for the payment of the nursing home, we sought every bit of financial help available and applied for a subvention; I was constantly filling in forms and discussing plans with officials.

When, on 10 May, we visited Cathal and found him in a wheelchair and barely able to speak, we became worried. We learned that he had fallen twice and injured his hip. It seemed that he had also suffered yet another TIA. On 14 May we called in to see him and found him sleeping at an awkward angle in his bed. A chest infection had led to a fever. My mother, Anthony Harrison and I were due to go to Sligo for a holiday on the following day, but we did not go; Cathal was rushed into Blanchardstown Hospital in a critical condition. I found him connected to a drip and a monitoring device, shaking like a leaf. He was moved into a ward with other patients, then transferred to a private room, where he was placed on a water mattress so that he was not in pain. I was told that such a combination of complications would have carried off most men of his age.

He now drifted into a light coma and lay there for a week with his eyes closed most of the time, the right side of his body paralysed. Nonetheless, he signalled his recognition of voices by a flickering of his eyes under his eyelids. By this, I realized that he recognized some of his favourite music – Brahms's *Zwei Gesänge* (Two Songs) for contralto, viola and piano – which was being played on the radio one evening. As this type of existence was pointless, my mother and I prayed that he be taken out of his misery as quickly as possible.

Just as we were preparing for bed on the night of 22 May, the telephone rang. It was a nurse from the hospital, who told me that my father was unlikely to last the night. We spent that entire night and much of the following day observing him fight valiantly for life, his chest heaving as he gasped for breath. He was not giving up easily – I was astounded at his strength. It was only when left on his own, on the evening of the 23rd, that he gave up the struggle. At home, I had just fallen asleep; my mother woke me and told me that he had died and that a nurse wanted to speak to me on the telephone. I reluctantly drove to the hospital to bid him my final farewell but had to shut the door almost immediately, for I could not bear to see him as a corpse. I wanted him to remain alive in my memory.

Two days later, Cathal's body was removed to the simple little church at Porterstown, St Mochta's, where he used to attend Mass. On the following day, Wednesday, 26 May 1999, after ten o'clock Mass, he was buried in the graveyard of St Brigid's Church, Castleknock. Quite a number of Cathal's friends and relatives attended. During the Mass, various favourite songs of his were sung and June Stuart, the widow of his best friend, William, spoke warmly about him.

Just as Cathal had entered the world, he left it to the sound of music. As his coffin was taken from the church, my third cousin Judith Gannon once again played my father's 'signature tune': the Nocturne No. 5 by John Field. I felt that it was a fitting way to say goodbye to him. Walking behind his coffin, I noticed several people in tears.

The funeral was not a miserably sad occasion – my mother's composure was exemplary – it was, in fact, a wonderful day during which everyone remembered my father with fondness and laughed at the various things that he had said and done. It was just how he would have wished it to be, for he never wanted any fuss or ceremony at his passing away. Unfortunately, he had been denied the two things that he had always wanted: a speedy death, free of pain and suffering, and the chance to see the year 2000. Nevertheless, he had managed to live a good, long and interesting life.

Epilogue

*O*ver the coming days we received a flood of cards and letters from friends and relatives, many of which contained words of comfort for us and fond recollections of Cathal. Whilst there had been an emptiness in the house ever since he had left for the nursing home – my mother had often found herself gazing at his empty armchair – the silence now became more profound. Surprisingly, my father's passing away did not affect me too much – probably because I had been expecting it and, indeed, I had almost been longing for it to happen so that it might relieve him of any suffering. I discovered that I could still stay in contact with him by writing this book and listening to the many recordings that I had of him speaking. He was still very much alive in my memory.

Whilst Cathal's death lifted a heavy burden from my mother's shoulders, she most certainly was saddened by his loss, for he had been her constant companion for the best part of fifty-seven years. Judging by the number of times she told her friends about the circumstances of Cathal's removal to the nursing home and his death, it was clear that she thought about him constantly. She laid low and dressed simply for twelve months, then began to blossom. To relieve the silence and emptiness of the house at Knockmaroon, I bought her a budgie one Christmas. Another followed about a year later and these cheerful little birds provided her with companionship at home. Because of her increasing deafness, social intercourse became difficult and she turned constantly to the television as a means of entertainment and keeping in touch with the world. She celebrated her ninetieth birthday in style, with another wonderful party in June Stuart's house in Celbridge. Then, six days after her ninety-first birthday, on 21 November 2002, she suddenly died whilst preparing to go to bed. She had the good fortune to die without pain or suffering – the type of death that Cathal had wished for himself, sadly in vain. As my parents' good friend Bernadette Agnew tearfully said to me over the telephone, it was the end of an era.

Despite Cathal's outspoken criticism of the treatment of the musical instruments in the Kildare Street branch of the National Museum of Ireland in former times, his very first harpsichord (the one modelled on the Kirckman instrument of 1777 in London) was fetched out of the harness room in Knockmaroon and moved there in July 2001. It is currently in storage at the Collins Barracks branch, awaiting restoration.

Towards the end of his interview with Ray Lynott in 1983, Cathal mentioned that he would be happy to donate most of his instruments to a museum of keyboard instruments in Dublin, which, as he said, 'every civilized city in Europe has'. Referring to the collection in the National Museum of Ireland, he said, 'They shouldn't be in the museum – they should be in a Georgian house where people can go in and play these instruments as in Fenton House in Hampstead.'

A small but significant step in the direction of this vision of an institution where pianos and harpsichords could be played and not only examined in glass cases was made on 25 May 2003, when the Cathal Gannon Early Music Room was officially opened at the Royal Irish Academy of Music by John O'Conor and Gillian Smith. The small room, adorned with panels of printed information and photographs, contained the harpsichord that Cathal had made for the Academy, the Broadwood grand piano of 1809 that he had restored for Trinity College, and a Clementi square piano that had been purchased from a Mr Campbell of Blackrock, County Louth and restored to playing condition by the eminent English piano expert David Hunt. The room and its contents, I believe, are a fitting tribute to the memory of my late father.

Afterword

*I*n 1983 when he was well into his seventies, Cathal Gannon was asked during an RTÉ interview with Ray Lynott how he maintained his youthful spirits. He replied, 'Well, I think I've got an interest in life and I enjoy every moment of it, and I like young people; and most of my friends are younger – much younger than myself.'

I was one of those 'younger' friends. In the seventies I used to visit him frequently when I would cycle across Dublin to his home on Lord Moyne's estate in Castleknock. I can still see him blithely hopping over the fence separating his house from the sylvan surroundings of his workshop in which I was invited to look at work in progress, whether a harpsichord being constructed or a fortepiano being restored. All this took place in an atmosphere of considerable hilarity engendered by his anecdotes and risqué jokes. Afterwards we would return to the house for an excellent lunch or afternoon tea prepared by his wife, Margaret.

The first harpsichord I owned was built by Cathal. Thirty years later I am daily reminded of him by the chimes of a fine old clock that he restored to working order for my wife, Susan, and which now stands on the mantelpiece in our music room. Strangely, this connection between harpsichords and clocks had already become established in my mind when I went to Amsterdam in 1980 for a year of study with Gustav Leonhardt. Often my lessons took place around midday and the unsynchronized chimes of several antique clocks would fill Leonhardt's magnificent seventeenth-century house as an accompaniment to my interpretations of Bach and his contemporaries.

In the sixties and seventies international performers like Leonhardt and John Beckett gave concerts in Dublin on 'Gannon' harpsichords. The so-called 'early music movement' was slow in becoming established in Ireland but how much slower it would have been without Cathal Gannon. He was one of those enlightened harpsichord builders who realized the importance of copying the construction methods of seventeenth- and eighteenth-century masters.

His life spanned most of the twentieth century; or to put it another way, he once told me how as a child he heard corncrakes at Dolphin's Barn, now a densely populated part of Dublin city. He himself was a rare bird – a crafts-man of great skill and integrity of whom Ireland can justifiably be proud.

Malcolm Proud, July 2006

Postscript

I first met Cathal Gannon in the late 1930s. At that time we were both members of the Old Dublin Society. I was a schoolboy and Cathal a young carpenter working in Guinness's Brewery. There was an age gap, but we certainly must have been about the youngest members of the society, and this helped bring us together.

Cathal was a quietly spoken young man, with a lively interest in local history and the arts, especially those of the eighteenth century. We found much in common in the history and traditions of Dublin. Cathal was an alert and pleasant companion on walks of exploration in the city and the surrounding countryside, a countryside that came so much closer to the city in those now distant days. At that time, I was not very aware of his musical interests, although I had heard that he had shown much skill in repairing old musical instruments. It was local history and archaeology that were our shared interests, and when the Old Dublin Society, in September and early October 1937, held a Loan Exhibition in the Municipal Gallery of Modern Art, in Charlemont House, both Cathal and I were contributors to it. According to the Catalogue, 'Wormwood Gate, *c.*1855. Wash drawing by Alexander Williams, RHA', was exhibited by Mr C.W. Gannon. He also exhibited a collection of Dublin watches and watch movements 'all in good working order', and dating from 1788 to *c.*1860. My contribution was more modest: it was a modern map of Dublin on which I showed the area of the old walled city, the areas that had been 'recovered' from the sea and the sites of a number of ancient monuments and places of historical interest. Both of us were members of the Hanging Committee for the exhibition. It was Alderman Tom Kelly, the president of the Society, who first suggested the exhibition and he had been associated with the gallery since its inception. It was hoped that the exhibition might open the way to a properly endowed city museum. We still await that happy event. The 1937 exhibition proved a success in terms of public response.

It was Cathal Gannon who introduced me to Grace Gifford, the talented artist who had married Joseph Mary Plunkett on the eve of his execution in 1916 and he brought me to meet Carl Hardebeck, that great interpreter of Irish music in his little house – a man who deserved better of the nation. All this took place in the late 1930s and 1940s. Elsewhere in these pages can be found an account of how Cathal and I dropped out of the Old Dublin Society, though many years later I rejoined it. After that we kept in touch with one another, but I had no involvement in his great work for music, especially the building of instruments. My academic commitments and the fact that I had to spend, as a result, time outside the country tended to lessen the opportunities for us to meet. However, in more recent times we had several meetings, which brought back the brightest memories of those earlier years. Cathal Gannon will always be for me the bright young Dublin artisan with so much wit and knowledge. It was good to have known him.

Kevin B. Nowlan, April 2006

Appendix A

KEYBOARD INSTRUMENTS MADE BY CATHAL GANNON

CLAVICHORD, begun in 1948

Using 'bad photographs and descriptions', Cathal attempted to make a clavichord but left it unfinished. He completed it in the late 1950s or early 1960s and gave it to John Beckett, who practised on it whilst recovering from a car accident in hospital. For some time it was in the music department of King's Hospital, Palmerstown, Dublin and is now in the Royal Irish Academy of Music, Dublin. It has four and a half octaves, the construction is basic and the wood is plain and unpainted.

HARPSICHORD NO. 1, 1951–2

Based on an 1777 instrument by Jacob and Abraham Kirckman in the Benton Fletcher Collection of Early Keyboard Instruments, Fenton House, Hampstead (originally at Cheyne Walk, Chelsea). Featuring two manuals and 'dog-legged' jacks, Cathal made his instrument shorter than the original, which was 7 ft 9 in. Painted in black and Dutch orange with the motto 'Musica magnorum est solamen dulce laborum' (Music is the sweet solace of work) on the lid. Following Kirckman's usual colour scheme, the naturals on the keyboard were covered in white celluloid and the accidentals in black. The soundboard was made of Sitka spruce. Having examined a Dolmetsch harpsichord, which Radio Éireann had purchased, Cathal modified the work that he had done, then corrected it after hearing a talk on the radio given by Raymond Russell. For many years it belonged to Dr Stan Corran. In 1986 it returned to Knockmaroon and now is in storage at the Collins Barracks branch of the National Museum of Ireland.

> Compass: 5 octaves, F_I to f^3.
> Registration: 8′ top, 8′ bottom, 4′ bottom, Lute top, Harp (Buff) top, Harp (Buff) bottom, coupler.
> Case (excluding lid): length 7′3″ (2235 mm), width 3′$\frac{1}{2}$″(927 mm), depth 1′ (305 mm).

CLAVICHORD, 1952

This instrument was an improvement on the first but still not up to Cathal's standard. It was made using plans printed in *Newnes Practical Mechanics* in September 1949 and the *Woodworker* magazine in 1950. The clavichord, veneered in mahogany, was given to David Owen Williams around 1960.

VIRGINAL, *c.*1959

Based on a 1664 instrument by Robert Hatley in the Benton Fletcher Collection of Early Keyboard Instruments, Fenton House, Hampstead. As Cathal did not like it, he gave it to his friend Michael Clifton, now deceased.

HARPSICHORD NO. 2, 1962

Based on a Kirckman harpsichord of 1772 discovered in Townley Hall the previous year. Configured in the same manner as the first harpsichord, this instrument was an exact copy of the Kirckman, which was in very poor condition. Cathal's instrument was given a handsome mahogany case. Contrary to Kirckman's usual practice, the naturals on the keyboard were covered in ebony and the accidentals in ivory. The scaling and plucking points of the jacks, the thickness of the soundboard and the positions of the bridges were all carefully copied from the Townley Hall instrument. Cathal's instrument was used as a model for subsequent harpsichords made in Guinness's Brewery and was kept at home until 1972, when it was purchased by Guinness's Brewery and donated to the Gardner Centre, University of Sussex, England, where it remains.

HARPSICHORD NO. 3, 1964–5

Using the 1772 Kirckman instrument as a model, Cathal constructed this elegant instrument in Guinness's Brewery. It was donated to the Royal Irish Academy of Music in April 1965. Following the pattern of the former instrument, the jacks were made of holly and the plectra of Delrin plastic. The soundboard was made of silver spruce and the case was decorated with tulip, mahogany and rosewood. The instrument remains in the Royal Irish Academy of Music and is kept in the Cathal Gannon Early Music Room.

> Compass: 5 octaves, F_I to f^3.
> Registration: 8′ top, 8′ bottom, 4′ bottom, Lute top, Harp (Buff) top (also available on bottom).
> Case (excluding lid): length 7′9″ (2362 mm), width 3′1$\frac{7}{8}$″ (962 mm), depth 1′ (305 mm).

HARPSICHORD NO. 4, 1965

Constructed in Guinness's Brewery, this instrument was sold to Harrods of London, where it was displayed during the Irish Promotion Month in August. Cathal made this instrument 2$\frac{1}{2}$ inches longer than the original in order to improve the quality of the bass. The lowest strings of the four-foot stop were also longer than the original model. The case was veneered with panels of Cuban mahogany, cross banded with Honduras mahogany and inlaid with ebony and boxwood stringing. The keyboard surround was veneered with panels of burr walnut, cross banded with tulip wood. In private ownership, UK.

HARPSICHORDS NOS 5–7

Starting on 15 November 1965, Cathal built three plain walnut copies of the 1772 Kirckman harpsichord, with added manual couplers. These are detailed below.

HARPSICHORD NO. 5, 1966

First of above copies sold to Radio Éireann on 20 September. RTÉ still owns this instrument.

HARPSICHORD NO. 6, 1967

Second of above copies; in private ownership.

HARPSICHORD NO. 7, 1967

Third of above copies sold to John Beckett, who subsequently sold the instrument when he moved to London. Now in private ownership.

HARPSICHORDS NOS 8–14

In September 1972 Cathal began making seven single-manual Italian-style harpsi-chords, based on a Zuckermann kit assembled and loaned by Bernard Hayden. The keyboards were bought from Pyne's of London. Sold to Cathal's friends.

Compass: $4\frac{1}{2}$ octaves: 54 notes (one extra added by Cathal), B_1 to e^3.
Registration: 2 x 8 '.
Case (excluding lid and mouldings): length 6 ' (1829 mm),
    width $32\frac{15}{16}$" (837 mm), depth 8" (203 mm).

HARPSICHORD NO. 8, 1973

Made for David Lee. This instrument was later sold to Malcolm Proud and subse-quently sold again. In private ownership.

HARPSICHORD NO. 9, 1973

In private ownership, Dublin.

HARPSICHORD NO. 10, 1973

In private ownership, Dublin.

HARPSICHORD NO. 11, 1974

Made for the Dublin Baroque Players.

HARPSICHORD NO. 12, 1974

In private ownership, Dublin.

HARPSICHORD NO. 13, 1974
In private ownership, Dublin.

HARPSICHORD NO. 14, 1974
In private ownership, Dublin.

HARPSICHORD NOS 15–17

In November 1974 Cathal began the construction of three copies of a Pascal Taskin harpsichord, 1769, housed in the Russell Collection, Edinburgh. Frank Hubbard's book *Three Centuries of Harpsichord Making* and other sources were used as references, for he never saw the original instrument. All three instruments had two manuals and were painted a delicate shade of green, like the original, with lines made of gold leaf. The jacks for two of the instruments were ordered from Mark Stevenson.

> Compass: 5 octaves, F_1 to g^3.
> Registration: 8′ top, 8′ bottom, 4′ bottom, Harp (Buff) top, Harp (Buff) bottom. Coupler – top manual slides forward.
> Case (excluding lid): length 7′7″ (2311 mm), width 3′1$\frac{1}{2}$″ (952 mm), depth 11$\frac{11}{16}$″ (297 mm).

HARPSICHORD NO. 15, 1976
With decorated soundboard and hand-made jacks. In author's home at Knockmaroon.

HARPSICHORD NO. 16, 1976
With plain soundboard; made for Emer Buckley, who sold the instrument when she moved to Paris. In private ownership.

HARPSICHORD NO. 17, 1976
In private ownership, Dublin.

FORTEPIANO, 1976–80
In April 1976 Cathal began to assemble a Frank Hubbard fortepiano kit, modelled on an instrument by Andreas Stein, which was shipped from Boston. Cathal added a fine mahogany case. Although completed in late 1978, modifications were made to the hammers and hammer shanks in 1980 and the name plate was added. Cathal was not satisfied with this instrument and disliked the sound. It was kept upstairs in his bedroom at Knockmaroon and remains there.

HARPSICHORD NOS 18–20

Three simplified versions of the Pascal Taskin model with one manual and two eight-foot stops.

Compass: 5 octaves, F_1 to f^3.

Registration: 2 x 8 ′, Harp (Buff).

Case (excluding lid): length 7 ′ 2$\frac{1}{2}$″ (2197 mm), width 36 $\frac{10}{16}$″ (930 mm), depth 11 $\frac{12}{16}$″ (298 mm).

HARPSICHORD NO. 18, 1977

Built and sold to Mr Norman Finlay, who subsequently sold the instrument. In private ownership, Northern Ireland.

HARPSICHORD NO. 19, 1977

Donated to Trinity College, Dublin by the Russian cellist Mstislav Rostropovich, who was conferred with an honorary degree in December. The instrument remains in TCD.

HARPSICHORD NO. 20, 1979–86

A painted soundboard was installed, but the instrument was not finished for some considerable time. It was finally completed in 1986. In private ownership, Dublin.

HARPSICHORD NOS 21–4

Up until now, Cathal had been working on three simplified single-manual Taskin models and one full-size double-manual Taskin, which he never completed. He only made the cases, which were stored on their sides in his bedroom. They were finally shipped to Mr Patrick Horsley of Derbyshire, England, who finished them.

HARPSICHORD NO. 21, 1986

In September, one of the three single-manual Taskin models, completed by Patrick Horsley, was brought to Dublin and delivered to Knockmaroon. In May 1987 it was presented to St Patrick's College, Maynooth along with an 1827 Clementi grand piano, which Cathal had restored. The inauguration was marked with a recital by Malcolm Proud, who played both instruments. The instrument remains in St Patrick's College, Maynooth.

HARPSICHORD NO. 22, 1986

A single-manual Taskin model with red and black case, completed by Patrick Horsley, who kept the instrument for a year or two and then sold it. In private ownership, UK.

HARPSICHORD NO. 23, 1987

Double-manual Taskin model with blue and black case, with seven-sided legs and seven-sided stars (the so-called 'Seal of Solomon') painted on the soundboard, inscribed GANNON HORSLEY 1987. In private ownership, London.

HARPSICHORD NO. 24, 1992

Single-manual Taskin model with red and black case, inscribed GANNON HORSLEY 1992. In private ownership, UK.

Cathal's first harpsichord, based on a Kirckman of 1777, completed in 1952. In storage at the National Museum of Ireland, Collins Barracks.

Harpsichord No. 3, made in the Guinness Brewery for the Royal Irish Academy of Music, completed in 1965. Based on a Kirckman of 1772.

Harpsichord No. 13, in private ownership. Italian style with single manual.

Harpsichord No. 15, based on a Pascal Taskin of 1769. At Knockmaroon.

Appendix B

HISTORIC KEYBOARD INSTRUMENTS RESTORED OR
ACQUIRED BY CATHAL GANNON

1936: GRAND PIANO BY ROUND, JONES & CO, LONDON, c.1810
Bought for £3 in Jackson's furniture shop in Grafton Street. Six octaves, a mahogany case, four reeded legs and a satinwood nameboard incorporating the Prince of Wales plumes (painted in colours). In good order; Cathal restrung it and put new coverings on the hammers. It had a good sound. He kept it in the conservatory at the back of the house in Crumlin Road and sold it, for the same price, to a second-hand shop in 1939.

c.1940: BROADWOOD SQUARE PIANO, c.1825
Bought in the Iveagh Market for 30s. It was not in very good condition; Cathal restrung it and put new leather on the hammers. No special features except an iron plate, to which the strings were attached. It had a reasonably good sound and appearance. Cathal gave this piano to his brother Jack, now deceased, around 1960. He then gave it to Billy Sexton, Cathal's helper in Guinness's Brewery and he in turn gave it to another person who treasured it and took great care of it.

1940: ALEXANDRÉ HARMONIUM
Bought for £2 at Lalor & Briscoe's, the auctioneers on the quays, this instrument had fourteen stops. Unplayable; Cathal restored it to playing condition and kept it in his bedroom at Crumlin Road, along with the Broadwood square piano, until he moved to Herberton Road. He got it French-polished for £2. He kept it, with the previous Broadwood square, in the sitting room of Herberton Road. It had a very good sound. In 1945 he sold the harmonium to Pigott's of Grafton Street for £25.

1958: CLEMENTI SQUARE PIANO, 1815
Bought from the Misses Bullards' shop in Chancery Place for 30s. The piano was in bad shape, though everything was there. Cathal restored it to playing condition. He was quite happy with the sound. He kept it for a while in the sitting room at Herberton Road, then stored it on its side in 1963. It was moved to Knockmaroon

and subsequently given to friends as a wedding present. It is now in private ownership, Dublin.

1960: BROADWOOD GRAND PIANO, c.1802
Cathal restored this instrument for Desmond Guinness at Leixlip Castle. He worked at it over a period of eight consecutive weekends.

1960: BROADWOOD SQUARE PIANO, c.1814
Bought at Battersby's Auctions, Westmoreland Street (now gone) for £25 plus auction fees. In reasonable condition; needed restringing. As it turned out to be a good piano, Cathal retained it until 1978, when he gave it to friends. It is now in private ownership, Dublin.

1965: LONGMAN & BRODERIP SQUARE PIANO, LONDON, c.1796
Bought at a house in Donnybrook for £16. It was in poor condition – most of the strings were missing, along with many of the hammers and ivory key coverings. Cathal replaced missing notes, re-leathered all the hammers and restrung the instrument in 1967, having stored it for two years. The result was very satisfactory and it proved to be the best of the square pianos that Cathal purchased and restored. With five and a half octaves and a sustaining pedal, it stands on four legs with a large shelf between them and the mahogany case and legs are inlaid with tulip wood and boxwood stringing. The nameboard over the keys is made of satinwood and bears an enamel plaque bearing the inscription, 'New Patent, Longman and Broderip, London'.

After its restoration it was played by John Beckett in Knockmaroon House for some RTÉ recordings. It was also featured in one of John O'Conor's *Piano Plus* series, shown on RTÉ in 1988. This instrument is kept at Knockmaroon and is still in playing condition. According to the eminent English piano restorer David Hunt, the piano may actually have been made by Southwell of Dublin.

1965: BROADWOOD SQUARE PIANO
In July, Cathal restored this historical instrument, once owned by the poet and composer Thomas Moore, which belonged to Lord and Lady Elveden (later Iveagh) of Farmleigh House. Lord Elveden's father had bought it in 1900. The piano had been used by Moore when he had lived in Kent, where he wrote many of his poems. After Moore's death, it passed through several hands before Lord Iveagh purchased it.

1967: BROADWOOD GRAND PIANO, 1809
In December Cathal began to restore this handsome instrument, which had been found in Townley Hall, near Drogheda, by Trinity College. The piano was in an unplayable condition, but nothing was missing. The restoration involved restringing the instrument, working on the action and replacing the doe-skin coverings on the hammers. Cathal reckoned that he spent some 300 hours working on the instrument. He was disappointed in the resulting sound. Nevertheless, it was inaugurated at the Provost's House on 5 June 1968; Prof. Brian Boydell made an introductory

speech and it was played by Prof. Anthony Hughes. This instrument is now in the Cathal Gannon Early Music Room in the Royal Irish Academy of Music, awaiting further restoration.

1971: ROBERT WORNUM UPRIGHT CABINET PIANO, LONDON, c.1813

Originally sold by Isaac Willis of Westmoreland Street, Dublin (old label, badly rubbed, on top of case). Number 510 stamped on wrest plank but 513 on other internal parts such as the case and action. Gills of Nassau Street (a music shop, now gone) was about to dump this piano in the late 1950s, but Mr Paul Egerstorff, who was friendly with Mr Gill, stopped the workmen, acquired the instrument and kept it at his house in Wellington Place. It was in very bad condition. In 1971 he offered it to Cathal, free, on condition that he restore it, which he did. The job took 340 hours to complete. Woodworm had attacked the instrument in places. A new bottom was made and fitted, a portion of the hitch-pin rail was replaced, the piano was restrung and its hammers re-leathered, and missing hammers were made. This piano remains at Knockmaroon.

1972: SAMUEL MORLAND SQUARE PIANO, DUBLIN, c.1830

Bought from Mr Williams (an employee of Lord Iveagh, Farmleigh House), for £10. Cathal discovered Morland's signature and the date inscribed on the back of the bridge, on the soundboard. He also found 'Ned, June 1829' written on the inside of the uppermost key. This instrument was kept in the workshop at Knockmaroon for many years and never restored.

1972: BROADWOOD UPRIGHT CABINET PIANO, c.1830

This instrument was given to Cathal by Sir George Mahon (who then lived in Castleknock) in lieu of payment for restoring his virginal, made in 1950 by by Alex Hodsdon of Lavenham, Suffolk. This piano was kept in the workshop at Knockmaroon for many years and never restored. It was finally was given to a friend. In private ownership, Dublin.

1973: BROADWOOD GRAND PIANO, 1828

This instrument (No. 11658) was found in Townley Hall, near Drogheda, by Trinity College and restored by Cathal in 1973. This Broadwood grand was in better condition than the previous one but many of the ivory key coverings were missing. Fortunately Cathal had a supply of spare ivories in stock. Despite being an interesting piano from a historical point of view, Cathal was disappointed with the result. The instrument remains in Trinity College.

1978: ROBERT WEARR SQUARE PIANO, c.1790

Cathal restored this instrument in November. Entry in workbook: 'Restringing all brass and steel, removing covered and replacing same ($23\frac{1}{2}$ hrs). Re-hinging all hammers, re-felting bass dampers, renewing felt where necessary total 60 hrs. 16th Nov.– Sat 2nd Dec. Received £75.00.' In private ownership, Dublin.

1979: LICHTENTHAL PIANINO, *c.*1840

Purchased at an auction in Tormey's Auction Rooms. Restoration was completed in 1980. This attractive inlaid instrument (Lichtenthal, Facteur de Pianos du Roi, Bruxelles) was featured in one of John O'Conor's *Piano Plus* series, shown on RTÉ in 1988. This instrument is still at Knockmaroon.

1979: CHRISTOPHER GANER SQUARE PIANO, LONDON, 1785

Cathal spent 115 hours over one month restoring this piano for a friend, now deceased. In private ownership, Dublin.

1980: ALPHONSE BLONDEL SMALL UPRIGHT PIANO, *c.*1860

Cathal bought this unusual French instrument for £50 in Scally's auction rooms on the quays. The case was made of rosewood. The inside was very dirty and quite damaged. He got to work on it immediately. He acquired a handsome pair of brass candlesticks for it in another shop on the quays by trading in a preserving pan for them. When finished, he sold the instrument to friends in Castleknock. Cathal saw another piano by Blondel in Keane, Mahony and Smith's auction rooms in March 1982 but he did not buy it; he regarded it as being quite hideous.

1982: CLEMENTI GRAND PIANO, 1827

Marion Hayden gave Cathal this instrument in gratitude for the help that he had given her father, Hughie Doherty, whilst making a harpsichord for her. The piano, a concert grand, had six and a half octaves, was 8 ft long and would have cost 100 guineas in its day. It was typical of the type of piano that John Field and Frederic Chopin would have played. Cathal got to work on it immediately and by early October it was restored and in playing condition. Unfortunately, despite its magnificent appearance, the sound was of poor quality. This piano was ultimately donated to St Patrick's College, Maynooth, where it remains.

1985: CLEMENTI, COLLARD AND COLLARD SQUARE PIANO, *c.*1760–70

Cathal was given a square piano that was believed to have been in Dardis and Dunn's (the house that had featured in James Joyce's short story 'The Dead') by friends in Castleknock. After Cathal had restrung the instrument and got it working, he returned it to his friends.

1985: ROBERT WORNUM GRAND PIANO, 1848

Cathal bought or acquired this highly unusual instrument, with a Viennese down-striking action, from someone (never identified) living in Celbridge. The piano was in very poor condition. It remained on its side in the laundry at Knockmaroon until May 1987, when it was moved to the workshop. It was never restored and eventually, when the workshop collapsed, it was brought back to the laundry, where it remains.

1986: HOUSTON GRAND PIANO, LONDON, *c*.1794

This fine instrument belonged to Cathal's best friend, William Stuart, and had originally belonged to Gerard Shanahan. William believed that this was the earliest piano of its type in Ireland. Cathal restored this instrument at Knockmaroon and returned it to William; it remains in Kildrought House, Celbridge.

1986: BRODERIP AND WILKINSON SQUARE PIANO, *c*.1805

Cathal bought this instrument at the same time that William bought the Houston mentioned above; the square piano had also belonged to Gerard Shanahan. It featured a hand-painted nameboard. Cathal never restored it but gave it to a neighbour, who attempted to have it restored. In private ownership, Dublin.

Bibliography

Boalch, Donald H., *Makers of the Harpsichord and Clavichord 1440 to 1840* (George Ronald, London, 1956)

Boylan, Henry (ed.), *A Dictionary of Irish Biography* (Gill & Macmillan, Dublin, 1998)

Byrne, Al, *Guinness Times – My Days in the World's Most Famous Brewery* (Town House, Dublin, 1999)

Closson, Ernest, *History of the Piano* (Paul Elek, London, 1976)

Craig, Maurice, *Dublin 1660–1860* (Allen Figgis Ltd, Dublin, 1980)

Craig, Maurice and the Knight of Glin, *Ireland Observed* (The Mercier Press, Cork, 1970)

Douglas-Hume, Jessica, *Violet – the Life and Loves of Violet Gordon Woodhouse* (The Harvill Press, London, 1996)

Ehrlich, Cyril, *The Piano: A History* (J. M. Dent & Sons, Ltd, London, 1976)

Fingall, Elizabeth, Countess of, *Seventy Years Young* (The Lilliput Press, Dublin, 1995)

Guinness, Desmond and William Ryan, *Irish Houses and Castles* (Irish Georgian Society/Thames and Hudson Ltd, London, 1971)

Hubbard, Frank, *Three Centuries of Harpsichord Making* (Harvard University Press, Cambridge, Massachusetts, 1965)

Kearns, Kevin C., *Dublin Tenement Life – An Oral History* (Gill & Macmillan, Dublin, 1994)

Magan, William, *The Story of Ireland* (Element, Dorset, Boston & Melbourne, 2000)

Moody, T. W. and F. X. Martin (eds), *The Course of Irish History* (RTÉ/The Mercier Press, Cork, 1994)

O'Neill, Marie, *Grace Gifford Plunkett and Irish Freedom – Tragic Bride of 1916* (Irish Academic Press, Dublin & Portland, OR, 2000)

Pearson, Peter, *The Heart of Dublin – Resurgence of an Historic City* (O'Brien Press, Dublin, 2000)

Peck, Carola, *Mariga and Her Friends* (The Hannon Press, Ballivor, Co. Meath, 1997)

Russell, Raymond, *Catalogue of the Benton Fletcher Collection of Early Keyboard Instruments at Fenton House, Hampstead* (Country Life Limited for The National Trust, London, 1957)

Russell, Raymond, *The Harpsichord and Clavichord* (Faber & Faber, London, 1959)

Scuffil, Catherine (ed.), *By the Sign of the Dolphin –The Story of Dolphin's Barn* (Dolphin's Barn Historical Society, 1993)

Spencer, C.P., Paul Francis, *To Heal the Broken Hearted – The Life of Blessed Charles of Mount Argus* (Gill & Macmillan, Dublin, 1988)

Somerville-Large, Peter, *Dublin – The Fair City* (Sinclair Stevenson, London, 1996)

Zuckermann, Wolfgang Joachim, *The Modern Harpsichord* (Peter Owen, London, 1970)

Index